CRIMINAL JUSTICE
AT THE CROSSROADS

Criminal Justice at the Crossroads

*TRANSFORMING CRIME
AND PUNISHMENT*

William R. Kelly

 COLUMBIA UNIVERSITY PRESS   NEW YORK

COLUMBIA UNIVERSITY PRESS
Publishers Since 1893
New York   Chichester, West Sussex

cup.columbia.edu
Copyright © 2015 Columbia University Press
All rights reserved

Library of Congress Cataloging-in-Publication Data

Kelly, W. R. (William Robert), 1950–
    Criminal justice at the crossroads : transforming crime and punishment / William R. Kelly.
        pages cm
    Includes bibliographical references and index.
    ISBN 978-0-231-17136-6 (cloth : alk. paper) — ISBN 978-0-231-17137-3 (pbk. : alk paper) —
    ISBN 978-0-231-53922-7 (electronic)
    1. Criminal justice, Administration—United States. 2. Criminals—Rehabilitation—United
States—Evaluation. 3. Recidivism—United States—Prevention. 4. Crime—United
States—Prevention. I. Title.

    HV9950.K45 2015
    364.973—dc23

                                                                    2014029752

Cover design: Archie Ferguson

References to websites (URLs) were accurate at the time of writing.
Neither the author nor Columbia University Press is responsible for URLs
that may have expired or changed since the manuscript was prepared.

The real measure of civilization in any society can be found in the way it treats its most unfortunate citizens—its prisoners.
—Fyodor Dostoevsky, *The House of the Dead*

CONTENTS

ACKNOWLEDGMENTS

I AM VERY FORTUNATE TO have the support and encouragement of a number of wonderful people. First and foremost is my wife Emily, the love of my life, the one who has believed in me and supported this effort from day one. She motivated me and my writing in uncounted ways. She was ever graceful during working weekends and vacations and talking me down during my bouts of doubt and insecurity. I am truly blessed to have her in my life.

I also want to acknowledge the support and understanding of my dear friends of twenty-plus years Bill and Sabrina Streusand. They have been extraordinarily supportive and willing to listen to me opine about American criminal justice at the many dinner parties they hosted. Bill is a child and adolescent psychiatrist and provided invaluable advice and insight on psychiatric and neurocognitive issues. Bill and Sabrina also provided Casa de Streusand de Durango to us during the summer of 2013, where I was able to make the big push to finish the manuscript.

Robert Pitman, a very good friend, formerly the United States Attorney for the Western District of Texas and just confirmed as a federal district judge, was very supportive and encouraging throughout. He has played a critical role in providing drafts to key policymakers in the U.S. Department of Justice. Robert has also encouraged me to write a book about criminal justice reform for a broader audience. That project is currently underway.

I would like to thank De Sellers, who was instrumental in this project in a variety of ways. In addition to being supportive and encouraging, De motivated my interest in neurodevelopment and neurocognitive functioning, which plays a central and ever-growing role in my understanding of crime and behavioral change.

Sheldon Ekland-Olson, longtime friend, colleague, and co-author, read the manuscript and provided invaluable feedback and much-needed encouragement. Sheldon's comments have played a big part in this project as well as the next two books that are in the pipeline. He has always been there and I really appreciate that.

Dan Mears, also a co-author and a prior graduate student of mine, read the manuscript and suggested important changes to early drafts. Dan has been terrific over the years in the role reversal of student supporting professor and for that I am most grateful. My colleague Mark Warr also read a draft of the manuscript and offered helpful suggestions.

The editors at Columbia University Press, especially Jennifer Perillo and Stephen Wesley, have been a true delight. Jennifer was excited and supportive about this project from the very beginning. Stephen was great with the logistics of getting the draft to the final product with as little pain as possible. I also must thank the anonymous reviewers of the manuscript. They all understood what I was hoping to accomplish with this book and essentially gave me free reign to do that. They also made terrific suggestions that improved the book in important ways. My experience with Columbia University Press during this process has been a true pleasure, for which I would like to express my sincerest gratitude.

I also must thank the thousands of students who have listened (sometimes with interest) to my lectures, as I have presented in class much of the evidence (research and real world experiences) and many of the ideas that follow. A good bit of what is in this book has seen some limited vetting in the classroom. Thanks to my students for being involuntary and unwitting judges of some of these ideas over the years.

CRIMINAL JUSTICE
AT THE CROSSROADS

THIS IS A BOOK ABOUT a remarkable policy failure, perhaps the greatest in American history. Over the past forty-plus years, elected officials and policymakers throughout the United States have failed the public, taxpayers, crime victims, the criminal justice system, the mentally ill, the drug-addicted, criminal offenders, their families, and their communities. They have also compromised public safety and contributed to millions of preventable criminal victimizations. It is a failure that has resulted in state expenditures on corrections of over a trillion dollars since 1980. That failure is called "crime control," a theory of public safety premised on greater severity of punishment for criminal offenders and defined by tough rhetoric like "lock 'em up and throw away the key" and "do the crime, do the time." It is a policy that has resulted in the United States having the highest incarceration rates in the world. It is a policy that has led to over 7 million individuals under correctional control, a number larger than the combined populations of Los Angeles and Chicago.

It is a failure that was prosecuted by the careful leveraging of fear (e.g., the Willie Horton TV ads of the 1988 presidential campaign that artfully combined violence, race, and partisan politics) by political self-interest and by an apparent disregard for what the evidence suggested in regard to the effectiveness of the primary policies and initiatives in place to address public safety. This failure has been compounded by neglect of basic public institutions such as education, the mental health system, healthcare, and social problems such as drug and alcohol abuse, poverty, unemployment, homelessness, and community disorganization, among others. The consequences of this neglect are higher crime and victimization rates, which in turn place more offenders in a revolving-door criminal justice system. To be clear, criminal offenders make serious mistakes. They engage in crimes that cause harm—sometimes devastating harm. The failure of the justice system and other public institutions is not excusing crime and criminal offending. What is necessary is to recognize and appreciate that there is shared responsibility for crime. It is time that the United States as a civil society accepts that failure and that shared responsibility—and moves forward to correct it.

So this is also a book about opportunity. Rather than just focusing on the negative, I will discuss a viable, evidence-based, cost-efficient path forward. The research indicates that not only are the alternatives proposed herein more effective (unlike punishment, they actually can change behavior), they are also considerably less expensive.

The scientific community has, over the past twenty-five years or so, accumulated substantial knowledge regarding the criminogenic circumstances of criminal offenders. A considerable amount is known about what situations, conditions, impairments, and deficits are related to criminal offenders and recidivism. Substance abuse, poverty, compromised mental health, cognitive and intellectual deficits, neurodevelopmental impairments, trauma, poor education, lack of employable skills, and many other factors comprise the list of dynamic (changeable) criminogenic factors.

Today, more than 20 percent of America's children grow up in poverty. The United States is thirty-fourth out of thirty-five developed nations in relative child poverty (UNICEF). The United States ranks above only Romania and is well below all of Europe, Canada, Australia, New Zealand, and Japan. The Annie E. Casey Foundation compiles data on child well-being on a variety of dimensions. The *2013 Data Book: State Trends in Child Well-Being* ranks states on dozens of measures of child welfare. The bottom ten states are New Mexico, Mississippi, Nevada, Arizona, Louisiana, South Carolina, Alabama, Georgia, Texas, and California. Of those ten, eight have incarceration rates above the average incarceration for all states combined. Put differently, of the twenty states with incarceration rates above the national average, all but four are below the median ranking on child welfare. Eleven of the states with above-average incarceration rates are in the lower one-third in terms of child welfare. This is neither scientific nor dispositive; it is suggestive of a relation between the use of incarceration and how well the United States cares for its disadvantaged.

The science is rapidly accumulating regarding the effects of poverty or low socioeconomic status on neurocognitive functioning. Children who grow up in impoverished environments tend to have greater exposure to environmental toxins, experience greater chronic stress, have detrimental exposure to inferior cognitive skills, and experience and observe impaired social and emotional relationships. As a consequence, children who grow up in these environments have significantly poorer brain development and more impaired cognitive development than children who grow up in non-poor environments. The consequences include lower IQ and "executive function" (the broad term for cognitive processes that manage other cognitive processes such as planning, organizing, strategizing, paying attention, and working memory), self-control, and impulse regulation, poorer language skills, and an impaired ability to focus attention and ignore distraction. There are real cognitive skill deficits associated with growing up and living in poverty. The environment of poverty often induces trauma. Today the consequences of trauma are better understood, as well as how trauma can lead to PTSD and how it affects cognitive functioning. The Substance Abuse and Mental Health Services Administration (SAMHSA) has taken the lead in promoting the identification of trauma and providing trauma-informed care in a variety of settings. Moreover, these deficits and disorders can and often do persist into adulthood. One of the stark realities is that there is nothing about crime control policy, especially the enhanced severity of punishment, that can correct or overcome these types of neurocognitive and developmental deficits.

However, this is a new era, a new era in which there are vast amounts of actionable, policy-focused research and evaluation on a wide array of interventions that target behavioral change. There is a relatively comprehensive inventory of evidence-based practices that have been validated by dozens of meta-analyses. These evidence-based practices have a demonstrated record of significant behavioral change and recidivism reduction. There are a variety of examples of innovation and problem solving in the justice system, programs in local jurisdictions that sprung up out of recognition that business as usual was not working. The United States now has the opportunity to reverse a failed policy and get smart about crime and public safety.

Where we go from here depends on whether and in what ways these initiatives are translated into policy, programs, and procedures. It is based upon an appreciation that as more and more is understood about criminal behavior it is also understood that changing that behavior is a complex undertaking. It requires resources and expertise that historically have not had much involvement in the American justice system. It is the recognition that criminal justice as traditionally defined cannot accomplish public safety. Absent the elimination of poverty, mental illness, inadequate public education, physical health problems, homelessness, and so on, the American justice system will continue to be placed in the position of dealing with the failures of these institutions. The evidence makes it clear that the task requires a collective effort to address the complexities of criminal offending. That is what smart policy looks like—being smart about what is needed to accomplish public safety, being innovative and creative about where and how to obtain the proper resources and expertise, and understanding going forward that the key is collaboration with a wide variety of players. At the end of the day, this will involve a substantially different way of approaching the business of criminal justice. It will be an approach that is designed to understand and identify the complexity of reasons why criminal offenders are criminal offenders (the diagnosis phase); address the relevant, primary criminogenic deficits and conditions (the treatment phase); and provide the ongoing supports necessary to retain the treatment effects (the continuing care phase). As much as we may not like to put the U.S. criminal justice system in this position, it is the only approach that will cost-effectively enhance public safety, reduce victimization, and reduce recidivism short of eliminating the structural conditions and institutional failures that play a large role in crime in this country.

Much of what I discuss here cannot be easily legislated at the state or federal level. Granted, statutory changes will be required and funding will need to be redirected. However, justice policy going forward should not rely primarily on top-down mechanisms. In 2003 Oregon passed legislation requiring that 75 percent of the Department of Correction's program funding should be used to support evidence-based programs. This is an important initiative, but such legislation does not necessarily address the extent and fidelity of the adoption of evidence-based practices, nor does it necessarily create a culture of innovation. State support is important; however, much of the substance of these changes requires *local* adoption and implementation. They also require significant changes in ways of thinking about crime and justice, public safety, and behavioral change, as well as substantial cultural change where they are implemented. Moreover, policy makers and elected officials will need to set aside the traditional political consequences of criminal justice policy (few public officials lost elections by being tough on crime) and adopt a smart, prudent focus on advancing public safety and avoiding needlessly placing victims at risk of preventable crimes.

Effective and appropriate implementation requires changing how criminal justice is funded. The current model is one in which the state pays for incarceration in prison, whereas the burden of paying for diversion (problem-solving courts, probation) and community-based rehabilitation is generally placed on local jurisdictions or is a combination of state and local funding. Financially, there is an incentive to send offenders to prison (no local cost) compared to community-based treatment. That must change. And there are innovative approaches available for states to evaluate and adapt. For example, California and several other states employ performance incentive funding to reduce recidivism and redirect funding to local jurisdictions. California counties that reduce the recidivism of probationers are provided a portion of the funds averted by not incarcerating them. The lower the probation recidivism rate, the more the county receives from the state for avoided incarceration costs.

The likely resistance to developing and paying for costly evidence-based diagnostic and treatment programs and facilities for those who break the law must be overcome. The sentiment is understandable—break the law, get help. What makes sense about that? The answers are money and public safety. If such interventions are not implemented, we will simply continue to pay the financial and the social costs of a criminal justice system that fails to change behavior and perpetuates unacceptably high levels of recidivism and victimization.

For those who follow U.S. criminal justice policy, the story is all too familiar. Between 1960 and 1992, violent crimes in the United States increased by 570 percent. National Crime Victimization data indicate substantial increases in violent victimization between 1973 (the inaugural year of the victimization survey) and 1992. The nation responded with a massive investment in law enforcement, the toughening of sentencing laws, a focus on possession and distribution of illegal drugs, and a massive, unprecedented expansion of incarceration and correctional control. The Bureau of Justice Statistics reports that between 1982 and 2006 (the most recent statistics), state and local criminal justice spending (including law enforcement, prosecution, courts, and corrections) increased from $32 billion to

$186 billion, a 480 percent increase. Today, the United States has a prevalence rate of mentally ill prison and jail inmates nearly three times that of the general population, and an ageing inmate population (the percent of inmates age sixty-four and over is increasing at a rate ninety-four times that of the general population). Today, 10 percent of all children in the United States have a parent that is in prison, in jail, on probation, or on parole. Seven percent of minority children have a parent in prison. U.S. criminal justice is a very large, extraordinarily expensive system that produces a three-year rearrest rate for inmates released from prison of between 55 percent and 65 percent, and a reincarceration rate between 45 percent and 50 percent.

We, as a nation, have been participating in one of the most ambitious public policy experiments, in terms of scope, cost, and impact, that the United States has ever witnessed. Forty years ago, the United States had an incarceration rate (number of individuals in prison per 100,000 U.S. population) that mimicked those of most other nations in the world. The same could be said of our overall rate of correctional control, which includes prison, jail, probation, and parole. Today, the United States has the highest rate of incarceration (prison and jail) and correctional control in the world. How we got here, what we have accomplished, and, most importantly, where we should go from here are the topics of these pages.

Today, we find ourselves at a criminal justice crossroads. Crime is at the lowest level in decades. Many aspects or components of U.S. criminal justice are or recently have been at all-time record highs: criminal justice expenditures, prison and jail populations, community control populations (probation and parole), and incarceration rates. Some policy makers and elected officials exclaim that the substantial crime reductions experienced over the past few decades are a direct result of the massive expansion of criminal justice. More careful observers know that the story is a lot more complex and that there are many reasons for the crime reduction, only one of which is the impact of criminal justice policies and activities. The simple interpretation—that our past success with crime reduction is nearly exclusively a result of correctional policies—keeps us generally locked onto that path.

The harsh reality is that we are now encountering the fiscal challenges of crime control and are realizing we cannot afford it, especially when we consider that the public safety accomplishments of crime control are modest at best. The recession of 2008 triggered significant changes in state and local spending, including criminal justice spending. Reports by the National Association of State Budget Officers, the National League of Cities, and the Office of Community Oriented Policing Services indicate significant declines in criminal justice spending on law enforcement, prosecution, and corrections. News reports occasionally document the shuttering of prisons as the fiscal realities of the recession confront the high cost of crime control. It does not matter whether we begin heading down a path of smarter criminal justice policy because of a consensus that crime control does not work or because of the fiscal realities of crime control. The goal is to be willing for whatever reasons to redesign criminal justice policy according to the evidence, revamp practices and procedures, reorient funding, and implement significant statutory changes. The evidence is pretty clear that going down that road will reduce crime and recidivism, reduce victimizations, enhance public safety, and save money.

On August 12, 2013, Eric Holder, the Attorney General of the United States, spoke at the annual American Bar Association's meeting of the House of Delegates. The topic was sentencing reform in the federal justice system. As I will discuss later in this book, in the late 1980s, Congress set in motion the massive and punitive restructuring of sentencing for individuals convicted of federal crimes. So were born the Federal Sentencing Guidelines, probably the most severe sentencing laws in the nation. The federal guidelines have lead to substantial increases in admissions to federal prison, for much longer sentences. Part of this was accomplished by a wide variety of mandatory sentences (as the name implies, situations in which the judge has no choice but to do as the guidelines indicate). Also key to advancing punishment at the federal level was the elimination of parole, requiring federal inmates to in effect serve the entire sentence imposed.

Enough background for now. In General Holder's own words to the Bar Association:

> As it stands, our system is in too many respects broken. The course we are on is far from sustainable . . . with an outsized, unnecessarily large prison population, we need to ensure that incarceration is used to punish, deter, and rehabilitate—not merely to warehouse and forget.
>
> Today, a vicious cycle of poverty, criminality, and incarceration traps too many Americans and weakens too many communities. And many aspects of

our criminal justice system may actually exacerbate these problems, rather than alleviate them.

Even though this country comprises just 5 percent of the world's population, we incarcerate almost a quarter of the world's prisoners. . . . And roughly 40 percent of former federal prisoners—and more than 60 percent of former state prisoners—are rearrested or have their supervision revoked within three years after their release, at great cost to U.S. taxpayers

This is why I have today mandated a modification of the Justice Department's charging policies so that certain low-level, nonviolent drug offenders. . . . By reserving the most severe penalties for serious, high-level, or violent drug traffickers, we can better promote public safety, deterrence, and rehabilitation—while making our expenditures smarter and more productive.

Finally, my colleagues and I are taking steps to identify and share best practices for enhancing the use of diversion programs—such as drug treatment and community service initiatives—that can serve as effective alternatives to incarceration.

The point is that the changes implemented by the Attorney General and the discussions that will continue with Congress further help to clarify that we are at an important juncture in the history of U.S. criminal justice policy. What the Attorney General proposes for the federal government today and what may follow in the near term from these initiatives is heading down the road of smarter, more effective, and more cost-effective justice policy. And the fact that the U.S. Attorney General is on board and is carrying the banner of justice reform is highly symbolic for the rest of the nation. Having said that, the fact that General Holder resigned in the fall of 2014 may mean that these efforts are derailed or at least demoted, depending on the priorities of his successor.

We begin with a relatively brief overview of U.S. criminal justice policy—where we have been and why, and where we are today. This overview is necessary in order to place current policy in context, and is brief because there are many excellent, comprehensive discussions of how we got to where we are today (Beckett 1997; Beckett and Sasson 2004; Western 2006).

We then turn to a discussion of what the past forty years of unprecedented expansion of correctional control, especially incarceration, have accomplished. We have fundamentally reengineered criminal justice into a system with a nearly singular focus on control and punishment. The obvious question is: What have we achieved? We will consider the wisdom of continuing to punish offenders well after the justice system is through with them (for example, by prohibiting access to licensing and employment in a wide variety of occupations). We will ask questions like: What do we expect (not want, but expect) offenders to do once they are discharged from correctional control, no better, and often worse than when they arrived? What are the odds for convicted felons gaining legitimate employment? What do we expect when the parole system is largely a sorting mechanism for identifying violators, rather than a safety net for enhancing successful reentry and reintegration into the community? How do we expect released offenders to find sustainable housing if they lack resources and have a felony conviction? What do we expect when the clear majority of prison and jail inmates are addicted to controlled substances and alcohol, but very few receive any treatment while in the justice system and after release? The same issues apply to offenders with other mental health problems. The prevalence of mental illness in the U.S. criminal justice system is extraordinary, unprecedented, and shameful, largely a consequence of the failure of public mental health treatment and the willingness of the justice system to serve as the "asylum of last resort." But when mentally ill offenders are released from custody with little treatment, what do we expect? What do we expect when they are released with two weeks' worth of medication, when it usually takes two to three months to get an appointment with a psychiatrist in the community? These questions are not excuses for bad behavior. Criminal offenders do bad things. The point is, how smart is it to continue down a path for which the desired outcomes are rarely achieved? How smart is it to continue to assume that punishment will change behavior? How can punishment find housing or employment, or address addiction and mental illness?

Most discussions of U.S. criminal justice policy typically focus only on criticisms of where we have been, how and why we got here, and what is wrong with it. In 2011, James Austin criticized criminologists for the failure to provide a path forward for reforming the justice system and reducing incarceration. "Criminologists seem content to study and lament the origins of mass incarceration but not to orchestrate its demise" (Austin 2011: 632).

This book is different than many in that most of what we discuss is how and where we go from here. The process of creating today's criminal justice system required substantial changes at all levels of government and included reframing how we think about crime and punishment; dramatic revisions of penal codes and sentencing statutes; massive redirection of public expenditures for law enforcement, courts, and corrections; construction of prisons and jails; and much more. Moving forward in the appropriate direction will require considering all of that again.

It is difficult to find many informed observers who will admit that the current justice system is effective and a prudent investment of public resources. Thus it should come as no surprise that we are going to recommend a different direction here. Just as getting to where we are today required substantial changes in a variety of areas, turning the current system around will not be a simple matter. Thus our discussion of a path forward will focus attention on most of the key components of the justice system, highlighting the fact that an effective and cost-effective future for U.S. criminal justice is multidimensional.

We will address the primary areas in need of reform or change, including: sentencing and the roles of prosecutors and judges in that process; diversion from traditional criminal adjudication and punishment; how probation should operate; how prisons should be used; how to address the problems associated with prison release and community reentry; and how to deal with the drug problem. Law enforcement does not receive much attention here not because it is unimportant, but because the vast majority of the necessary reform and reinvention involves what happens after someone is arrested.

These reforms will also require significant changes to how we think about crime and punishment and how we engage solutions. Much of what is effective in reducing crime and recidivism is tangible—structural, statutory, and financial. Equally important are two less tangible components—a cultural shift in which all individuals and agencies involved in this enterprise accept responsibility for reducing recidivism, and the practice of routinely embracing a problem-solving posture in doing the business of criminal justice.

The decisions and conclusions reached in this book are based on valid, reliable evidence provided by the scientific community regarding what is effective and what is ineffective in terms of criminal justice policy and practice. We are, in 2014, in a very fortunate position of having a couple of decades of scientific research that has focused precisely on the questions of what does and what does not work in terms of enhancing public safety. We are finally in a position to go beyond what sounds reasonable and effective (for example, boot camps, Scared Straight, DARE, the deterrent effect of punishment severity) to what scientific research demonstrates is effective.

One of the primary challenges in developing policy recommendations involves the complexity of the U.S. justice system. There are in effect fifty-two different, largely autonomous justice systems and jurisdictions—fifty states, the District of Columbia, and the federal system. Within the fifty state jurisdictions are over 3,100 counties or county equivalents with differing concerns, problems, financial means, and challenges with regard to crime, and varying approaches to public safety.

Most jurisdictions share the difficulty of significant fiscal constraints. This book is written at an opportune moment for implementing meaningful changes to U.S. justice policy, due to constrained state and local revenue streams. Fiscal conditions in part appear to be motivating legislatures to rethink the costs of "tough on crime" policies. This has led to a variety of initiatives such as accelerated early release of prison inmates (for example, in California), to modification of mandatory sentencing laws (for example, New York's mitigation of the Rockefeller drug laws), to ramping up diversion resources (for example, Texas has foregone more prison expansion in favor of increased funding for probation). These changes appear to be consistent with justice reform, however they are a far cry from the systemic, nationwide shift in policy, statutes, funding, and thinking about crime and punishment of the extent and scale necessary to effectively reduce recidivism and victimization. After all, the Pew Charitable Trusts report released in November 2014 shows that most states anticipate increases in their prison populations over the next four years.

When the U.S. criminal justice system underwent the unprecedented changes that resulted in a nearly unilateral focus on punishment, there was essentially no scientific evidence supporting such a path. It was based largely on common sense and intuition. And there was little push back, because to oppose it was to oppose conventional wisdom. Today, we are in a much different position of having the evidence to support an effective, smart, and cost-effective strategy. What will catch the attention of policy makers and the public is not so much what the science indicates. Framing the path forward in terms of *smart* policy and *cost-effective* policy should help provide much needed traction.

I will provide what the scientific evidence indicates is best practice or evidence-based policy reform. I will then take that discussion a fair amount beyond what is typical of presentations of evidence-based practices. It appears that public opinion is generally supportive of this type of initiative and that the fiscal climate has forced states to start thinking about the cost of criminal justice. What is left is mustering the political support to facilitate real change in order to substantially reduce recidivism, crime, and victimization, as well as the cost of doing so.

U.S. Criminal Justice Policy, 1960-2013

THERE ARE TWO QUESTIONS ADDRESSED in this chapter: 1) Where has the United States been in terms of criminal justice policy and 2) where does it stand now? I begin by providing statistical information on changes over time in U.S. correctional policy and practice. I then try to make sense of one of the most extensive policy shifts in U.S. history, focusing on the "whys" and "hows" of the evolution of crime control and the dramatic growth in corrections.

One more thing before I begin. The term "crime control" is used throughout this book to refer to a set of policies and laws that focus on crime reduction primarily through the mechanisms of punishment and control. Crime control, which has characterized federal- and state-level criminal justice policy for four decades, is premised on the assumption or belief that punishment and control will deter and incapacitate. Under this approach, punishment severity is assumed to specifically deter the individual being punished (specific deterrence), and generally deter others (general deterrence), presumably because they observe or are aware of the consequences of offenders' actions. And correctional control, in the more extreme version of prison and jail and to a lesser extent probation and parole, is assumed to prevent crimes by eliminating or reducing opportunity, thus the term "incapacitation." In chapter 2 I will address the extent to which punishment and control have reduced crime and recidivism in recent U.S. history.

BY THE NUMBERS

Undoubtedly, the defining characteristic of U.S. criminal justice of the past forty years is the growth in incarceration. The prison population has risen by an extraordinary 535 percent over that period. Figure 1.1 is a visual depiction of the growth in U.S. incarceration reflected by the number of state and federal prisoners between 1936 and 2012 (data are from the Bureau of Justice Statistics, 1988, 2002, and 2012).

The headlines are all too familiar and are from a wide variety of sources—liberal, conservative, and neutral—including the *Washington Post, The Economist, Time Magazine, U.S. News and World Report, CNN, Science, Newsweek, The Atlantic, Business Week,* the *Wall Street Journal,* the *National Review, The New York Times,* and many, many more.

"1 in 100 Incarcerated"
"America's Soaring Prison Population"
"Incarceration Nation"
"U.S. Incarceration Highest in the World"
"U.S. Prisons Largest in the World"
"Inmate Count in U.S. Dwarfs Other Nations'"

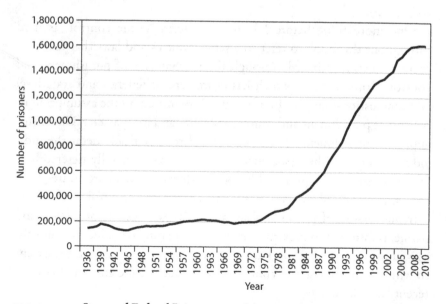

FIGURE 1.1   **State and Federal Prisoners, 1936–2012**

"U.S. Prison Population Sets New Record"

"Rough Justice: America Locks Up Too Many People, Some for Acts that Should Not Even Be Illegal"

"Prisons: Cruel and Unusual Punishment"

"As Crime Rate Drops, the Prison Rate Rises and the Debate Rages"

"Too Many Laws, Too Many Prisoners: Never in the Civilized World Have So Many Been Locked Up for So Little"

While incarceration gets most of the attention and press, the bigger picture of America's crime control policy is the expansion of correctional control in general—prison, jail, probation, and parole. Although they vary in the degree of control or loss of liberty, all of the forms of correctional control exploded over the past four decades, which is testament to the ability of the justice systems of the states and the federal government to respond to the call for crime control. This is where I begin.

In 1980, there were 1,840,000 individuals in the United States under correctional control or supervision. By the end of 2012, the correctional population had exploded to 6,937,600, representing an increase of 280 percent. The individual components of the correctional explosion increased at unprecedented rates. Between 1975 and 2012, the parole population in the United States increased by nearly 475 percent. Between 1978 and 2012, the local jail population in the United States increased by over 370 percent, from 158,400 to 748,700. Probation populations in the United States increased from 816,500 in 1977 to 4 million in 2012, a growth of 390 percent. Finally, in 1975, there were 240,000 prison inmates in the United States. Over the next thirty-five years, the prison population increased to over 1.5 million, an increase of 535 percent. Figure 1.2 shows the growth in the correctional population over the period from 1980 to 2012 (2012 is the most recent year the data are available; data are from the Bureau of Justice Statistics, Correctional Populations in the United States).

Trends in correctional spending at the state level correspond to the expansion of incarceration and corrections more broadly. In 1982, states spent $9.7 billion on prison operations; by 2010, that increased to $37.3 billion (these cost figures are inflation-adjusted to 2010 dollars). This change in institutional spending represents a 285 percent increase. Total state corrections expenditures increased from $15.1 billion to $48.5 billion, a 221 percent increase over nearly thirty years.

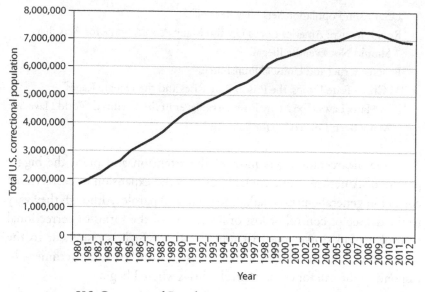

FIGURE I.2 **U.S. Correctional Population, 1980–2012**

In terms of sheer numbers, the community supervision population (probation and parole) far exceeds the prison and jail population. In 2013, while there were 2,285,000 individuals in custody in local jails and state and federal prisons, there were nearly 5 million individuals on community supervision (state and federal probation and parole). In addition to the officially counted 6.9 million under correctional control today, there is survey evidence indicating that there are nearly 1 million individuals not counted in the correctional population census. These are individuals that are on conditional release and supervised while on pretrial status, individuals participating in diversion courts and alternative sentencing programs, and other types of diversion (Pew 2009a). Additionally, Pew estimates that there are another 100,000 offenders (not typically counted in official statistics) in prisons in U.S. territories, Immigration and Customs Enforcement (ICE) facilities, and in juvenile programs. Perhaps a more realistic and inclusive estimate of the current correctional population is closer to 8 million.

The correctional boom involved the participation of the federal correctional system as well as the systems of all fifty states and the District of Columbia. However, as the states exercise sovereignty over their individual justice policies and face crime and justice problems at different levels of intensity and concern, as well as different fiscal priorities and constraints, they participated in the correctional boom at differing levels of intensity. Based on yearend 2009 statistics, variation in correctional rates across states is substantial. At the high end: Georgia (1 in 13 individuals is under correctional control); Idaho (1 in 18); Texas (1 in 22); Massachusetts (1 in 24); Ohio (1 in 25); Indiana, Rhode Island, Minnesota, Delaware, and Louisiana (1 in 26); Michigan (1 in 27); and Pennsylvania (1 in 28). At the low end: New Hampshire (1 in 88); Maine (1 in 81); West Virginia (1 in 68); Utah (1 in 64); North Dakota (1 in 63); Iowa (1 in 54); and New York and Kansas (1 in 53).

While there are substantial differences in how and at what level the states participated in the correctional boom, there is uniformity with regard to the impact on various demographic groups. As the Pew Center on the States (2009a) calculates, one in thirty-one individuals in the United States is currently under correctional control. However, this ratio is different for various demographic groups. One in eighty-nine women, but one in eighteen men is under correctional control. One in forty-five whites is under correctional control, compared to one in twenty-seven Hispanics and one in eleven blacks. Drilling down farther, one in three young black males is currently under correctional control. Micro-analyses by the Pew Center demonstrate that correctional control is unsurprisingly concentrated geographically within urban areas, with the highest correctional rates in a small number of urban zip codes and neighborhoods. For example, of the 72,168 offenders released from the Texas prison system in 2008, 30 percent of them returned to seven zip codes in Harris County, Houston, Texas. One in sixty-one residents of Michigan is under correctional control—prison, jail, parole, or felony probation. However, in Wayne County, which is the state's most populous county, it is one in thirty-eight. In Detroit, which is the largest city in Wayne County, the ratio is one in twenty-five. The East Side of Detroit has a further concentration of offenders (one in twenty-two). Finally, in Brewer Park, an area in the East Side of Detroit, the ratio of residents under correctional control is one in sixteen.

The most often cited trend in the history of U.S. criminal justice is the incarceration boom. For the first three-quarters of the last century (1900 to 1975), U.S. incarceration rates were fairly stable, ranging between

100 and 200 incarcerated individuals per 100,000 Americans. The U.S. incarceration rates were so stable during this seventy-five-year period that most experts predicted continued stability in incarceration for the foreseeable future. However, things changed.

Between 1975 and 2011, the U.S. incarceration rate (jail and prison, state and federal) increased from 165 per 100,000 to 730 per 100,000, amounting to a 345 percent increase. In 1980, U.S. prisons and jails held just over 500,000 inmates. By 2011, the incarcerated population had increased to 2,266,800, a jump of 350 percent. The federal system grew at a greater rate than that of the states. Over the past thirty years, the federal prison system population has increased from 25,000 inmates to nearly 220,000, representing an increase of 790 percent.

Just as is the case with correctional control in general, prison incarceration rates vary considerably by region and by state. In 2012, the aggregate prison incarceration rate among the states was 480. Regional incarceration rates ranged from a high of 551 for the South and a low of 302 in the Northeast. Among states, the range was from a high of 893 (Louisiana) to a low of 145 (Maine). The top five were Louisiana, Mississippi, Alabama, Texas, and Oklahoma. The five lowest were Maine, Minnesota, Rhode Island, New Hampshire, and Massachusetts. Differentials like these were evident throughout much of the corrections boom. For example, in 1994, the state aggregate prison incarceration rate was 367. The South had the highest regional rate (462) and the Northeast the lowest (298). The District of Columbia led the nation (1,935), followed by Texas (637). The states with the lowest prison incarceration rates were North Dakota (84), Maine (119), and Utah (158).

Imprisonment rates differ dramatically by demographic groups. The aggregate (state and federal) prison incarceration rate again was 480 in 2012. However, when broken out by gender, age, and race/ethnicity, there are phenomenal differences. The male incarceration rate is 932; the female is 65. The white male rate is 478; the black male rate is 3,023; the Hispanic male rate is 1,238. Adding age to the breakout, even more striking differences are seen. Young black males are an extraordinarily high-risk group for imprisonment. Black males between ages twenty and forty-four have incarceration rates ranging from 4,702 to 7,517 (again, compared to the overall rate of 502). Black men today have a one in three lifetime likelihood of imprisonment.

There are many ways to place the U.S. expansion of corrections into historical and comparative context. For example, back in the late 1990s and early 2000s, newspaper headlines began to appear to the effect that nearly 50 percent of young black males in cities like Baltimore, Atlanta, and Detroit were involved in the criminal justice system. Or, as the Pew Center on the States has told us, 1 in 100 is incarcerated and 1 in 31 is under correctional control. Or, the United States has 5 percent of the world's population, but 25 percent of the world's prison inmates. Or, the United States incarcerates about 400,000 more inmates than the twenty-six largest European nations (with a total population 2.6 times that of the U.S. population).

Perhaps the most compelling statistic is that the United States today has the highest incarceration rate in the world. The 2012 U.S. jail and prison incarceration rate was 716. By way of initial comparison with the U.S rate, the world incarceration rate (if there was such a thing) would be 146/100,000 population. Exemplary incarceration rates for other nations include China (121), Russia (475), Rwanda (492), Australia (130), Kazakhstan (351), Iran (291), Singapore (265), Spain (147), the United Kingdom (153), Germany (79), Japan (58), Saudi Arabia (178), Pakistan (40), Argentina (151), Canada (118), Mexico (200), and South Africa (316) (Walmsley 2011).

Regardless of how it is viewed, these increases in correctional control and the current and recent levels of U.S. incarceration are unprecedented in U.S. history and unprecedented in the history of any other nation for which there are basic data, absent perhaps the Russian Gulag in its heyday. In short, the U.S. correctional boom is a uniquely U.S. experience. The United States has come a long way from Alexis de Tocqueville's 1831 observation in *Democracy in America* that "In no country is criminal justice administered with more mildness than in the United States." I now turn to the "whys" and the "hows" of the correctional boom.

TRACING THE EVOLUTION OF CRIME CONTROL AND THE CORRECTIONAL BOOM

The U.S. correctional boom depended on many factors falling into place. All fifty states participated (to varying degrees), as did the federal justice system. It required massive expansion of prison and jail capacity, increases in probation and parole caseloads, changes to penal codes, changes to sentencing and prison release laws, reorientation of federal, state, and local government funding, and changes in beliefs and attitudes about the causes and prevention of crime, among others. In addition, the political significance of crime control or tough on crime cannot be overestimated.

Barry Goldwater, 1964

The beginnings of the correctional boom in the United States can be traced to Barry Goldwater, the Republican candidate in the 1964 presidential election. Goldwater is credited with putting crime and punishment on the national agenda during his campaign against Lyndon Johnson, and was the first to use the substantial political leverage that crime and punishment provided for future generations of elected officials at the national, state, and local levels. Goldwater, in his speech accepting the Republican nomination for president stated:

> The growing menace in our country tonight, to personal safety, to life, to limb and property, in homes, in churches, in playgrounds and places of business, particularly in our great cities, is the mounting concern, or should be, of every thoughtful citizen of the United States. Security from domestic violence, no less than from foreign aggression, is the most elementary and fundamental purpose of any government and a government that cannot fulfill that purpose is one that cannot long command the loyalty of its citizens. History shows us—demonstrates that nothing—nothing prepares the way for tyranny more than the failure of public officials to keep the streets from bullies and marauders.

Lyndon Johnson, 1963–1968

Goldwater lost the election of 1964 to Lyndon Johnson, but the message was clear—crime and public safety had hit the national stage as a central concern. The Johnson administration did address crime and disorder both through communications, such as campaign speeches and State of the Union addresses, and through appointments of study commissions. In communications, Johnson referenced crime as "a sore on the face of America" and a "menace on our streets" (Calder 1982). In 1965, Johnson created the Commission on Law Enforcement and the Administration of

Justice, which also included a variety of study panels focusing on new solutions to the problems of public safety, law enforcement, and corrections, among others. The Commission's findings were presented in early 1967 and Johnson compelled Congress to make the implementation of these recommendations a "matter of the highest priority."

While Johnson placed crime control high on the list of priorities, as the story plays out, Johnson's presidency was consumed by Vietnam, a situation made more challenging by the frequent and distracting domestic protests against the administration's Vietnam policies, as well as massive civil disorder, as race riots swept across the United States, primarily during the summer months of 1965 onward. As Calder (1982) aptly concludes, Johnson suffered a "crisis of confidence," which significantly contributed to the end of his presidency in 1968 and the end of his crime control initiatives.

The 1960s and Richard Nixon

Although Lyndon Johnson declared a war on crime and condemned crime and lawlessness in the streets in his State of the Union speech, it was Richard Nixon who had the "evidence" to really begin to effectively make the crime and punishment link, and to make crime and punishment work politically. Official crime data supported a growing unease regarding predatory crime in U.S. cities. The Uniform Crime Reports (UCR) official crime statistics reflected what the national news media were reporting—crime, especially violent crime, was on the rise. The UCR violent crime rate rose by an unheard of 85 percent between 1960 and 1968 (from 161 in 1960 to 298 in 1968). The robbery rate more than doubled in that eight-year span. The murder rate increased 35 percent, rape was up 65 percent, and aggravated assault had increased by 67 percent. Finally, property crime more than doubled between 1960 and 1968. Figure 1.3 presents the trends in the Uniform Crime Reports violent crime index and property crime index for the period 1960 to 2011 (data from The Disaster Cener, http://www.disastercenter.com/crime).

This was new in the U.S. experience, and although the average resident is not aware of levels and changes in crime statistics, media coverage of the upswing in crime planted the seeds of public fear that drove much of the political dialog and public policy on crime over the next forty years.

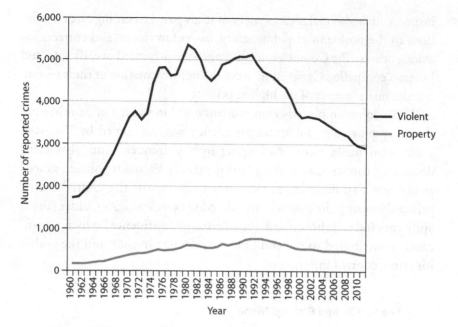

FIGURE 1.3   **Uniform Crime Reports Crime Rates, 1960–2011**

However, it was not just traditional predatory street crime that fueled fear. The 1960s was a decade of tremendous civil upheaval associated with the civil rights movement and the Vietnam War. Beginning in 1965 in Watts, Los Angeles, and continuing through the remainder of the 1960s, essentially every major city and many more, smaller cities experienced massive race-related civil disorders. The list of cities affected includes Newark, Detroit, Chicago, Omaha, Buffalo, Milwaukee, Minneapolis, Baltimore, Louisville, Washington D.C., and Tampa, to name but a few. The scale of these disorders was monumental—hundreds killed, thousands injured, tens of thousands arrested, and billions in property damage. On top of this unrest, there were frequent anti–Vietnam War protests on college campuses around the nation. And, in 1968, Martin Luther King, Jr. was assassinated, spurring another massive wave of violence in urban America. In 1968, Robert Kennedy was also assassinated. Anyone who was paying any attention during the decade of the 1960s likely exhibited some anxiety about the state of disorder, lawlessness, and crime. Every evening, especially during the summers of 1965, 1966, 1967, and 1968, Walter Cronkite reported the extent of the violence to the nation. For the first time since its birth, the United States was experiencing alarming levels of crime and violent disorder in essentially every city in the country.

The 1960s and 1970s also saw the initiation of drug use on college campuses and in urban areas across the United States. In part a function of veterans returning from Vietnam with established patterns of drug use, and in part an attribute of the counterculture movement, the result was increasing drug use and the anxiety and fear associated with it. So concerned was Washington about drug use, in 1971 President Nixon declared drugs "public enemy number one" in launching the War on Drugs.

The ingredients for the launch of crime control can be found in the events of the 1960s. The law and order, crime and punishment, crime control response to these events was simple, logical, intuitive, and proactive. What the United States had been doing in the past to deal with crime and disorder clearly was not working. The evidence was consistent and vivid, in living rooms every evening on the television news. It was time to chart a new course.

What the United States had been doing in the 1940s, 1950s, and 1960s in terms of addressing crime was a somewhat more balanced focus on control and rehabilitation. It was not the case that incarcerated offenders simply spent days in group therapy or in rehabilitation classes. Instead, the focus of penology in the day was that of attempting to change offender behavior through treatment, intervention, rehabilitation, and punishment, while at the same time providing risk management through correctional control.

Correctional rehabilitation was such an important component of justice policy then that it drove the implementation of indeterminate sentencing statutes. In 1975, the federal system and every state system sentenced convicted felons (and misdemeanants) under indeterminate sentencing laws. These statutes were called indeterminate for two reasons. One, the penal code provided for fairly wide ranges of punishment upon conviction of a particular offense or class of offense (for example, first degree felony, class E felony). So the sentence was indeterminate because it was not precisely determined until the sentencing judge imposed the sentence (for example, fifteen years, life, probation). The other and more relevant reason that such sentencing laws were labeled indeterminate is because the actual time served of the sentence imposed was up to the parole authorities, who in theory were to monitor the progress of an inmate's rehabilitation and determine when the inmate was "better" and could therefore be released. In fact, indeterminate sentencing was a statutory framework that facilitated correctional rehabilitation, based on the simple observation that different individuals, with different experiences and different circumstances, progress at different rates. Therefore, a fixed sentence was not appropriate when the goal was to change behavior.

It is unclear precisely when correctional rehabilitation came into disfavor. Many observers cite the 1974 publication of what has come to be known as the Martinson Report, which concluded that "nothing works" in correctional rehabilitation. It is fair to say that this publication, which represented input from the scientific community regarding the effectiveness of correctional rehabilitation as practiced in the 1940s, 1950s, and 1960s, had a profound negative impact on the future of correctional rehabilitation. However, the wheels of change were already spinning well before the Martinson Report.

What is said of politics is true of crime—it is local. It happens on local streets in local neighborhoods, investigated by local police, prosecuted by local district attorneys, sentenced by local judges, and punished by local (probation, diversion, jail) or state (prison) officials. However, the role of the federal government and federal officials in determining, defining, and establishing criminal justice policy not only at the federal level but at the state and local level is critical in understanding where the United States has been and how and why the United States traveled that road. It is not that the federal government sets state and local policy, but federal initiatives and federal funding certainly influence state and local decision making. I now turn to a brief discussion of the impact and influence of the national administrations that presided over the massive restructuring of America's criminal justice system. I begin with the 1968 presidential campaign.

The Nixon–Humphrey campaign of 1968 was the platform for Richard Nixon to establish himself as the leader of the crime control initiative by putting law and order squarely on the public agenda. By way of example, a popular Nixon campaign TV ad portrays a middle-aged white woman walking alone at night. The voiceover is by a male who has a quite concerned tone to his voice when he says the following:

> Crimes of violence in the United States have almost doubled in recent years.
> Today a violent crime is committed every sixty seconds, a robbery every two

and one half minutes, a mugging every six minutes, a murder every forty-three minutes, and it will get worse unless we take the offensive. Freedom from fear is a basic right of every American. We must restore it.

Then the closing caption reads "This Time Vote Like Your Whole World Depended On It—NIXON." A number of other Nixon TV campaign ads showed images of student protesters, rioters, burning buildings, street criminals, and victims (all with anxiety-producing music), and then candidate Nixon's voice stating that it is "time to take an honest look at order in the United States . . . and so I pledge to you that we shall have order in the United States."

It appears that the point of the ads is to provoke fear. Nixon's solution: "Doubling the conviction rate in this country would do more to cure crime in America than quadrupling the funds for Humphrey's war on poverty." The language of crime control that evolved focused on arrests, convictions, and narcotics enforcement. The Nixon administration was the first to explicitly place drug use on the national criminal justice radar, linking drug use and property crime. The Nixon administration went several steps further in declaring a War on Drugs in 1971 and established the Drug Enforcement Administration (DEA) in 1973.

There is evidence that this focus on crime and punishment had substantial political consequences. Beckett and Sasson (2004) offer a credible argument that the Republican crime control initiative was a concerted strategy to sway white southerners. The migration of blacks to the north and northeast, especially during the 1930s, 1940s, and 1950s, while acquiring voting rights, provided a challenge for the Democratic Party to simultaneously maintain the allegiance of southern whites (a traditional ally of the party), as well as the growing block of black voters in the north and northeast. For a variety of reasons, the Democratic strategy led to the focus on northerners and blacks, which left southern whites available to the Republicans. And race played a prominent, though often subtle role in the so-called Republican "southern strategy." As Beckett and Sasson conclude (2004: 54):

The discourse of "law and order" is an excellent example . . . of racially charged fears and antagonisms. In the context of increasingly unruly street protests, urban riots, and media reports that the crime rate was rising, the capacity of conservatives to mobilize, shape and express these racial fears and tensions became a particularly important political resource. As the traditional working-class coalition that buttressed the Democratic Party was ruptured along racial lines, race eclipsed class as the organizing principle of American politics.

Whether this impact on white southern voters was deliberate or simply a collateral consequence of crime control policies is less relevant than the fact that it appears to have produced significant political advantage.

Ronald Reagan, 1980-1988

Much of the 1970s were a lot quieter in terms of urban racial violence and Vietnam War protests. While the crime rates continued to rise during the 1970s, the administrations of Gerald Ford and Jimmy Carter reflected a relative lack of attention to crime control in Washington.

Between 1968 (when Nixon assumed the presidency) and 1980 (when Ronald Reagan became president), the violent crime rate doubled and the property crime rate increased by 75 percent. There was still plenty of fuel for the tough on crime agenda. President Reagan launched his own version of crime control, which included a focus on arrest, conviction, incarceration, and drugs, as well as explicitly rejecting socioeconomic or criminogenic explanations of crime. Under Reagan, crime was a choice, and, as a response, crime control and the corrections boom began in earnest. The period 1980 to 1988 saw substantial increases in federal assistance to the states for prison construction, changes in sentencing laws, and closing perceived loop holes in time served (the "truth in sentencing" issue, which targeted the often large gap between sentence imposed and actual time served). This was done by encouraging states to revise sentencing laws by moving away from indeterminate sentencing; imposing more and more mandatory sentences, especially for violent crimes and drug crimes; changing parole statutes and discretionary parole release policies, resulting in inmates serving longer sentences; and the reorientation of federal law enforcement away from white collar crime toward predatory street crime.

The Reagan administration also presided over the passage of the federal Sentencing Reform Act of 1984, which was the legislation that enabled the development and implementation of the Federal Sentencing Guidelines.

The federal guidelines that resulted include substantially more severe sentences at the federal level. The Federal Guidelines will be discussed in more depth later in this chapter.

A key element of federal crime control policy has been the focus on illegal drugs, a focus that helped the Reagan administration counter some of the impact of constitutional limits on federal power. The War on Drugs placed the federal government in a key policy role in addressing not only drug crimes, but also the violent and property crimes that were presumed to be associated with drugs.

The Reagan administration faced several significant drug-related challenges in the 1980s, including the 1981–1982 rise of the Medellin cartel (the Columbian cocaine trafficking organization), the 1982 pact between Pablo Escobar, the head of the Medellin cartel, and Manuel Noriega, the president of Panama, allowing cocaine to be transported through his country, and the 1985 crack explosion in New York, which quickly spread to other urban areas. The crack epidemic and the initial violence associated with the distribution and street-level sales of crack rekindled with considerable enthusiasm the antidrug initiatives launched by the Nixon administration. The administration's responses included the passage of the 1986 Anti-Drug Abuse Act, which provided for mandatory minimum sentences for drug offenses, the Federal Sentencing Guidelines with substantially enhanced sentences for drug law violations, and the Nancy Reagan "Just Say No" campaign.

George H. W. Bush, 1988-1992

It was probably quite obvious even to the casual observer that the 1988 presidential campaign had much to do with crime and punishment. The infamous Willie Horton ad is illustrative of the focus on crime, fear, and punishment. Willie Horton was an inmate in the Massachusetts prison system, and Bush's opponent in the 1988 presidential campaign was Michael Dukakis, the governor of Massachusetts. As such, Dukakis was perceived as responsible for the furlough program that let Willie Horton out of prison for a weekend and in turn Horton's failure to return to prison and his subsequent crimes of assault, armed robbery, and rape.

The 1988 campaign further highlighted the political liability of being perceived as soft on crime. George H. W. Bush continued the focus on drugs with the establishment of the Office of National Drug Control Policy and requests for substantial increases in funding for the War on Drugs.

Throughout the decades of the 1960s, 1970s, and 1980s, conservatives essentially owned "tough on crime." This is not to say that Democrats ignored crime and disorder or were silent on concerns about the problem. Instead, the Democrats were simply outdone by their more conservative counterparts. This was accomplished with a masterful combination of discrediting correctional rehabilitation and the social causes of crime and promoting the intuitive logic of punishment. The problem was crime and disorder, and the solution was simple: punishment deters and incapacitates. If old rehabilitative policies were working, crime rates would not have risen to unprecedented levels during the 1960s and 1970s. It was as simple as that and the electorate got it. Crime control became a wedge issue that provided conservatives tremendous political leverage for decades. Then the political landscape changed in the early 1990s.

Bill Clinton, 1992-2000

The 1992 presidential campaign gave birth to a "new generation" of Democrat (as a Clinton/Gore 1992 TV ad labeled them). Clinton/Gore are "a different kind of Democrat . . . they don't think like the old Democrats," the ad continued. The 1992 presidential campaign attempted to brand Clinton/Gore as tough on crime Democrats in favor of welfare reform, among other issues. The campaign made clear that Clinton/Gore supported the death penalty; they advocated putting more police on the streets. The 1992 campaign even had ex-governor Clinton returning to Arkansas to witness an execution. With a combination of symbolism and substance, Clinton/Gore would change the political control of tough on crime that in turn served to further its momentum.

As the story would unfold, the days of sole Republican ownership of crime control were numbered. Campaign rhetoric aside, the real question was: What did the Clinton administration do to demonstrate the new Democratic brand of crime control? It did not take long. In response to a 1993 House Republican crime control legislative package, the Clinton administration, in collaboration with the Democratic leadership, crafted their own crime control bill that reflected many of the initiatives proposed by the Republicans—federal funding for local law enforcement and for expansion of state prison systems if states adopted "truth in sentencing" legislation (again, referring to changes in laws that require prisoners to serve greater percentages of their sentences before consideration for parole release). The Violent Crime Control and Law Enforcement Act of 1994, with a final allocation of $30.2 billion, provided nearly $14 billion for enhanced law enforcement and nearly $10 billion for the expansion of state prisons. While the longer-term impact of the Violent Crime Control and Law Enforcement Act of 1994 is questionable (Turner et al. 2006), the political impact was clear—crime control or tough on crime became a bipartisan issue.

The post-1994 Clinton/Gore administration saw continued federal involvement in shaping criminal justice policy. The Republican Contract with America was a document that was released during the 1994 midterm Congressional elections and was based considerably on President Reagan's 1985 State of the Union Address. It was a policy statement on a number of topics including crime and crime control. The Taking Back Our Streets Act, which was a key anticrime bill within the Contract With America, provided for enhanced funding to states for the expansion of prison capacity, as long as states met the truth in sentencing requirements (typically, requiring that violent offenders serve 85 percent of their sentence before parole consideration). Beckett and Sasson (2004) note in their analysis of the Contract with America legislation that the Republican party proposed the elimination of all funding for crime prevention programs, enhancement of the federal death penalty, and imposition of new mandatory minimum sentences. The political importance of crime control is illustrated by the following quote from Beckett and Sasson (2004: 58):

> The goals advanced in the Contract With America were subsequently embodied in a series of bills passed easily in the House in February 1995. Although President Clinton and the Democrats did manage to retain separate funds for community policing efforts and the ban on assault weapons, the 1995 legislation largely embodied the get-tough approach to crime and decimated federal support for crime prevention programs. Asked to explain President Clinton's failure to provide any real alternatives to proposals, one administration official said, "You can't appear soft on crime when crime hysteria is sweeping the country. . . . " Since that time, few congressional representatives have been willing to deviate from the bipartisan consensus in favor of "getting tough."

By the end of Clinton's second term, crime rates had declined dramatically. The Great American Crime Decline (Zimring 2007), as it has been labeled, consisted of a roughly 40 percent decline in homicide, rape, robbery, burglary, and auto theft between 1990 and 2000, and more modest declines (in the 25 percent range) in aggravated assault and larceny. These UCR trends in crimes known to the police are confirmed by National Crime Victimization Survey data. For a variety of reasons, including declining crime rates, crime and crime control played a less prominent role on the national agenda in the 2000 presidential campaign. Candidate Gore maintained the stance of the Clinton/Gore administration in advocating for more local law enforcement, tougher punishment for offenders (including the death penalty), and mandatory drug testing for all prison inmates and parolees. Candidate Bush maintained support for the death penalty, restrictions on early release from prison, and mandatory sentences, among other crime control initiatives. While both candidates advocated tough on crime positions, aside from mentions in a few speeches and answers to interview questions, crime just was not at the forefront of the campaign as it had been in recent decades.

George W. Bush and the War on Terror, 2000-2008

As governor of Texas, George W. Bush presided over the second-largest prison system in the United States and one of the largest in the world. When Bush took office as Governor, Texas was in the middle of one of the most ambitious prison capacity expansion programs in history, launched by his Democratic predecessor Ann Richards. In a little over six years, the Texas prison system grew by approximately 100,000 beds. During Bush's term, Texas had the third-highest incarceration rate in the nation (behind the District of Columbia and Louisiana). Clearly, George W. Bush was a tough on crime governor and tough on crime presidential candidate. At the time of the 2000 election, the two major political parties were trying to "out-tough" each other. The Democratic message that was delivered at the 2000 Democratic National Convention was that "Clinton and Gore fought for and won the biggest antidrug budgets in history. . . . They funded new prison cells and expanded the death penalty for cop killers and terrorists. . . . But we have just begun to fight the forces of lawlessness and violence." The Republican message that was delivered at the 2000 Republican National Convention was that "we renew our call for a complete overhaul of the juvenile justice system that will punish juvenile offenders and for no-frills prisons for adults." Moreover, the popular press continued to support the premises of punishment and crime control (*Newsweek* November 13, 2000):

> The answer seems obvious to most Americans: Yes, of course punishment reduces crime. Punishment converts criminal activity from a paying proposition to a nonpaying proposition, and people respond accordingly. . . . The logic of deterrence is pretty obvious, and the evidence is powerful too. First, consider the September 18 issue of Forbes, which asks John Lott, senior research scholar at Yale Law School and author of More Guns, Less Crime, "Why the recent drop in crime?" His answer: "Lots of reasons—increases in arrest rates, conviction rates, prison sentence lengths."

By 2000, the great crime decline of the 1990s was well established and violent and property crime rates were the lowest they had been since the 1970s. Moreover, public fear of crime was at a near historic low. Despite these objective indicators of relative calm, just nine months into President Bush's first term, September 11, 2001, dramatically changed the landscape regarding anxiety, fear, threat for personal safety, and crime as it was traditionally known.

The September 11 attacks shifted public attention and government efforts and resources toward domestic terrorism and homeland security. Traditional predatory crime rates continued to decline into the decade of the 2000s and fear of crime remained at relatively low levels. Much of the public anxiety and fear associated with the risk of criminal victimization shifted to the new and now more realistic threat of terrorism. That risk was reinforced by the Bush administration time and time again.

Public opinion polls (Pew Research Center for the People and the Press 2011) confirm that while reducing crime was a priority of respondents before September 11, 2001 (76 percent stated that reducing crime was a "top priority," placing it third behind strengthening the nation's economy and improving education), reducing crime as a priority dropped considerably after September 11 to 47 percent in 2003, 46 percent in 2009, and 44 percent in 2011. On the other hand, defending against terrorism was the top public priority for the nation for most of the decade after 9/11.

The most significant piece of legislation to come out of the Bush administration regarding predatory crime and crime control was the USA Patriot

Act of 2001. The Patriot Act had broad significance for criminal investigation, whether criminal refers to terrorist activity or traditional predatory crime. The Patriot Act in some regards reminds us of Justice Holmes's argument in *Northern Securities Co. v. United States,* in which he stated (paraphrasing) that hard cases make bad law. The Patriot Act was passed some forty-five days after the September 11 attacks. David Cole's (2002) analysis suggests that the scope of the Act was in part a function of the perceived seriousness of the attacks:

> The Administration's final line of defense maintains that unprecedented risks warrant an unprecedented response. The availability of weapons of mass destruction, the relative ease of worldwide travel, communication and financial transfers, the willingness of our enemies to give their own lives for their cause and the existence of a conspiracy that would go to the previously unthinkable lengths illustrated on September 11 require a recalibration of the balance between liberty and security.

That recalibration of the balance between liberty and security has resulted in several provisions of the Act having direct application in traditional (that is, nonterrorist) criminal investigations. Those provisions that are most problematic for criminal justice activities include: the expansion of the definition of terrorism, which can be any act involving a weapon or dangerous device that was not committed for personal gain; reduction of judicial oversight in initiating and supervising wiretaps; the expansion of the government's ability to track internet use and conduct surveillance of libraries and bookstores without probable cause; expansion of the use of sneak and peak searches; and roving wiretaps without probable cause. As Cole (2002) and others opine, the Patriot Act is in many respects an end run around the Fourth Amendment's protection against unreasonable searches and seizures, as well as the requirement for probable cause as the basis for issuing warrants for lawful searches and seizures.

Barack Obama, 2008-Present

Candidate Obama presented a more balanced approach to crime during the 2007 and 2008 campaign. By balanced, I mean emphasizing tough sanctions for violent offenders, but also providing programs like job training, mental health and substance abuse treatment for ex-offenders; more police, but also resources for stronger families and support for the death penalty, with the recognition that it does not deter; supporting diversion programs; alternative sentencing and rehabilitation; and enhancing reentry programs.

That was candidate Obama. What about President Obama? Until very recently, the Obama administration had not really engaged in much highly visible legislative initiatives regarding crime policy. The president did sign a new federal hate crime bill, and presided over the reduction in the powder-crack cocaine disparity in the federal sentencing guidelines (until it was recently changed to eighteen to one, possession of one gram of crack resulted in the same federal sentence as 100 grams of powder cocaine). On balance, perhaps the best characterization of the Obama administration's efforts to promote a more balanced crime policy was wait and see. While the Attorney General has announced that the federal government will not pursue marijuana possession cases in Colorado and Washington, the two states that in 2012 legalized possession of personal amounts of marijuana, there seems to be an appreciation for the political risk involved in significant criminal justice policy change. As Doug Berman of Ohio State comments in *Politico* (Gerstein, September 11, 2010):

> Obama wants to do something, I think, big on criminal justice and I think he is absolutely afraid to. Democrats are right to continue to fear tough on crime demagoguery. The lessons of Clinton continue to resonate. . . . This really is, inevitably, low priority, high risk kind of stuff.

Having said that, there are recent signs (late 2013, early 2014) that the Obama administration may be taking some lead in the area of criminal justice reform. The U.S. Attorney General Eric Holder recently launched the Smart on Crime initiative, aimed at significant changes to sentencing laws and policies, developing alternatives to incarceration for low-level, nonviolent offenders, prioritizing prosecution to focus more on serious offenders, and improving reentry from incarceration.

THE MECHANICS OF CRIME CONTROL AND THE CORRECTIONAL BOOM

The "whys" of crime control and the correctional boom are fairly evident based on the historic realities of the 1960s and 1970s—high levels of predatory crime, massive urban civil disorder, Vietnam War protests, increasing illicit drug use, and the conclusion that what the United States had been doing to address crime and disorder was not working. In short, a broad and serious lack of law and order combined with what at the time seemed to be a failed policy. The key ingredients were in place for a radically new approach, one that would define U.S. justice for decades.

I now focus on how all of this was accomplished, beginning with incarceration. Increases in incarceration of the magnitude experienced in the United States were primarily accomplished by expanding prison capacity and correctional control; changing sentencing and release laws and policies; casting a wider net in terms of what types of offenders are incarcerated; and using fear and anxiety to get the public on board for a massive investment in the new policy.

Bricks and Bars

Incarceration capacity has increased dramatically over the past forty years. In 1970, the United States had approximately 580 state-level correctional facilities. By 2005 (the most recent data available for the number of correctional facilities), the states had 1,720, representing a 200 percent increase. In 1970, state correctional facilities in the United States had a capacity for 240,000 inmates. In 2008, the capacity of state facilities in the United States was 1,272,300, a 430 percent increase.

It is important to point out that the state-by-state distribution of the growth in prisons is not uniform and, as expected, most of the growth is lodged in a relatively small number of states. An analysis by the Urban Institute (Lawrence and Travis 2004) demonstrates that nearly two-thirds of the growth in prison capacity occurred in ten states: Texas, California, Florida, Michigan, Georgia, Illinois, New York, Ohio, Colorado, and Missouri. Texas was the outlier among the states, with an increase in the number of facilities over this time period of over 700 percent.

In 1990, 1995, and 2000, state prison systems were operating at an average of 100 percent of rated capacity. By 2005, that had increased to an average of 108 percent, but there was considerable disparity across regions as well as within regions. For example, states in the west averaged 120 percent of capacity, in the Midwest 110 percent, and in the South, 104 percent. However, California was operating at 141 percent,

Washington at 131 percent, Florida at 128 percent, Ohio at 122 percent, and Illinois at 136 percent.

The federal prison system also expanded capacity during the corrections boom. Federal data are not very consistent over time, but here is what can be pieced together. Between 1990 and 2005, the capacity of the federal prison system increased from 42,180 to 106,700, an increase of over 150 percent. Interestingly, while several states were in the midst of federal litigation during this era, litigation challenging, among other things, overcrowding of their prison systems, the federal prison system was operating at a level well over its rated capacity. In 1990, the federal prison system was operating at 135 percent of capacity; in 1995, it was 124 percent; in 2000, 134 percent; and in 2005, 137 percent.

Community Supervision Caseloads

The majority of individuals under correctional control are on parole or probation, both of which are supervised release. Probation, defined as conditional supervised release to the community, is diversion from incarceration, but probationers are subject to revocation to prison (for felons on probations) or jail (for misdemeanants on probation) if they violate the conditions of supervision. Parolees, individuals released from prison early, are also subject to revocation to prison if they violate the conditions of their release. Revocation from probation or parole is generally discretionary. In the case of probation, the offender is brought before a judge for a revocation hearing. In the case of parole, the case is brought before the parole authorities, generally a parole board or parole commission.

In 2011, there were 2.75 times as many probationers as prisoners. And while incarceration grew at a faster rate than probation and parole between 1975 and 2011 (incarceration increased by 535 percent, while parole increased by 475 percent and probation increased by 390 percent), the sheer volume of community supervision, primarily probation, required substantial changes as well. One of the primary methods for "expanding" probation and parole during the past three decades to meet increasing supervision demands was simply to increase officer caseloads. The American Probation and Parole Association recommends probation officer caseloads for regular probation supervision of 50. Nationally, the average is somewhere between 130 and 150. In California, one of the largest probation systems in the nation, probation caseloads range from 100 to 200. In Texas, the average caseload is 160. In some jurisdictions in the United States, probation caseloads of 750 to 1,000 have been reported.

While parole caseloads are lower than probation, the parole population is generally higher risk than probation, since parolees have served a period of incarceration. Typical parole caseloads in the United States have increased from forty-five per officer in the 1970s to seventy and higher in more recent years (Travis, Solomon, and Waul 2001). In Texas, state law requires that the maximum parole caseload be sixty. However, the typical Texas parole officer supervised eighty or more parolees in 2010.

Probation and parole caseloads are just one metric for measuring how well community supervision delivers or provides intended risk management and community-based services. What is evident in recent research on probation and parole (DeMichele 2007; Jalbert et al. 2010; Jalbert et al. 2011; Paparozzi and DeMichele 2008) is that community supervision budgets have been steadily declining and caseloads have been steadily increasing.

Available financial data at the state and national levels indicate that criminal justice expenditures increased by over 300 percent between 1988 and 2008. The Pew Center for the States (2009b) estimates that total state-level expenditures for criminal justice in 2008 exceeded $52 billion. The bulk of that—88 percent—was spent on prisons. The irony, as the report points out, is that prisons account for about one-third of the growth in correctional control over the past few decades, but prisons account for the vast majority of criminal justice spending.

Changes to Sentencing Laws and Procedures

Crime control requires punishment, which means punishing more offenders more severely. Thus the strategic issue is how to accomplish that. This is where sentencing reform, an essential mechanism of the crime control strategy, comes into play.

Forty years ago, state and federal criminal defendants were sentenced under indeterminate sentencing laws. Indeterminate sentencing consists of statutes that provide broad authority or discretion to the court in sentencing an individual. The typical indeterminate sentencing statute provides for a relatively wide range of punishment upon conviction of a particular offense (for example, aggravated armed robbery) or class of offense (for example, first degree felony). By way of example, in Texas, a state classified as indeterminate today, the punishment range for someone convicted of a first degree felony is five to ninety-nine years of incarceration or probation (if the offense qualifies for probation). Clearly, a range of five to ninety-nine is considerable and provides the sentencing judge with considerable discretion.

Indeterminate sentencing was called indeterminate primarily because when the offender was admitted to prison, it was unclear (that is, not determined) how long that offender would be incarcerated. How much an offender served of the sentence imposed by the court was up to the parole authorities.

In theory, indeterminate sentencing allows sentencing of the offense and the offender. That is, the court may consider the elements and characteristics of the offense, prior criminal history, and a relatively broad array of mitigating and aggravating circumstances in arriving at an appropriate punishment. The court may sentence for the harm done in the commission of the instant offense, the harm done in the past, and any offender-based aggravating factors that may indicate a harsher sentence, and mitigating factors that may indicate more lenient treatment. Under indeterminate sentencing, the court was generally free to consider a variety of goals of sentencing—specific deterrence, general deterrence, incapacitation, retribution, rehabilitation, something else, and any combination of the above. The court was also generally free to consider, weigh, and evaluate evidence as he/she sees fit. There was no set formula that says: here are the aggravating factors, here are the mitigating factors, and here is a list of the more important and less important considerations for sentencing. In short, judges have substantial discretion in sentencing, and that was historically viewed as an advantage in forging the appropriate sentence for individual offenders. And who better to do that than judges who have the experience in considering the totality of the circumstances and arriving at an offender-based sentence?

And therein lies part of the problem. Sentencing reform was spearheaded by three concerns. One, when judges are allowed such wide latitude in sentencing as that provided by indeterminate sentencing, extralegal factors can enter into the sentencing calculus, which can lead to sentencing disparity and, in the extreme, sentencing discrimination. Disparity has been defined in practice as similarly situated offenders convicted of similar offenses receiving different sentences. Discrimination is the use of clearly unlawful factors, such as race, in the sentencing decision. The second concern, perhaps less frequently articulated but just as present in the crime control/sentencing reform movement, was the perception that when judges are afforded such wide latitude, they tend to "error" on the lenient side of the sentence. Clearly, what is a disparate or lenient sentence is in the eyes of the beholder. Two offenders who appear similar may in fact exhibit relevant differences that the court considers important. What appears lenient to one observer may simply be a case of mitigation.

The third issue is referred to as truth in sentencing. This is also a consequence of indeterminate sentencing and focuses on the gap between the sentence imposed by the court and how much of that sentence the offender actually serves. Indeterminate sentencing was designed to allow offenders to be released when they had progressed to the point at which the parole authorities believed further incarceration was not warranted. Parole release, based on good conduct credit or good time, was also a mechanism prison officials used to manage the prison population—an incentive for good behavior based on the universal currency of those in prison, getting out sooner.

Truth in sentencing essentially means that sentencing should be honest—when the court imposes a sentence of ten years, that means ten years, not two, not five, not seven. What the truth in sentencing advocates promoted was narrowing that gap between what the court says and what actually occurs in terms of time served.

These concerns, disparity/discrimination on one side and leniency of sentence and time served on the other, formed the perfect union. The liberal side of the political aisle embraced the disparity/discrimination concern, and the conservative side embraced the leniency and truth in sentencing concerns. The remedy for both was the same: control or restrict judicial discretion in sentencing. With clear bipartisan support, sentencing reform was launched.

The direction it took was toward determinate or structured sentencing. Determinate sentencing, also called fixed sentencing and including sentencing schemes such as guidelines, is designed to limit judicial discretion by restricting what may be considered by the court at sentencing (the aggravating and mitigating factors common in indeterminate sentencing) and by providing for more specific sentences (rather than wide ranges) for particular offenses.

Several states, including California, Washington, Maine, Minnesota, and Oregon, had begun moving in the determinate sentencing direction in the 1970s and early 1980s. One of the earlier and decidedly more visible and controversial results of sentencing reform were the Federal Sentencing Guidelines.

In 1984, Congress passed the Sentencing Reform Act, legislation drafted in an era of a congressional focus on crime control strategies, including punishment enhancements for narcotics law violations and mandatory minimums for violent offenders. As Stith and Koh note (1993: 259):

> The renewed congressional interest in mandating heavy sentences for drug offenses and violent crimes, reflecting Congress' increasing determination to demonstrate its anticrime sentiment, ultimately resulted in the passage in the 98th Congress of an assortment of statutes imposing minimum terms of imprisonment.

It is important to point out that while the Sentencing Reform Act of 1984 passed both the House and Senate with overwhelming support, there was dissention, especially in the House. Opposition focused on the rigidity and punitiveness of the proposed guidelines, the fact that they were to be mandatory, and that they restricted the court from tailoring sentences to the particulars of individual cases.

The support for this legislation was significantly a function of the fact that it was attached to the continuing appropriations resolution in September 1984. The passage of the Sentencing Reform Act came when the fiscal year was about to end (October 1) and there was an impending national election on November 6, 1984. Both of these considerations played significant roles in the massive overhaul of federal sentencing. Essentially, once the bill was attached to the appropriations bill, it was guaranteed to be enacted, if for no other reason than the immediacy of continuing federal appropriations.

Language in the original legislation and amendments indicate that the Federal Sentencing Commission, which was created by the Sentencing Reform Act, was encouraged to develop mandatory guidelines that enhanced punishment, both across the board, as well as for several targeted segments of the offender population—violent offenders, repeat offenders, drug offenders, and offenders who commit crimes while on bail, among others.

The Federal Guidelines are probably the most drastic version of determinate sentencing in the United States. They are harm based and utilize a quantitative system (effectively, a scorecard) that scores the offense in terms of various measure of harm (physical harm, financial loss, the defendant's role in the offense, the defendant's use of a weapon, quantity of drugs, etc.). Most of the traditional offender attributes that judges may have considered mitigating under indeterminate sentencing laws, such as mental health, intellectual capacity, addiction, poverty, and so on, are "not ordinarily relevant" under the federal guidelines. The focus is on the harm reflected in the instant offense (the offense-level score), and the harm perpetrated by the defendant in the past (the criminal history score). The guideline matrix consists of forty-three rows consisting of offense levels, which are statistical scores reflecting the harm done during the commission of the conviction offense. The six columns of the sentencing matrix are composed of scores reflecting criminal history. The matrix has 258 cells, corresponding to the combinations of offense levels and criminal history categories. All but 21 of the 258 cells dictate a sentence of incarceration. Those twenty-one (8 percent of the cells) are subject to diversion on probation. Truth in sentencing issues were quickly resolved by the Commission's entire and swift elimination of parole in the federal system. The bottom line is that the sentencing role of federal judges was dramatically restricted, most of the opportunities for mitigation were removed, sentences of probation were significantly restricted, sentences are effectively more severe, and time served is greatly increased by the elimination of parole.

The significance of the federal guidelines is not found in the number of individuals sentenced in federal court or in the reach of federal law into sentencing and punishment in the states. The federal system accounts for a small proportion of all individuals sentenced in the United States (approximately 6 percent to 7 percent of felony sentences in a given year in the United States are federal cases). The constitutional limits on the federal government's authority in local law enforcement, prosecution, sentencing, and punishment highlighted what the Nixon administration saw as a leadership role rather than a direct legislative role for the federal government with regard to crime fighting. The significance of the federal guidelines in terms of U.S. criminal justice policy is the example set. One of the primary goals of the federal sentencing reformers was to create a model for other states to follow (Stith and Koh 1993). And that they did.

The federal system was unique with regard to the sweeping changes the guidelines had on sentencing law, discretion of the court, and the severity of punishment. While no state developed guidelines in the mold of the federal version, the message was clear. In terms of policy, the federal guidelines represented a quite visible standard for the states. The federal government was putting its money where its mouth was in terms of tough on crime. The federal guidelines have been referred to as the "prison guidelines," a reflection of their overall punitiveness (Hoelter 2009).

The United States went from essentially uniform indeterminate sentencing in all of the states, the District of Columbia, and the federal system prior to 1975, to fifty-two varied, fragmented, hybrid systems of determinate sentences, structured sentences, fixed sentences, guideline sentences, indeterminate sentences, mandatory sentences, mandatory minimum sentences, habitual offender sentences, and elimination of or statutory restrictions on early release. What is clear after sentencing reform is that no state or the federal system in the United States today sentences like it did in 1975, and no two jurisdictions share the same sentencing laws.

It is a bit challenging to classify the sentencing systems in the United States today, mainly because there are no "pure" types. A useful classification by Stemen, Rengifo, and Wilson (2006) is used here to flesh out where states are today after thirty-five years of sentencing reform. Stemen et al. define determinate sentencing as a system that does not have discretionary parole release. Using this definition of determinate sentencing, they classify seventeen states as determinate, meaning the elimination of discretionary parole release. Eighteen states have developed and adopted some form of required or structured sentencing, either in the form of presumptive sentences or presumptive guidelines. Presumptive sentences and guidelines are presumptive because there is the expectation or requirement that the recommended sentence or the guideline sentence will be used, unless there is proper cause and written justification for a departure. An additional eight states had voluntary sentencing guidelines in 2002. What these statutory changes mean in effect is that thirty-five states removed discretion from the court and/or from the parole authorities (seventeen determinate states and eighteen structured/guideline sentence states). Ten states eliminated discretionary parole release and implemented structured sentencing or presumptive guideline sentencing. Twenty-seven states neither eliminated discretionary parole release nor created guidelines or structured sentencing, rendering their sentencing systems discretionary on the part of the court for upfront sentences, and discretionary on the part of the parole authority at release. And while they still, strictly speaking, have discretionary parole, many of these states have altered the statutes governing eligibility for discretionary release (requiring longer percentages of sentences be served before eligibility) and have altered discretionary release decision policies regarding who and how many are released.

While those twenty-seven states did not implement guidelines or dramatically restrict the discretion of the court in sentencing, it is nevertheless the case that those states do not have the sentencing systems they had in 1975. Twenty-three of those states enacted mandatory minimum sentences for a variety of drug law violations; fifteen have mandatory minimums for weapons offenses, nine have them for habitual offenders, nine for certain violent offenders, and nine for sex offenses and/or pornography.

In addition to those states just mentioned, approximately thirty states have or had mandatory minimum sentences for drug offenses, twenty-five had mandatory minimums for crimes involving a weapon, eighteen had mandatory minimums for habitual offenders, seventeen for violent, and eighteen for sex/pornography offenses. The federal government has mandatory minimum sentences for weapons offenses, drug offenses, habitual offenders, and organized crime, among others.

One more matter needs to be addressed while discussing sentencing reform and that is truth in sentencing (TIS) legislation. TIS involves a variety of statutes and sentencing practices all aimed at increasing time served at least for certain types of offenders. One of the provisions of the 1994 Crime Act was the availability of federal grant money to states that implemented TIS provisions. The grant money was designed to fund prison expansion in the states for the incarceration of violent offenders. One requirement attached to the funds was the implementation of truth in sentencing laws.

All told, forty-one states plus the District of Columbia passed some form of TIS law. While twenty-one states had a TIS law in place prior to the passage of the 1994 Crime Bill, twenty-one states either implemented new laws or made at least modest changes to TIS laws. Nine of these states implemented new TIS legislation after 1994. Twenty-nine states implemented the 85 percent rule, requiring that violent offenders serve at least 85 percent of the sentence imposed. The remaining twelve TIS states that did not impose the 85 percent rule did impose a percentage (less than the 85 percent) requirement for time served prior to eligibility for release consideration (data are from Sabol et al. 2002).

The end result is that state legislatures and Congress increasingly took control of sentencing and release decisions, and across the board, this translated into more severe punishments for increasing numbers of offenders. It resulted in more sentences of incarceration (admissions to prison), with longer sentences imposed, and greater time served. These results of sentencing reform provide one of the key mechanisms for accomplishing the incarceration boom.

Drug Control Policy: Casting the Net More Widely

The scale of the correctional boom, in terms of the rate of growth in incarceration and probation and the resulting size of the incarceration and probation populations, was additionally and significantly aided by net widening. Net widening refers to expanding the population of individuals coming in the front door of the criminal justice system. The War on Drugs did just that. The enhanced focus on enforcement of drug law violations, in conjunction with changes in drug sentencing laws, provided a new and growing segment of offenders for the correctional system. Caplow and Simon (1999:71) suggest that there were simply too few nondrug offenders to fuel a correctional boom on the scale that was experienced.

> "Tough on crime" policies produce prison population increases only to the degree that offenders are available to be imprisoned. The growth in nondrug crime has simply not been sufficient to sustain the rapid growth in imprisonment.

The logic is twofold. First, drug offenses have been subject to a wide variety of state and federal enhancements in the form of mandatory minimums, mandatory sentences, and repeat offender statutes. These mandatory sentences increase admissions to prison as well as length of sentence and time served. All three of these components—increases in admissions, length of sentence, and time served—will increase incarceration rates and prison populations. The second element in the argument is that drug offenses, to a greater extent than violent and property offenses, are capable of providing a nearly inexhaustible supply of offenders. This is true in part because of the voracious demand for drugs in the United States, the enormous profit to be made, and an ever-present supply of drugs. Moreover, when a drug dealer is arrested, the dealing is not typically removed from the street just because that dealer is in custody. There is usually an eager cohort of replacements ready to fill that vacancy.

So what is the evidence regarding the extent of the role of the War on Drugs in facilitating the correctional boom? Between 1975 and 2002, the number of drug offenders incarcerated in state and federal prisons and jails rose from 40,595 to 480,519, an increase of 1,083 percent! The overall incarceration population increased by slightly more than 400 percent over this period. If drug offender admissions were no different than other offenders, one would expect the increase in drug offenders incarcerated to be somewhere around 400 percent. Instead the increase in incarceration of drug offenders was 2.7 times that of the overall incarceration population. The increase in drug offenders in state prisons and jails was 1,140 percent between 1975 and 2002; for federal prisons and jails, the increase was 1,030 percent.

In addition to this descriptive evidence, research by Stemen, Rengifo, and Wilson (2006) supports this link between incarceration and the War on Drugs. Their analysis demonstrates that the effects of drug arrests likely outstrip the negative effects of declining crime rates on incarceration rates. During the past twenty years, a period in which crime rates declined by 42 percent, incarceration rates increased by 66 percent. Drug incarcerations contributed substantially to the increase in incarceration rates during a period of declining overall crime. Drug offenders have also comprised a significant proportion of individuals sentenced to probation in the United States. In 1990, drug offenders constituted 36 percent of the probation population. In 2000, it was 24 percent, and in 2011 it was 26 percent.

One final point on the issue of incarceration and drugs merits emphasizing. Some observers may inject a conspiratorial element into this argument, suggesting that the War on Drugs was launched to help maintain such large-scale incarceration. The position here is not a conspiratorial one. Instead, the correctional boom and the War on Drugs both occurred within the context of crime control policies and the extent to which drug offending helped support the scale of the incarceration and corrections boom is important, but largely a collateral consequence.

PUBLIC OPINION ABOUT CRIME: THE ROLE OF THE EXECUTIVE AND LEGISLATIVE BRANCHES

The launch and longer-term sustainability of crime control, sentencing reform, and the correctional boom warrant an assessment of the role of public opinion. It is no mistake that public opinion is placed here under the heading of the mechanics of crime control, rather than under the prior section on the drivers of these policies. The evidence does not really support a conclusion that crime control policies were a response to a groundswell of public pressure about crime.

Public opinion polls have tracked a variety of measures including fear of crime and crime as a significant problem, whether crime seems to be increasing or decreasing in their area. For example, one of the more common metrics of crime as a problem is the Most Important Problem (MIP) question, which has been asked annually since 1945. It simply asks: "What is the most important problem facing this nation today?" The MIP question presumably takes more of a national focus (the most important problem facing the nation today) and does not define what it is about crime that is the problem or concern. Fear of crime is also tracked over time and is based on questions like: "Is there any area near where you live—that is, within one mile—where you would be afraid to walk alone at night?" This question has a local focus and asks about personal concerns about safety.

The trends indicate that crime as the MIP was essentially off of the public radar until the late 1960s and 1970s. There was a slight increase in the percentage of respondents indicating that crime was their top priority in 1968 and that continued until 1977. In relative terms, however, these percentages (10 percent to a high of 17 percent) are small. However, in 1988, crime as the MIP jumped to 40 percent, likely in part a response to the violence associated with crack markets as well as the 1988 presidential campaign and influences such as the George H. W. Bush campaign's Willie Horton TV ad. Crime as the MIP quickly dropped in 1989–1990, but then peaked in 1994 at 52 percent. Crime continued to be at the top of the list of the most important problem facing the nation in 1995, 1997, 1998, and 1999. Beginning in the early 2000s, crime once again slipped off of the public radar (MIP data are from Gallup, various years).

The fear of crime time series is relatively stable over time. Fear, as measured by the "walking alone at night" question, was highest in 1982 with

48 percent affirming such fear and lowest in 1967 at 31 percent (Bureau of Justice Statistics 2010). Over the long term (1965 to 2011), the trend reflects a bump in fear between 1972 and 1993, but between 1994 and 2011 it is essentially stable, fluctuating around an average of 35 percent.

Another measure is whether respondents believe that there is more or less crime in their area than a year ago. Time series data for the period 1972 to 2011 indicate significant fluctuation. Half of respondents in 1972 reported that crime was higher in their area. That was down to 37 percent in 1983, back up to 53 percent in 1989, and 54 percent in 1992, then down to 31 percent in 1998. It remained in the 30 percent to 40 percent range until 2004, then rose and fluctuated between 44 percent and 51 percent up to 2011 (fear of crime and crime increasing data are from the Sourcebook of Criminal Justice Statistics 2011).

This cursory glance at public opinion about crime and fear of crime indicates that the public was sufficiently fearful or concerned about crime to perhaps be "supportive" of a crime control/correctional control initiative. However, there is little evidence in the public opinion data to indicate that the public was growing increasingly and substantially concerned and fearful in the years preceding the launch of crime control or even in the earlier years after crime control was in place.

Political scientists and sociologists have focused on the role of executive, legislative, and political campaign communications in the formation of public opinion about crime. There is a well-established research literature on presidential influence on public opinion (Cohen 1995). An obvious question at this point is: What has been the influence of elected officials and their party platforms in shaping public perception about crime as a problem and crime control as a solution? The research is pretty clear: changes in public opinion about crime and punishment follow public rhetoric by elected officials. That is, the research indicates that the content of national executive, congressional, and party platform speech in turn shapes public opinion, not the other way around. As Bosso (1987: 261) explains:

> The presidency is the single most powerful institutional lever for policy breakthrough and is the political system's thermostat, capable of heating up or cooling down the politics of any single issue or of an entire platter of issues.

Beckett and Sasson (2004: 110–111) assert that public opinion about crime and crime solutions is substantially influenced by political and media discussion/coverage of crime, not the reverse:

> The public worries about crime and drugs, but this worry is not the driving force behind the massive political and media attention to these issues. On the relatively rare occasions when the public has put crime or drugs at the top of its list of concerns, it has done so in the context of massive political initiative and media coverage.

ARE AMERICANS A VENGEFUL LOT?

During the September 7, 2011, Republican primary presidential debate before a Tea Party audience, mention was made of the fact that Texas governor Rick Perry had overseen a record 234 executions while governor. Many in the audience cheered. Viewed from afar, an observer would likely conclude that Americans indeed thrive on revenge. A quick glimpse at the U.S. justice system would certainly add support to that, and the evidence regarding what tough on crime has accomplished would also lead to a revenge for revenge's sake argument. At the same time, as of May 2013, eighteen states have outlawed the death penalty, including six states since 2007.

In the late 1990s, I had the opportunity to collaborate with some faculty at the Institute of Criminology at Cambridge University in the United Kingdom. Part of the collaboration was my touring a British maximum security prison, not far from Cambridge. Part of the tour was to sit in on an inmate discussion called a dialog group. The dialog group I attended consisted of about thirty-five or forty inmates, sitting in a room with no guards present. The purpose of the discussion group was the opportunity for the inmates to discuss their concerns and fears, strategies for managing life while incarcerated, and how to prepare for release and reentry. The inmates had been informed that I was from the United States, and in particular from Texas. The two-hour dialog group took a one-hour detour that day when the inmates asked me all about the U.S. justice system, whether it was as tough as they had heard, how tough the punishment is, and whether it was true that Texas was about a tough as they get. Most of their observations or impressions of the U.S. justice system focused on what appeared to them to be revenge. British inmates, serving (for the British system) long sentences, were quite impressed (not in the favorable meaning of the word) by the tough on crime approach of the United States.

Many things struck me about this experience, but two are particularly relevant here. One, it is quite unlikely that this type of a discussion or dialog group would ever take place in a similar institution in the United States. Second, the takeaway by British inmates was that the U.S. system was largely revenge based, as evidenced by the no-nonsense, tough on crime punitive approach.

So what is the answer? Are Americans vengeful? Is that what crime control has been about? Are Americans bloodthirsty? Do Americans seek an eye for an eye? To try to answer this, I return to public opinion data.

The short answer is not as much as one would expect based on things such as U.S. incarceration rates, the size of the correctional population, and decades of tough on crime rhetoric. Americans' attitudes do not reflect a simplistic, unidimensional view toward harsher and harsher punishment. The public opinion evidence that suggests that Americans favor punitiveness tend to be based on abstract, simplistic questions that provide little context, or in response to a particularly horrific crime (Unnever and Cullen 2010). When asked appropriately, Americans' attitudes regarding punishment are rather complex and conditional. For example, Americans' attitudes about the death penalty tend to be selective; Unnever, Cullen, and Roberts (2005) report that over half of Americans who support the death penalty do so with reservations. Moreover, Americans continue to embrace rehabilitation of criminal offenders, especially juveniles. The National Center for State Courts 2006 Sentencing Attitudes Survey revealed that while Americans favor tough sentencing for violent offenders, they overwhelmingly believe that many offenders can and should be rehabilitated, and that rehabilitation is a higher priority than punishment. But most believe that prisons are unsuccessful at rehabilitation. The public is also quite supportive of alternatives to incarceration such as probation, job training, and treatment. When Americans do hold punitive attitudes, those attitudes are most pronounced among individuals who perceive that crime rates are worsening, that society is in some form of moral decline, and who have biased views about minorities (Unnever and Cullen 2010).

While public attitudes are more complex than the casual observer might conclude, Americans have been willing participants in crime control. To a considerable extent, Americans have allowed policymakers to continue to ramp up punishments for criminal offenders, a role that Useem and Piehl (2008) describe as "willing co-conspirators." Cullen, Fisher, and Applegate (2000: 1) review and assess public opinion data about crime and punishment and note that while Americans can and do hold punitive attitudes, they are selective and more balanced in their views:

> Support for get tough policies is "mushy. . . ." Especially when nonviolent offenders are involved, there is substantial support for intermediate sanctions and for restorative justice. . . . In the end, the public shows a tendency to be punitive and progressive, wishing the correctional system to achieve its diverse missions of doing justice, protecting public safety and reforming the wayward.

Overall, it does seem that the beliefs and attitudes of the U.S. public are a bit out of sync with the rhetoric of crime control. While elected officials appear to have been pursuing a nearly singular solution of more and more punishment, the public has had a broader, more balanced perspective that incorporates multiple strategies for achieving public safety.

Despite public celebrations upon news of the death of bin Laden or water cooler talk about the preferred method of execution for Jodi Arias, it appears that Americans are rather utilitarian in thinking about how best to accomplish public safety. That includes an element of revenge, and often that vengeance seems to surface when referencing a particular individual. But at the end of the day, Americans seem to prefer and support a variety of approaches.

THE FEDERALIZATION OF CRIMINAL JUSTICE POLICY

Looking back over the past forty years of crime control, sentencing reform, and the correctional boom, it is a wonder that all fifty states engaged in this most profound of criminal justice policy transformations. A fundamentally important factor in understanding the evolution of crime control is the role of the federal government in this process.

In the February 1967 report "The Challenge of Crime in a Free Society," the President's Commission on Law Enforcement and the Administration of Justice stated that "crime is a national, as well as a state and local phenomenon" (Presidents Commission 1967). As a result of the Commission's findings, Johnson proposed grant programs to states and local jurisdictions for funding law enforcement. Subsequently, in June 1968, at Johnson's urging, Congress passed the Omnibus Crime Control and Safe Streets Act, which provided grants to state and local jurisdictions for law enforcement expansion, training, recruitment, and infrastructure, among other things.

The President's Commission and the administration's Omnibus Crime Control and Safe Streets Act of 1968 signaled the beginning of the federalization of crime control, both defining crime as a national problem and asserting federal responsibility for assisting the states in crime control. Subsequent Congressional legislation reinforced the federal role in local crime control. The 1984 Comprehensive Crime Control act established the grant-making arm of the U.S. Department of Justice. The 1990 Crime Control Act authorized nearly $1 billion in grants to states to assist with improving and expanding prisons, enhancing the functions of criminal justice agencies, and enforcing drug laws. The Violent Crime Control and Law Enforcement Act of 1994 provided $30.2 billion for increases in local law enforcement and expansion of prison capacity.

The federal government, including the president, the Attorney General, and the Justice Department, Congress, and the national political party organizations have all been fundamentally important in setting the national crime control agenda. This has been accomplished in a variety of ways, including campaign rhetoric; State of the Union Addresses; other executive and legislative communications; legislation (such as the Omnibus Crime Bills, providing highly visible examples such as the implementation of the Federal Sentencing Guidelines, mandatory sentences, and truth in sentencing legislation); prosecuting the War on Drugs; and providing federal funding and technical assistance to states and local jurisdictions for implementing numerous crime control initiatives.

Research by Oliver and colleagues (Marion 1994, 1997; Marion and Farmer 2003; Oliver 1998, 2002; Oliver and Marion 2008) demonstrate that presidential communications about crime (speeches, State of the Union Address, printed statements) bear a significant statistical relationship with crime as the MIP trends. For example, the relatively small spikes in crime as the MIP in 1967 and 1968 can be attributed to President Johnson's push for the Omnibus Crime Control and Safe Streets Act, and the persistence of the small spikes, but spikes nevertheless, in crime as the MIP in 1969, 1970, 1971, and 1972 are due in part to the 1968 presidential campaign and the Nixon administration's focus on law and order once in office. The sizable uptick in crime as the MIP beginning in 1988 through 1991 is due in part to the Bush campaign's focus on crime. Finally, the significant increase in crime as the MIP starting in 1994 and lasting through much of the crime decline of the 1990s is attributed to the Clinton administration's focus on crime and Clinton campaigning for passage of the Violent Crime Control and Law Enforcement Act of 1994 (Oliver 1998).

Research by Oliver and Marion (2008) suggests that political parties, like presidents, have used crime control as a symbol to define crime as a problem, assure the public that they will do something about it, and used crime control as a model for states to emulate. Further, they conclude that the use of crime control in this manner has led to the "federalization" of crime. Oliver and Marion (2008: 411) conclude that

> this study demonstrates that political parties have also become increasingly engaged in advocating a larger role for the federal government in crime control . . . crime as a national political issue appears to be well entrenched on the institutional agenda of our federal government, and has been further propagated by the modern political parties, demonstrating that crime has become an important policy issue for winning elections.

Marion and Farmer (2003) document that at the end of the crime decline of the 1990s, when crime rates were at their lowest in the prior twenty years, crime was still a key topic during the 2000 presidential campaign.

Acknowledging that in fact the vast majority of crime is local, one of the concerns about the federalization of crime control is that a federal approach of "tough on crime" is essentially imposing a one-size-fits-all solution to a problem that is extraordinarily complex, a function of some common causes or correlates, but also due to many unique location- and situation-specific factors. While a fairly unidimensional, uniform federal crime control approach may be well intentioned, the expectation that it is appropriate for all is simply wrong.

SUSTAINABILITY OF CRIME CONTROL AND THE CORRECTIONAL BOOM

On balance, given the significant challenges to public safety at the time (high crime, racial violence, student protests, increasing drug use, a perceived general lack of law and order, and a perception that the justice system was failing), it is relatively easy in hindsight to understand the launch of crime control. There was anxiety and fear born of the realities of the 1960s and 1970s and that concern was reinforced by the media and elected officials. There was pressure to find a solution to restore law and order. There was the perception that what the United States had been doing in the past was not working, thus it was time for a new course, a sea change in criminal justice policy. That new course, control and punishment, made sense to policymakers, elected officials, and the public. It was simple and intuitive to those proposing the new path and to those voting for its proponents.

One can understand the birth of crime control as a seemingly realistic, logical, and, at the time, just solution to a significant problem of disorder, crime, and public safety. However, crime control and the correctional boom have been front and center in U.S. criminal justice policy for the past forty years. So what does the longer-term picture of crime and disorder in the United States on the one hand, and crime control and the correctional boom on the other look like? More specifically, if the correctional boom and crime control were a response to a crime problem, how are we to understand their longevity? How do we explain the ongoing existence of the correctional boom in 2014?

A simple, descriptive trend analysis of crime and the correctional boom would conclude that while crime and disorder were at historically high levels in the 1960s and 1970s, both began significant declines in the early 1980s, the period of the beginning of the substantial surge in incarceration. Just looking at simple trends, it is difficult to reconcile crime and punishment in a meaningful way.

Several researchers have addressed this question over the past twenty years. Blumstein and Beck (1999, 2005), Raphael (2009), and Raphael and Stoll (2009) have all conducted time series analyses of trends in incarceration rates utilizing the primary predictors of crime rates, arrests, admissions to prison, and length of sentence/time served. For the time period 1980 to 1996, only 12 percent of the trend in incarceration rates is statistically due to crime. Instead, the vast majority of the trend in incarceration (88 percent) is due to commitments to prison (51 percent) and time served (37 percent). A subsequent analysis by Blumstein and Beck (2005) utilized the same approach on a somewhat different time period (1991 to 2002) and found that crime rates played no statistical role in accounting for change in incarceration. Instead, the most important factor in this later period of the incarceration boom for explaining incarceration changes was time served.

Using a somewhat different approach that incorporates the impact of incarceration on crime, Raphael and Stoll (2009) determine that for the time period from 1984 to 2002, increases in crime account for 17 percent of the increase in incarceration rates. Eighty-three percent of the change is statistically attributed to time served and prison admissions.

What these statistical analyses clearly indicate is that over the longer term of crime control, crime rates play a minor role in explaining the growth in incarceration. The conclusion is that what sustained the correctional boom and the incarceration boom and crime control policies over the long term was not increases in crime or arrests, but enhanced punitiveness (increased admissions to prison and increases in time served, both of which are a result of sentencing reform). So the question now is that if crime was not driving the longevity of crime control and the correctional boom, what was? Why is the United States still pursuing a set of policies and continuing to spend extraordinary amounts of money on an approach that (1) is neither effective nor cost-effective at reducing crime and recidivism, as I will show in chapter 2; and (2) does not appear to have a clear, contemporary rationale or justification? Why is it that the United States still pursues a nearly unilateral focus on punishment and control, when public opinion supports a more balanced, multidimensional approach? Part of the answer, which is not really an answer, is inertia. It is just hard to turn around such as large, entrenched enterprise. There are also economic interests at play. When prisons close, jobs are lost, and over the past thirty years or so, correctional facilities have been economic drivers in many, many smaller, rural areas in the country. There is also the correctional industry that consists of such large, publicly traded corporations as GEO (formerly Wackenhut), Corrections Corporation of America, and Cornell Companies, to name but a few. These companies have a clear financial interest in keeping corrections scaled up and no doubt lobby legislatures to preserve their interests. And there are the ever-present political considerations. Tough on crime still resonates; it still sells. And elected officials apparently find it difficult to package correctional change in a way that does not come across as soft or lenient.

SUMMARY

I have shown that the launch of crime control was in response to increasing predatory crime rates, massive racial violence in the nation's urban areas, protests over the Vietnam War, the assassinations of Martin Luther King, Jr. and Robert Kennedy, and increasing use of illegal drugs. In short, plenty of evidence for concluding there was a substantial lack of law and order.

It seems that throughout their duration, crime control, sentencing reform, and the correctional boom took on a life of their own, driven in part by the realities of electoral politics. The political leverage that crime control first afforded the Republican Party was strategically used in a variety of ways, in the effort to recruit southern whites to the fold of the party and becoming a wedge issue differentiating the two major political parties. And a highly effective wedge it was, until the Democratic strategy of the early 1990s wrestled exclusive ownership of tough on crime from Republicans.

The crime control initiative required, among other things, massive capital investment in correctional facilities and expansion of community supervision caseloads, dramatic changes to sentencing laws that increased the numbers of offenders entering prisons, on longer sentences, and serving greater amounts of those sentences (the truth in sentencing initiatives) before inmates are eligible for consideration for discretional parole release or discharge their sentence. While not directly involved in state law making, the federal government exercised significant influence throughout this period as both financial incentives and policy-making assistance came to the states from Washington. I have shown that the War on Drugs played an important role in increasing the scale of the corrections boom, contributing large numbers of offenders to help occupy the newly constructed facilities and serve on community supervision caseloads. I have also considered the role of opinion formation in managing the evolution of crime control as well as the phenomenal importance of tough on crime in the political process.

At the end of the day, what is left is a massive criminal justice system that requires hundreds of billions of dollars annually to keep running. It is, in effect, a system that feeds itself, a perpetual motion machine of sorts. Offenders come in the front door, go through the system, are sent out the back door and after some period of time (often a fairly short period of time), come around to the front door again, and the process repeats— usually several times.

One obvious question that any prudent CEO or CFO would pose is: What is the return on investment? Crime rates declined throughout part of the correctional boom and public officials were quick to imply cause and effect. However, as I will show in chapter 2, crime control has been oversold.

Crime Control

WHAT HAVE WE ACCOMPLISHED?

IN THIS CHAPTER, I EXPLORE what the past forty years of sentencing reform, crime control, and the correctional boom have accomplished. One of the challenges in analyzing the effects of policy is assuring that the appropriate range of goals, outcomes, and impacts, both intended and unintended, have been identified. Some of the goals will be obvious, such as enhanced public safety, reductions in crime rates, and reductions in recidivism. Others perhaps less so, such as the challenges of prisoners returning to the free world after a period of incarceration, the variety of costs (both financial and collateral) of crime control, and the extent to which sentencing reform actually reduced sentencing discretion. I begin with a discussion of the impact of crime control on public safety.

DID IT WORK?

At first glance, the trends in incarceration and crime rates provide compelling evidence for success. Assuming that a primary goal was to reduce crime, some might look at the trends—increasing incarceration and declining crime—and conclude that punishment reduced crime. Consider the following from the popular media, a May 23, 2005, *Forbes* article by Dan Seligman entitled "Lock 'Em Up":

> A big story, inadequately memorialized by the media is that crime in America has become a much smaller story. . . . Counterintuitive as it might seem, this happy result came about via a massive social program. The program did not

promote job training or administer therapy to thugs. Instead it consisted of putting them behind bars. . . . The connection of incarceration to crime is hard to ignore. The number of Americans in prison during 1984–2003 correlates –.71 with the number of violent crimes in in the country. That powerful negative coefficient says that increases in the prison population go hand in hand with declines in crimes committed.

And frankly, this conclusion makes sense. Punishment is intuitive, it is logical, and it is something easily understood. Punishment is something everyone has experienced, and it worked most of the time.

However, the world is just not that simple. In fact, looking at the evidence from a variety of vantage points, the unmistakable conclusion is that any public safety impact of crime control, sentencing reform, and the correctional boom is quite modest. While it is difficult to know what the expectations for public safety have been as a consequence of crime control policies, it seems plausible to assert that the crime reductions that can realistically be attributed to crime control are relatively underwhelming. That is not to say that crime rates have not declined substantially over the course of crime control policies. How much of those declines are due to tough on crime policies is rather limited. I now turn to the evidence.

THE CRIME DECLINE OF THE 1990S

The sustained decline in crime since the early 1990s was relatively consistent throughout the United States. That is, crime declined in all states and in all major metropolitan areas. As Michael Tonry notes (2004: 119) in his excellent analysis of the crime decline:

> Crime trends in cities and states that adopted especially celebrated crime control policies can be compared with trends in comparable cities and states that did not. When such comparisons are made, it becomes clear that the comparable trends occurred everywhere. Including in cities that did not adopt aggressive zero-tolerance policing styles, and in states that adopted neither truth-in-sentencing nor three strikes laws.

The U.S. crime decline that began in 1992 was not a uniquely U.S. experience. Far from it. The International Crime Victimization Survey (ICVS) data (van Dijk, van Kesteren and Smit 2007) consist of periodic crime surveys of European and non-European industrialized nations. The report presents analyses of trends between 1988 and 2005 in property and personal crimes. The trends in the fifteen participating industrialized nations (United States, Canada, Australia, New Zealand, Belgium, England and Wales, Estonia, Finland, France, Netherlands, Northern Ireland, Poland, Scotland, Switzerland, and Sweden) are remarkably similar. While these nations have experienced varying levels or rates of offending, they share the rather dramatic and persistent decline in crime that began in the early 1990s. Those declines are comparable in relative magnitude to those experienced in the United States.

What can be learned from this? Analyses of international crime policies and practices (for example, Padfield, van Zyl Smit, and Dunkel 2010; Tonry 2004; Tonry and Frase 2001) show that none of the comparison nations implemented U.S. crime control policies. The simple conclusion is that whatever has driven the crime decline of the 1990s and 2000s, the outcome was not largely dependent on sentencing reform, crime control, and a correctional boom.

The comparative U.S. and Canadian experiences are particularly informative. In his book *The Great American Crime Decline*, Zimring (2007) devotes an entire chapter to the U.S.–Canadian comparison and notes: 1) the crime declines in both nations occurred at the same time and shared all of the relevant defining characteristics of size, breadth and length; and 2) the punishment policies of these two nations could not be more different—the Canadian incarceration rate varied between 98 and 116/100,000 between 1980 and 2000, while the U.S. rate tripled. The U.S. incarceration rate was 45 percent higher than the Canadian rate in 1980; by 2000, the U.S. rate was four times higher than the Canadian rate.

These comparative analyses of Canada and the European and non-European nations at least bring into question the wholesale assertion that the U.S. crime decline was largely a consequence of crime control policies, massive incarceration, and correctional control.

WHY SHOULD PUNISHMENT REDUCE CRIME?

Crime control is premised on the expectation that punishment will reduce crime and recidivism through the mechanisms of deterrence (specific and general) and incapacitation. I begin with a discussion of deterrence.

Deterrence theory identifies two types of deterrence: specific and general. Specific deterrence suggests that the experience of punishment will deter future offending on the part of the individual being punished. General deterrence posits that the likelihood of offending by others is a function of awareness of the punishment that follows committing a crime and getting arrested. When a court sentences in order to discourage others from engaging in crime, the intent is general deterrence.

Deterrence theory further stipulates that in order to deter, punishment must be swift, certain, and severe. The punishment must quickly follow the commission of the act, it must have a high probability of occurring, and it must be sufficiently severe.

General Deterrence

What is known about the effectiveness of general deterrence? Perhaps the most familiar version of this debate is the death penalty. As recently as the late 2000s, national media and conservative policy organizations have promoted the idea that the death penalty deters (*Associated Press,* June 11, 2007; The *Wall Street Journal,* June 21, 2002;; The Heritage Foundation, August 28, 2007). Despite recent statements by economists asserting the deterrent effect of the death penalty, the scientific consensus (Apel and Nagin, 2011; Bailey and Peterson 1999; Doob and Webster 2003; Radelet and Akers 1996) is clear—there is no valid, reliable scientific evidence supporting the conclusion that the death penalty deters homicide.

Moreover, despite over forty years of federal, state, and local policy based on the premise that punishment severity deters crime—after all, crime control has been about enhancing the severity of punishment—the conclusions from the scientific community are clear. While it may feel appropriate and justified under the circumstances when the District Attorney or judge announce that they are sending a message to the community by imposing a severe sentence, the research indicates either the community is not listening, or if they are, it does not alter their behavior.

Over a decade ago, an exhaustive review of a very impressive amount the scientific research (Doob and Webster 2003) focused on the general deterrent effect of sentence severity. The assessments of the scientific research on general deterrence of specific offenses, offense categories, or crime more broadly lead to the same conclusions, and those conclusions are shared by the vast majority of experts in the field. As Doob and Webster (2003: 187, 189) state:

> Can we conclude that variation in the severity of sentences would have differential (general) deterrent effects? The reply is a resounding no. We could find no conclusive evidence that supports the hypothesis that harsher sentences reduce crime through the mechanism of general deterrence. Particularly given the significant body of literature from which this conclusion is based, the consistency of the findings over time and space, and the multiple measures and methods employed in the research conducted, we would suggest that a stronger conclusion is warranted. . . . The effects are consistent: the severity of sentence does not matter.

Does this mean that sanctioning of criminal offenders has no general deterrent effect? No, it does not. Crime rates are likely to increase if there are no consequences for offending. What it means is that the increasing severity of the sanction appears to be irrelevant as a general deterrent.

A more recent assessment of general deterrence by Apel and Nagin (2011) provides evidence that general deterrence can work, if the focus is on the certainty of punishment rather than severity. Moreover, the research clearly indicates that the deterrent effect of sanctioning is conditional on a number of factors, including the particular sanction used, the particular individual being sanctioned, and the jurisdiction. Apel and Nagin help refine the focus by directing away from questions like: Does greater sanction severity generally deter? (No.) Does general deterrence work? (It can.) Directing instead toward questions like: Under what conditions does a particular sanction deter, if at all? Is the sanction sufficiently cost-effective to warrant implementation?

Specific Deterrence

The other side of the deterrence argument is that harsher penalties, especially incarceration, will deter the future offending of the particular individual being punished. In essence, the negative effect of punishment will cause the individual to reconsider the next time around. In the aggregate, punishment or the threat of punishment raises the costs of engaging in crime and when the costs of crime increase, its frequency declines, thus harsher punishment leads to lower crime rates. At the individual level, the argument is in terms of reducing probabilities of reoffending based on the severity of punishment. As the costs to the individual increase, the likelihood of engaging in crime is diminished, all else equal. So the theory asserts. Let's look at the evidence.

One incomplete, but telling bit of evidence regarding the ability to deter reoffending is recidivism of offenders released from prison. Recidivism is measured in a variety of ways: rearrest, reconviction, and reincarceration are typical. Reincarceration reflects the stronger measure or more serious version of recidivism because it requires an arrest, a reconviction, and a recommitment to prison or a violation of parole, and a subsequent revocation of parole and return to prison. It is also important to point out that recidivism is a measure of official response, meaning first that law enforcement must be aware of a crime (or a parole officer must be aware of a parole violation if the individual is under parole supervision). For that reason, official recidivism measures are underestimates of overall reoffending because crimes known to the police represent approximately 50 to 60 percent of crimes committed.

Recidivism data (rearrest and reincarceration) are available for offenders released from state prisons in 1983 and 1994 (Bureau of Justice Statistics 2002). These will serve as "baseline" statistics. The Pew Center on the States (2011) recently published a report on state-specific recidivism of inmates released from U.S. prisons in 1999 and 2004. All studies follow releases for three years subsequent to release.

It is important to emphasize that comparing the BJS and Pew recidivism data is just illustrative because they consist of different states reporting rearrest and reincarceration statistics. It is also important to note that these rates are aggregations of state rates and that there is considerable variation across states in recidivism rates, release laws and policies, revocation policies, and so on.

Comparison of the 1983 and 1994 release data with the 1999 and 2004 release data indicate the following four things:

1.   Approximately 45 to 50 percent of inmates released in 1983, 1994, 1999, and 2004 were reincarcerated within three years, either for a new offense or for a technical violation of parole.
2.   Reincarcerations for a new offense increased 12 percent between 2002 and 2007, the end years for the 1999 and 2004 Pew release cohorts. This was during a period of declining crime rates and increasing incarceration rates.

3. These recidivism statistics have remained essentially unchanged for the past thirty years, the period of crime control and the corrections explosion.

4. The most important predictors of recidivism are age (younger), number of prior arrests, and offense type (primarily property offenders).

While this is not a strong test of the impact of crime control, the fact that recidivism rates remained stable over time is suggestive. After decades of sentencing reform, increased incarceration, longer sentences, truth in sentencing resulting in greater time served, and dramatic increases in correctional control—all of which presumably were designed to reduce recidivism—it does not appear that the investment has produced noticeable dividends. Again these are aggregate statistics and thus do not reflect interstate variation, as well as varying recidivism probabilities associated with demographics, prior criminal history, and so on. However, the point is telling—it does not appear that the harshest form of punishment the United States metes out (short of the death penalty) deters all that much. It is not known what policymakers in years past expected with regard to the level of deterrence when they implemented crime control. There were no bold statements on the record that X percent drop in crime or Y percent drop in recidivism should be expected. However, it seems likely that the results seen today in terms of recidivism would be viewed as underwhelming.

One ironic discovery in reviewing the research on the specific deterrent effects of incarceration is how relatively little informative research has been conducted, especially farther back in time (Nagin, Cullen, and Jonson 2009). What is ironic about this is the fact that crime control was premised on the deterrent effect of harsher punishment. As discussed in chapter 1, the massive expansion of prison capacity, unprecedented increases in incarceration rates and correctional control, and dramatic changes in sentencing statutes all characterize and define U.S. criminal justice policy. *All of this, with very little scientific evidence to support the purported and often articulated merits of these policies.* We are not naive to the point of expecting policymakers to consult the scientific community regarding each policy decision made. Policy formation is a product of many influences and inputs. Scientific evidence is only one of those. However, for policies of the scale, expense, and longevity of those focused on here, it is a bit disconcerting that decision makers did not occasionally seek such guidance. Apparently, the intuitive, common sense appeal of crime control was sufficient to launch and sustain it for decades, despite mounting, contrary evidence.

Relatively exhaustive reviews of the scientific research literature on the specific deterrent effects of imprisonment have been completed over the past fifteen years or so (Gendreau, Goggin, and Cullen 1999; Nagin, Cullen, and Jonson 2009; Villettaz, Killias and Zoder 2006). These reviews and assessments of the state of the scientific knowledge impose screening standards for studies in their assessments (to assure their scientific validity and rigor) and carefully consider the scientific merit of the research. The most informative research is comparative or controlled, contrasting recidivism outcomes for individuals receiving a sentence of imprisonment versus a noncustodial sentence such as probation. On balance, three things are known. First, there is a remarkable lack of scientific support for the assertion that harsher punishment deters those who experience it. Second, compared to noncustodial sentences, incarceration is either no different in terms of future offending (that is, recidivism), or has a crime-promoting or criminogenic effect (Bales and Piquero 2012; Nagin, Cullen, and Jonson 2009). Finally, there is sufficient evidence to give scientific credibility to the common assertion that criminals who go to prison typically come out even worse.

In terms of the policy relevance of these findings on deterrence, a discussion I will return to in detail in the subsequent chapters, Nagin, Cullen, and Jonson (2009: 183) echo the concerns of the scientific community in their concluding remarks:

> There is little convincing evidence on the dose-response [severity of punishment] relationship between time spent in confinement and reoffending rate. Because imprisonment is so costly, $30,000 per person-year or more, knowledge of this relationship has important implications not only for public safety but also for the state, local and federal budgets.

So how does one make sense of the failure of punishment to deter criminal offending and recidivism? How does one reconcile the fact that science smacks right up against common sense and individual experiences with punishment?

There are a few ways of understanding the lack of a general deterrent effect of punishment severity. Most of us are law abiding (exceptions for the occasional traffic ticket, ordinance violation, or minor misdemeanor). Thus it is reasonable to suggest that for most Americans, the severity of the punishment is irrelevant because they are disinclined to engage in crime in the first place. Many Americans have grown up and live as adults in a world in which crime is neither a desirable nor necessary option.

For others, who are more crime prone, the null effect of sentence severity might be understood in terms of the series of predicate events that are required before an offender is punished: law enforcement must become aware of the offense, then must apprehend/arrest the offender, then the prosecutor must indict, adjudicate, convict, and then the court must impose a severe sentence. The odds are generally in the offender's favor. First, only 50 percent of violent crimes and 40 percent of property crimes are actually reported to law enforcement. Of those reported, 47 percent of violent crimes are cleared (that is, lead to an arrest) and 18 percent of property crimes are cleared. Obviously, there is considerable variation in arrest rates by type of felony, a reflection largely of seriousness. The likelihood of reporting a crime to the police is largely a function of its seriousness, as is the likelihood of an arrest. Moreover, the vast majority of indictments are plea negotiated and, most typically, it is a form of charge bargaining in which the offender pleads guilty to a lesser charge in exchange for less punishment. Offenders know how this system works. They may not have precise probabilities at hand, but in all likelihood, they have some general impressions about their odds of getting caught and punished. Given these probabilities, it is generally true that crime pays.

Moreover, there is the assumption (at least implied in deterrence theory) that individuals would: 1) have access to information regarding outcomes like conviction and sentences; and 2) make decisions in a rational manner. It is probably reasonable to suspect that neither of these conditions is uniformly present among the offender population.

What about the apparent lack of a specific deterrent effect? Why is it that personal experiences and logical reasoning do not seem to apply to offenders considered to have been harshly punished by the justice system? Once again, there are several explanations that are relevant. One is that the punishment is not sufficiently harsh. This line of reasoning leads to the conclusion that it is not the theory that is faulty, but the implementation of it. There are a number of problems with this argument. First, there is no scientific evidence to support it. In today's political and fiscal climate, it would be extraordinarily difficult to muster much support for going down that road. Moreover, there is always the concern with constitutional challenges (Eighth Amendment cruel and unusual punishment issues, equal protection issues, due process issues).

A more reasonable explanation for the disconnect between the common sense of deterrence and the reality is that while nonoffenders can apply the threat or imposition of punishment in their own lives and rightfully conclude that it would work for them, this logic misses the fact that typical offenders are not like nonoffenders. Research has consistently and decisively shown that there is a very strong link between poverty and disadvantage and criminal involvement. Criminal offenders typically do not have the resources, the opportunities, and the alternatives that nonoffenders have. Nor do they typically have access to the education and employment resources that many Americans have. Drug and alcohol abuse are prevalent among the offender population, as is mental illness. Most have prior criminal justice involvement, which creates additional barriers to desistence from crime. The point is that with the typical barriers and challenges that offenders face, it is not surprising that they view crime as a viable, often necessary option.

In most states and for some federal programs, there is usually an ongoing effort to punish offenders well after they have been discharged from the justice system by, for example, preventing them from being employed in certain types of jobs and obtaining certain types of occupational licenses, denying access to things like public assistance and public housing, Pell grants for educational advancement, and health care through Medicaid. Research reported by the Pew Center on the States (2010) indicates that before incarceration, two-thirds of male inmates were employed and one-half were the primary source of support for their families. After release from incarceration, inmates work nine fewer weeks annually and earn 40 percent less than prior to incarceration. Moreover, society continues to punish by restricting where ex-inmates can live and work. Landlords deny housing to individuals who do not pass the criminal background criteria set up by management, and employers deny employment to individuals with criminal backgrounds (despite the fact that there are laws in place preventing such actions). The point is simply that once someone enters the justice system, his or her options, opportunities, and alternatives diminish rapidly, simply as a consequence of their justice system involvement. These restrictions and ongoing barriers tend to further perpetuate a life of crime.

This is not an apology for criminal offenders. Instead, the reality of the criminogenic circumstances and deficits that offenders present with, combined with the additional limits and restrictions the justice system and society place on them, begs the question: What do we expect? What is expected of a parolee who has few resources, limited family ties, employment and housing challenges, and substance abuse problems, for whom there are few resources or forms of assistance available either from the parole system or the public sector? Is it really surprising that many offenders return to crime after they have been punished? Is it really surprising that harsh punishment does not work? Again, this is not an exercise in feeling sorry for criminal offenders. Instead, it is a realistic look at a system that is premised on several very basic principles, a system that just seems to miss a very fundamental point. When someone has limited options, it is rational that they take the one that seems most available and viable. If anything, it is surprising that official recidivism rates are not higher than they are.

A similar reasoning applies to specific deterrence as to general deterrence regarding the probability of experiencing subsequent punishment. This involves the reoffender's perception of the likelihood of getting caught. Deterrence theory holds that in order for punishment to deter, it must be swift, certain, and severe. The certainty of punishment is contingent on the perceived probability of apprehension, which is somewhere well south of 100 percent. Moreover, there is not much about processing criminal defendants that can be characterized as swift. Absent the ability to address the swift and certain attributes of deterrence, it probably makes sense that policymakers chose severity (if they are or were aware of deterrence theory at all).

Finally, punishment may not specifically deter for the simple fact that punishment does not target the reasons individuals engage in crime, and therefore punishment does not alter behavior. As Cullen and Gendreau (2000: 146, 154, 155) note early on in the scientific scrutiny of crime control policies:

A central policy issue is whether the movement to "get tough" on crime has enhanced public safety. In particular, the massive rise in the prison population . . . has created an intense interest in whether the extensive use of imprisonment has a meaningful incapacitation effect, or, at the aggregate level, deterrent effect. Punishment does not target criminogenic needs and thus is one of the most ineffective, if not counter-productive, strategies . . . there is no evidence that punishment-oriented "treatment" programs specifically deter or otherwise reform offenders.

Perhaps thirty years ago it was reasonable for state and federal officials to make promises that enhanced punishment will pay crime reduction dividends because it will deter reoffending. So too the tough on crime prosecutor who recommends a maximum sentence in order to send a message to the community and to a specific offender that this kind of behavior will not be tolerated. Those assertions and the subsequent implementation of tough on crime punishments had little basis in terms of scientific evidence pointing to their likely success, but at the same time, there was little scientific evidence indicating that they would not work. Certainly, there are examples of individuals who were deterred from reoffending because of the punishment they received. There are individuals who have decided not to engage in crime because of the threat of punishment. Nevertheless, in the aggregate, these deterrence strategies are ineffective.

Even if the evidence pointed toward a crime-deterring effect of severity, there is little basis for knowing or even determining how severe the punishment must be in order to produce a marginal deterrent effect. The amount of punishment has been determined for decades in terms of harm perpetrated by the offender, not generally in terms of any particular understanding of the individual's circumstances that might inform the proper dosage of punishment. The severity of punishment is in the eyes of the giver (the sentencer) and the receiver (the convicted offender), and it is presumptuous to think that the appropriate level of severity could be determined on a case-by-case basis.

So is there any reason not to just bury the deterrence argument and move on? Yes. Research indicates that punishment may deter if it is swift and certain (Farabee 2005; Grasmick and Bryjak 1980; Nichols and Ross 1990; Paternoster 1989; Rhine 1992; Taxman, Soule, and Gelb 1999). In practice, the swift and certain attributes of sanctioning or punishment appear to be producing enhanced compliance and accountability among probationers. The HOPE Court, developed in Hawaii in 2004, is based on the premise that deferred and low-probability threats of severe punishment are less effective than immediate and more certain threats of mild punishment. Probationers participating in the HOPE Court program receive an initial warning by the court that spells out what will happen when anyone violates any conditions of probation. When a violation occurs, the offender is immediately brought before the judge and typically a short sentence in jail is imposed and the individual is immediately taken to jail. The length of jail time is increased for successive violations. Evaluation research indicates dramatic reductions in rearrest, drug use, missed appointments with the probation department, and revocations. I will discuss the HOPE Court model in more detail in later chapters.

In 2009, Mark Kleiman published a book entitled *When Brute Force Fails*. The title is a bit misleading, as some readers probably figure this is a book about alternatives to deterrence-based approaches. Instead, the premise of Kleiman's book and the premise of subsequent discussions along the same lines (for example, Durlauf and Nagin 2011) is that a greater police presence can deter crime by increasing the perceived certainty and swiftness of punishment. The logic is based in part on the well-established lack of a general or specific deterrent effect of the severity of punishment and the criminogenic effect of incarceration (Apel and Nagin 2011; Nagin, Cullen, and Jonson 2009). The recommendation is to shift resources away from severe incarceration sentences to a greater police presence. Reducing the severity of punishment is evidence based. Increasing the presence of police is less so. As Tonry (2011) notes, the evidence is problematic regarding the crime-reducing impact of police crackdowns, zero-tolerance policing, and increased police presence. The coincidence of police initiatives and crime rate declines is at least partly spurious, as crime began declining before the police initiatives were introduced. Tonry states (2011: 148): "Fifteen years later, the clear weight of opinion concerning these [certainty enhancing] policies [the three-strikes law in California and zero-tolerance policing in New York City] is that they do not deserve major credit for the crime declines in those places." Moreover, there is significant concern about whether the findings of drug market crackdowns and hotspot policing are generalizable across time and space, and whether there are sizable crime-reduction effects net of displacement. As Tonry (2011: 148) concludes "If crackdowns have no long-term effects, then they are little different from castles of sand built on ocean beaches: the waves will wash them away as if they never existed." Tonry expresses substantial reservations about the potential civil rights and racial profiling concerns with this strategy. He cites law enforcement's track record in this regard for a lack of confidence in mitigating these concerns.

Finally, there is little in Kleiman's strategy that results in changes to major criminogenic circumstances, so it is hard to know how longer-term reductions in crime are achieved.

In short, there is considerable appeal to the concept of implementing strategies that increase the certainty and celerity of punishment. It is intuitive and there is research to support a deterrent effect. There are some programs that are based on this premise that appear to be effective and are gaining widespread attention in research and policy circles (Hawken and Kleiman 2009). There is mounting evidence that the certain and swift sanction model, in conjunction with therapeutic interventions, have very promising potential. However, absent the therapeutic intervention, swift and certain punishment is unlikely to change behavior in the longer term.

Incapacitation

Crime control also promotes the incapacitation function of correctional control, especially incarceration. Incapacitation is the removal of criminal opportunity, the effect of preventing criminal offending in the free world while an offender is incarcerated. The intuitive appeal of incapacitation is compelling. Lock up the criminal, lock up the crime.

The scientific evidence on incapacitation is consistent in one respect: the incapacitation effect is relatively small. Where the evidence is inconsistent is in terms of how small (somewhere in the 10 to 25 percent range, meaning incarceration accounts for somewhere between 10 and 25 percent of crime declines over the past twenty years). In a thoughtful review of the research, and assessment of a variety of statistical and methodological concerns and challenges, Spelman (2000: 485) concludes:

> In a nutshell then, what the studies of the past ten years tell us is that crime responds to prison capacity and that continued expansion of prisons nationwide will reduce the crime rate. What the studies don't tell us is whether the reduction is large enough to warrant continued expansion.

A recent analysis by Western (2006) concludes that incapacitation accounts for 2 to 5 percent of the reduction in serious crime during the 1990s and 10 percent overall. Three studies have addressed some of the more compelling methodological difficulties of prior research (Spelman

2000, 2005; Levitt 1996) and their estimates of the incapacitation effect converge (Steman 2007). The range of estimates produced by these studies is 2 to 4 percent, meaning that a 10 percent increase in incarceration will produce a 2 to 4 percent reduction in crime. Zimring (2007) argues that the incapacitation effect is problematic in light of the comparison of the U.S. and Canadian crime declines during the 1990s. As discussed earlier, both nations experienced similar crime reductions, but Canada did not dramatically expand incarceration.

Some research further indicates that the scale of incarceration matters in that as scale increases, the marginal return of reduced crime erodes dramatically (Liedka, Piehl, and Useem 2006). Put differently, incarceration does appear to have a modest crime-reducing effect at low levels, but as incarceration increases, the negative effect on crime is diminished.

Another consideration regarding the presumed crime-reduction effect of incapacitation has to do with the extent to which criminal offending is eliminated when an offender is removed from the street and incarcerated. It is the idea that the incapacitation effect, to the extent that it exists, is dependent at a minimum on the type or nature of crime that was being committed. For example, in the case of gang-related or organized crime, simply incarcerating a gang member may not eliminate the crime. It is reasonable to expect that the crime for which the incarcerated gang member was responsible will continue, simply being committed by another gang member.

A similar argument applies to the drug trade. Taking a street-level dealer off of the street will probably not disrupt the distribution of drugs. That incarcerated dealer will in all likelihood be replaced by one of any number of dealer wannabes who have been waiting for the right opening or opportunity. There is clear ethnographic evidence that this is in fact what happens (Johnson et al. 1990; Padilla 1992; see also Blumstein 1994). The overall caution here regarding incapacitation effects is that they are conditional, in part depending on the nature of the crime. Some criminal activity is like a labor market. If a worker is removed, another takes his or her place. The irony is obvious. Prison sentences for some mean opportunities for others.

Strictly speaking, incarceration does not always prevent or incapacitate those in prison from being involved in crime on the outside. Prison gangs are extraordinarily prevalent in the nation's prisons, and many have street equivalents. These gangs are organized by race or ethnicity. White gangs include the Aryan Brotherhood, the Nazi Lowriders, the Aryan Circle, Dead Man Incorporated, and the Confederate Knights of America. Typical Hispanic gangs are the Mexican Mafia (or La Eme), Nuestra Familia, Barrio Azteca, and the Texas Syndicate. Black gangs include the Crips, the Bloods, the Black Guerilla Family, United Blood Nations, and Folk Nation. While these gangs provide protection for their members while incarcerated, they are primarily criminal enterprises that have extensive connections in the free world and are often heavily involved in drug trafficking and money laundering, among others. While they may not be physically committing free-world crime themselves, members of prison gangs can influence and/or direct crime on the outside.

Enthusiasm for the incapacitation effect of incarceration is reflected in mandatory sentences, especially habitual offender laws (commonly known as three strikes laws). Such repeat offender laws are, in part, a statutory attempt to implement selective incapacitation—a strategy based on the fact that the majority of crime is committed by a relatively small number of repeat offenders. Selective incapacitation is the attempt to incarcerate those offenders responsible for the bulk of crime. One substantial challenge to selective incapacitation is that it is difficult to accurately identify these offenders. The success of selective incapacitation depends on the presumption that an offender will continue offending and therefore incapacitating him or her will reduce crime. Not only is there an error rate in selective incapacitation (false positives deprive individuals of liberty for lengthy periods of time, when in fact they are not the repeat offenders who were targeted), there are errors involved in the implementation of the repeat offender or three strikes laws. The likelihood of those false positives combined with cases in which the mandatory sentence was radically inconsistent with the conviction offense has led to a reduction in the use of such laws in most states.

Another consideration associated with mandatory sentences and the incapacitation effect is as the prison population ages as a function of length of incarceration, we run the risk of incarcerating larger and larger numbers of inmates who have aged out of offending. To the extent this is the case, an incapacitation effect should not be expected from those individuals who are taking up space that might be more productively used for offenders still in the crime-prone age span. Recent data indicate that between 2007 and 2011, the number of U.S. prison inmates ages sixty-four and over increased at a rate ninety-four times the rate for those ages in the general, free-world population. The prison population is graying at a very rapid rate, a trend that further limits the ability of incarceration to effectively and cost-effectively incapacitate. As increasing numbers of older inmates are incarcerated, the marginal ability to incapacitate declines.

So part of the disconnect between the intuitive, common sense appeal and the scientific reality of the incapacitation effect is that removing an offender from the street does not always remove the crime in which he was engaged. The disconnect is also a function of how well the justice system accurately identifies who needs to be incapacitated. This raises what will become a common concern as I move forward in my discussion. Effective sentencing (in a utilitarian sense) is really a matter of accurately sorting offenders into one of a limited number of categories: diversion, probation, prison, and so on. Part of the failure of incapacitation to live up to expectations, whatever they may have been, may reflect a historic inability to make optimal, utilitarian decisions about who should go into which category. Clearly, although there may be merit to the incapacitation function of incarceration, the implementation has not been terribly effective.

THE CONSEQUENCES OF SENTENCING REFORM

In this section, I focus on the consequences of two pivotal aspects of sentencing reform: the implementation of mandatory sentences and the shift to determinate sentencing. These attributes of sentencing are important for reform because absent such changes, crime control and the corrections explosion would have been mere shadows of themselves. I begin with mandatory sentencing.

Mandatory Sentencing

In 1970, Congress repealed virtually all of the mandatory minimum drug sentences that had been implemented some twenty years earlier under the Boggs Act of 1952. This repeal of mandatory minimums was based on the observation that "lengthening prison sentences had not shown the expected overall reduction in drug law violations" (quoted in Mascharka 2001). It was a short fifteen years later that Congress reversed course in the Sentencing Reform Act, which paved the way for a variety of federal mandatory minimum sentences, many of which are aimed at drug law violations. By 1994, all fifty states had at least one mandatory sentencing law in place. The Anti-Drug Abuse Act of 1986 instituted new mandatory sentences for a variety of drug law violations. The Rockefeller Drug Laws, the quite severe mandatory sentences for drug offenses in New York, were put in place in 1973. Michigan followed suit in 1978. Over the next twenty years, thirty-seven states implemented harsher drug law provisions. At the same time, opposition to mandatory minimum sentences was broad, including the Federal Sentencing Commission, the Judicial Conference of the United States, the Federal Courts Study Commission, the Federal Judicial Center, the American Bar Association, and the vast majority of federal judges, as well as Supreme Court justices Rehnquist, Kennedy, and Breyer (Mascharka 2001).

Mandatory minimum sentences and other mandatory sentences, such a habitual offender laws, have been in place for decades and constitute a characteristic element of the U.S. criminal justice landscape. Mandatory sentences have been an essential mechanism for accomplishing the goals of crime control because they enhance the punitiveness of criminal sentences by increasing the number of offenses for which incarceration is the sentencing outcome (therefore increasing admissions to prison), as well as length of incarceration, increasing both the up-front sentence as well as time served. The evidence supports the conclusion that one of the important consequences of the imposition of mandatory sentences is growth in incarceration rates. Stemen, Rengifo, and Wilson (2006) conclude that states with more mandatory sentences had higher incarceration rates. Truth in sentencing reforms also appear to be related to increases in inmate populations in the states. Research by Sabol et al. (2002) shows that states that implemented truth in sentencing laws experienced increases in prison population, however they caution that this effect of truth in sentencing laws is tied to broader sentencing reforms that states implemented, such as mandatory sentences.

But what about public safety? What is the impact of mandatory sentencing on crime and recidivism? Once again, Michael Tonry (2009) has provided us with an excellent review and critique of the existing research on the deterrent effects of mandatory sentences. Referencing three sources of evaluation research—National Advisory bodies, surveys of the research literature, and evaluations and impact assessments—Tonry underscores the convergence of the conclusions that there are no detectable deterrent effects of mandatory sentences. Because mandatory sentences focus on severity of punishment exclusively, one would not expect a deterrent effect based on the research on punishment severity and deterrence. Several National Academy of Sciences panels, research by the British Home Office and the Canadian Sentencing Commission, to name but a few, all concur. In fact, it is ironic that the Home Office and Canadian Sentencing Commission recognized in the late 1980s and early 1990s that "deterrence cannot be used with empirical justification, to guide the imposition of sentences" (Canadian Sentencing Commission 1987: xxvii). The research communities' assessment of the marginal deterrent effect of increasing punishment severity through mandatory sentence enhancements is consistent with that of national advisory bodies: "the effects of severity [of punishment] estimates and deterrence/sanctions composites, even when statistically significant are too weak to be of substantive significance" (Pratt et al. 2006: 379). Finally, with regard to individual state-level evaluations, Tonry (2009: 95) concludes: "No individual evaluation has demonstrated crime reduction effects attributable to enactment or implementation of a mandatory minimum sentence."

What about an incapacitation effect of mandatory sentencing? In theory, this is a plausible expectation. However, many of the mandatory sentences are for drug law violations, and removing drug dealers from the street typically does not remove the offending. Moreover, mandatory sentences, especially habitual offender laws, are an attempt at selective incapacitation—lock up the career offenders for a lengthy incarceration and crime reduction benefits should be realized. The problem is that a statutory mechanism for implementing selective incapacitation is fraught with error. Just because the three strikes laws work well as a baseball metaphor does not mean they are effective at capturing true habitual offenders. What is the logic behind using a law rather than clinical assessments to determine who is more or less likely to reoffend? What is magical or predictive about three? And then there is the inefficiency at the other end of the sentence, where there is an increasingly aging inmate population. Twenty-one percent of prison inmates in the United States are serving a sentence of at least twenty years; 10 percent are serving a life sentence. With mandatory sentences, offenders are kept well past the age of desistence from offending.

A RAND study published in the late 1990s (Caulkins et al. 1997) focused on assessing the relative cost-effectiveness of mandatory minimum drug sentences. The researchers found that mandatory minimum drug sentences were not justified on cost-effectiveness grounds. Their research indicated that incarceration, whether through mandatory minimum sentences or indeterminate sentences, is less cost-effective than drug treatment for problem users. More on cost-effectiveness later.

Determinate Sentencing

It appears that the conclusions are the same when the movement to determinate sentencing is considered. There were two primary drivers of determinate sentencing: to reduce leniency in sentencing due to judicial discretion and to reduce sentencing disparity/unfairness due to judicial discretion. Regarding the former, the jury has rendered that verdict. There is little evidence to support the assertion that judges tend to be too lenient. Secondly, in the aggregate, enhanced sentence severity does not deter either generally or specifically and if there is an incapacitation effect, it is minimal.

Where are we with regard to sentence disparity? Many observers (including Alschuler 1979; Engen 2008; U.S. Sentencing Commission 1991; Forst and Bushway 2010; Mascharka 2001; Miethe 1987; Piehl and Bushway 2007; Tonry 2009; Vincent and Hofer 1994) have pointed to the obvious and troubling consequence that sentencing reform did not eliminate sentencing discretion, it simply displaced it from the bench to the prosecutor. Determinate sentencing and mandatory sentences remove much of the latitude from the judge at sentencing, but the sentencing-relevant characteristics of the case are largely established by the prosecutor through decisions such as what charges to indict, what evidence to use, what to negotiate in the inevitable plea bargain, and what to recommend at sentencing. Jurisdictions that restrict discretion by judges simply enhance the discretion that prosecutors exercise in influencing sentencing outcomes. One of the key concerns expressed by the shifting of discretion to prosecutors is that decision making moves from the "neutral, fair adjudicator" to the adversarial lawyer who represents the state. I shall return to this issue of prosecutorial discretion in chapter 4.

SUMMARY

On the one hand, crime control has a very logical, familiar, intuitive basis. It just feels right. It seems just, deserving, appropriate. If someone errs, we do what we do with children: we punish. Punishment may not work the first time, but eventually this approach will probably produce the intended results. It worked for us, it works in our everyday lives, thus it has real-world validation.

And therein lies the problem. Criminal offenders are not "us." The wisdom of crime control fails when similar results are expected from individuals whose lives are significantly different. Most criminal offenders do not enjoy the opportunities and options that most of us have and that policymakers and legislators who write the laws have.

There was very little scientific basis for the efficacy of crime control. In fact, there is evidence that sentencing policy developed, at least in part, based less on scientific evidence and more on logic and personal preference. Hoelter (2009: 54) relays the experiences of one Federal Sentencing Commissioner who lamented the fact that sentencing policy was based on personal preference and opinion, rather than scientific evidence.

> The personal preferences of sentencing commissioners as to what is "good" or "right" or "just" should not be the basis for the Commission's policy decisions. The basis for those decisions must be information, and information of the costs and benefits of various policy options. What concerns me about these unsupported amendments is not only that the substantive changes may not be warranted but also that the Commission's process for generating guideline amendments is developing in such a way as to hinder rational policy-making.

One can appreciate the difficult situation that gave traction to crime control in the late 1960s and 1970s and even the 1980s. But at some point, the wisdom of crime control came into question, as the simple argument of "incarceration goes up and crime goes down means it works" was no longer credible to those who looked carefully at the issues.

Thirty years ago phrases like "lock 'em up and throw away the key" and "do the crime, do the time" were common. The states and the federal government seemed as if they could not build enough prisons. Rural communities competed for prisons because they were viewed as an economic boon, and in many respects they were. However, of late, it seems some Americans have awakened after a thirty-five year sleep with a really bad hangover and the realization that not only has this experiment failed, it has wasted enormous amounts of public resources, jeopardized public safety, and resulted in hundreds of thousands of avoidable victimizations.

A 2004 study of felony defendants from the seventy-five largest metro areas demonstrated what many observers already knew, that 75 percent of the felony defendants had a prior arrest history, and over 50 percent had at least five prior arrests (Kyckelhahn and Cohen 2008). It is truly a revolving door. What policymakers appear to ignore, or at least not appreciate sufficiently, is that each time someone reoffends and law enforcement arrests them, the public cash register rings once again, as costs are incurred by law enforcement, the jail, the prosecutor, the judge at a preliminary hearing, pretrial services, the grand jury, the arraignment judge, defense counsel (more than likely assigned counsel or a public defender), the trial court, and corrections. Moreover, ineffective policies result in future victims being irresponsibly placed in jeopardy. It is as inappropriate as it is unnecessary.

The Scientific Case for Alternatives to Crime Control

EVIDENCE-BASED PRACTICES AND WHERE NEUROCOGNITIVE IMPLICATIONS TAKE US FROM HERE

THIS CHAPTER PRESENTS A BRIEF OVERVIEW of the scientific evidence in support of alternatives to crime control. While research continues to clearly indicate that the U.S. policy of severe punishment is ineffective, including three National Academy of Sciences Panels (Blumstein, Cohen, and Nagin 1978; Blumstein et al. 1986; Reiss and Roth 1996) as well as the research reviewed in chapter 2, the United States steadfastly plods down that road. It is time to rethink this.

There is a clear need for incarceration for those offenders who pose monumental risks either through their offending or through the inability of our best rehabilitative efforts to change their behavior. For these individuals, incarceration (incapacitation) is an appropriate sentence; thus, prisons are clearly necessary. But let's also be clear why we have them. They should not be used as or promoted as *correctional* facilities. Prisons have one primary purpose and that is to separate offenders from the public. It is time to be honest about what prison can and cannot achieve. So this is not a discussion about closing U.S. prisons. It is about using fewer prison resources more wisely, while reducing crime.

For those offenders that are not incarcerated, the direction that the evidence indicates is appropriate is an approach emphasizing a balance between behavioral change on the one hand and risk management, compliance, and accountability on the other. Many criminal offenders come to the justice system with a variety of deficits, impairments, disadvantages, and circumstances that are related to their offending. Thus, part of the direction forward is a concerted and comprehensive effort to effectively change behavior. For those, I propose efforts at behavior change through diversion, intervention, treatment, and rehabilitation, and risk management and compliance through smart sanctioning based on swift and certain punishment, supervision, and accountability.

Efforts should be focused on the implementation of programs, policies, procedures, and interventions that have passed scientific muster as effective in changing criminal behavior (evidence-based practices). The good news is that in 2014, we know, and have known for at least twenty years, that there are effective alternatives to punishment and control, effective both in terms of outcomes and cost. And over time, we learn more and more. We have the tools to significantly impact crime and recidivism. The first step is to sketch out the road map and demonstrate the effectiveness and cost-effectiveness of these alternatives. That is what the next five chapters are about. The second step is to understand the barriers and challenges to implementing these policies on an appropriate scale, and then to develop strategies for addressing these barriers and challenges. I will turn to these issues in the concluding chapter.

While there are exceptions to the norm of punishment, these efforts at behavioral change often involve just going through the motions, only loosely approximating anything with any evidence-based validation, and involve incredibly low standards for "success." Judge Marcus describes an often too accurate picture of what this process looks like in practice (Marcus 2003: 770):

> That this is symmetry rather than science—that we cannot cite these practices as evidence of a responsible pursuit of crime reduction—is obvious from these circumstances: we never ask the programs whether their graduates reoffend; we make no effort to determine which offenders actually benefit and which do not. Instead, we are satisfied when programs communicate effectively with the system to document completion—which we

deem "success"—or indicate failure (regardless of any lack of recidivism). Because we make no effort to track the impact of these sentences on criminal behavior, we fail to motivate the programs to compete on the basis of crime reduction; we fill many with offenders they cannot improve, fail to send many offenders to programs that would work for them, sustain some programs that work on no one, and—worst of all—fail to preserve some programs remarkably good at crime reduction. Like "reformation" in general, programs are simply part of the liturgy of the sentencing mantra, rather than a responsibly deployed strategy to serve public safety.

What Judge Marcus is describing is not a lack of information or scientific evidence or evidence-based practices. What he is describing is the disconnect between what we know and how we use it. It describes the inappropriate and inadequate application of "what works." It describes going through the motions without a serious intent to actually produce measurable results. The failures to adequately address recidivism and crime are not due to a lack of knowledge of what to do, but a failure to fund and properly implement what we do know.

The point is simple, but tremendously important. Knowing what works is necessary, but not sufficient to reduce crime and recidivism. We must also properly implement what we know on a scale that produces measurable impacts on the big picture of crime and recidivism. Let me reinforce this point by way of example. I, in collaboration with a couple dozen or so other stakeholders, was involved in developing a community court. We assessed all of the evidence regarding what such a court should look like, we conducted needs assessments, we consulted with leading experts on community courts, and we took approximately eighteen months to design the court. The court was funded (well below our estimates, but funded nevertheless) and launched in 1999. For the next ten years, it was a dismal failure. The failure was largely due to one significant error in hiring. The individual selected by the city administration to be the court administrator did not understand or embrace therapeutic jurisprudence; he did not believe in rehabilitation. For ten years, he essentially ran the court as a criminal court, and repeatedly gave rehabilitation funds back to the city, which kept his supervisor (the city manager) happy with his performance. While the process of designing the court was quite deliberate and research informed, the effort failed because of a significant flaw in implementation.

So we have to get it right. We have to design it properly, we have to implement it according to the evidence, we have to operate it as designed, we have to evaluate it on a regular basis, then we have to make the changes indicated by the evaluations, and we have to fund it at a level at which it becomes meaningful in terms of crime reduction. Too often, such initiatives have more symbolic value than substantive impact. Drug courts are very popular in the United States, and we know that they work. The problem is that despite their prevalence, drug courts are very limited in terms of capacity, and overall address approximately 5 percent of the need. It is the unfortunate reality today that alternatives to punishment tend to have symbolic significance rather than constitute a primary component of efforts to address crime and recidivism.

THE PRINCIPLES OF EFFECTIVE CORRECTIONAL INTERVENTION AND EVIDENCE-BASED PRACTICES

The evaluation results of effective correctional rehabilitation, treatment, diversion, and intervention started becoming mainstream (mainstream meaning not just academic, but available to and accessible by practitioners and policymakers) twenty-five years ago. Published work by Andrews and colleagues (1990), Andrews and Bonta (1994), Andrews and Dowden (1999), Cullen and Applegate (1997), Gendreau (1996), and Gendreau, Little, and Goggin (1996) constitute the foundation for the principles of effective correctional rehabilitation or intervention. They are based on and supported by hundreds of research studies and meta-analyses, and constitute the evidence-based practices of effective contemporary offender rehabilitation. Meta-analyses have demonstrated recidivism reductions between 25 and 30 percent from the implementation of these principles, and as high as 50 percent for particularly effective configurations.

These principles are not foolproof and they are not *the* solution to crime and public safety. Interventions based on the faithful implementation of these principles will not always produce typical results. However, the scientific evidence demonstrates without equivocation that these intervention principles produce dramatically greater reductions in recidivism than any other known strategy, and clearly greater reductions than purely punitive approaches.

While some authors group the principles differently, they are, in essence, the following:

1. Conduct thorough, accurate, actuarial-based assessments of risk and dynamic, criminogenic needs
2. Assess treatment readiness and enhance treatment motivation
3. Target interventions:
   a. on dynamic (changeable) criminogenic needs (need principle)
   b. on multiple criminogenic needs
   c. on medium- and high-risk offenders (risk principle)
   d. to the personality, learning style, and intellectual capabilities of the participants (responsivity principle)
   e. with social learning and cognitive-behavioral modalities, the primary evidence-based approaches to effective behavioral change
   f. with the appropriate dosage for the appropriate participants
4. Increase positive reinforcement
5. Adhere to fidelity of design, implementation, and operation, and engage in quality control
6. Provide a continuing care, aftercare, or relapse prevention component
7. Monitor and evaluate programming and create structures for feedback
8. Engage ongoing support in natural communities
9. Provide extensive skill training for staff

1. Conduct Thorough, Accurate, Actuarial-Based Assessments of Risk and Dynamic, Criminogenic Needs

Using validated, standardized screening and assessment instruments to measure crime risk and criminogenic needs has been a primary component of evidence-based practices in criminal justice for over two decades. Today, accurate risk and needs assessments are a well-established best practice that is used to mitigate the risk to public safety, to determine what criminogenic needs should be addressed with what level of intervention, to more efficiently and effectively allocate intervention resources, and to measure or monitor treatment progress. The most recent generation of risk and needs assessment instruments (fourth generation) permit the measurement not only of the presence of particular criminogenic needs, but their severity as well (Andrews, Bonta and Wormith 2006;

Ferguson 2002; Jones et al. 2001). Dynamic needs assessments are also useful for measuring treatment or intervention progress (for example, the Addiction Severity Index or ASI).

The importance of using accurate, validated, standardized risk and needs screening and assessment instruments is directly related to the effectiveness and cost-effectiveness of correctional treatment. Absent accurate diagnoses of offender needs and appropriate classification of an offender in terms of risk, "offenders enter a treatment lottery in which their access to effective interventions is a chancy proposition" (Latessa, Cullen, and Gendreau 2002: 48).

As of 2007, validated needs assessment instruments were used by approximately 58 percent of prison, jail, and community corrections officials for substance abuse screening, and by 34 percent for a risk assessment (Taxman et al. 2007). Use of standardized instruments varies by facility type: roughly 75 percent of drug treatment prison facilities use them, 50 percent of general prison facilities, 40 percent of community correction facilities, and 20 percent of jails.

Regardless of the challenges involved, criminal justice practitioners, from prosecutors and defense lawyers to judges to corrections officials, should be making decisions based on valid information. Subjective judgments do not and should not take the place of validated risk and needs assessments. However, the use of judgments or information other than validated assessments still seems to be as likely as not in many correctional settings.

While using such assessments is clearly indicated as a correctional best practice, such information is also essential to prosecutors, defense attorneys, and judges in making diversion decisions and sentencing decisions. There are no systematic data on the prevalence of the use of assessments for diversion and sentencing. Virginia appears to be one the few states (as of 2009) to systematically use a standardized risk assessment for sentencing adult offenders. A survey of agencies involved in pretrial diversion indicates that all survey respondents used either eligibility criteria or a risk assessment to determine appropriate individuals for diversion (National Association of Pre-Trial Services Agencies 2009). The survey also reported that 58 percent use "other assessments" to fashion supervision plans and treatment needs.

It is important to emphasize the need to use scientifically reliable and valid assessments. What some jurisdictions and agencies use may be considered "validated" in some regard, when in effect, the assessments are inappropriate. For example, the assessment instrument used by the Texas Parole Commission to assess the risk of reoffending for sex offenders (the Static 99), and in turn to assist with release decisions, has an item for age that simply differentiates those above and below the age of twenty-five. In essence, a ninety-year-old sex offender will have the same risk as he did at age twenty-six (all of the items are static, meaning unchangeable, therefore the assessed risk does not change over time). The likelihood of reoffending is associated with a number of factors, including the obvious and very important effect of age. The problem seems clear. "Validated" does not necessarily mean accurate.

2. Assess Treatment Readiness and Enhance Treatment Motivation

Simply ordering someone to treatment is shortsighted, counterproductive, and an inefficient use of expensive treatment resources. Assessing treatment readiness is an effective and productive way of determining who among those in need of a particular intervention is appropriate, and who is inappropriate for treatment at a given point in time. Treatment readiness has been shown to predict program retention and completion, and is useful for matching individuals to particular levels or intensities of treatment (Osher and Kofoed 1989; Peters, Bartoi, and Sherman 2008). Matching individuals to particular stages of treatment is based on the premise that stage-specific interventions will enhance retention and completion. Treatment readiness instruments can also be used to monitor changes in motivation and readiness over the course of treatment.

There are several validated instruments that assess readiness for substance abuse treatment, psychiatric treatment, co-occurring disorder treatment, and cognitive skills training, among others. The most common instruments are designed to assess readiness for substance abuse treatment, instruments such as the Circumstances, Motivation, Readiness, and Suitability (CMRS) Scale (DeLeon and Jainchill 1986); Readiness for Change Questionnaire (RCQ) (Rollnick et al. 1992); Stages of Change Readiness and Treatment Eagerness Scale (SOCRATES) (Prochaska and DiClemente 1992); and the University of Rhode Island Change Assessment Scale (URICA) (DiClemente and Hughes 1990).

Motivation for treatment can be enhanced by utilizing a variety of incentives and sanctions, as well as approaches like motivational interviewing, by providing a respectful, empathetic, encouraging environment for the screening and assessment process, and by maintaining positive and encouraging attitudes throughout treatment (Castonguay and Beutler 2006).

3. Target Interventions

Targeting interventions in terms of needs, risk, responsivity, and dosage highlights the fundamental importance of accurately assessing needs, risk, and treatment readiness. Absent this information, intervention is often a waste of resources.

DYNAMIC (CHANGEABLE) CRIMINOGENIC NEEDS (NEED PRINCIPLE)

Focusing on dynamic criminogenic needs presumes a needs assessment process that identifies the existence of problems and deficits and provides sufficient information on severity to allow prioritization of needs. The goal is to intervene with regard to the primary needs that are related to criminal offending. Determining which needs are more or less related to the propensity to engage in crime is not always intuitive. But there is a growing research base of evidence that indicates which typically are and are not criminogenic. Research has demonstrated, for example, that antisocial attitudes, antisocial friends, substance abuse, lack of empathy, and impulsive behavior are criminogenic circumstances. Research has also demonstrated that anxiety, low self-esteem, poor physical conditioning, medical (nonpsychiatric) needs, feelings of inadequacy, and depression are generally noncriminogenic.

MULTIPLE CRIMINOGENIC NEEDS

It is a rare circumstance in which a criminal offender presents with only one primary criminogenic need. Crime is a product of many factors, including disadvantage, poverty, unemployment, educational deficits, mental illness, drug abuse or dependence, neurocognitive deficits and impairments, among others. But correctional treatment or intervention, when provided at all, typically focuses on just one need or deficit.

The reality is much more complex. Psychopathology is typically the result of heritable vulnerabilities interacting with the environment. Biological vulnerability, when combined with high-risk environments (poverty, parental neglect or abuse, exposure to violence), can produce a variety of psychopathologies. Co-morbidity rates are quite high among offenders, especially with regard to substance abuse. For example, individuals who present with externalizing disorders such as conduct disorder have a reasonably high vulnerability to internalizing disorders such as depression and substance abuse. Awareness of these considerations at the diagnostic phase can be very useful in identifying co-morbidities.

The research is clear: addressing multiple primary criminogenic needs produces substantially greater reductions in recidivism than just addressing one or two (Andrews and Bonta 2007; Andrews, Dowden, and Gendreau 1999; Carey 2011; Dowden 1998; French and Gendreau 2006). Carey (2011) reports that meta-analysis demonstrates that addressing six criminogenic needs reduces recidivism by 50 percent; addressing 5 reduces recidivism by 30 percent; four by 25 percent; three by 20 percent; two by 18 percent; and addressing one results in minimal impact. The research also clearly indicates that prioritizing criminogenic needs in terms of level of need/severity produces better recidivism reduction outcomes. For example, someone who is abusing drugs will likely need to have the substance abuse addressed first because drug abuse probably interferes with other therapeutic interventions.

Moreover, research confirms that while there are a wide variety of criminogenic needs, there are eight that are most consistently related to recidivism, and four of them have been identified as having the greatest impact (Andrews, Bonta, and Wormith 2006). The so-called central eight needs, with the primary four listed first, are: antisocial behavior, antisocial attitudes, antisocial peers, and antisocial personality; the remaining four are family stressors, substance abuse, lack of employment and education, and poor use of leisure time. These eight needs do not preclude identifying and treating others that may be precursors of these, independent of them, or aggravators.

MEDIUM- AND HIGH-RISK OFFENDERS (RISK PRINCIPLE)

The risk principle is based on long-term research, which indicates that low-risk offenders do not require nor do they benefit as much as medium- and high-risk offenders from extensive and intensive treatment and case management (Andrews and Bonta 2003; Clear 1981; Palmer 1995). At the same time, there is research that indicates that extremely high-risk offenders may not respond well to treatment and are disruptive to therapeutic interventions.

On balance, the risk principle indicates that the optimal targets for correctional intervention are those assessed as medium and high risk. Treatment intervention and case management should be used in an effort to reduce risk.

RESPONSIVITY PRINCIPLE

In addition to matching risk level, treatment readiness, and level of motivation to the appropriate treatment programming, the responsivity principle also includes the consideration of additional factors that likely impinge on the success of treatment. It is clear that one size does not fit all. There are a number of offender characteristics that are relevant to consider before intervention. These include cognitive abilities, gender, mental health status, language fluency, and intellectual/learning capacity, among others. The point is simple: Do what it takes in terms of appropriately fitting offenders and programs such that barriers to successful outcomes are minimized. As Beauchaine and colleagues (2008) note, neurobiological considerations, as a consequence of heritable tendencies and interaction with the environment, can produce psychopathologies that impinge on an individual's abilities to understand, comprehend, and communicate. Understanding and taking into consideration these biosocial vulnerabilities can facilitate more efficient and effective matching of offenders to programming. Matthys, et al. (2012) note that neurocognitive dysfunctions associated with oppositional defiant disorder (ODD) and conduct disorder (CD) among children and adolescents likely compromise the effectiveness of social learning interventions. The neurocognitive implications of ODD and CD include compromised ability to understand consequences of behavior, problem solving, attention, cognitive flexibility, and decision making. Thus, the effectiveness of a cognitive-behavioral therapy (CBT), social learning intervention may be limited by these characteristics of participants. Success is enhanced by incorporating these factors in the decision-making process. Failure to consider them can hinder success (Andrews and Bonta 2007; Cullen and Gendreau 2000).

Research by Andrews, Dowden, and Gendreau (1999) indicates that adhering to the three principles of risk, needs, and responsivity reduced recidivism by an average of 25 percent; adhering to only two of the principles reduced recidivism by an average of 18 percent; and adhering to just one essentially did not reduce recidivism.

COGNITIVE-BEHAVIORAL MODALITIES

Another evidence-based finding is that the most effective intervention modalities for behavioral change are social learning, cognitive-behavioral approaches. Cognitive-behavioral therapies (CBT) are the most appropriate for changing antisocial thinking and cognitive distortion, and developing problem-solving skills, new ways of thinking, and other prosocial skills. CBT is based on the observations that thinking affects behavior, antisocial and distorted thinking can lead to criminal behavior, ways of thinking can be influenced, and changing how and what we think changes how we feel about ourselves and our behavior (Latessa n.d.).

Cognitive-behavioral programming should be highly structured, focusing on social learning and modeling and the acquisition of new skills, behaviors, and attitudes. They target peers, attitudes, values, anger, substance abuse, and so on. Training family on appropriate behavioral techniques is also important. Successful family-based approaches, among others, include Functional Family Therapy (Alexander et al. 1998), Multi-Systemic Therapy (Borduin et al. 1995; Schaeffer and Borduin 2005), and the Teaching Family Model (Kingsley 2006).

Most importantly, meta-analyses have confirmed that cognitive behavioral therapy reduces recidivism by least 25 percentage points more than other therapeutic modalities (Landenberger and Lipsey 2005; Lipsey, Landenberger, and Wilson 2007).

APPROPRIATE DOSAGE FOR THE APPROPRIATE PARTICIPANTS

How long an individual is in treatment should be driven by clinical decisions of the severity of the need and the risk level, not by funding, policy, or the simple decree of a prosecutor or judge. It is a waste of resources for someone who has been homeless and addicted to alcohol and drugs for fifteen years to be placed in an outpatient treatment program or even a thirty-day residential program. In all likelihood, the dosage is simply inadequate. This seems obvious to many, but this scenario of inappropriate treatment dosage is played out on a daily basis in probably every jurisdiction in the United States.

Higher-risk offenders require more structure and intervention than lower-risk offenders. As general guidelines, higher-risk offenders should be in structured, prosocial activities between 40 and 70 percent of the time over a three- to nine-month intervention period. Higher-risk offenders need 200 to 300 hours of intervention over a six- to twelve-month period. Medium-risk offenders generally require 100 hours over a three- to nine-month intervention period (Andrews and Bonta 2007; Bourgon and Armstrong 2005; Gendreau and Goggin 1995). These are suggestive dosage guidelines, designed to reflect the fact that individuals differ in important ways and that these differences must be taken into account. At the same time, there will be exceptions. That is why is it vital to get as much information as possible, similar to a medical diagnosis or emergency department triage. Guesswork can be quite counterproductive.

4. Increase Positive Reinforcement

While criminal offenders will, from time to time, require punitive responses to violations of rules and conditions, research clearly supports the minimization of negative reinforcement in correctional rehabilitation. When punishment/sanction is necessary, it should be quick and expected (swift and certain are the two aspects of punishment for which there is evidence of a deterrent effect).

Behavior change is facilitated and motivated by a balance of positive and negative reinforcement. Research by Andrews and Bonta (2006), Gendreau and Goggin (1995), Gendreau (1996), Gendreau, Little, and Goggin (1996), and Gendreau and Paparozzi (1995) indicates that the optimal ratio of positive to negative reinforcement is four positives for every one negative. The point is that an exclusively negative, punitive environment is not conducive to positive behavior change.

5. Adhere to Fidelity of Design, Implementation, and Operation, and Engage in Quality Control

Program integrity is fundamental for program success. Research clearly indicates a significant relationship between successful program outcomes and the fidelity used in developing and operating a program as the evidence shows it should be developed and operated (Latessa and Lowencamp 2006). This is not to say that local jurisdictions cannot or should not adapt programs to local circumstances and needs. However, in so modifying programs, it is important that the primary or key components remain intact or are modified in ways that research evidence supports.

6. Provide a Continuing Care, Aftercare, or Relapse Prevention Component

Common sense and evaluation research converge on the issue of continuing care or relapse prevention. One of the more common and avoidable "cracks" that individuals fall through is the failure to provide ongoing support and relapse prevention. The direct treatment effect is dramatically weakened or lost if ongoing support is not in place. This is particularly the case with substance abuse treatment and mental health treatment. For much of the history of correctional intervention, it seems that the philosophy that we have "done enough" by providing direct drug treatment has been the working assumption. The evidence indicates, however, that the resources spent on that treatment are wasted without an effective relapse prevention program in place.

Aftercare or continuing care typically requires developing collaborative relationships with community-based providers. Obviously, it is important that aftercare programming is evidence based, so an important criterion for establishing these relationships is to assure that programs utilize evidence-based methods.

7. Monitor and Evaluate Programming and Create Structures for Feedback

Presumably, correctional programming is designed, implemented, and operated with certain expectations and goals in mind, both process and outcome expectations and goals. All too often, "assessments" of performance are either general observations or seat-of-the-pants guesses. From an administrative perspective, goals are often in the form of money spent and people processed.

Valid, systematic process and outcome evaluations may seem like overkill to some, but it is the only way to know if and how the program is operating as intended, what is working more and less well, and importantly, how it can be improved and rendered more cost-effective. Developing appropriate, relevant metrics for evaluation is critical to the process and requires a clear understanding of the program. For example, appropriate metrics for a drug diversion program probably include program retention and program completion (and of course, any clues regarding who stays in the program and who graduates). But should recidivism be an outcome measure? For policymakers, recidivism is the metric, the end game, the common currency that all understand. Whether recidivism is an appropriate outcome measure for a drug diversion program depends on the types of interventions and programming that are provided. If the programing is primarily drug and alcohol treatment, recidivism is likely not appropriate (except reoffending involving drugs or alcohol). Most offenders have a variety of criminogenic circumstances, and unless the programming addresses these, recidivism reduction is unrealistic. Relapse should be the outcome measure instead.

Assuming that evaluation processes are in place, it is fundamentally important to make constructive use of the findings by providing feedback channels. Program fidelity, quality control, and staff performance, among others, are critical to meeting the goals and objectives of the program. Proper evaluation data are the only mechanism for taking corrective action, knowing if the program is operating as designed/intended, and if the staff is performing to expectations.

8. Engage Ongoing Support in Natural Communities

The logic is simple and intuitive: place offenders in prosocial environments in which there are existing networks that provide meaningful, productive connections, both people and activities, and help offenders strengthen their own prosocial skills and behaviors. Research indicates that recidivism is reduced when offenders' families are engaged in their activities and when offenders have positive, meaningful connections to a prosocial environment (Bonta et al. 2002; Clear and Sumner 2002; O'Connor and Perryclear 2002; Shapiro and Schwartz 2001).

9. Provide Extensive Skill Training for Staff

This is another obviously important component of successful correctional rehabilitation: assure that the staff is competent, motivated, and properly trained to provide cognitive-behavioral and social learning strategies, and assure that behavioral change is reinforced. This requires extensive training and retraining, and not all probation officers, parole officers, prison and jail staff, diversion court staff, among others, have the aptitude and the motivation to acquire and maintain the appropriate skills. There is the added challenge of the historic priority of risk management among those staff in charge of diverted and released offenders, for example, the cop versus social worker dichotomy that has been pervasive among parole and probation officers.

These are the current evidence-based tools or best practices that have been shown to reduce recidivism. Which of these are more and less important in reducing recidivism is a question that science is unable to answer with precision at this time. Clearly the risk principle (the who of correctional intervention), the need principle (what is targeted), the treatment principle (how to change behavior), and program integrity (how well behavior is changed) are the key elements. The evidence points to the conclusion that all of these principles should be implemented for maximum benefit. What should guide program development and operation is an overall *problem-solving perspective*. A problem-solving approach is one based on enhanced, accurate information (risk and needs); a focus on individuals and individual circumstances and needs, not categories of people and not one size fits all; community engagement; collaboration with community stakeholders; enhanced expertise at key decision points (for example, referral to diversion, sentencing); accountability; and importantly, creatively addressing (problem solving) the barriers and challenges to successful outcomes.

There are a growing number of meta-analyses of evaluations of what works to reduce crime and recidivism. These usually focus on particular programs such as drug courts or in-prison vocational training. One of the more comprehensive such analyses was conducted by Aos, Miller and Drake (2006b) at the Washington State Institute for Public Policy. Aos and colleagues not only estimate average effect sizes (crime/recidivism impacts), they are also able to attach economic benefits to categories of programs and produce net economic benefits. Their analysis is based on a statistical review of 571 evaluations of programs that passed muster as a "rigorous" evaluation. The primary criterion for being considered rigorous is that the evaluation must include a nontreatment or treatment-as-usual comparison group that is well matched to the treatment group. This Washington State Institute for Public Policy report is one of the more useful consolidations of existing research on what works. It provides direction to policymakers in terms of the types of interventions or programs for optimal recidivism reduction and cost-effectiveness. The specifics of the design, implementation, and operation of particular programs and the incorporation of the principles of effective correctional interventions require consulting other source materials.

The overall results, while general and approximate, are quite encouraging in providing viable, effective and cost-effective, evidence-based alternatives to traditional incarceration and community supervision.

To keep this in proper perspective, the goal here is to strike a balance between (1) incarceration and tough correctional control for those who are particularly dangerous, high-risk, habitual offenders for whom behavioral change has failed or is not deemed possible or appropriate, and those who commit particularly reprehensible crimes and are deserving of retributive punishment; and (2) concerted efforts at behavioral change through scientifically demonstrated effective policies and programs aimed at addressing criminal circumstance and criminogenic need. The evidence is clear. We know how to better and more cost-effectively reduce recidivism and, in turn, victimization.

At the same time, this is an uphill battle as adoption and implementation of these evidence-based practices (EBPs) is limited. Recent surveys of justice agencies and community-based providers of treatment and intervention for justice-involved adults and juveniles show sporadic adoption of EBPs for drug treatment programming. Most justice agencies and community-based providers for correctional drug treatment that employ any EBPs employ, on average, 60 percent of those indicated by the research. In addition, research indicates that the least-used EBPs are those modalities that have the greatest research support and that have been repeatedly shown to have the greatest impact on drug treatment outcomes (for example, cognitive-behavioral therapy and therapeutic communities [Henderson, Taxman, and Young 2008]).

Community-based treatment providers adopt EBPs more often than correctional organizations. Factors associated with adoption include being community based, absence of a punitive focus, being an accredited provider, and being connected to a broader network of providers. Moreover, the adoption of EBPs in correctional settings is significantly related to organizational leadership and culture. Leadership with background and experience in social/human services and favorable beliefs and attitudes about treatment and rehabilitation, as well as a culture of performance enhancement, training, and internal support for innovation, are characteristics of those institutions with greater adoption of EBPs (Friedmann, Taxman, and Henderson 2007).

IMPLEMENTATION OF EVIDENCE-BASED PRACTICES

Just because there is scientific evidence that a set of practices reduces recidivism does not mean that implementing those practices in a particular venue or setting will produce the same results. There is substantial evidence showing that real-world applications of effective demonstration programs can and do fall short in terms of treatment effects (for example, Andrews 2006; Bourgon et al. 2009). As Andrews notes (2006: 595):

> Implementation of effective human service is not simply a matter of selecting an evidence-based program off the shelf. Even well-researched ("blueprint") programs such as Aggression Replacement Training, Functional Family Therapy, and Multisystemic Therapy failed in Washington State when not well implemented. . . . The negative experience of England and Wales with the large-scale implementation of cognitive skill programs such as Reasoning and Rehabilitation is an intriguing and challenging story. . . . One cannot read the transcript of a roundtable discussion on the lessons of Project Greenlight without feeling the sting experienced by the Vera Institute of Justice and New York corrections team. . . . How is it, they ponder, that a reentry program designed with reference to "what works" could actually increase recidivism rates?

As Lowenkamp, Latessa and Smith (2006) tell us, there is a significant and substantial relationship between program characteristics (fidelity or accuracy of implementation and operation) and program effectiveness. Unlike the Nike tagline, it is not a matter of just doing it. It is a matter of doing it correctly. Technology transfer is one of the most significant challenges facing corrections today. There are two primary components to effective technology transfer: the technology itself and the transfer process. Thus, it is the responsibility of researchers and practitioners involved in development and implementation of EBPs to demonstrate not only what works, but also how it works. Knowing that a pilot or demonstration program works in a controlled environment is quite different from implementing it in real-world settings in which a variety of constraints and barriers challenge the fidelity of implementation. The point is simple but often missed: evidence-based programs and practices are not self-implementing or self-executing. Yet agencies and organizations routinely launch programs or sets of practices without careful consideration of the particulars of, for example, the organizational change process or the culture of the agency.

Fixsen et al. (2005) conducted an extensive review of the implementation of human service programs and practices in a wide variety of public and private settings. On balance, they affirm what was just discussed: proper implementation (fidelity) is far more difficult than developing the practices and programs themselves, and that the technology is much better understood than the technology transfer process. Their review and analysis is designed to improve effective implementation of evidence-based practices through identification of primary barriers and challenges to implementation, as well as key efficiencies in the implementation process.

Programs and practices have measurable outcomes and so does implementation. Integrity/fidelity can be measured, and determining whether implementation has been done correctly can assist program managers in refining the operation of programming. The primary outcomes of successful implementation (Fixsen et al. 2005) are: changes in the behaviors, attitudes, knowledge, and skills of professional practitioners and other relevant organizational staff; changes in organizational structures and cultures (changes in values, beliefs, attitudes, ethics, philosophies, policies, goals, procedures, decision making) that support the behavior change of the professional staff; and changes in the relationships with consumers, clients, patients, stakeholders, and partners.

The stages of the process of implementation identified by Fixsen and colleagues' research include: exploration and adoption, program installation, initial implementation, full operation, innovation, and sustainability.

Exploration and Adoption

There are many reasons why local jurisdictions adopt and attempt to implement an innovative or evidence-based practice or program. Often it seems that a new idea is adopted because of the perception that everyone else is doing it. Community policing and broken windows initiatives come to mind, as do drug courts. Often these programs are adopted before there is much evidence that they are effective in what they are designed to do, and often before there is much implementation experience or shared implementation knowledge to assist the adoption and installation process. Sometimes implementation of evidence-based programs is mandated from above, for example when a state legislature requires drug courts in jurisdictions that meet a certain population size criterion, but provide little guidance for adoption and implementation (the Texas legislature did this with drug courts in 2001).

In the best of circumstances, exploration is a segment of the process that focuses on assessing local community needs, the match between community needs and the program/innovation, the availability of local resources, and a deliberate and informed decision whether or not to proceed. That decision should not be based on the perception that the innovation is a good idea, but whether it is a significant value add, the extent to which it is needed, and whether it is feasible in terms of available resources. Making these decisions should typically involve conducting needs assessment research, sizing or scaling the need, identifying appropriate programs or interventions that best address those needs, assessing the fit between the program and the needs, and laying the ground work for a decision to proceed (if that is decided). The process should be need driven and not program driven.

One of the key functions or roles in implementation is the "purveyor," "change agent," or "program consultant." This is the person, persons, or organization that is responsible for the idea or concept of the practice or program. "A purveyor works in more or less organized ways with the intention to implement a specified practice or program at a particular location" (Fixsen et al. 2005: 14). Individuals or organizations that fill the purveyor role over time can gain important experience and knowledge regarding the implementation process and can therefore expedite the successful implementation of programs and practices. Organizations that at least partially fulfill that role are the Center for Court Innovation, the Bureau of Justice Assistance, and Community Oriented Policing Services, among others.

A critical element of the exploration and adoption phase is gaining political support at all appropriate levels, from state and local government to relevant stakeholders and interest groups, service providers, and consumer groups. This support is initiated in the exploration and adoption phase, but is essential for the entire implementation process, as well as for the sustainability of the initiative.

Fixsen and colleagues (2005) reviewed the implementation of programs and practices in "community" settings and identified several factors supported by research that facilitate successful implementation. In this context,

I use the term "community" to mean stakeholders external to the organization or agency in which the program is being implemented. These include:

- Mobilizing local interest, consensus, and support, and identifying local champions; articulating how the innovation contributes to the big picture; developing a marketing strategy.
- Encouraging community participation in decision making.
- Developing understanding and commitment to the initiatives.
- Clarifying feasibility by identifying how the innovation fits into existing organizational structures or how new structures and operational mechanisms will work.
- Assuring that stakeholders have an ongoing monitoring function and that they participate in long-term sustainability.
- Assuring program/practice implementation readiness by enhancing awareness and familiarity and benefits, and identifying barriers and strategies to addressing them.

Program Installation

The installation phase, which follows the decision to proceed, involves the nuts and bolts of the process, including the commitment of resources, structural supports, any relevant legal changes, and so on. Collateral elements include funding streams, human resource considerations, development of policies and procedures, creation of referral mechanisms, reporting requirements, securing physical space and required technology, among others.

Initial Implementation

Implementation requires varying levels of change in skill levels, organizational capacity, organizational structure, roles and responsibilities, and organizational culture. As Fixsen and colleagues (2005) note from their research, implementation is often confronted by fear of change, a culture of and investment in the status quo, and "diamond-hard inertia." These barriers are often encountered while attempting to engage the inherently difficult task of developing and implementing something new and innovative to the organization or agency. Overcoming these difficulties requires careful planning, key political support, appropriate purveyors, the relevant implementation elements, an effective marketing plan to sell the ideas internally and externally, the ability to communicate effectively with a variety of audiences, effective organizational leadership to move things forward, and mechanisms and processes to change internal beliefs, attitudes, and ways of thinking and doing (culture change). By way of example, the culture change could involve creating an environment in a justice agency whereby every individual embraces the responsibility for recidivism reduction, much in the same way that the Nordstrom culture is one in which all employees care about and deliver an exceptional customer experience. It is the idea that the culture creates ways of thinking and believing that result in actions and behaviors that produce consistent, productive, mission-driven results.

Full Operation

Full implementation is reached "once the new learning becomes integrated into practitioner, organizations, and community practices, policies and procedures" (Fixsen et al. 2005: 16). This is the point at which the program is at staffing and client capacity, referral channels are fully operational, practitioners are fully engaged in implementing evidence-based practices with skill and fidelity, the organization is providing all relevant supports, and the community embraces the innovation. Over time, the definition of treatment as usual changes to reflect the new ways of doing business, program benefits begin to be realized, and the new policies and procedures become routine. As program fidelity hits prescribed criteria, outcome targets should approximate the levels of the demonstration or original EBP.

Innovation

One size does not fit all, thus it is reasonable that implementation will differ by site depending on the unique characteristics each site exhibits. Implementation is an opportunity to learn both positives and negatives, what is successful and what is not. Implementation sites differ and offer different barriers and efficiencies to implementation. How the barriers are addressed and the efficiencies are leveraged provide opportunities to innovate. As Fixsen et al. (2005: 17) note:

> They [unique conditions at a site] also present opportunities to refine and
> expand both the treatment practices and programs and the implementation

practices and programs. Some of the changes at an implementation site will be undesirable and will be defined as program drift and a threat to fidelity. . . . Others will be desirable changes and will be defined as innovations that need to be included in the "standard model" of treatment or implementation practices.

The key of course is differentiating between fidelity drift and innovation. The prescribed path is to first implement the program as described and then to innovate as indicated. That way, the innovation is not based on an effort to circumscribe perceived difficult fidelity standards. Research clearly indicates that innovation after full implementation was more successful than modifications made before full implementation.

Sustainability

The environment changes, funding ebbs and flows, well-trained staff and practitioners leave, leadership changes, stakeholders and partners come and go, political alliances evolve, and champions/advocates move on. The goal is to sustain the effort in the context of a changing environment.

There are six identified core components of implementation that research shows create, support, and enhance high-fidelity, EBP behavior and actions (Fixsen et al. 2005; Bourgon et al. 2010a). One is practitioner and staff selection. It sounds simple. Create a set of guidelines and qualifications and it's done. However, getting the criteria and qualifications right and properly/correctly identifying staff is often more challenging. Identifying staff and practitioner criteria requires a fundamental understanding of the EBPs for which staff are being hired. Some jurisdictions may have a larger pool of candidates than others, so those with limited availability of qualified candidates will have to address that issue. Some compromise may be required, thus knowing the potential impact of such compromises needs to be on the radar of the key decision makers.

Training is another core component. Preservice and in-service training not only teach the proper protocols, roles and responsibilities, and rules and procedures, they also teach and reinforce what is often a new agency or departmental culture. Getting all relevant participants on the same page regarding mission, vision, philosophy, and values is critical. Knowing what to do, when to do it, and how to do it does not in fact assure it gets done and done properly. On the job training is the more effective way to teach more specific job skills.

Ongoing staff evaluation is key to knowing how well practitioners and support staff are engaging the EBPs. Evaluation not only serves to assess performance and fidelity, it can also provide corrective action to remedy deficiencies that can be addressed in hiring, training, and coaching. Facilitative administration refers to a management perspective and approach that provides key leadership and support, leaders that understand and agree with the premises of the initiatives and programs being implemented, and support for the mission and culture required to produce the desired outcomes. Facilitative leadership also promotes a learning and problem-solving environment, and a culture of professional development. Clearly, facilitative administration is an ongoing focus and process that continually assesses and improves. Finally, systems interventions are linkages with external resources necessary to maintain ongoing funding and human resources and other organizational needs.

With all of these pieces in place, the core components and the proper phases or stages of implementation will substantially improve the likelihood of success. However, it is important to emphasize that all components and all phases are important. Programs have failed due to a lack of appreciation for a seemingly minor detail or element. Success generally requires that all factors are considered and addressed. Failure only requires one mishap.

One of the major sources of variation in the quality of human service provision is that many are practitioner centered, thus all hinges on the expertise of the practitioner and the type and nature of services provided. Successful intervention programs should be evidence-based program-centered or evidence-based practice-centered, rather than practitioner centered.

One additional factor that is implicit in some of the discussion above is the role of politics. Assuring buy in by internal staff and administration, local stakeholders, elected officials, and policymakers can be critical for the viability of an initiative. Lack of appropriate funding can easily render a program or initiative ineffective or compromised. Thus, having key community leaders on board with an initiative may be an important component in persuading local county or city elected officials to properly fund a program. Assuring that all relevant stakeholders are informed can prove important down the road. Thus, a new EBP for offender rehabilitation may require an in-depth understanding of the local political arena and contact with interested parties and stakeholder groups (such as law enforcement, prosecutors, the defense bar, judges, the religious community, victims groups, county and city elected officials and administrators, probation officials, local political party officials, the mental health community, housing authorities, the medical community, and the many components of the nonprofit sector, including treatment providers, the school district/board, and so on). Obtaining local support from all relevant sources is critical for the success of many initiatives, especially community-based initiatives. Fixsen and colleagues (2005: 68) summarize the issues surrounding implementation as follows:

> Implementation practices function in a complex ecology of best intervention practices, organizational structures and cultures, policy and funding environments, and community strengths and needs. Given the preponderance of evidence from a variety of sources, implementation appears to be a crucial component of moving science to service with fidelity and good outcomes for children, families, and adults.

Andrews (2006) has identified additional key components of the implementation of the risk-need-responsivity (RNR) principles and some barriers to effective implementation and operation of EBP programming. Use of structured, validated risk and need assessments is critical, but the impact of their use is mitigated if the information they provide is not routinely and comprehensively incorporated into case and program planning and management. Another is the perception that the highest-risk offenders are untreatable and thus are sometimes excluded from services. Another barrier to successful intervention is that high-risk offenders may be less motivated to participate in treatment. Understanding that higher- and moderate-risk offenders are not equally motivated to participate in programming is important. So is utilizing techniques to enhance motivation and treatment readiness.

Not all cognitive-behavioral programs and therapists are created equal. Some programs that are labeled cognitive behavioral fall far short of the criteria for true cognitive programming. Moreover, there is a profound shortage of qualified cognitive behavioral therapists in the free world, and there is reason to believe the situation is similar if not worse in corrections. While some therapists/counselors may be considered or call themselves cognitive behavioral, the reality may be quite different. Assure that the therapeutic staff is properly qualified and engage ongoing training and supervision of clinical and other staff involved in programming.

Finally, Andrews (2006) emphasizes the importance of ongoing assessment or monitoring, feedback, and corrective action. Part of this process is the assessment of program integrity/fidelity over time and identification and implementation of changes as warranted to remain in compliance with EBPs.

THE BIGGER PICTURE OF BEHAVIORAL CHANGE: WHERE WE GO FROM HERE BASED ON OUR EMERGING UNDERSTANDING OF NEUROCOGNITIVE IMPAIRMENTS

The preceding discussion constitutes what is currently known about general evidence-based practices for behavioral change of criminal offenders. I discuss specific EBPs in more detail in later chapters. I am now going to take the discussion of behavioral change beyond the core correctional practices to focus on what the evidence suggests is needed in the future. The point is that EBPs are necessary for efforts at behavioral change and recidivism reduction. Necessary, but not sufficient. There is much more that is research based that has not worked its way to the level of discussion and consideration in criminal justice policy, let alone as EBPs. These include addressing the complexity of criminogenic, collateral cognitive, and behavioral impairments with which criminal offenders present, the inadequacy of current screening and assessment, and the lack of true clinical diagnosis, among others.

There are many mental health conditions that are relevant to understanding criminal involvement and/or relevant to the behavioral change process. In addition to the criminogenic factors that assessments are intended to identify, there are many developmental, cognitive, and mental health conditions or disorders that may or may not impact criminal offending, but which may significantly and substantially impact the intervention, treatment, and rehabilitation process. Mental illness is clearly implicated in the commission of violent crime. Individuals with diagnoses of major depression, bipolar disorder, anxiety disorders, and schizophrenia are at greater risk of committing violent crimes than individuals without those conditions. The risk increases in the presence of multiple psychiatric disorders. This is especially evident when co-occurring disorders include substance abuse, and antisocial personality disorder, and/or psychopathy.

Substance abuse/addiction and mental health problems can lead to or cause cognitive and behavioral impairments, impairments related to psychosocial and interpersonal functioning, and executive functioning. Functional impairments are important to assess because they can and do impact the ability to effectively interact with treatment and supervision staff, engage and participate in treatment, and successfully complete treatment and supervision. In turn, the presence of such impairments challenge effectively adhering to the responsivity principle discussed previously.

Peters, Bartio, and Sherman (2008) assert that cognitive and behavioral impairments are not typically a focus of screening and assessments, although they are often more important in predicting treatment outcome and identifying the nature of particular treatment interventions. As Peters, Bartoli and Sherman (2008: 13) note, "an understanding of functional impairment, strengths, supports, skills deficits, and cultural barriers is essential to developing an informed treatment plan and to selecting appropriate levels of treatment services." While it is critical to identify (screen and assess) criminogenic deficits, it is also critical for effective and successful intervention to identify collateral impairments that are vital to informing the intensity, duration, type, and scope of treatment, as well as supervision strategies.

The point is that criminal offenders often present with very complex developmental, cognitive, and mental health challenges. To be effective, behavioral change intervention processes must appreciate this complexity, utilize screening and assessment procedures and instruments that are designed to capture the variety of circumstances and deficits, develop treatment plans that reflect primary and secondary intervention priorities, and then engage the variety of evidence-based interventions relevant to the individual's circumstances. I now turn to a more detailed discussion of neurobiological and neurocognitive factors involved in criminality and in the intervention process.

Neurobiological and Neurocognitive Considerations

The past ten to fifteen years have ushered in a remarkable amount of knowledge about the role of neurobiological and neurocognitive disorders and criminal offending. Much of this has been driven by enhanced technology such as the electroencephalograph, functional magnetic resonance imaging (fMRI), positron emission tomography (PET), transcranial magnetic stimulation (TMS), and diffusion tension imaging (DTI), among others.

There are several terms that are used to describe this focus on the brain and crime: the neurobiology of criminal behavior, neurocriminology, and biosocial criminology. Regardless of the label, the basic premise is that a broader understanding of crime and criminality should incorporate the fact that humans have brains, genes, hormones, and an evolutionary history. In turn, the knowledge from these disciplines (behavior genetics, neurobiology, evolutionary science) should be integrated into theories of crime as well as intervention, rehabilitation, and prevention strategies. Such an approach takes away from the naïve nature versus nurture position to one of nature by way of nurture—the interaction of biological tendencies with the social and physical environment. Humans have genetic predispositions, not genetic determinism. There are no criminal genes, but there are genes that predispose some to low IQ, low empathy, low self-control, and impulsiveness, factors that have been identified as criminogenic. Thus, genes facilitate behavioral tendencies that are conditioned by and respond to the environment.

Neuroscience addresses the mechanisms whereby interactions and experiences in the environment affect or condition behavioral tendencies. Neurobiology focuses on the cells of the brain (neurons) and communication among neurons through substances called neurotransmitters. Our interactions, experiences, observations, thoughts, and feelings are registered in our brains through new connections among brain cells. These neural connections, some of which are established early in development through the influence of genes and other inputs (which are established on an ongoing basis through interaction with the environment) determine how we think, perceive, feel, interpret, and react to the social and physical environment. The neural connections shape our thoughts, emotions, and feelings, our self-identity and our personality. They are experience dependent, shaped by the environment in interaction with genetic influences.

Neurocriminologists are primarily interested in the fact that while basic human functions such as heart rate and breathing are hardwired in the brain, most other behavior is acquired through interactions and experiences in the environment. These interactions and experiences largely shape the neural connections in our brains, which in turn influence out thoughts, perceptions, and behaviors. As Walsh (2012: 139) describes it:

> Neural networks are continually being made and selected for retention or elimination in a "use it or lose it" process governed by the strength and frequency of experience. Retention is biased in favor of networks that are most stimulated during early development. . . . This is why bonding and attachment are so vital to human beings, and why abuse and neglect are so injurious. Hormones released by chronic stress can cause neurons to die, and children with high levels of these hormones experience cognitive and social development delays. . . . As Perry and Pollard (1998) point out, "Experience in adults alters the organized brain, but in infants and children it organizes the developing brain" (p. 36). Brains organized by stressful and traumatic events tend to relay events along the same brain pathways laid out by early events because pathways laid down early in life are more resistant to elimination than pathways laid down later in life. A brain organized by negative events is ripe for antisocial behavior.

Neuroscience research has consistently demonstrated that exposure to adverse events and experiences can have long-term impacts on neural networks, which have substantial consequences for behavior. Exposure to poverty, low social status, violence, abuse, neglect, hostility, and academic failure is registered in the brain and can lead to substantial levels of anxiety, anger, hostility, fear, and in turn antisocial behavior.

In the most basic sense, we are able to successfully navigate the social environment when we appropriately respond to rewards and punishments with a socially appropriate approach and avoidance behavior. Central to this premise is the regulation of behavior though the behavior activating system (BAS) and the behavior inhibiting system (BIS), both of which are part of the limbic system, with extensions into the prefrontal cortex of the brain. The BAS is largely associated with the neurotransmitter dopamine and thus the pleasure areas of the brain. The BAS is like an accelerator, motivating the individual to pursue rewarding stimuli. It is influenced by the pleasure principle and is the "biological raw material representing drives for acquiring life sustaining necessities and life's pleasures" (Walsh and Bolen 2012: 20). The BIS, which is associated with the neurotransmitter serotonin, reflects the moral and social rules and norms that an

individual internalizes during socialization. The BIS is sensitive to punishment and serves as the brake that, when properly operating, prevents
us from excess. The neurotransmitter dopamine facilitates goal-directed,
rewarding behavior, and serotonin functions to moderate behavior. If the
BAS/BIS is out of balance, whereby the BAS dominates (excess dopamine
and insufficient serotonin), that imbalance can result in sensation-seeking
behavior, impulsiveness, low self-control, low empathy, and behavior driven
by reward and relatively insensitive to punishment or consequences. The
outcomes can include addictive behavior, antisocial behavior, and criminal
behavior. "Serotonin and dopamine are powerful regulators of behavioral
and cognitive functions, thus any aspect of reduced or enhanced seroto-
nergic or dopaminergic functioning results in emotional, behavioral and
cognitive dysregulation" (Walsh and Bolen 2012: 20). Moreover, as Berman, Tracy, and Coccaro (1997) report in their review of the research on
serotonin levels among criminal offenders, low serotonin activity is related
to aggressive behavior. A meta-analysis conducted by Moore et al. (2002)
reports that the effect size for the relationship between serotonin levels
and antisocial behavior is −.45, indicating an effect of medium magnitude.
Hormones also play a role in criminality. For example, cortisol is part of the
body's stress reaction system and works to mobilize the body's resources
in times of stress. Many studies have documented lower cortisol levels
among antisocial children, adolescents, and adults, indicating that such
individuals may be less influenced by stressors and may be less concerned
with any potential consequences for their actions (Rudo-Hutt et al. 2011).
Rudo-Hutt and colleagues (2011: 25) conclude from a review of research
and meta-analyses that "overall, these findings suggest that hormones and
neurotransmitters often interact with social and environmental factors to
increase the likelihood of antisocial behavior."

A third behavioral system of relevance here is the fight or flight system (FFS), regulated by the neurotransmitter epinephrine or adrenaline.
A properly functioning FFS will mobilize the body for appropriate action
under various circumstances; for example, flight when confronted with fear.
However, a weak FFS can contribute significantly to antisocial behavior
because the FFS functions to inhibit behavior via conditioned and uncon-
ditioned fear. Inappropriate responses to fear include antisocial behavior.

The prefrontal cortex (PFC) is the part of the brain that is responsible for executive functions, including planning, analyzing, synthesizing,

making moral judgments, and modulating emotions (Walsh 2012). The PFC requires optimal levels of dopamine, among other things, thus improper levels of dopamine can impact PFC functioning, executive functions, and criminality. So can injury to the PFC, as well as other deficits and disorders. Attention deficit hyperactivity disorder (ADHD) has been implicated in weaker PFC activation, increasing the risk of antisocial behavior. fMRI and PET scans have consistently found links between lower PFC functioning and impulsive criminal behavior. Deficits in prefrontal functioning are quite common among violent, aggressive, and antisocial groups, and reduced prefrontal lobe activity is associated with antisocial individuals (Fabian 2009). Prefrontal lobe functioning is related to understanding and processing information, communication, interpreting others' reactions, abstract reasoning, impulse control, emotional regulation, and empathy, among others.

A primary takeaway at this point is that our brains capture the variety of interactions we have in the social and physical environment. The fact that our brains register these events and experiences, some of which are negative, toxic, and/or dangerous and threatening, creates the potential for implicating neurological factors in antisocial behavior. The consequences of these neurological factors include intellectual and cognitive impairment, compromised executive function, lack of empathy and self-control, addiction, and aggression, among others. The sources of these neurological consequences are as varied as alcohol and nicotine consumption by the mother while pregnant, poverty, lack of proper maternal attachment, trauma, and violence, among others.

EXECUTIVE DYSFUNCTION

Executive function is an umbrella term that refers to cognitive processes that facilitate goal-directed behavior. Executive processes are fundamental to higher brain function, including goal setting, planning, analyzing, goal-directed activity, attention, response inhibition, self-monitoring, understanding consequences, and complex cognition. It allows individuals to be self-sustaining and self-reliant, and is considered necessary for proper adult conduct. Executive functioning, which is associated with the prefrontal cortex of the brain, can have substantial consequences for cognition and behavior. Executive dysfunction has been consistently linked to cognitive development disorders, psychotic disorders, affective disorders, and conduct disorders. Factors that interfere with normal brain development can affect the prefrontal cortex. Toxins such as alcohol, drugs, lead, and tobacco can enter the fetus and disrupt brain development, including affecting the PFC, resulting in compromised executive functioning and a heightened risk of antisocial behavior (Beaver, Wright, and Delisi 2007).

Executive dysfunction is also implicated in criminal behavior. A meta-analysis of thirty-nine studies and over 4,500 participants on the relation between executive dysfunction and antisocial behavior (Morgan and Lilienfeld 2000) revealed a robust and statistically significant relationship. The effect size is medium to large. More recent research by Barbosa and Monteiro (2008) finds a clear relation between criminal recidivism and executive dysfunction (impulsivity, distraction, lack of self-control, difficulty using environmental feedback in regulating behavior, exhibiting behavior that is inappropriate for the social context). Moreover, Hancock, Tapscott, and Hoaken (2010) report a significant relationship between executive dysfunction and violent criminal offending.

Another meta-analysis investigated the relationship between post-traumatic stress disorder (PTSD) and executive functioning. Polak et al. (2011) reviewed eighteen studies involving 1,080 subjects and over 600 controls that showed that PTSD subjects had significantly impaired executive functioning. Hawkins and Trobst (1999) show from their review of research that there is a relationship between weak executive functioning and aggression and violence. Another review by Brower and Price (2001) finds similar evidence for a significant link between frontal lobe dysfunction (executive dysfunction), and aggression and antisocial behavior. Brower and Price (2001: 724) conclude:

> The studies surveyed in this review indicate that clinically significant frontal lobe dysfunction is associated with aggressive dyscontrol. Subjects with both traumatic and neurodegenerative disorders primarily involving the prefrontal cortex display increased rates of aggressive and antisocial behaviour compared with subjects who have no, or non-frontal brain injury. Studies employing neuropsychological testing, neurological examination, EEG, and neuroimaging have also tended to find evidence for increased rates of prefrontal network dysfunction among aggressive and antisocial subjects.

The research on executive dysfunction and antisocial behavior shows a clear link between lack of control and elevated impulsivity, and antisocial behavior and aggression. Executive dysfunction is also linked to schizophrenia, ADHD, autism spectrum disorder, and bipolar disorder. There are a number of standardized tests or assessments for executive function that are widely used and validated. These include the Clock Drawing Test, the Stroop Test, the Wisconsin Card Sorting Test, and the Train-Making Test.

INTELLIGENCE

The deficit in IQ among criminal populations has been well documented (Savage, Ellis, and Kozey 2013) and recent research has uncovered a common genetic basis for low IQ and antisocial behavior (Koenen et al. 2006). Moreover, low IQ is quite likely a function, in part, of cognitive deficits or impairment (Yoshikawa 1995). While IQ per se is related to criminal offending, the subscales of Verbal and Performance IQ have been shown to differ among individuals engaged in antisocial behavior. Specifically, there is a tendency for offenders to exhibit not only lower IQ, but also lower Verbal compared to Performance IQ. Verbal IQ measures fact-based knowledge and Performance IQ focuses on spatial and nonverbal reasoning (Walsh and Bolen 2012).

Research by Moffitt (2006) and many others implicates intellectual functioning with chronic offending. Moreover, Moffitt reports that long-term chronic offending (life-course persistent) is associated with low intellectual ability, reading difficulties, and lower scores on neuropsychological tests.

POVERTY, NEGLECT, AND DISORDERED ATTACHMENT

We have long known about the link between poverty/disadvantage and crime. Criminal offenders are predominantly lower income and crime tends to cluster in areas of socioeconomic disadvantage. We also now have a clearer understanding of how poverty affects the brain. For one, recent research (Hook, Lawson, and Farah 2013) shows that poverty is related to executive functioning both directly as well as indirectly through poverty's impact on parenting. The research is clear: children who are exposed to poverty score lower on a variety of cognitive and behavioral assessments, including memory, attention, language skills, impulse regulation, achievement, IQ, and functional literacy. Nobel, Norman, and Farah (2005) conducted a comprehensive study of socioeconomic status (SES) and cognitive functioning among kindergarten children. The research focused on the potential effects of SES on five neurocognitive domains or systems, including the prefrontal/executive system and the language system. The findings indicated that SES is significantly related to the executive and language systems. While language effects are important, the executive functioning deficits among those in poverty are of direct relevance to antisocial behavior and crime. Farah and colleagues (2006) focused on identifying the neurocognitive systems responsible for the poverty-IQ link, or as they put it, "how and why might a sociological construct, SES, be associated with brain function?" They found substantial disproportionate effects on the prefrontal/executive function systems of working memory and cognitive control, as well as language and memory, which involve the left perisylvian and medial temporal areas of the brain.

Research has revealed a strong correlation between income and child neglect/abuse (Sedlak and Broadhurst 1996). Loughan and Perna (2012) investigated the effects of poverty and neglect/abuse (physical, sexual, and emotional). Unsurprisingly, their analysis revealed significantly below-average IQ, academic ability, memory, and executive functioning. The combination of poverty and neglect/abuse is also associated with significantly higher diagnoses of developmental delay, ADHD, conduct disorders, anxiety disorders, PTSD, personality disorders, learning disabilities, and emotional/behavioral disorders.

Psychopathy, sociopathy, and antisocial personality disorder are generally synonymous terms that describe a clustering of traits or characteristics such as narcissism, irresponsibility, sensation seeking, risk taking, deception, impulsiveness, lack of remorse, lack of empathy, lack of self-control, and shallow affect. Walsh and Bolen (2012: 163–164) indicate that under the right (or wrong) circumstances,

> [a]buse and neglect, combined with prenatal insults to normal brain development, both of which are more common in lower-SES environments, lead to early predisposition to antisocial behavior which, with the right genetic profile, may reach psychopathic/sociopathic proportions. . . . Thus, this study, along with many others that have looked at the neurobiological consequences of abuse and neglect, shows that children who suffer early socioemotional deprivation can indeed develop a number of the neurobiological abnormalities seen in psychopathy.

Recently, considerable attention has been focused on the prevalence, nature, and consequences of disordered attachment, which tends to be associated with neglect, poverty, parental substance abuse, and other parental psychological disorders. Research has revealed that a lack of a proper attachment relationship (a close, secure emotional bond) between an infant and the primary caregiver has very important consequences for behavior, especially antisocial behavior and violence. The development of a secure attachment relationship intervenes against or mitigates subsequent antisocial behavior and cognitions. A proper attachment relation can mitigate subsequent antisocial and violent behavior by promoting or facilitating the regulation of impulses and emotions, development of empathy and prosocial values, effective management of stress, and development of a positive self-image (Levy and Orlans 2000). Absence of a proper attachment relationship can have substantial consequences for cognitive, intellectual, emotional, and social development, as well as affective and behavioral regulation. The common consequences of disordered attachment include impulsivity, anger, aggression, lack of conscience and empathy, and extreme oppositional behavior.

EXPOSURE TO VIOLENCE

Exposure to violence is largely, though not exclusively, a consequence of poverty, disproportionally affecting low-SES, urban, minority youth. Research indicates that the vast majority of youth living in poor, inner-city neighborhoods have witnessed violence, and over two-thirds have been victims of violence (Fitzpatrick and Boldizar 1993; Scarpa 2001). There are a variety of negative consequences of exposure to community violence, including aggression, PTSD, anxiety disorders, depression, dissociation, impaired academic functioning, lower IQ and reading ability, and lower high school graduation rates (Stein et al. 2003). Clinical research on exposure to violence shows consistent neurological and physiological effects, including dysregulation of the hypothalamic-pituitary-adrenal axis (HPA), which is responsible for regulating the stress response. This dysregulation of the HPA axis can lead to chronic hyperarousal (contributing to hypervigilance), or a dissociative response of reduced responsiveness, which can contribute to depression. Exposure to violence has been shown to result in various externalizing problems, including antisocial behavior, aggression, and violence. Exposure to violence is also associated with internalizing problems such as depression and anxiety (Lynch 2003).

TRAUMA AND POSTTRAUMATIC STRESS DISORDER

Research by Breaslau et al. (1998) estimates the lifetime exposure to one or more DSM-IV defined traumatic events at 90 percent. The most common is the unexpected death of a relative or friend. Assaultive violence is more common among men, low-SES individuals, and nonwhites. Over 50 percent of inner-city residents experienced assaultive violence, compared to 33 percent for residents of other, non-inner-city areas. The estimated probability of any traumatic event leading to PTSD is approximately 9 percent. Assaultive violence poses the greatest risk of PTSD (21 percent). In most cases, research shows PTSD symptoms lasted more than six months.

Additional research utilizing a hospital intercept approach of low-income, nearly exclusively African-American males and females seeking care in primary care and OBGYN clinics at an urban public hospital (Gillespie et al. 2010) found lifetime PTSD prevalence of over 46 percent. The primary source of the originating trauma was interpersonal violence. Alim and colleagues (2006) found similar lifetime PTSD rates (51 percent) for urban African-American subjects in a primary care intercept setting. These high PTSD prevalence rates among poor, urban, minority populations have been replicated time and time again. Moreover, co-morbidity of PTSD with other mental disorders is common. The National Co-Morbidity Survey revealed that among those with PTSD, the co-morbidity rate was 48 percent for major depressive disorder, 22 percent for dysthymia, 16 percent for generalized anxiety disorder, and 30 percent for phobia. Women exhibited more panic disorder and men exhibited co-morbid alcohol and drug abuse, and conduct disorder.

PTSD consists of four primary behavioral clusters: reexperiencing the traumatic event(s), for example having flashbacks; avoiding situations or places that remind one of the event(s); feeling emotionally numb, experiencing memory problems, and trouble concentrating; and feeling anxious or hypervigilant, angry, irritable, and engaging in self-destructive behavior such as substance abuse. Trauma exposure and PTSD can manifest as well in self-destructive behavior, aggression, and mood and personality shifts. Research is clear that traumatic events alter the structure of the brain, fundamentally alter brain development, and can have substantial impacts on the limbic system, which is responsible for controlling emotions, among other things. Freidman (2000) notes in a review of PTSD and brain abnormalities that PTSD is related to impaired cognitive capabilities.

Meta-analysis cited by Polak et al. (2011), as well as research by others (Gilbertson et al. 2001; Johnsen and Asbjornsen 2008; Stein et al. 2003), demonstrate a clear link between PTSD and impaired cognitive and executive functioning. There is additional evidence that the severity of PTSD symptoms is more influential on executive functioning impairment than the character or frequency of the trauma.

The relationship between trauma and antisocial behavior has been well documented. Violent victimization and exposure to violence both heighten the risk of committing antisocial acts and violence, with the common element of trauma. Aggression and criminal behavior are statistically linked to child abuse and its associated traumatic effects. As Ardino (2012) notes, the more common risk factors for PTSD and posttraumatic reactions, antisocial behavior, and aggression are poverty, abuse and neglect, sexual molestation, and exposure to violence in the community or household.

Criminal offenders present with a significantly higher prevalence of trauma and posttraumatic stress disorder and related symptoms. The prevalence of trauma and PTSD among offender populations varies considerably from study to study, with low end rates from around 4 percent to as high as 65 percent lifetime prevalence of PTSD, but more recent research (Goff et al. 2007) found estimates between 4 and 21 percent. There is also clear evidence of co-morbidity of PTSD with substance abuse, and recidivism rates for the combination of disorders are significantly higher than each disorder separately (Ardine 2012).

Looking at this differently, a very high percentage of individuals with PTSD have criminal justice involvement. Donley and colleagues (2012) researched a sample of inner-city individuals at primary care clinics in a metropolitan hospital. The vast majority were African American and poor. The authors found that 88 percent of male civilians with PTSD had been arrested, 87 percent had been jailed, 36 percent had been imprisoned, and 37 percent had been charged with a violent offense, rates much higher than non-PTSD controls. The results show that trauma exposure and PTSD symptoms are both related to significant justice system involvement, although the design was not able to determine whether trauma/PTSD led to justice involvement, justice involvement led to trauma/PTSD, or both.

ATTENTION DEFICIT HYPERACTIVITY DISORDER

Attention Deficit Hyperactivity Disorder (ADHD) seems to be the diagnosis de jure for children engaged in challenging behaviors. However, whether ADHD is overdiagnosed is not the issue at hand. Our concern is the prevalence of ADHD in the criminal justice population, and in turn what we know about the neurological and neurocognitive implications of ADHD. Study after study, in the United States and other nations, among juvenile and adult populations all confirm the hard fact that ADHD is a substantially important risk factor in criminal offending. Prevalence rates among prison inmates range from roughly 25 percent to as high as 65 percent. Co-morbidity for substance abuse is also common, with estimates as high as 85 percent among prison inmates (Walsh and Bolen 2012).

ADHD is clinically defined as ongoing inattention and/or hyperactivity or impulsive behavior occurring in various settings, and uncharacteristic in frequency and severity in terms of the individual's developmental stage. There are three types of ADHD: the primarily inattentive, the primarily hyperactive/impulsive, and the combined, hyperactive and inattentive. The combined is the most common of the three. Although typically considered a childhood and adolescent disorder, it is clear that depending on the definition and symptoms, significant proportions of cases will persist into adulthood.

The relation between ADHD and crime can be better understood by investigating the neurological implications. ADHD is consistently and substantially linked to deficits of the PFC (again, that part of the brain responsible for executive functioning, moral judgment, and social cognition), including reductions in gray matter volume as well as alterations in PFC circuits and impaired PFC activation in behavior and attention regulation. Behavioral manifestations of ADHD that are relevant for understanding criminality include general executive function deficits, impulsivity, lack of self-control, being present oriented, and an inability to delay gratification.

What Does It All Mean?

First, it does not mean that implicating the brain, genes, and the environment through these examples excuses criminal behavior. This is not an effort to minimize or mitigate culpability or responsibility, or to create new affirmative defenses for defendants going to trial.

What it does mean is that the landscape of criminal circumstance is much broader and deeper than most discussions of criminogenic factors and correctional rehabilitation/treatment. The concern here is not the one-off offenders who make a few bad decisions that lead to limited criminal involvement (the adolescent limited offenders). They will not require the attention and resources that I am discussing. However, many chronic, persistent, habitual offenders have neurocognitive and psychosocial impairments, including spatial and verbal impairments, impairments of memory and nonmemory cognitive function, intellectual impairments, executive dysfunction, and so on. Raine and colleagues (2005) conclude that longer-term habitual offenders (life-course persistent) have pronounced and profound neurocognitive and psychosocial impairments that distinguish them from others. Brain scans comparing antisocial individuals with controls reveal significant reductions in the frontal lobe of the brain (between a 9 and an 18 percent reduction), that part of the brain responsible for executive functioning, among other things. Comparisons of the brains of psychopaths with controls showed deformations in the amygdala and up to an 18 percent reduction in the volume of the amygdala, which is a part of the limbic system responsible for memory and emotional regulation. Other research implicates the amygdala in borderline personality disorder, psychopathy, binge drinking, aggression, and anxiety. A 2005 review of neuroimaging studies of aggressive, violent, and antisocial individuals by Bufkin and Luttrell (2005) shows consistent patterns of brain dysfunction and criminal activity, involving the prefrontal lobe, the temporal lobe, the relative balance of the activity between the prefrontal cortex and the subcortical structures, and the neural circuitry regulating emotion in aggressive and violent behavior. They conclude (2005: 187): "Research emanating from affective, behavioral, and clinical neuroscience paradigms is converging on the conclusion that there is a significant neurological basis of aggression and/or violent behavior over and above contributions from the psychosocial environment."

These are just examples of the neurological involvement in crime, not an exhaustive discussion of the neurocognitive, neurobiological, and genetic issues relevant to a more comprehensive and accurate understanding of crime, its origins, and correlates. What this means is that it is necessary to look more broadly in terms of understanding criminal risk, screening and assessment of criminogenic needs, and intervention, treatment, and rehabilitation. This accumulating knowledge about neurocognitive and neurobiological implications in criminal behavior provides a greatly enhanced opportunity to obtain much more and much better clinical and criminogenic information. Some of the neurocognitive and neurobiological knowledge will be relevant to assessing criminal risk. It will be relevant for assessing criminogenic needs as well as better understanding the etiology of various criminogenic conditions. Neurocognitive and neurobiological impairments and deficits will constitute some of the criminogenic circumstances that will be the targets of interventions (discussed shortly). This knowledge will inform treatment planning and intervention, in compliance with the responsivity principle of matching treatment to the abilities and circumstances of offenders. For example, Fishbein et al. (2006) and Van Goozen and Fairchild (2008) suggest that neurobiological impairments may negatively disrupt cognitive processing in therapeutic interventions. Cornet and colleagues (2013) suggest that such neurobiological impairments may be a significant source of variation in outcomes of CBT interventions with criminal offenders, in addition to fidelity issues, treatment setting, and other individual offender characteristics.

Neuroplasticity: The Brain Changes

The obvious question as knowledge continues to accumulate about the involvement of the brain and brain functioning in crime is: What can we do? Can this information move beyond just a broader understanding of crime to implementing this knowledge to reduce crime and recidivism? The answer is an unequivocal yes.

Plasticity is a fundamental and intrinsic property of the human nervous system. It refers to changes in neural pathways and synapses, rewiring of neuronal circuits, which result from training, changes in behavior, the environment, neural processes, and bodily injury. Plasticity is the process that permits the brain to modify its genomic restrictions by adapting to environmental stimuli and experiences. This process is one of reorganization and adaptation, whereby the circuits or connections among neurons are established, eliminated, or reinforced. These changes to the connections or pathways among neurons, which occur throughout the lifetime, are a product of stimulation from the environment in a variety of forms. As Pascal-Leone et al. (2005: 377, 396) describe this process:

> Behavior will lead to changes in brain circuitry, just as changes in brain circuitry will lead to behavioral modifications. . . . Plasticity is the mechanism for development and learning, as much as a cause of pathology and the cause

of clinical disorders. Our challenge is to modulate neural plasticity for optimal behavioral gain, which is possible, for example, through behavioral modification and through invasive and non-invasive cortical stimulation.

In effect, plasticity means that the brain can and does adapt and reorganize itself according to experience-dependent changes. Robertson and Jaap (1999) outlined a rehabilitation process for individuals with brain impairments, based on the observation that "recovery of neuropsychological functions is achieved largely by the reorganization of surviving neural circuits to achieve the given behavior in a different way" (1999: 544). In developing this rehabilitative process, they note: (1) the brain is capable of a large degree of self-repair through synaptic turnover (synaptic connections changing over time, synapses connecting, disconnecting, reconnecting); (2) synaptic turnover is to a certain extent experience-dependent and is a key mechanism for learning and recovery of function; (3) recovery processes following brain damage share some mechanisms with normal learning; and (4) experiences and inputs available to damaged circuits will shape synaptic interconnections and therefore assist recovery. In effect, reorganization, brain plasticity, neuroplasticity, or nervous system plasticity all refer to a process of regeneration and recovery that is similar to how normal learning occurs, and plasticity is a lifelong characteristic of the brain and the central nervous system.

More recently, Vaske, Galyean, and Cullen (2011) identified research that supports their contention that cognitive-behavioral therapy (CBT) is appropriate for rehabilitation of many criminal offenders. This is based on the processes of brain plasticity and the knowledge that cognitive-behavioral therapy involves areas of the brain that are implicated in criminal offending due to particular structural and functional deficits in those areas, deficits that lead to behavioral manifestations of poor problem-solving, coping, and social skills. Research shows that CBT leads to changes in brain functioning in areas of the brain that are associated with a variety of these skills. Vaske, Galyean, and Cullen (2011: 97) provided compelling testimony about the importance of CBT for correctional interventions:

The ability to show that interventions, such as CBT, activate if not reshape neuropsychological processes opens fresh vistas for demonstrating why treatments are capable of effective, meaningful offender change.

Accordingly, efforts to move toward a biosocial theory of offender rehabilitation may provide a powerful rationale for why treatment intervention must be a core goal of the correctional enterprise.

Neuropsychologists have extended the logic of recovery from brain injury to treatment of neurocognitive deficits in criminal justice or correctional populations. As discussed above, executive functioning is often compromised among the offender population as a result of a variety of causes. Those executive functioning deficits are often implicated in crime and recidivism (for example, deficits in planning and decision making, inhibition, cognitive flexibility, and understanding consequences). It is suggested that these deficits are not only related to offending, but also interfere with offenders' ability to benefit from psychosocial interventions (Ross and Hoaken 2010). These researchers note that there is little evidence to indicate that correctional rehabilitation programs effectively identify, target, and address executive functioning deficits among criminal offenders. They suggest that the effective practices for intervening with executive functioning deficits in those with acquired brain injury (ABI) can be used to develop protocols for treating correctional populations, citing the similarities in the ABI and correctional populations regarding executive functioning. The primary approach is twofold: cognitive retraining, which is designed to assist the brain's ability to recover functioning through reorganization and regeneration of neural circuitry, and teaching compensatory skills to replace and/or compensate for deficits (Ross and Hoaken 2010). The research on interventions with ABI and schizophrenia patients provide several evidence-based practices (Rohling et al. 2009) and indicate substantial applicability of nonforensic cognitive rehabilitation (such as plasticity-based computer programs and paper and pencil exercises). The research indicates three primary recommendations going forward: individualized functional assessment of executive functioning; individualized functional rehabilitation utilizing a broad-based, multimodal approach that addresses not only the manifested problem, but also the potential contributors; and opportunities for relevant application of skills in the real world. Ross and Hoaken (2010) concluded that implementing appropriate screening and assessment methods with problem-solving skills training and computerized or paper and pencil cognitive rehabilitation programming that focuses on identified deficits and has opportunities for feedback about progress, with application in real-world settings and contexts, should add significant value to the rehabilitation of offenders with executive functioning deficits.

The bottom line is this. Heritability may set an individual's path in the direction of antisocial behavior and that may or may not be reinforced by experiences, observations, and activities in the environment. Or, independent of any genetic implication, an individual's experiences may create neural pathways that facilitate antisocial tendencies. The brain can tend toward antisocial behavior and can be further trained toward antisocial behavior by interactions and experiences, an experience-dependent process. Trauma, lack of attachment, brain injury, or growing up in poverty and abuse may create antisocial behaviors. However, neuroscience shows us that the brain is malleable, ever changeable. Knowledge of how neural connections form has provided us with additional tools for behavioral change. By developing new neural pathways or reinforcing others, experience-dependent plasticity can redirect a brain from an antisocial trajectory to a prosocial lifestyle.

By way of example, what is now known about the impact of trauma and PTSD on brain structure and function clearly indicates that the justice system should embrace the tenants of trauma-informed care, which is being disseminated by the Substance Abuse and Mental Health Services Administration (SAMHSA). SAMHSA's protocol includes a concerted effort to screen and assess for trauma and PTSD, and incorporate such information into treatment plans. Trauma-informed care treatment services are "interventions designed to address the specific behavioral, interpsychic, and interpersonal consequences of exposure to sexual, physical and prolonged emotional abuse" (SAMHSA 2011)

While cognitive behavioral programming is a primary focus of justice evidence-based practices, the findings from neuroscience indicate that correctional CBT (when implemented according to the EBP standards) may not be enough to effectively change antisocial behavior. In many situations, medication may be indicated. In addition, neuroscience has shown that some actions are deeper in the brain than the prefrontal cortex. These automatic thoughts, feelings, and emotions should be considered in the bigger picture of correctional rehabilitation. Many CBT programs concentrate on thinking and reasoning and tend to ignore the role of emotions. A broader understanding of the role of emotions and how emotions and thoughts impact each other will enhance programming designed to mitigate antisocial behavior.

The point is not to replace CBT. Instead, these observations from neuroscience should be incorporated to enhance and improve CBT. Research indicates significant variation in the outcomes of CBT. Some of that is due to inadequate implementation and failure to adhere to other principles of effective interventions. Some of it is due to not considering and addressing neurodevelopmental and neurocognitive factors. Reasoning and Rehabilitation 2 (R&R2) was developed in Canada at the Cognitive Centre of Canada, University of Ottawa. R&R2 is a neuroscience- and neurocriminology-informed, revised CBT intervention program, which is designed to promote prosocial neurological development. R&R2 is based on research conducted over the past twenty years on motivating individuals, the relationship between antisocial behavior and cognition, the role of emotion in prosocial competence, developing empathy, prosocial modeling, crime desistence, cognitive neuroscience, and relapse prevention. There are several modules focusing on different subgroups. Evaluation results indicate substantial increases in program retention and completion as well as substantial recidivism reductions for a variety of subgroups (Cognitive Centre Canada, cognitivecentre.ca/content/news).

GETTING IT RIGHT

It is time for criminology to embrace the biosocial paradigm. More importantly, it is time for practitioners, professionals, decision makers, and policymakers to appreciate the added complexity of crime due to the evolving understanding of neurocognitive and neurodevelopmental factors and, in turn, what this evolving understanding tells us about what it takes to effectively reduce recidivism. We have been saying for several years now that we have the tools to reduce recidivism. That was premised on the evidence-based practices outlined at the beginning of this chapter. We are now getting the tools necessary to address the neurodevelopmental issues that are so clearly implicated in criminal behavior, as well as desistance from crime. What is left is to get it right.

The opportunity is here for the U.S. criminal justice system to get serious about rehabilitating criminal offenders. Clearly, not all offenders can be treated, and there are many whom we cannot treat or for whom we will not want to try. However, the remaining majority of offenders are those that current (and evolving) knowledge about EBP and neurodevelopmental interventions should be directed.

The evidence is clear regarding what risk factors, disadvantages, situations, circumstances, experiences, histories, deficits, and impairments should be screened and assessed. There are also sufficient knowledge and tools for effectively intervening in many cases. What is required is funding, expertise, and a culture conducive to effective rehabilitation. We need to clarify how we sort those who go to prison and those who we decide to rehabilitate (this is discussed in later chapters). Once we decide to rehabilitate, we need to get serious. Donald Andrews, who is one of the key figures in developing effective correctional rehabilitation principles and programming, says it precisely: program/intervention quality must be a matter of policy (Andrews 2006).

In 2006, the American Psychological Association developed a policy statement on evidence-based practices in psychology (APA 2006). The goal of evidence-based practices in psychology (EBPP) is "to promote effective psychological practice and enhance public health by applying empirically supported principles of psychological assessment, case formulation, therapeutic relationship, and intervention" (2006: 280). The following is extracted from the section of the policy statement regarding assessment, diagnostic judgment, systematic case formulation, and treatment planning (APA 2006: 276).

The clinically expert psychologist is able to formulate clear and theoretically coherent case conceptualizations, assess patient pathology as well as clinically relevant strengths, understand complex patient presentations, and make accurate diagnostic judgments. Expert clinicians revise their case conceptualizations as treatment proceeds and seek both confirming and disconfirming evidence. Clinical expertise also involves identifying and helping patients to acknowledge psychological processes that contribute to distress or dysfunction. Treatment planning involves setting goals and tasks of treatment that take into consideration the unique patient, the nature of the patient's problems and concerns, the likely prognosis and expected benefits of treatment, and available resources. The goals of therapy are developed in collaboration with the patient and consider the patient and his or her family's worldview and sociocultural context. The choice of treatment strategies requires knowledge of interventions and the research that supports their effectiveness as well as research relevant to matching interventions to patients.

There are many elements of the APA EBPP statement that are fundamental to successful intervention, behavioral change, and recidivism reduction. These include evidence-based assessment and diagnosis that reflects the individuality and complexity of cases; developing case treatment plans based on individual pathology, complexity, assets and characteristics; matching treatments to individual characteristics; and modifying the treatment protocol over time. These are basic principles that should be embedded in all aspects of behavioral change interventions in correctional settings.

Many other professional associations and organizations involved in behavioral health care have similar policy statements regarding professional conduct and evidence-based practices. These include the American Psychiatric Association, which has similar clinical guidelines that reflect evidence-based practices for psychiatric diagnosis, development of a treatment protocol, and ongoing clinical treatment, as well as professional social work, and drug and alcohol treatment. Why should practitioners involved in behavioral change in the criminal justice context be exempt from the practices and guidelines developed for professionals engaged in behavioral change in the free world? Why should efforts at behavioral change in criminal justice be limited in terms of expertise and standards of care? Clearly, they should not, but the current status of correctional rehabilitation indicates they fall short.

In addition to what the research indicates are EBPs, it is obvious that given what we currently know and what we are learning on an ongoing basis, there is a critical need to enhance clinical expertise in addressing the criminogenic needs of offenders. This need is at the beginning of the process in assessment, diagnosis, and development of a treatment plan, as well as in the treatment and aftercare phases. Given the scientific evidence implicating the impacts of poverty, trauma, abuse/neglect, among others on cognitive, emotional, neurodevelopmental, and behavioral functioning, and the numbers of offenders with multiple criminogenic needs (among other considerations), the clinical picture becomes quite complex.

That complexity requires substantial changes regarding clinical expertise in the process of assessment, diagnosis, treatment planning, and intervention. It is not just that probation officers, drug court judges, or prosecutors or trial court judges need to be aware of the complexities of offenders' situations. They need to recognize where their experience and expertise is insufficient and be able to consult with appropriate clinical experts. This requires not only the ability to know when a situation requires enhanced clinical expertise, but also requires having the resources and the available experts to bring on board. The same considerations apply to correctional treatment programs, whether institutional- or community-based. Treatment providers will need to have the expertise to deal with populations of individuals with complex situations. For example, treatment providers will need to be trained to recognize the impacts of trauma and be able to address those impacts in, for example, a substance abuse treatment protocol.

The point is a simple one to make. If we do not ramp up efforts to proactively and effectively address significant criminogenic needs of offenders with appropriate, evidence-based strategies and expertise, as well as going beyond the standard evidence-based practices in understanding, identifying, and treating offenders' neurocognitive and neurodevelopmental impairments, we will simply continue to see the revolving door spin. Moreover, we need to be able to identify the spectrum of needs, prioritize them, and develop treatment plans that consider the severity of needs, as well as the appropriate sequence of treatment (that is, in many instances it makes sense to treat substance abuse first because substance use often compromises other interventions). A simple point to make, yet challenging to implement. But if the United States can build the largest prison system in the world, implement substantial changes to sentencing laws nationwide, dramatically change the culture, beliefs, and attitudes about crime and punishment, and launch and fight a monumental War on Drugs, efforts that required massive resources, public support, cooperation, and collaboration of many different constituencies and interests, and significant statutory changes, certainly it can muster the will and the resources to follow what the evidence indicates and get it right. *There are many reasons why the stakes are quite high in this effort, not the least of which is the fact that with appropriate and adequate behavioral interventions, we have the ability to prevent millions of avoidable criminal victimizations, reduce crime, and save public revenue.*

CHAPTER 4

Sentencing Reform Reconsidered

"There is a better way. We need to move from anger-based sentencing that ignores cost and effectiveness to evidence-based sentencing that focuses on results— sentencing that assesses each offender's risk and then fits that offender with the cheapest and most effective rehabilitation that he or she needs."
—Hon. Ray Price, Missouri Chief Justice, in his State of the Judiciary speech, 2010

"Sentencing has been a ceremony of punishment for a very long time. We wear robes and conduct what is in large part a morality play—maintaining a secular equivalent of a state church. . . . If our job is to deliver an appropriate sermon, we need only work on our delivery and steer towards severity."
—Hon. Michael Marcus, Multnomah County District Court Judge, Portland, Oregon, 2003

THE WAVE OF SENTENCING REFORM in the United States that began around 1980 transformed the sentencing process in the federal system and all fifty states. Sentencing changed from a focus on offenses and individuals, from weighing aggravating and mitigating circumstances and sometimes criminogenic deficits, from tailoring sentences to particular goals that the court deemed appropriate under the circumstances, to a system in which mitigation is discouraged or prevented, in which the intent is to sentence the harm of the instant offense and the harm of prior bad deeds, and in which the focus is on the primary goals of deterrence and incapacitation. Sentencing reform had two things in mind: punishment and control.

By way of example, an August 10, 2013, opinion piece by Nicholas Kristof in the *New York Times* relayed the story of how Edward Young had been sentenced to fifteen years in federal prison (for which there is no parole) for ostensibly helping a neighbor. Young had been convicted of several burglaries in the past, was incarcerated and then released in 1996. He turned his life around, married, worked six days a week, and raised four children. The problem began when his neighbor's husband died and she asked Young to help her clear things out of her house for a garage sale (apparently her husband was a hoarder). Among the items were seven shotgun shells, which Young took home for safekeeping. For some reason, the local police suspected Young of burglaries again and searched his home. They found the shotgun shells Young had hidden to keep away from his children. The U.S. Attorney charged Young under a federal statute forbidding convicted felons from possession of guns or ammunition. That charge has a mandatory fifteen-year sentence. Because the U.S. Attorney chose to charge Young that way, the court had no choice in the sentence. When the U.S. Attorney was asked why he charged Young, he stated, "The case raised serious public safety concerns." Young had never possessed a weapon, the neighbor explained everything to the court, and the local authorities dropped their burglary suspicions that initiated the search. Young's wife proclaimed, "I can't believe my kids lose their daddy for the next 15 years. He never tried to get a firearm in the 16 years I was with him. It's crazy. He's getting a longer sentence than people who've killed or raped."

Kristof proceeds to use this example to represent what he says is wrong with the U.S. justice system—what he calls the irresponsibility of mass incarceration, and the problems with mandatory sentences. He concludes: "Some day, Americans will look back and wonder how we as a society could be much more willing to invest in prisons than in schools. They will be astonished that we sent a man to federal prison for 15 years for trying to help a widow."

Determinate sentencing, mandatory sentencing, and truth in sentencing are all antithetical to rehabilitation of individuals. As the dust has settled, and the scientific community has completed volumes and volumes of evaluations and assessments, it is difficult to believe that the positive impacts of these sentencing reforms are on a scale most would consider productive or effective. Crime is down, but mainly for reasons having little to do with crime control, sentencing reform, and the corrections explosion. Recidivism is still unacceptably high, having very much to do with crime control, sentencing reform, and the corrections explosion.

In 2014, and for the past several years, states have faced fiscal situations that have motivated their implementing reductions in criminal justice budgets. One impact of that search for cost savings has been on sentencing and release.

There are increasing examples of legislative changes to sentencing and release laws that, while largely piecemeal, when taken together reflect a modest retreat from some of the crime control initiatives put in place over the past thirty to forty years. These changes are in the right direction, if often for the wrong reasons (cost savings, rather than a more effective approach). I will briefly summarize where state statutes and legislative policy have been heading over the past ten years, and indicate that much more extensive statutory change is required to get the U.S. justice system to a place of significantly enhanced effectiveness and cost-effectiveness.

The Sentencing Project and the Vera Institute of Justice have compiled summaries of legislative changes at the state level regarding criminal codes, alternatives to incarceration, time served, and mandatory sentences, among other justice-related changes. The general trends that are reflected in legislative changes in some states over the period from 2001 to 2010 include the following: changes to criminal codes that in some cases reduced offense severity and sentence length; increases in alternatives to incarceration with a focus on drug treatment; and reduction in prison terms by changes to mandatory sentences and time served.

Recent examples are in order (King 2009; Porter 2010, 2011), and some are more notable and substantive than others. First, New York State scaled back the Rockefeller drug laws, perhaps the most punitive in the nation, by eliminating some mandatory minimums for first and second offenses. South Carolina, New Jersey, Colorado, Louisiana, Maine, Minnesota, Nevada, Arkansas, Hawaii, Massachusetts, and Rhode Island revised drug laws, generally by modifying/scaling back mandatory minimums and deprioritizing marijuana law enforcement. Other states reduced time served by altering laws governing release from prison. These states include Kentucky, Mississippi, Louisiana, Indiana, Kansas, New Hampshire, and Texas. Recently, the federal government, with the leadership of Attorney General Holder, has begun the process of implementing sentencing changes at the federal level under General Holder's Smart on Crime initiative.

However, some caveats are important to note. First, changes to sentencing and release have been limited to particular states. These changes have not been national in scale by any means. Second, while several states are revising some sentencing and release laws to help stabilize the states' prison populations, there has been a 22 percent increase in life without parole sentences between 2003 and 2008, due in large measure to an increased hesitancy to impose the death penalty. Third, many of the sentence reductions to the criminal code are limited to lower-level offenses. Finally, while some states are implementing modest sentencing and parole measures to reduce prison populations, several states are modifying/rolling back these provisions, failing to adequately fund collateral programs, and facing political pushback. For example, Washington, Delaware, and Kansas have reduced spending on prisoner reentry programming to help address short-term budget problems; Illinois, Wisconsin, and New Jersey rolled back early release programs that allowed well-behaved inmates early parole; Arkansas passed legislation reducing the punishment for selected nonviolent and drug offenders, earlier release for some inmates, and reduced sanctions for parole violators. These changes were not embraced by all. As one legislator said about the reduction in punishment for certain drug offenders, "We have a very, very low tolerance for drug offenses of any type"; and a sheriff asked, "Where is the deterrent?" (Arkansasnews.com, August 15, 2011)

Clearly, some limited change is underway. Prison population growth slowed in the late 2000s and has declined modestly in the past three years, due to some states shuttering prison units. However, the United States still has the world's largest prison population and the world's highest incarceration rate and projections indicate state prison populations will increase by an average of 3 percent over the next three years. Moreover, while there have been some modest changes to state sentencing and release statutes and policies in the past few years, the characterizations of state sentencing laws provided earlier are accurate. The sentencing reform that occurred in the United States during the 1980s and 1990s that served as a primary mechanism for accomplishing crime control is alive and well.

Partially because of the sustained crime decline beginning in the early 1990s, partially because of the fiscal need to reduce prison costs, and partially because other issues and concerns have taken priority, the rhetoric of tough on crime has died down and the language of justice policy today involves more and more phrases and terms like "smart policy," "smart practices," and "evidence-based practices." This focus on "smart" is probably in part a reflection of the volumes of scientific evidence that have accumulated in recent years regarding the effectiveness of alternatives to crime control. However, despite the availability of effective alternatives to the nearly singular policy of harsher and harsher punishment, the term "smart" is still primarily rhetorical, and the reform of sentencing and release is still uphill. There are several reasons for this challenging assessment. One is the widespread belief that the crime decline of the 1990s was a result of tough on crime policies. It is understandable that many policymakers and elected officials abide by the mantra "if it ain't broke, don't fix it." Another concerns the political realities of tough on crime, even in light of a sustained decline in crime and much discussion about criminal justice reform. Traditional political values still play a very significant role and the risk of being perceived or labeled as soft on crime is to be avoided. As I discussed earlier, fear has played a substantial role in fashioning criminal justice policy, and while official crime statistics indicate that we are "safer," other risks, such as threats of terrorist attacks, help keep the fear level elevated. The bombing at the Boston Marathon in April of 2013, the Sandy Hook Elementary School shooting, the Aurora Colorado movie theater killings, and many, many others, in combination with the obsessive coverage of such events on the cable news channels, keep fear and concern at heightened levels. There has been much "tough" rhetoric associated with terrorism. Perhaps public fear about threats to safety, whether associated with predatory crime or with terrorist attacks, keeps crime control in a preferable position in the political arena.

Some suggest that U.S. criminal justice policy is path dependent, or inertia driven, meaning that the policies in place are difficult to change due to their own momentum (Fernandez 2011; Sharp 1999). By way of example, Mark Mauer, the executive director of the Sentencing Project, points to the impact of *U.S. v. Booker* on federal sentencing outcomes. *Booker* rendered the federal sentencing guidelines "advisory," rather than mandatory, after a Sixth Amendment challenge pertaining to the relevant conduct provision of the guidelines. Relevant conduct allows sentencing for criminal conduct for which a defendant need not be indicted nor convicted. One might expect significant departures from the guidelines by judges in sentencing offenders, especially downward departures because many judges have and still do perceive the guideline sentences as too severe in many cases. Data from the United States Sentencing Commission (2013) indicate that nongovernmental sponsored downward departures (meaning downward departures initiated by the court) increased after *Booker*, but only modestly. Judicial downward departures increased in 2006 to 12 percent, in 2011 to 15 percent, and in 2013 to roughly 18 percent. Despite the opportunity to implement sentencing changes, judges tend to stay close to that with which they are familiar—an inertia of sorts.

There are also institutional barriers to reform. For example, in May of 2011, Texas closed a prison unit for the first time. The vast majority of the 112 units in the Texas prison system, as is the case in many states, are located in rural areas of the state, in or near small towns that depend heavily on the revenue that prisons bring to those communities. Rightly or wrongly, correctional units are perceived as economic engines in local communities, and therefore closing units can have significant economic, and perhaps even more importantly, political consequences. Recall the closing of U.S. domestic military bases in the 1990s and the contention in Congress created by the process. It is political, and there is reason to expect that the closing of prison units will involve similar concerns and issues.

SENTENCING REFORM PART II

Sentencing in the United States today consists of a fragmented array of fifty-two different sets of laws, procedures, and regulations. The states and the federal system are a mix of structured, determinate, indeterminate, presumptive, or mandatory guidelines, advisory or voluntary guidelines, mandatory statutes, habitual offender statutes, and mandatory minimum statutes, among others. The states and the federal system also differ in terms of parole release laws and policies. Some states and the federal government abolished parole and others heavily restricted the numbers released early. Truth in sentencing laws, designed to maximize time served, are less prevalent today, but are still in effect in many jurisdictions. In 2014, sentencing in the United States can range from broad minimum and maximum sentences and early release after serving a relatively small fraction of the sentence, to prescribed, fixed, or mandated sentences and no early release. In some jurisdictions, for example Texas, judges still have the lion's share of the discretion in determining the sentence; however, Texas law also includes a wide array of mandatory sentences for everything from murder to burglary and robbery, to repeat offender three strikes laws. In others, for example the federal system, judges have a considerably more limited role under the federal guidelines, and this appears to be the case even post-*Booker*.

The fragmentation of sentencing and release laws, policies, and regulations serves to underscore the clear lack of common understanding, let alone consensus, regarding what we as a nation are trying to accomplish with sentencing, and what principles or theories about sentencing guide policy. At the same time, the one theme that has and does characterize sentencing in the United States is enhanced severity of punishment.

The evolution of punitive sentencing is in part a consequence of the shift in the enhancement of sentencing responsibility to the legislative branches of state and federal government (a consequence of sentencing reform). As such, legislators and sentencing commissioners think about offenders, crime, and punishment in the abstract and ex ante; they are removed from considering individual culpability, the individual offender, and any particular circumstances that may play a role in criminality. In deliberating crime and punishment in the state house rather than the courtroom, it is perhaps easier for legislators to think of criminal offenders as categories (first-degree felons, aggravated sexual assaulters, burglars), rather than as individuals. This perhaps also facilitates the near-demonization of some types of offenders (sex offenders, drug offenders). Ultimately, as offenders are thought of as offenses (rather than as offenders), a culture of punishment is facilitated and perpetuated. Whether the sentence is determined by legislative fiat or by a judge, it is puzzling how those legislators and judges know how much punishment is enough to deter offenders.

At the end of the day, sentencing reform has produced changes to statutes, values, and culture. As I discussed earlier, these changes also impacted public opinion about crime and punishment.

The U.S. justice system consists of many moving parts and three primary sets of agencies and individuals. Law enforcement governs the front door, determining who gets in. Prosecutors review cases and determine whether or not they should be carried forward to indictment and prosecution. When the time comes, the cases are adjudicated typically by a negotiated plea (5 to 10 percent of cases are adjudicated by trial). After the sentencing hearing, the convicted offender is transferred to corrections. Each stage of processing a felony defendant involves judgment and discretion. Decisions are routinely made regarding what to investigate, whether and who to arrest, what to charge, whether to indict and with what evidence, how to plea a case out, what sentence to recommend, what sentence to impose, and ultimately how and under what conditions to carry out that sentence. All of these decision gates are important. If law enforcement does not decide to arrest, the individual will not end up in the system. The same goes for the decision to prosecute. But when we view the big picture regarding the longer-term viability of the justice system, the ability of the justice system to accomplish the primary goals of enhanced public safety and limited recidivism, the decision regarding the sentence looms large in terms of the business of criminal justice.

Does effective policing enhance public safety? Does arresting individuals promote the peace? In some respects, yes, arresting an individual can remove that crime from the street. At least momentarily. However, the extent to which this individual and the hundreds of thousands like him or her simply cycle in and out of the justice system, on and off of law enforcement's radar, begs the question: Are we really accomplishing longer-term public safety, or are we playing an expensive game of cat and mouse? The same goes for indictment, prosecution, and conviction. Criminal indictments, prosecutions, and convictions all aim to promote public safety. Once again, if the offenders we indict, prosecute, and convict today simply cycle back in the courts in six weeks, three months, or a year or two, are we really accomplishing public safety?

The sentencing decision is critical to the effectiveness of the justice system. Sentencing determines how we attempt to correct offenders, which in turn determines the overall success (recidivism reduction) of the justice system. In some cases these are guideline sentences in which judges play a minor role and prosecutors wield the greater influence. Sometimes these are unstructured, indeterminate sentences in which the court exercises wider discretion. Regardless of the statutes or the realities of sentencing in a particular jurisdiction, the question is the same: On balance, are the sentences that are handed down productive of public safety or are they just as likely or more likely to be oil for the revolving door of U.S. justice? Certainly, having a convicted offender under correctional control or supervision potentially contributes to the short-term enhancement of public safety (depending on how much of an incapacitation effect is assumed). However, if in the long term "corrected" offenders leave criminogenically no better or, as growing evidence indicates, worse than when they went in, public safety will be compromised. Add to that our current inability to effectively enhance the odds of successfully reintegrating offenders into the free world upon release from incarceration, and we appreciate again the persistently high recidivism rates that characterize the U.S. corrections systems.

Sentencing is sorting offenders into one of a limited number of bins: incarceration, diversion, probation; high risk, medium risk, low risk; highly antisocial bad person, run of the mill offender, one-off, potentially can be rehabilitated. How well offenders are sorted depends on a number of factors, including who does the sorting, how much and what kind of information is available at sentencing, the purposes of the sorting process, and finally how many options (bins) are available to the court for sentencing. Two things among many that are a consequence of sentencing reform are that the judge generally has less of a decision-making role, and the number of bins into which the court is permitted to sort offenders has been remarkably reduced.

Traditionally and currently, sorting has been assisted by presentence investigation (PSI) reports, which summarize for the court details such as the characteristics of the instant offense, prior criminal involvement, victim impact, social/family history, work and employment history, substance use, among others. The PSI also typically contains a sentencing recommendation. The relevance of this information largely depends on the statutes that govern sentencing. In some jurisdictions that still have indeterminate sentencing, offering wide sentencing ranges and the considerable influence of aggravating and mitigating circumstances, PSIs can be important. In determinate sentencing and guideline jurisdictions, the PSI's relevance is often in terms of providing the appropriate data and calculations for a structured or guideline sentence or evidence in support of a mandatory sentence.

Much of the focus of sentencing reform of the past forty years has been on controlling judicial discretion. What the story about Edward Young illustrates is the discretion exercised by prosecutors and the profound impact that discretion has on sentencing outcomes. Key decisions made by prosecutors are fundamentally linked to sentences—decisions such as what charges to bring against a defendant, what evidence and what charges to bring before a grand jury for indictment, what to negotiate in a plea agreement, and what sentence to attach to a plea agreement. The sentence is then essentially determined by the conviction offense, prior criminal involvement, and some, often limited, aggravating and mitigating circumstances.

So what do we know about how and what judges think about sentencing, punishment, deterrence, incapacitation, rehabilitation, crime, and public safety? The answer is that we know a limited amount. Most of the research on judicial opinions about sentencing has been conducted by the United States Sentencing Commission and consists of surveys of federal judges. The most recent Sentencing Commission survey of federal judges (United States Sentencing Commission 2010) indicates a widespread belief that mandatory minimum sentences are too harsh, that the guideline sentences for many drug and pornography offenses are too harsh, and that many factors determined in the guidelines to be "not ordinarily relevant" for sentencing are considered relevant by the clear majority of judges surveyed. Federal judges believe that the current federal guidelines have reduced unwarranted sentencing disparities and increased fairness. Unfortunately, judges were not asked whether they believed that the guideline sentences reduce recidivism or are achieving public safety.

The limited survey data on the opinions of state judges (for example, Alexander and Carroll 2006; Warren 2009b) do indicate a number of interesting concerns and priorities. The National Council on State Courts' (NCSC) 2006 multistate survey of chief justices' opinions regarding sentencing reform found three conclusions. Sentencing should: aim to promote public safety and reduce recidivism through the enhanced use of offender risk and needs assessments and evidence-based practices; reduce overreliance on incarceration as punishment for those offenders who do not pose a substantial danger to the community or have not committed the most serious offenses; and promote alternatives to incarceration such as community-based alternatives.

Warren (2009b: 277) reports that the NCSC survey results also indicate the following:

> The ineffectiveness of probation and current sentencing practices and resulting high rates of offender recidivism, the overuse of incarceration and the lack of effective sentencing alternatives were also among the most frequently cited subjects of complaint from state trial judges hearing felony cases.

Judges also expressed concern about the relative lack of judicial discretion in sentencing, the belief that prosecutors exercised too much discretion, and that prosecutors overcharge defendants too frequently. Additional survey research (Alexander and Carroll 2006; Elikann 1996) reveals judges' overwhelming objections to mandatory minimum sentences, mandatory sentences in general, and the loss of judicial discretion as a consequence of changes to sentencing statutes over the past few decades.

As a whole, judges appear to share some serious concerns about the state of sentencing in the United States. While judges offer opinions about such matters when asked to do so in a survey format, they do not routinely become involved in policy debates or policy recommendations. As Warren (2009b) indicates, the judicial role is not making law and policy, but interpreting and applying law and policy. While the perspective from the bench is to be highly valued, it is not often that knowledgeable judges are found who risk the foray into justice policy and speak loudly about their concerns.

There are several judges who have been particularly outspoken about crime, punishment, sentencing, recidivism, and public safety. Much of the sentiment is represented well by Hon. Roger Warren, President Emeritus, National Center for State Courts, and Hon. Michael Marcus, Circuit Court Judge, Multnomah County, Portland, Oregon. Marcus and Warren have not only written extensively on what is wrong with sentencing today, but they have also offered some suggestions for moving forward. Here are the cases they make.

Judge Marcus is quite critical and quite vocal about the failures of contemporary sentencing and corrections in the United States. Marcus's primary concern is the inability of current policy, law, and practices to reduce crime and recidivism. In his own words (Marcus 2004: 19):

It didn't take long for me to realize after taking the bench in 1990 that the first offender is a rare occurrence in our system. It became immediately obvious that most of those we sentence have been sentenced before, and that most would probably offend and be sentenced again—often having produced another victimization. The notion that we were actually managing criminal careers occurred to me early in my own career as a judge. That notion was soon followed by the suspicion and then the conviction that we could surely do a better job of diverting offenders from criminal careers if we made some substantial effort to do so—by employing data, evidence, and anything better than our various philosophies, assumptions, and untested beliefs about how people work . . . there is no question that recidivism rates are abysmal. There are many measures, but they surely represent the impact of sentencing that is not responsibly aimed at crime reduction.

Judge Marcus (2003) notes that that there is built-in inertia to perpetuate the sentencing patterns of the recent past. He views sentencing behaviors of judges as a consequence of the "archaic adherence to the myth of deterrence, the ritual of retribution and the façade of rehabilitation" (2003: 78). He indicates that the safe place for judges, who are elected officials in most jurisdictions, is to tend toward severity. Further, because judges are not assessed on their ability to reduce crime and recidivism, their sentencing practices have been primarily judged in terms of their harshness. The public presumably believes either that tough sentences lead to recidivism reduction, or tough sentences just feel morally right. The public does not necessarily need evidence regarding whether it enhances public safety in order to believe it does.

Judge Warren (2009a: 1) echoes the concerns of Judge Marcus, focusing on the recidivism rate as evidence of a failure of sentencing and corrections, including the failure of probation:

Recidivism rates among these felony defendants are at unprecedented levels. Almost 60 percent have been previously convicted and more than 40 percent of those on probation fail to complete probation successfully. The high recidivism rate among felony probation pushes up state crime rates and is one of the principal contributors to our extraordinarily high incarceration rates.

RECONSIDERING THE SENTENCING PROCESS

"Our persistence in ignoring research when exercising sentencing discretion exceeds even offenders' persistence in crime."
—Hon. Michael Marcus, Multnomah County District Court Judge, Portland, Oregon, 2003

The Role of the Court

Judges' experience in the day-to-day practice of sentencing has highlighted a number of significant concerns. That perspective from the trenches, when coupled with the consensus emerging from scientific research and evaluation, points to clear remedies. So what appears to be the evidence-based path forward for sentencing? I first focus on changes to the sentencing process in the courtroom, then turn to sentencing structures and statutes.

Based on the scientific literature on evidence-based sentencing and, in part, on recommendations made by judges Warren, Marcus, and their colleagues, the following appear to be productive strategic changes to the sentencing process:

1. Establish crime and recidivism reduction as an explicit goal of sentencing, and utilize evidence-based strategies for accomplishing that goal
2. Introduce and utilize problem-solving concepts in the sentencing process based on collaborative decision making
3. Utilization of accurate, comprehensive, valid, newest-generation risk and needs assessment instruments to gauge the assessed risk and identify criminogenic needs
4. Substantial revision of the presentence investigation report
5. Utilize technology to assist in data informed sentencing

ESTABLISH CRIME AND RECIDIVISM REDUCTION AS AN EXPLICIT GOAL OF SENTENCING

Judge Marcus does not mince words on this matter (2009: 751):

> [T]he single most daunting impediment to meaningful sentencing improvement: our wholesale surrender to undifferentiated just deserts as *mainstream* sentencing's only responsibility. That surrender is a demonstrably dysfunctional, cruel, and wasteful allocation of the bulk of corrections resources—jail and prison included. Our use of jail and prison under the resulting paradigm frequently does more harm than good. The harm consists of accelerated recidivism by offenders whose criminality would be better addressed with wiser sentencing choices, by victimizations that smarter sentencing would have avoided, the excessive punishments that serve neither society nor the offender, of an enormous waste of public resources, and a continuing erosion of public trust and confidence.

It does not take much effort to realize that public safety, crime, and recidivism reduction are not realistic goals of current sentencing, once the results of sentencing reform over the past thirty-plus years are understood. Whether we consider explicit sentencing guidelines like those found in the federal system, determinate sentencing, mandatory sentences and mandatory minimums, truth in sentencing laws, and reductions in parole release—the outcomes of sentencing reform—the message is clear. Sentencing in this era is harm based and a harm-based system is a just deserts-based system. Once we acknowledge that punishment does not deter, it becomes evident that one of the problems we face going forward is the sentencing process itself.

Accomplishing this goal of making crime reduction an explicit priority in sentencing requires statutory changes, changes to correctional resources, and attitudinal and cultural changes, among others. I will address the statutory and correctional resource issues later. How do we change beliefs, attitudes, and the culture of the courtroom and the sentencing process? It sounds trite, but in the case of judicial beliefs and attitudes, it is probably, in part, a matter of education—consistently and routinely providing scientific evidence to the judiciary regarding what works in reducing recidivism and crime. It will also require that judges forego the concern with political risk of not following the traditional tough on crime mantra.

Judges are probably in a unique position of serving as community opinion leaders, individuals who, due to their position, presumed impartiality, experience, and expertise in the law, can function to facilitate changes in public attitudes as well as the attitudes of those in the justice system who play a role in sentencing, in particular prosecutors. The data are not terribly conclusive on the extent to which prosecutorial discretion is largely responsible for the enhancement of punishment in jurisdictions in which judicial discretion has been significantly curbed. Regardless, whether statutory changes have shifted sentencing discretion from judges to prosecutors, it is reasonable to presume that as an advocate for the state in the litigation of a criminal matter, it is often the prosecutor's goal to aggravate a sentence. Whether through a sentence recommendation for enhanced punishment, through charging decisions or plea negotiation decisions, or through factual findings relevant to sentencing enhancements or mandatory sentences, there are a number of ways in which prosecutorial decisions impact sentencing. To the extent that prosecutors believe that deterrence works and that incapacitation is a very effective crime-fighting tool, it will be difficult to place crime reduction as a viable sentencing priority.

Part of the bigger picture here is the use of evidence-based practices in sentencing criminal defendants. Part of that model is to provide decision makers—prosecutors, defense bar, and judges—with the scientific evidence regarding what does and what does not reduce crime and recidivism. It also requires making key changes to sentencing statutes and criminal procedure. However, it is not as simple as providing information to prosecutors, judges, and defense lawyers, and changing law and procedure. Instead, all three, the government, the court, and the defense bar, need to be on board with the goals and objectives. This requires consensus and cooperation, as all the players remain focused on implementing sentences that have proven to be effective at reducing recidivism. Accomplishing this will require a cultural shift in how the key parties to this process think about and accomplish recidivism reduction. Because of their position, judges can be particularly effective in leading this initiative.

This sounds simple, but it often will not be. The statutory and procedural changes are difficult enough, because they will involve the cooperation of state legislatures. Moreover, while necessary, statutory changes are insufficient for producing real change in attitudes, beliefs, and, in turn, decision making. Discretion looms large in this process. Therefore, in combination with changes to laws and procedure, there needs to be a concerted local effort at persuasion combined with mechanisms that motivate compliance (incentives and disincentives). A prosecutor or judge cannot directly compel a defendant (and his or her defense counsel) to accept a sentence of diversion to treatment court or probation with treatment. However, it is possible to set up the choices such that the diversion or probation is the clearly more attractive option. Not everyone wants treatment, and not everyone is ready for treatment. This is where the careful assessment of individuals is essential to identify who are truly reasonable candidates for diversionary sentences. Once appropriate candidates are identified, the prosecutor, the judge, the defendant, and the defense counsel then negotiate the desired outcome using whatever lawful carrots and sticks are available.

This will not be uniform across jurisdictions. In some communities, prosecutors exercise the majority of the power and influence, while in others it is the judges, and in still others, the defense bar is in the driver's seat. This will all need to be locally negotiated. But the first step is to get all parties on the same page regarding what a particular plea agreement and sentencing process is aiming to accomplish.

So what this looks like is an implementation process that includes structural changes (changes to statutes and criminal procedure as necessary), as well as a concerted process of bringing all of the relevant parties on board. The end goal is to institute a cultural shift in how we think about crime and punishment. Again, judges can be very effective lobbyists and leaders in the process of implementing statutory change and the revision in how the key players think about crime and punishment. After all, judges have played prominent roles in a variety of reforms and initiatives in the U.S. justice system, either by using the bench as a bully pulpit of sorts, or by taking the lead in change (for example, Judge William Wilkins in developing the Federal Sentencing Guidelines; Judge James Gray in his book *Why Our Drug Laws Have Failed and What We Can Do About It: A Judicial Indictment of the War on Drugs*; Chief Judge Gerald Wetherington and Judge Herbert Klein in developing the Miami Dade County Drug Court, the first problem-solving, diversion court implemented in the United States; Supreme Court Justice Kennedy who declared that in too many cases, mandatory sentences do more harm than good; Judges Warren and Marcus cited previously; Judge Judith Kaye for advocating for problem-solving approaches and her role in the Midtown Manhattan Community Court; Judge Steven Alm for developing the HOPE Court; among many, many others).

What makes this particularly challenging is that judges are typically elected officials (federal judges are exceptions because they are presidential appointments). Historically, tough on crime has played well in many parts of the country and is still an important consideration today. One method for countering this trend is to change the rhetoric about crime and punishment from tough on crime to smart and cost-effective on crime. Public opinion research indicates that the public is more than willing to think beyond a punishment-only crime policy.

INTRODUCE AND UTILIZE PROBLEM-SOLVING CONCEPTS IN THE SENTENCING PROCESS BASED ON COLLABORATIVE DECISION MAKING

Criminal sentencing should be a matter of considering and balancing three potentially competing interests: public safety, cost, and potentially negative consequences to the individual being sentenced (so called iatrogenic effects, or negative side effects that are criminogenic). These considerations enhance the complexity of the sentencing process compared to what we have been doing with mandatory sentences, mandatory minimum sentences, guideline sentences, retributive sentences, and heavy-handed attempts at deterrence. That complexity potentially requires a good deal of information as well as participation by a variety of experts in the process. It requires thinking more broadly about sentencing and engaging problem solving and collaboration.

There is a research basis for changing the mode of operating a conventional court in a manner that can provide more informed, relevant, recidivism-reducing sentencing outcomes. A good deal of scientific research and evaluation has demonstrated that problem-solving strategies reduce recidivism and reduce overall criminal justice costs (Berman and Gulick 2003; Cissner and Rempel 2005; United States Government Accountability Office 2005; among many more). Moreover, a collaborative approach introduces a variety of expertise into the sentencing decision, including clinical input, screening and assessment personnel, recidivism experts, community treatment and rehabilitation resources, community supervision personnel, and others.

Problem solving, which is the hallmark of alternative or diversion courts, can be applied to conventional courts in ways that offer the court sentencing-relevant processes and information. The concepts are fairly straightforward, but may not always be easily adaptable to traditional courts. However, the research available on the idea of applying problem-solving concepts to traditional criminal courts indicates the general advantages and feasibility of doing so (Center for Court Innovation 2007; Farole et al. 2005; Farole 2009; Kaye 2004; Nolan 2003; Wolf 2007, 2011).

So what does problem solving look like? It can be conceptualized both as an overall approach or perspective of a court, as well as the application of specific concepts or principles. A useful definition of problem-solving judging is provided by Farole (2009: 60):

> Methods of judging that aim to address the underlying problems that bring litigants to court. Such methods could include the integration of treatment or other services with judicial case processing, ongoing judicial monitoring, and a collaborative, less adversarial court process.

The key elements of problem solving are: relevant, accurate information; community engagement; collaboration; individualized justice; and accountability. The following practices are characteristic of problem solving: a proactive, problem-solving, solution-seeking focus or orientation by the judge; a team-based, nonadversarial, collaborative approach; integration of social services in the court; ongoing judicial supervision; and direct interaction between the judge and the defendant. The point of problem solving is to have the information necessary to understand why a defendant is where he or she is today (What are the criminogenic circumstances?), what the evidence and experts indicate is the best way to reduce the likelihood of the defendant returning, and having the appropriate community or justice resources available to address those needs while ensuring compliance and accountability. It involves thinking creatively (within legal boundaries) to address/solve problems. It involves acceptance of responsibility for resolving a problem, not just passing it on or concluding "it is not in my job description."

One of the best recent examples of problem solving in practice is the development of a new court in Hawaii. It started with the problem of enforcing conditions of probation leading to high rates of noncompliance. In 2004, Judge Steven Alm of the First Circuit in Hawaii started an experiment—the Hawaii Opportunity Probation with Enforcement (HOPE). The strategy is creative yet simple and is grounded in evidence regarding punishment and deterrence, which is that swift and certain (but not severe) punishment can deter. The logic behind HOPE is to be clear from the very beginning (referred to as a warning hearing) where expectations are clearly set regarding what will happen when a probationer violates conditions (the judge informs all participants that the first violation will immediately result in X days in jail, the second violation will result in Y days in jail, and so on). When a violation occurs, the probationer is quickly brought into the HOPE court. The probationer is informed about what is going to happen, and is immediately taken to jail. There are provisions for serving the jail sentence on weekends if the individual is employed. The evaluation evidence indicated dramatic increases in compliance and substantial reductions in revocations. A simple yet creative approach to solving a problem.

Focus group research by Farole and colleagues (2005) and the national survey of judges (Farole 2009) indicate general support for the application of problem solving to conventional courts. Approximately 75 percent of the judges surveyed report that they approve of the application of problem-solving principles in their current court assignments. Nearly 70 percent indicate that they practice some problem-solving principles in their court.

According to judges who participated in the research, the proactive, problem-solving judge is, in practice, a judge who asks questions, seeks additional information, and explores a greater range of solutions for cases. It is as simple as: Here is a case that presents a problem in terms of public safety/recidivism. What is the best way to problem solve? What is the best way to bring this to a positive resolution? Direct interaction with the defendant was determined by judges to be an essential component of motivating an individual to comply with orders. One of the easiest principles to apply in conventional courts, according to judges, is ongoing judicial supervision of individuals, especially probationers, in order to monitor progress, assess compliance, and enhance accountability. Traditional monitoring of probationers amounts to a revocation hearing when the probation office files a motion to revoke, well after there has been failure to comply with conditions or a new offense has occurred. At that point, it is generally too late for judicial intervention; the only real choice, considering how conventional courts operate, is the decision to revoke or not. While judicial monitoring is likely desirable, the reality of heavy caseloads presents a significant challenge. Judges recommended prioritizing those cases that require such monitoring. While the focus group research did not address this point, it might be productive to think of a HOPE type of sanction court that runs parallel to a problem-solving court, designed as a means or mechanism for enforcing orders/conditions and holding individuals accountable.

The integration of social services in the courtroom is seen as very valuable by most of the judges in the survey, especially for defendants with commonly identified criminogenic needs such as drug addiction, mental illness, and educational and employment deficits.

Both the focus group discussions and the subsequent judicial survey results indicate some potential pushback or obstacles to implementation of problem solving in conventional courts. The most common obstacle is in the form of limited resources, articulated in terms of lack of sufficient support staff and appropriate services, and the ever-present heavy caseloads. Additionally, the collaborative, team-based, decision-making model is relatively radical for some judges who value their independence, expertise, and experience in making difficult decisions. Getting past that, however, opens the door to smarter sentencing, sentencing based on enhanced information (through the use of actuarial risk and needs assessments), and an array of expertise (clinicians, social workers, case managers, mental health experts, and others) who can participate in the decision-making process as needed and provide assertive case management (a major barrier to the effective use of integrated social services is the lack of case management staff in the courts). Other prominent considerations include the observation that problem solving compromises the neutrality of the court, that it would require additional knowledge and skills, and the belief that it is not appropriate for all cases.

While making the case of applying problem-solving principles in conventional criminal courts is not entirely uphill, there are realities that must be confronted in the process. It is unclear whether some of the pushback from judges is based on a lack of information or insufficient justification for doing business is a new manner. One important step is to provide to judges the scientific basis, the evidence, that problem solving can be a more effective way of addressing public safety and recidivism.

Clearly, it is important that judges have the necessary tools for effectively practicing problem-solving principles, tools that include the sentencing options that are required for the variety of offenders and criminogenic needs that judges will encounter. Some of this is statutory, requiring changes to sentencing laws, and much of it is local, requiring the availability of diversion resources such as mental health treatment, substance abuse interventions, employment training, education programs, among others.

This model is one that involves dramatic change in a variety of local resources as well as statutory changes to sentencing. Judges can be quite effective lobbyists, especially when presenting a united front. Even more compelling is the collaboration of District Attorneys and the defense bar. The Affordable Care Act will likely assist with access to behavioral health treatment and as demand increases, it is reasonable to assume that capacity will expand. That will help provide additional community-based resources.

UTILIZATION OF ACCURATE, COMPREHENSIVE, NEWEST-GENERATION RISK AND NEEDS ASSESSMENT INSTRUMENTS TO GAUGE THE ASSESSED RISK AND IDENTIFY CRIMINOGENIC NEEDS; SUBSTANTIAL REVISION OF THE PRESENTENCE INVESTIGATION REPORT; UTILIZE TECHNOLOGY TO ASSIST IN DATA INFORMED SENTENCING

I was particularly struck by a comment a federal judge recently made to me regarding sentencing. He indicated that from his perspective on the bench, sentencing was particularly difficult because he did not feel that he had sufficient, reliable, relevant information to make good sentencing decisions. He said something to the effect that "my job is to sort people but I don't feel like I have the information I need to make good decisions."

How sentencers go about preserving and enhancing public safety involves the consideration of a number of factors that may include: information provided in presentence investigation reports (PSIs); evidence litigated at a sentencing hearing, such as aggravating and mitigating factors and character references; a variety of goals of sentencing (deterrence, incapacitation, rehabilitation, retribution, risk management); statutes that affect how much of a role a judge has in the process; and guesswork about how well a sentence will produce the desired outcome. With regard to this last point, the court can impose conditions of probation and deferred adjudication, and can monitor progress while an offender is on community supervision. However, a sentence of incarceration is beyond the court's purview, effectively removing the individual from the jurisdiction and monitoring of the court. When a judge imposes a sentence of incarceration with certain expectations about, for example, participation in programs and services, such as mental health treatment or substance abuse treatment, education classes, length of sentence served, and so on, whether any of these expectations are met is up to the corrections department. The prison officials determine the conditions of incarceration, and it is up to (in most states) the parole authority to determine how long the individual will serve.

Sentencing has been and remains part science and part art. The research indicates that broadly considered, judges focus on three sets of concerns when sentencing: the blameworthiness of the offender; the practical implications of sentencing; and public safety (Silver and Chow-Martin 2002; Steffensmeier and Demuth 2000; Steffensmeier, Ulmer, and Kramer 1998). Blameworthiness reflects culpability and the proportionality of the sanction (that is, does the punishment fit the culpability of the offender and the crime?). The implications of the sentence involve considerations of collateral consequences (ties to family, children), as well as factors such as whether the offender can do the time imposed. Public safety involves considerations of future dangerousness and criminality. Steffensmeier and Demuth (2000: 709) report:

> Judges' assessments of offenders' future behavior (dangerousness, recidivism) are based on attributions predicated on the nature of the offense (e.g.,

violent, property, drug), case information, the offender's criminal history, and also perhaps, on characteristics of the offender such as education, employment, or community ties.

Ultimately, the sentencing decision probably involves, at a minimum, consideration of harm and risk. Harm is relatively straightforward: severity of the instant offense and prior criminal involvement. However, the research also shows that judges make little use of scientific risk assessment instruments to measure or estimate risk (Silver and Miller 2002). Instead, they appear to rely on "perceptual shorthand" or intuition (Steffensmeier, Ulmer, and Kramer 1998; Tonry 1987).

One of the key questions at this point is the extent to which science can improve determinations or predictions of risk compared to what is currently in place in many jurisdictions—"perceptual shorthand" and intuition. If this question had been posed twenty years ago, the answer probably would have been "not sure." Risk prediction instruments have historically produced high rates of false positive predictions (meaning the prediction of recidivism when in fact it does not occur), often as high as 50 percent. However, recent innovations in risk prediction have mitigated much of the concern about prediction errors. This is the case for primarily two reasons. First, risk assessment predictions are most reliable and appropriate when they are used to classify individuals into categories of risk, rather than being used to attach a specific probability of recidivism to a particular individual (Silver and Miller 2002; Silver, Smith, and Banks 2000). Second, a new approach that relies on multiple models rather than a single model of prediction enhances accuracy. Silver and Chow-Martin (2002) report that the use of multiple models produces significantly more accurate predictions than single-model approaches, and in turn, significantly more accurate predictions than judicial intuition.

In 2014, scientific risk prediction provides relatively easy to use and more accurate instruments for assessing risk and criminogenic needs (Berk et al. 2009; Hyatt, Bergstrom, and Chanenson 2011; Silver and Chow-Martin 2002). Several states have either explicitly incorporated new generation risk assessment protocols into the sentencing process (for example, Virginia has used actuarial risk assessments since 2004 for placing the lower-risk 25 percent of prison-bound offenders in alternative, nonincarceration sanctions) or are beginning the process (Pennsylvania and Missouri).

The experience in Virginia highlights the substantial advantages of having actuarial risk assessments. Research indicates that standardized risk assessment instruments accurately discriminate among low-risk offenders sentenced to diversion and higher-risk offenders sentenced to incarceration or more intensive supervision. The evidence indicates that the low-risk offenders did in fact recidivate at significantly lower rates than the higher-risk offenders (Kleiman, Ostrom, and Cheesman 2007). Moreover, the research indicates that judges in Virginia appear to be properly using the risk assessment information in their sentencing decisions.

Widespread use of scientifically based actuarial risk and dynamic needs assessments could represent a sea change in sentencing and corrections, if the information provided is properly used. The ability to reliably differentiate low-risk from high-risk offenders, to identify the criminogenic circumstances that brought offenders into the courtroom, and the ability to reduce risk by addressing criminogenic circumstances allow the court to engage in what Judge Marcus calls "smarter sentencing." It appears to be a matter of developing and implementing the right tools and assuring that they are properly used. There are several standardized, validated risk and needs screeners and assessment instruments currently available. The LSI-R (Level of Supervision Inventory—Revised) and ASI (Addiction Severity Index) are but two examples of widely used instruments.

In the course of developing the right tools, it seems that we need to reconsider the traditional presentence investigation report (PSI). PSIs have been in use for decades in state and federal courts. The typical PSI has a fairly standard format: characteristics of the instant offense, prior criminal involvement, victim impact, social and family history, employment and education, substance abuse, mental health, among other items. The PSI is usually prepared by a local probation office, and routinely includes a sentencing recommendation. Judge Marcus (2003: 78), relying on his experience, characterizes the typical presentence investigation report:

> Addressing sentencing, writers [of PSIs] dutifully report the demographic, medical, and criminal background of the offender; the circumstances and perspective of any victims; and any applicable legal principles such as guidelines. Then they craft a recommended sentence based expressly on aggravation, mitigation or impliedly on just deserts, with no greater connection to what is likely to reduce criminal behavior than a conclusion that the sentence

recommended is "appropriate." . . . It is most likely our fault as judges for creating the expectation that our drummer is just deserts, but we almost never get analysis based on what is most likely to work and why.

It seems useful to reconsider the role and format of the presentence investigation report, as well as who is involved in its preparation. One of the critical components of problem-solving sentencing is the collaborative team approach. The team should consist of a variety of experts, including clinicians, social workers, recidivism experts, and case managers. The preparation of the PSI should be the responsibility of those individuals who are involved in the assessment of the offender, who can recommend to the court, based on risk and needs and other input, what may be an appropriate sentence/sanction/referral designed to reduce the likelihood of recidivism for that particular offender. Probation officers are not clinicians and usually do not know what the research indicates regarding reducing recidivism, thus they are probably not the most appropriate to be interpreting the information and making sentencing recommendations.

Too often in the past and too often today, criminal justice practice involves the application of the "one size fits all" approach and the nominal, "moving through the motions" sentencing and corrections policy. Marcus (2004: 17) describes it very fittingly:

> We send thieves to theft talk, drunk drivers to alcohol treatment, bullies to anger counseling, addicts to drug treatment, and sex offenders to sex offender treatment. But we do this as a matter of symmetry rather than of science: we do not select offenders based on their amenability to treatment, but on the crime they have committed. We do not select providers on their impact on criminal behavior, but on their ability to provide timely paperwork. We may ask providers if offenders complete "the program" but we do not ask if they reoffend after treatment. Again, the issue is *responsible* pursuit of crime reduction—not nominal pursuit.

What this looks like is a process whereby the best information possible is available to the court regarding characteristics of the individual being sentenced, including risk and needs, and scientific evidence regarding what works in reducing recidivism. The latter point is not just some generic statement about, for example, drug courts working, rather it is what the odds are of this particular sanction reducing the probability of recidivism for this particular offender. It is a matter of putting the right information in the hands of the right experts, in order to make the best decisions under the circumstances regarding what is more appropriate for this particular individual given a variety of limitations, constraints, and uncertainties. Importantly, it requires a real sense of responsibility for resolving the individual's criminality, not what seems to be the current practice of just passing offenders from one agency to another.

Objections to the use of standardized, reliable, and valid risk and needs assessments may be countered by the observation that absent such data, what we are left with are the idiosyncratic, subjective, intuitive methods that research clearly shows perform poorly, compared to risk and needs assessments available today (Andrews, Bonta, and Wormith 2006; Bonta 2007). Not to mention the potential for sentencing disparity when there is little guidance in sentencing decision making. That was after all the prime motivation for the sentencing reform of the past forty years.

There are existing models of the use of these techniques that can be implemented and adapted as necessary. Moreover, the National Center for State Courts (Casey, Warren, and Elek 2011) assembled a national working group to develop guidance for judges for using risk and needs assessment information at sentencing.

Technology and statistical probability are playing an increasing role in sentencing. For example, Multnomah County, Portland, Oregon has developed statistical tools that provide everyone involved in sentencing data about how well particular sanctions work with which offenders (Marcus 2004). Missouri has developed a computer algorithm designed to provide the court with sentencing alternatives on a case-by-case basis, as well as information on the costs of various sentencing alternatives and the recidivism experiences of similar offenders. As Michael Wolff, Dean of the St. Louis University School of Law and Chair of the Missouri Sentencing Advisory Committee (the organization responsible for developing the algorithm), described the purpose: "It's about learning to use our prison resources for those we're afraid of, not for those we're mad at" (quoted in Kates, 2013).

The National Center for State Courts 2006 survey of judges, cited earlier, clearly indicates a willingness on the part of judges to pursue the goals of crime reduction and recidivism reduction through the use of evidence-based practices, offender risk and needs assessments, reduction of overreliance on incarceration, and increasing use of appropriate, effective alternatives to incarceration. Moreover, the same survey also queries the public and the results indicate that the public's priorities for sentencing reform are quite consistent with those of judges. If there are concerns about the political ramifications of implementing the ideas I have discussed here, it appears that those concerns are likely inflated, and may be mitigated by focusing on the effectiveness and particularly the cost-effectiveness of these strategies.

The Role of the Prosecutor

Sentencing reform brought many significant changes to U.S. sentencing. Among those is the assertion that as the discretion of judges has been limited (one of the primary goals of sentencing reform), discretion simply moved upstream in the process to the prosecutor's office. Some argue that the impact that prosecutorial decision making has on sentencing has increased substantially over time as a result of changes to sentencing laws (Cohen and Tonry 1983; Phelan and Schrunk 2008; Tonry 1996; Ulmer 2005) and that enhanced discretion is extraordinarily consequential in determining case outcomes. The discretion displacement argument reasons that the day-to-day decisions that prosecutors make more directly influence sentencing outcomes because judges have less discretion to set sentences.

One of the top two roles identified by prosecutors is as sanction setter (Phelan and Schrunk 2008). This requires prosecutors' consideration of sanctions at the earliest stages of case processing. Decisions such as what to charge, what evidence to use, what to indict, what to plea negotiate, what to recommend at sentencing, and referral to preindictment, pretrial, and postadjudication diversion are decisions that prosecutors make that either directly and substantially or indirectly and subtly impact sentencing outcomes.

What does the research indicate about the shift in discretion as a result of sentencing reform? First of all, most experts lament that there is very limited research on the topic (Engen, 2008; Miethe 1987; Reitz 2011; Shermer and Johnson 2009; Wooldredge and Griffin 2005). The research that has been conducted has produced inconclusive results. Some (for example, Forst and Bushway 2010; Piehl and Bushway 2007; Ulmer, Kurlychek, and

Kramer 2007) indicate at least partial empirical support for enhanced prosecutorial discretion, often in the form of circumvention around mandatory sentences, mandatory minimums, and guideline sentences. On the other hand, some research indicates little support for the discretion displacement hypothesis, or lack of support for it regarding limited aspects of sentencing.

While discretion displacement may be reasonable to expect, the evidence is inconclusive at the moment. From a policy perspective, we proceed with the observation that prosecutors do in fact exercise substantial discretion, and much of that discretion influences sentencing outcomes. While prosecutors cannot per se impose criminal sentences, their decisions and recommendations clearly influence the sentence. In addition, there is likely substantial variation across jurisdictions and even within jurisdictions in the extent to which prosecutorial discretion impacts sentencing. Nevertheless, it is important that we investigate the roles and responsibilities of prosecutors and in turn develop strategies for moving forward in the appropriate direction.

Given that prosecutors exercise a substantial amount of influence on sentence outcomes, it makes sense to ask how prosecutors view their roles and responsibilities, especially with regard to their direct and indirect impacts on sentencing and sentencing outcomes.

I have spent a fair amount of time consulting with prosecutors in various capacities. I have also served as an expert witness in criminal sentencing hearings. My takeaway from these experiences is that first and foremost, the prosecutors I have observed take a hard line regarding punishment as the primary tool of the justice system.

A recent case for which I served as a defense expert in the sentencing phase was an intoxication assault case. The defendant had a prior drug conviction, had an acknowledged problem with alcohol, hit two pedestrians while intoxicated, and then fled in his car. I was asked to testify to the jury about the likely outcome of incarcerating the defendant (he had pled to the charges). I proceeded to testify that the defendant likely needs substance abuse treatment, which he would probably not receive while in prison, that the parole system is not currently designed to provide rehabilitative services to enhance successful reentry, and that his chances of finding legitimate employment when released are limited. The prosecutor's cross-examination was designed to discredit that testimony and maximize the sentence that the court would impose. While this example is just that, one example, it is likely that the tough on crime persona is well embedded in the prosecutor role and clearly entrenched in the culture of the prosecutors' office.

Prosecutors are advocates for the government in an adversarial, litigious setting. Because punishment has been and largely continues to be the primary focus of sanctioning, one concern expressed by observers of sentencing reform is that in this role, prosecutors' interests and values are in the direction of maximizing punishment (Irwin and Austin 1994; Zimring and Hawkins 1994), focusing on incarceration as the appropriate punishment in most felony cases. Unfortunately, there has been little additional survey research conducted on prosecutors' beliefs and attitudes regarding crime, crime control, and punishment. We know more about how Canadian, British, and Hungarian prosecutors view crime control than we do about U.S. prosecutors. What we do know from surveys conducted by the American Prosecutors' Research Institute (APRI) is that prosecutors' self-described priority is prosecuting crime and punishing criminals (Nugent, Fanflik, and Brominksi 2004). The National District Attorneys Association's National Prosecution Standards (third edition) indicate that the primary responsibility of the prosecutor is largely to assure that the guilty are held accountable. Very little is known about how prosecutors make decisions regarding preferred sentencing outcomes. What we do know indicates that prosecutors' sentencing preferences are primarily driven by the availability of sentencing alternatives in a jurisdiction (Rainville 2001). Prosecutors in areas with a greater amount and variety of sentencing alternatives tend to prefer less restrictive sentences. A secondary effect was the personal belief of the prosecutor in the effectiveness of punishment versus the effectiveness of rehabilitation. Those who believe in punishment favor more punishment-focused sentences and those who believe rehabilitation is or can be effective favor less restrictive sanctions.

THE BIG PICTURE FOR PROSECUTORS

The success of any reforms to adjudication and sentencing involves the adoption of the big picture goals of crime and recidivism reduction. This is just as relevant to prosecutors as judges. For example, many negotiated pleas have sentences already determined by the prosecutor, thus enhancing the discretion and influence of prosecutorial decisions compared to judges. Moreover, recent evidence indicates that prosecutors have achieved even more discretion and influence over sentencing as a consequence of the implementation of harsher penalties, including mandatory sentences, and mandatory minimum sentences that have enhanced prosecutors' plea negotiation leverage, increasing the plea percentage a bit north of 96 percent. A September 25, 2011, *New York Times* article quotes a former federal prosecutor and now a law school professor: "We now have an incredible concentration of power in the hands of prosecutors." Or a former federal judge who is now a professor of law: "Judges have lost discretion, and that discretion has accumulated in the hands of prosecutors, who now have the ultimate ability to shape the outcome. . . . With mandatory minimums and other sentencing enhancements out there, prosecutors can often dictate the sentence that will be imposed."

The goals of sentencing and the scientifically based effectiveness of various sentencing options need to be clearly communicated. If a prosecutor believes that a particular case deserves or requires harsh punishment, that is entirely legitimate. Let's just be honest about what we are trying to achieve. Retribution without any particular utilitarian goal can be an appropriate consequence for a crime, as can accountability or incapacitation. But these outcomes have costs and limited benefits. It is that balance between cost and effectiveness that should drive decision making. Does a particular sentence outcome promote the big picture goals of crime and recidivism reduction? Is there anything in the sentence that can reasonably (that is, scientifically) be expected to change behavior? This is perhaps the new version of truth in sentencing.

Where does this investigation of prosecutors and the prosecutorial role leave us? Once again, we return to evidence-based practices with a focus on assessment, problem solving, collaboration, and community/problem-solving prosecution as a reasonable way to move prosecutorial decision making in the appropriate direction. What that means is that the District Attorney (typically, an elected official) and the line prosecutors need to understand what is effective for reducing recidivism and what is not. That should not be based on opinion, but scientific evidence. While there will be competing pressures on decision making, originating from a variety of sources—the public, the media, the victim, political issues—prosecutors need to identify on a case-by-case basis what the intended goal is (presumably, the typical goal will be reducing the likelihood of recidivism) and how best to accomplish it. So while some cases will involve retributive outcomes, many others (presumably) will be identified for diversion and rehabilitation, and others still for incapacitation. What is missing from these goals is deterrence, if by "deterrence" we mean "punishment severity." There is still the option of swift and certain sanctioning, but that would typically be in the context of a diversion sentence to probation or other types of diversion/community release programs such a problem-solving courts.

What follows is a series of scientifically supported recommendations that appear to be appropriate strategies for adoption by prosecutors. The United States Department of Justice, National Institute of Corrections and the Crime and Justice Institute (Fahey 2008) have developed a set of evidence-based practices for prosecutors. These appear to be thoughtful and informative, therefore they are incorporated into the following recommendations.

SHIFT FROM CASE PROCESSING TO PROBLEM SOLVING

The primary, traditional role of the U.S. prosecutor is that of case processor, a role that characterizes the vast majority of prosecutors' offices and prosecutors themselves. The focus is on the efficiency and effectiveness of processing large numbers of felony and misdemeanor arrests brought to the prosecutors by law enforcement. Extraordinarily large caseloads are typical in large urban District Attorneys' offices.

The case processor role is largely a passive one, involving reacting to cases provided by local police. Once a case arrives in the prosecutor's office, screening occurs to determine the merits of the evidence. Weaker cases are screened out or set aside for further investigation. Cases carried forward to indictment are then on track for efficient conviction. The vast majority of felony and misdemeanor indictments (95 percent and greater) are plea negotiated to conviction and approximately 75 percent of cases that go to a bench or jury trial end up in conviction. From the case-processing perspective, in which the primary metric for success is conviction, prosecution is accomplishing its goal. Conviction rates are quite high, but that should not be surprising because prosecutors screen the cases for prosecution.

Some forms of criminal prosecution are undergoing a bit of transition toward what is referred to as community prosecution or problem-solving prosecution. Community prosecution is characterized by three primary elements, compared to traditional criminal prosecution (Nugent-Borakove 2007; Nugent, Fanflik, and Brominski 2004; Nugent 2004). Community prosecution focuses on partnerships with a variety of government agencies and NGO community-based groups, the use of varied methods including problem solving to address crime and public safety, and community involvement in the problem-solving process.

The Bureau of Justice Statistics (BJS) and the American Prosecutors Research Institute have been researching and tracking how prosecutors view their roles in terms of traditional prosecution and punishment on the one hand, and community or problem-solving prosecution on the other. While there are many similarities between community prosecutors and traditional prosecutors, there are also key differences in the methods and strategies employed to achieve the desired goals. The key differences are that community prosecutors are more proactive, and rely on a broader array of problem-solving strategies. However, much of the focus of community prosecution is on quality of life crimes, low-level misdemeanors on a segment of the offender population characterized by chronic homelessness, mental illness, drug/alcohol addiction, unemployment, and poverty. One objective is to more systematically adapt the principles of community prosecution for more serious misdemeanor and felony cases.

The BJS survey series of Prosecutors in State Courts began inquiring about community prosecution practices in local prosecutors' offices in 2001. There are only two waves of the survey that report data on problem-solving prosecution practices, 2001 and 2005. The results indicate an increase over that period in self-reported use of community prosecution principles. However, the surveys provide no real indication of how much community prosecution effort is expended or how extensively the principles are practiced. One conclusion is that community or problem-solving prosecution is gaining traction. However, not much is known about how it is understood, developed, implemented, and utilized within or across jurisdictions, or about how it has or will impact prosecutors' perceptions of their roles and responsibilities, especially with regard to crime control policies and the severity of punishment.

Community prosecution is a step in a good direction. But like diversion courts and other justice initiatives, it has a relatively small presence in a very large system. What evidence-based practices call for is a substantial expansion of problem-solving principles into prosecution in general. As Fahey (2008) notes:

> There is a growing national movement to reform our current correctional practice, to reduce recidivism and protect public safety through the use of

evidence-based practices. Many of the EBP principles are inherently relevant to the work of a prosecutor. Diversion determinations, charging decisions, plea negotiations, sentencing arguments, and revocation requests are critical junctures in the processing of a criminal case, require discretionary decision-making.

If we begin with the premise that decisions made by prosecutors have, as the primary goal, the reduction of recidivism, then the scientific evidence (see Fahey 2008) clearly indicates the following. First, that the primary utilitarian function of custodial sentences (prison and jail) is incapacitation. We should limit the use of custodial sentences to serious violent offenders, habitual offenders, and others for whom it is determined that diversion/rehabilitation will be ineffective, and the use of such custodial sentences for offenders whose offending, culpability, and moral blameworthiness are of such a nature that a retributive custodial sentence is warranted. We should also obtain as much accurate risk and criminogenic needs data as possible through the proper use of actuarial risk and dynamic needs assessment instruments, and evaluate criminal cases in a collaborative manner with a variety of perspectives. Prosecutors are lawyers, not clinicians.

The end game in reengineering criminal prosecution is a structural and cultural shift away from the traditional approach of case processing, conviction, and maximizing the punishment. A focus on cases puts us in the position of simply devising ways to quickly move them through the pipeline. The alternative proposed here is to think in terms of problems and situations rather than cases, understanding the criminogenic circumstances of individual offenders, and facilitating outcomes that best promote (according to the evidence) recidivism reduction. Thinking in these terms potentially causes prosecutors to think differently about roles and responsibilities, and eventually heads us in the direction of a shift in culture.

A CULTURAL SHIFT IN THE PROSECUTOR'S OFFICE

The traditional role of the prosecutor is to represent the state's interests in the adjudication and sentencing of criminal offenders. Much of the focus of prosecutorial success is on conviction and punishment. Today, we know the limitations of punishment in terms of producing positive public safety outcomes. In order to move the criminal justice system in the direction indicated by the scientific evidence, various agencies and actors must think differently going forward about roles and responsibilities and, in turn, the culture of the organization. One of the primary changes for prosecutors is a clear acceptance of responsibility for reducing recidivism: not just "doing my part" in a process involving several different agencies and individuals, but globally taking responsibility for recidivism reduction.

The goal here is balance. The scientific evidence clearly indicates moving in the direction of a more balanced approach to recidivism reduction and enhancement of public safety. That balance considers traditional just deserts, incapacitation, retribution, and control and punishment on the one hand, and correctional rehabilitation and diversion on the other. Clearly, some offenders need to be removed from the community. That decision should be based on considerations of the potential to rehabilitate serious, chronic offending, moral or emotional justification for retribution, and the seriousness of the crime. However, for many others, there is a clear opportunity to actually change behavior. We can have alternatives in place, we can have the mechanisms for making better decisions, but if we do not have a culture that promotes balance and better decision making, it is all for naught.

RISK AND NEEDS-BASED DECISION MAKING

Earlier in this chapter, I referred to criminal sentencing as sorting individuals into appropriate categories. Proper or accurate sorting is challenging for a number of reasons, including lack of universal agreement about the goals of sorting and lack of information relevant to making optimal sorting decisions. Prosecution also involves sorting both in terms of adjudication of criminal cases as well as the impact that prosecutorial decisions have on sentencing outcomes. Prosecutorial sorting is, or should be, equally as challenging.

Because charging, fact/evidence, plea negotiation, and diversion referral decisions all have substantial impacts on sentencing outcomes and, in turn, on the big picture goals of crime and recidivism reduction, it seems reasonable to begin the process of learning key decision-relevant information about an offender as early on as possible. One of the universal evidence-based practices is accurate, actuarial-based risk *and* needs assessment. We seem to have fairly clear conceptions of an offender's harm or dangerousness, based on the evidence presented and criminal history, but we have paid much less attention at this point in criminal processing to what it would take to change an individual offender's criminal behavior.

The use of current-generation actuarial risk and dynamic needs assessments is critical to an accurate determination of risk, as well as the development of a strategy for recidivism reduction on a case-by-case basis. Unfortunately, this is a relatively foreign concept at the prosecution stage of processing. If one does not know, with a significant degree of accuracy, the totality of the primary criminogenic problems or needs that contributed to an offender being arrested, then a prosecutor is not in a position to make informed decisions other than case-processing decisions. If what the prosecutor knows is the evidence that the police have gathered in the instant offense, which in turn leads to the charging decision, then that prosecutor is probably unable to make informed decisions about diversion, referral, or other rehabilitative alternatives.

Implementing risk and needs assessments as early as possible in case processing simply provides the prosecutor with the totality of the circumstances at a point before key decisions are made. For example, referral to diversion courts should happen early in case processing, before a defendant goes too far down the hallway toward traditional criminal adjudication. Having accurate, valid information that is systematically collected for all defendants puts prosecutors in the position of better decision making, assuming relevant alternatives are in place, a topic I take up in chapter 5.

It is also important to take the screening and assessment process to the next level. This incorporates clinical assessment regarding factors such as trauma effects, neurocognitive and neurological impairment, and deficits that should have a significant role in prosecutorial decision making and, in turn, the impact those decisions have on case outcomes including sentencing.

COLLABORATION

The problem-solving model is based in part on collaborative expertise. Many offenders come into the justice system with a complex set of circumstances or criminogenic needs. Specialized expertise (for example, psychiatrists and psychologists, substance abuse treatment and addiction specialists, employment training specialists, and educators) is generally required to measure and understand the severity of the problem and to develop the appropriate intervention to effectively address it.

Prosecutors are lawyers, not psychologists, psychiatrists, clinicians, social workers, educators, or recidivism experts. Part of the rethinking of prosecution is the introduction of a collaborative decision-making process that includes expertise in a variety of areas of criminogenic need, such as mental health, substance abuse, trauma, intellectual deficits, education and employment, and others. The problem-solving approach envisions a collaborative staffing of cases to determine what is the most appropriate, cost-effective approach for each case. If the goal going forward is to more effectively reduce recidivism based on obtaining more extensive diagnostic information on a variety of domains or dimensions, it makes sense that the appropriate experts are involved in the decision-making process. Because the decisions that prosecutors make can and do influence sentencing outcomes, often in quite substantial ways, it makes absolute sense for prosecutorial decision making to become more deliberate, more informed, and collaborative, and based on a broad array of dispositions and sanctions.

On the other hand, this is a fairly radical change to how cases are typically prosecuted. For that reason, these changes cannot be implemented overnight and cannot simply be decreed. These changes are in part structural, but they are also changes in thinking about crime and punishment, thinking about roles and responsibilities, and thinking about the end game. In effect, it involves a new culture of prosecution.

Crime is not just a criminal justice concern with traditional criminal justice "solutions." In many instances, crime is a public health issue (for example, mentally ill offenders, substance abusing offenders, offenders with neurocognitive deficits), an employment or workforce issue, a public education issue, or an affordable housing issue. In order to effectively change behavior, and in turn reduce the likelihood of recidivism, a variety of criminogenic problems need to be identified and community resources need to be brought to the table to address them.

We might benefit from borrowing a concept from the civil side of the court docket. Civil litigation, like criminal prosecution, relies nearly exclusively on strategies that avoid litigating cases at trial. On the criminal side, that is a negotiated plea. On the civil side, it is case mediation and settlement. Perhaps one way to think about the collaborative, problem-solving strategy for the prosecution of criminal cases is the mediation model. There are clearly legal issues and those interests are represented by the state's attorney and the defendant's attorney. However, as we have been suggesting, there are potentially many more considerations than just the prosecution of a criminal matter.

The concept of mediation as we are considering it here is a significant rethinking of and revision to the plea negotiation process. Rather than the typical negotiation between the prosecutor and defense counsel, involving a plea offer in exchange for lesser punishment, a revised approach would include all relevant interests, such as diagnostic and clinical expertise, the judge, jail and probation, community treatment, intervention and rehabilitation resources, victim input, and whatever other parties are relevant and/or necessary for case resolution.

The process would involve a triage stage at the beginning in which cases are sorted perhaps into two categories: (1) criminal adjudication, for those cases that do not merit any kind of diversion from criminal prosecution or rehabilitation efforts, either because of the offense elements (such as a violent crime or sex offense, among others deemed appropriate) or characteristics of the offender (habitual offender, low likelihood of successful intervention); and (2) cases for which there is an identified reasonable opportunity for rehabilitative intervention, based on risk and needs assessment and other screening data. The cases identified for traditional criminal prosecution then proceed as they currently do and are plead out and sentenced in a more traditional fashion (essentially probation or prison/jail). Offenders in the second category then undergo a more extensive case assessment, identification of appropriate interventions, securing available resources, and determination of the appropriate disposition (drug court, deferred adjudication, probation, jail plus programming, and so on).

This collaborative decision making should begin early in case processing. Comprehensive risk and needs screening and assessment should have been completed prior to this point so that those assessments may serve as a basis for more informed decisions early on.

There are several challenges this approach will encounter. One is developing and implementing the necessary structural and cultural changes required. It is often easier to implement structural changes than changes in thinking, beliefs, and attitudes. For some, it will involve something like resocialization in the job of prosecutor, a reorientation from the concept of the case to the concept of the problem, and all of the changes that are necessary to effectively address these problems.

Funding will be an issue. What is proposed here will require additional resources as prosecution caseloads will change. Resources will also be required to conduct the necessary screening and assessments and hire the relevant experts for collaborative decision making.

It is also reasonable to expect resistance from defendants. Many will not want to engage in diversion, intervention, and rehabilitation. Many will want the more punitive approach (a prison sentence) so they do not have to go through treatment/rehabilitation. They can just get it done quicker if they follow a traditional path. There are validated ways to assess treatment readiness/willingness on the part of defendants, and such assessments should become routine in order to assure that rehabilitation resources are effectively used (these assessments are referred to as treatment readiness assessments). There are also methods for coaxing or encouraging individuals (for example, motivational interviewing) that can be important in engaging participation in alternatives to traditional sentences.

It is also reasonable to expect pushback from the defense bar. Defense lawyers often think in terms of minimal sanction or punishment as the goal for the defendant, and sometimes that may translate into rejecting a diversionary, rehabilitative option in favor of a straight punishment option. Moreover, defense attorneys, like prosecutors, are trained to think in adversarial terms, thus often by definition what the government wants may not be in the defendant's interest. Just as a cultural shift will be necessary in the prosecutor's office, a similar shift will need to occur among defense lawyers. Defense lawyers will need to be educated regarding what works and what does not and about the global goal of reducing recidivism. And defense lawyers will need to think differently about their role in this process. They, like prosecutors, will need to think in terms of a problem, rather than a case, and engage their roles and responsibilities in more of a problem-solving manner than perhaps they have in the past. And just like prosecutors, defense lawyers are lawyers, not clinicians, behavioral experts, or social workers. Thus, the decisions about what treatment or intervention a defendant may need, or how long the defendant should be in that treatment, is not something the defense lawyer is trained to address and should not address without expert assistance. Clearly, preservation of constitutional protections and assuring due process in the proceedings will be a primary responsibility of the defense lawyer. But so will collaboration and mutual problem solving.

Because 80 percent of defendants are indigent and require appointed counsel or public defenders, it may be necessary to develop public defender offices in those jurisdictions that have appointed counsel systems. Appointed counsel rotate into cases and the composition of lawyers is often changing. It will be particularly challenging (though not impossible) to reeducate and resocialize appointed counsel to get on board with these proposed changes. Logistically, it seems that it would be more effective with a public defender system.

LEADERSHIP

One of the primary reasons that sentencing reform of the 1970s, 1980s, and 1990s was embraced on the scale witnessed, including the widespread adoption of truth in sentencing, was due to the leadership, assistance, and incentives provided by the federal government. The same is the case, for example, with community policing and problem-solving courts. There are a variety of organizations that support community prosecution, including the National District Attorney's Association (NDAA), the National Center For Community Prosecution (NCCP), and the American Prosecutor's Research Institute (APRI). While there are local jurisdictions that engage in some of the practices that are recommended here, what is likely required for this concept to gain traction is the declaration of a focused agenda at the national level.

But such procedural and cultural transformations also require local leadership on the part of District Attorneys. DAs set the agenda in their offices, so the District Attorney must be a prime mover for such initiatives to be successful. Clearly, what I am recommending here will require substantial changes in resourcing, in procedure, perhaps in statutes, and clearly in thinking. It will also require political courage. DAs are typically elected officials and historically many have been elected with the crime control message. Perhaps changing the rhetoric from tough and punitive to balanced, smart, effective, cost-effective, and victim and victimization centered (for example, making the reduction of victimization the priority) can gain some political leverage. Again, the point is not to jeopardize public safety. In all circumstances, risk of reoffending is the driver of initial decision making. The question is not whether supervision and control should be a consideration. Instead, how much supervision and control is necessary is the first question, followed by the extent to which we can at the same time engage behavioral change strategies.

I now turn to a discussion of sentencing structure and statutes as I reconsider the big picture of criminal sentencing.

RECONSIDERING SENTENCING STRUCTURES AND STATUTES

The 2006 National Center for State Courts' survey of state chief justices found that the primary concerns or complaints of state felony trial judges are high recidivism, lack of appropriate and effective sentencing alternatives, and lack of sentencing discretion by judges to more effectively and fairly sentence individual offenders. One of the overarching themes from these comments is, among other things, dissatisfaction with fairly unidimensional, one-size-fits-all sentencing. This is consistent with characterizations of U.S. sentencing and corrections policy (for example, Beckett 1997; Beckett and Sasson 2004; Western 2006). As I discussed earlier, crime control is based primarily on punishment and control, to the relative exclusion of alternatives. I have also documented that sentencing reform over the past forty years has limited judicial sentencing discretion. Moreover, the concerns expressed by judges about recidivism are supported by current scientific evidence about the failure of current policies to reduce recidivism. In effect, the view from the trenches is quite consistent with research-based profiles of U.S. criminal justice policy, as well as scientific evaluations of the impact of punishment and recidivism.

The term that best applies to a reconsidered sentencing policy is, once again, "balance." Balance between sanctions of punishment, control, and accountability on the one hand, and strategies targeting behavioral change on the other. Warren (2008: 324) states it quite well:

Sanctions alone will not result in positive behavioral change or reduce recidivism. On the other hand, treatment alone may not provide the punishment or behavioral controls that are appropriate or necessary. Policies that expect to control crime solely by punishing the offender's past conduct, without any meaningful effort to positively influence the offender's future behaviors, are short-sighted, ignore overwhelming research evidence, fail to capitalize on opportunities for substantial cost savings and needlessly endanger future victims and public safety.

So where does this lead us? A number of considerations appear relevant to the discussion of where we go from here regarding sentencing statutes and structures. One involves enhancing the ability of judges to utilize effective, evidence-based alternatives to traditional punishment-oriented sentences. Research indicates a number of quite viable recidivism-reducing alternatives to incarceration. Thus, judges need the statutory flexibility to determine who is appropriate for alternatives and then the ability to impose those sanctions. Clearly, this also requires sufficient resourcing of these alternatives to provide adequate capacity and appropriate implementation levels and efforts. The latter point is that it is not sufficient to just have a drug court, for example. To be effective, the drug court should be large enough to accommodate demand and it needs to be designed and operated according to what the scientific evidence has discovered to be the effective components and characteristics of a successful drug court. Too often we have seen alternative sentencing options as symbolic gestures, insufficiently funded, operated by overburdened and uncommitted employees who go through the motions at best (see Marcus's point above about the *responsible* pursuit of crime and recidivism reduction).

The second consideration involves the ability or opportunity to sentence both the offense and the offender. That is, permit evidence regarding not just the offense (and thus the harm of the instant offense and the harm of prior criminal involvement), but to consider and evaluate characteristics of the offender that are relevant to recidivism reduction. Such a consideration would involve assessing criminogenic circumstances and conditions that should be addressed in order to effectively change behavior and, in turn, reduce the likelihood of recidivism and victimization.

I argued earlier that the sentencing decision is a pivotal point in the processing of criminal defendants. This has been historically true, at least for the past thirty-five to forty years, because the sentencing decision has dictated the longer-term aggregate consequences—successes and failures—of U.S. criminal justice policy.

It is also a pivotal point going forward because if the appropriate sentencing options are in place (meaning balanced sentencing options that address enhancement of public safety and recidivism reduction), then the sentencing decision is critical in determining that the right offenders get the right sentence, or more accurately, the right outcome. If that is generally the case, then research indicates that we can expect recidivism reductions, crime reductions, cost reductions, and the enhancement of public safety.

Obviously, evidence-based practices cannot drive all sentencing policy. Sentencing and punishment have emotional, moral, and ethical elements. Therefore, we need to keep the door open for retributive sentences. But choices should be based on the optimal balance of utilitarian and moral sentencing motives. Some cases are simply beyond the pale in terms of failed attempts at rehabilitation, habitual offending, the level of violence perpetrated, and/or willful disregard for civility and humanity. Retribution may be simply what the community wants and the case calls for, and there clearly is a place for that type of sentence, although presumably at a much lower frequency than today and what we have seen in the recent past.

But once again, it seems reasonable to suggest that these decisions should be on a case-by-case basis, considering not only the elements of the offense and prior criminal involvement, but the criminogenic circumstances that are related to why this person is engaged in crime and, in some instances, related to their culpability. What makes us think that all third strike offenders should receive the same punishment? What we have lost with the sentencing changes of the past several decades is much of the consideration of the characteristics of the offender in the sentencing process.

So what should sentencing look like going forward and what statutory changes are required to facilitate this? First, sentencing should be a collaborative process in which the crime is the problem and the goal is, on a case-by-case basis, to bring all of the relevant information and resources to the table to develop a strategy to solve that problem. This process should be presided over by the judge, but must involve the prosecutor, the defense counsel, clinical experts, and community-based treatment/intervention providers, as well as others. I now turn to what appear to be relevant statutory and structural changes to sentencing to accomplish what I have outlined here.

The statutory framework that can facilitate the sentencing model outlined above is probably a hybrid consisting of generally indeterminate sentencing combined with something resembling presumptive or suggestive guidelines. The guidelines could indicate (not precisely require, but presume) incapacitation for violent offenders, serious habitual offenders, and serious offenders for whom there is little chance of significant behavioral change, and risk management and behavior change for the rest.

It is fairly easy to use statutes to identify violent offenders (for example, murder, aggravated assault, sexual assault). However, when it comes to habitual offenders, prior statutory attempts (for example, three strikes) have fallen short for a number of reasons (Schiraldi, Colburn, and Lotke 2004; Zimring, Hawkins, and Kamin 2001). A common problem with a wholesale policy or statutes like habitual offender laws is the high presence of false positives. Whether the magic number is three, ten, or forty priors, such gross classification of offenders fails to consider individual variation that drives the likelihood of future offending, individual factors that often play a more important role in recidivism than prior criminal involvement (for example, age). Decisions about habitual offenders and those for whom behavioral change is unlikely require significant evaluation from a variety of perspectives. Simply legislating some set of criteria like number of prior convictions to qualify as a habitual offender and number of prior probations or other diversions to identify rehabilitation failures keeps us precisely where we are today, with state legislatures and Congress creating gross categories of offenders and tossing those who have one or two characteristics in common into the same category. That is what determinate sentencing essentially does. Under such sentencing statutes, there is little or no regard for individual circumstance or for variation among individuals. Such approaches seriously miss the point of getting smarter and more deliberate about who should be in prison (incapacitated) and who should be diverted and how.

A reasonable approach is one that combines diagnostic assessment of risk, criminogenic circumstance, and recidivism potential that can be used to inform the collaborative decision making within an indeterminate sentencing framework. Keeping sentencing generally indeterminate allows for more deliberate decision making on a case-by-case basis, and gets us away from the unnecessary incarceration of offenders. Indeterminate sentencing can facilitate the collaboration of multiple interests in the sentencing process, which generally reduces the likelihood of an overly significant impact of discretion by any one individual. Indeterminate sentencing places discretion back in the court, but under what I am proposing, with a very different collaborative approach in which sentencing is more of a collective decision.

Under this approach, there is less room for incarceration sentences. Sentences of incarceration should be reserved for a subset of offenders and offenses for which the only instrumental goal is separation from society. It should be clear that incarceration sentences function to incapacitate rather than deter. Incarceration sentences should reflect the moral disruption caused by particular types of crime, through their nature (for example, murder, predatory sexual crimes, abuse of the young or elderly, among others) or their severity (the amount of harm inflicted in the course of committing the crime). Clearly, these decisions about sentences of incarceration (or even the death penalty) should reflect community concerns, attitudes, and sentiments, absent the political rhetoric and factual error that has so typically characterized sentencing legislation over the past forty years. These decisions should be guided by moral questions about what behaviors are sufficiently offensive to civil society, culpability of offenders (including the mental health and intellectual capacity of offenders), community impact of the crimes, cost considerations, and the likelihood that when released, such offenders will not have many protective assets designed to reduce the likelihood of reoffending.

Crafting presumptive guidelines that provide the overall structure to the sentencing decision-making process should help clarify the general goals of sentencing and can serve to build awareness and eventually consensus with regard to priorities about public safety, incarceration, diversion and rehabilitation, and the most effective ways to reduce recidivism and victimization. Presumptive guidelines can also be an effective tool for clarifying the nature of the sentencing process. The guidelines provide structure, direction, and guidance to a generally indeterminate sentencing scheme.

Now the challenges. First, there are fifty-two different sovereign jurisdictions. It will be a massive enterprise to get these jurisdictions even close in terms of the revised sentencing processes discussed here. However, one important strategy (a strategy that was fundamental in the earlier round of sentencing reform) is federal leadership, assistance, and incentives. The existence of a clear example, whether federal or state, that other states can investigate, evaluate, and mimic or modify can facilitate adoption in other jurisdictions. Moreover, the federal government can provide incentives to the states to get smarter about criminal justice policies and practices, including sentencing, the use of incarceration (including admissions, sentence length, and time served), diversion programs, behavioral change strategies, and a host of other evidence-based initiatives.

There has already been some movement away from mandatory sentences, primarily because of the fiscal impact they have on state incarceration budgets. For example, New York State has made significant modifications to the Rockefeller drug laws. Oregon's House Bill 3194 proposes substantial retreats from the state's mandatory sentences. Georgia House Bill 349 proposes some modest changes to Georgia's mandatory sentences. At the federal level, the Justice Safety Valve Act gives federal judges more discretion in certain circumstances involving mandatory sentencing situations. This is movement in the right direction, but in many cases it is more symbolic than substantive. The path forward outlined here will require overhaul of sentencing statutes, not fine-tuning. An example of what appears to be substantive change is Attorney General Holder's efforts to reform federal mandatory sentences under the Smart on Crime initiative. How far it goes is yet to be seen, but the momentum is starting to build.

Another challenge is funding. If and when states move away from massive incarceration toward more diversion and interventions aimed at risk management and behavior change, there will be a shift in location of corrections as well as a shift in the responsibility for funding. Incarceration in prison is typically managed and funded by state government. Jail, probation, diversion courts, and other diversion alternatives are largely locally funded. The model proposed here is one that envisions many fewer offenders in prison and many more on diversion sentences and short-term jail incarceration (these are discussed in much greater detail in the chapters ahead). The challenge is that this model places a much greater burden on local jurisdictions (primarily counties), assuming current funding protocol remains in place. The burden is financial, as well as scale (increased numbers of offenders), management, and availability of local treatment and rehabilitation resources, among others. A significant portion of the funding challenge can be addressed if states redirect the cost savings from reduced prison populations to local jurisdictions in support of their increased caseloads. There are funding models in place that do precisely that (for example, California's performance incentive funding).

However, the extent to which state legislatures actually do shift funding is a very large question. It certainly makes sense. When the state burden declines as prison populations decline, some of the funds that were devoted to incarceration should be redirected to local jurisdictions to help support community-based treatment and rehabilitation. As we move toward reduced incarceration, the offenders that are diverted in its various forms will increase, thus increasing the financial burden on local jurisdictions. There is likely to be substantial pressure on legislators to allocate those funds across a variety of competing interests (education, health care, debt service, and so on). Thus, the success of criminal justice policy going forward depends on sufficient funding for sufficient capacity at the local level, and not to shift an undue burden for funding on counties and cities. Among the problem-solving issues on the list here is how to assure that more funding is redirected to local jurisdictions for administration of criminal justice.

Another challenge is that the states and then the local jurisdictions within the states will embrace these initiatives with varying levels of enthusiasm, fidelity, resourcing, comprehensiveness, constraints, and pushback. Some will be more effortful and successful than others. To assume differently is naïve. It is likely that the best we can expect is a general consistency in goals (reduce recidivism and victimization, reduce reliance on incarceration, increase alternatives designed for behavioral change), and general consistency in the policy and program direction it all takes.

CONTEMPORARY PUBLIC OPINION ABOUT
CRIME AND PUNISHMENT

Americans are typically viewed as punitive regarding crime. As Warr (2000: 22) concludes: "Americans overwhelmingly regard imprisonment as the appropriate form of punishment for most crimes." However, a closer look at the public opinion data suggests a broader sophistication of opinion, one that the political process and the media may have muted. There is a duality to public beliefs and attitudes about crime and punishment. On the one hand, there is the element of proportionality in punishment, reflecting a deep-seated belief that wrongdoing should be punished and that the severity of the punishment should be proportional to the harm inflicted. On the other hand, there is the utilitarian element that reflects the goal of recidivism and crime reduction, with a primary focus on correctional rehabilitation. While these two views—enhanced severity of punishment and correctional rehabilitation—have historically been adversarial positions in electoral politics and policy debates in the United States, the duality of public opinion about sentencing and punishment may simply reflect a more balanced approach to the administration of criminal justice.

The public's attitudes about sentencing, punishment, and rehabilitation are long-held views. While most of the scientific survey research on public attitudes about sentencing and punishment has been conducted relatively recently, there is good evidence (Doble 2002; Doble and Klein 2009) that public opinion on punishment has been, for decades, much more multidimensional than assumed by listening to electoral rhetoric during the 1980s, 1990s, and 2000s. It is ironic that crime control has existed for much of the past forty years as a partisan position. Politics appears to have forced the electorate to take sides, when in reality, the public's position on punishment and rehabilitation has been conditional and multidimensional. The public sees things in terms of tradeoffs. Electoral politics and the media have kept the debate at the level of an oversimplified dichotomy.

Summaries of public opinion research (for example, Roberts and Hough 2002) as well as opinion survey after opinion survey (Beldon, Russonello, and Stewart 2001; Doble and Klein 2009; Hart/Open Society Institute 2002; Hartney and Marchionne 2009; Kriesberg and Marchionne 2006; Pew Center on the States 2010; Princeton Survey Research Associates International 2006; Warren 2009b) demonstrate that when provided with relevant information and multiple options, the public does not prefer one size fits all, instead the public prefers multiple sizes depending on the specifics of the situation. Thus, it is essential that public opinion surveys on these issues are designed to provide respondents with more specific information about particular decisions, as well as alternatives, options, and the opportunity to consider tradeoffs when responding.

So what do we know about contemporary public opinion regarding crime, sentencing, punishment, rehabilitation, and public safety? Below is a quick summary compiled from the sources cited in the preceding paragraph.

The majority of Americans believe that a balanced approach to crime reduction is optimal, compared to a punishment-only approach, with most people in favor of alternatives to incarceration for many nonviolent offenders and drug offenders; the majority also favors mandatory treatment for drug addicted, nonviolent offenders, compared to incarceration. Most Americans believe that prison is criminogenic and/or believe that rehabilitation will significantly reduce crime and recidivism, compared to incarceration. Finally, the majority believes sentencing is in need of substantial change—much of the public opposes both mandatory sentences and mandatory minimum sentences, while believing that judges should have the discretion to set sentences, rather than be required to impose mandatory sentences.

The point is not that we should always develop policy around public opinion, but that the appropriate use for public opinion here is as a method to gauge support for particular initiatives and policy recommendations. In this case, there is clear public support for implementing a much more balanced approach to adjudication and sanctioning.

CHANGE AND CHALLENGES

Policymakers and elected officials interested in heading in a new direction regarding criminal justice policy, a direction informed by evaluation research on effectiveness and cost-effectiveness, should take notice of what appears to be considerable public support for smart change. The evidence is here and continues to provide more detail and guidance on the appropriate policy path forward. It is time to change the public discourse on crime and justice, moving away from the rhetoric like "lock 'em up and throw away the key" and "do the crime, do the time" to smart, effective, and less expensive. The public embraces a more balanced approach to public safety. It is time for policymakers, elected officials, and practitioners in the justice system to come to the table as well.

The basics of what statutory changes need to be discussed and implemented are before us. It is neither possible nor desirable to develop a single, precise blueprint for the states and the federal system to follow. States will need to negotiate the specifics themselves, presumably in the general direction of what the evidence indicates is appropriate. In addition, local jurisdictions will also need to work out the particulars within the framework of the statutes that prevail in that state. Different states and different jurisdictions within states will embrace these evidence-based practices and policies with varying fidelity, resourcing, comprehensiveness, expertise, and motivation. This is the reality and it is as it should be, although it may compromise consistency of policy and practice.

Many of the changes proposed here cannot be legislated. Yes, states can change sentencing and release laws, and potentially change criminal justice funding formulas. However, problem solving and collaboration are not particularly amenable to statute. Neither is the idea that recidivism is the collective responsibility of a variety of agencies and individuals. Getting individuals to embrace that concept is challenging, especially when their roles and responsibilities are relatively narrow in scope.

The criminal justice system essentially operates as a series of discrete silos, as a series of handoffs, where there is effectively no one responsible for the big picture of reducing recidivism and enhancing public safety. In oversimplified terms, the police hand off the offenders to the prosecutor, the prosecutors hand offenders off to the judges, the judges hand them off to corrections, corrections often hand them back to the court for revocation, then back to corrections, then when corrections is finished, the cycle typically begins over again. And again. And again. In order for this to work, there needs to be a broad acceptance of responsibility for the big picture of recidivism reduction.

The more social, psychological, and cultural changes are as important as statutory changes, policy and procedure changes, and reallocation of funding. Certainly, laws, policies, and guidelines can stipulate how jobs are to be done, how services are to be delivered, how probation officers and prosecutors are to do their jobs. But those guidelines and policies and laws cannot easily invoke problem solving and collaboration as the concept is intended here. Absent changes in ways of thinking, engaging, collaborating, communicating, sharing information, problem solving, taking initiative, and all of the other more subtle attributes of a radical cultural shift, this endeavor will fail to accomplish what could be achieved.

The challenges are significant. Within a local jurisdiction, there are multiple agencies that are used to operating relatively independently. There is turf and in turn "turf issues." There are elected officials (typically judges and District Attorneys) who are used to independence and autonomy, but who are also subject to significant political considerations and pressures. There is an existing culture of crime control and punishment that has been ingrained for decades. There are groups with historically competing interests (for example, prosecutors and defense counsel, tough on crime prosecutors and judges, and those advocating and delivering correctional rehabilitation). And there is a general lack of consensus regarding alternatives to accomplishing the mission of the justice system. Add on top of that the fact that there is variation across local jurisdictions (typically counties) within a state in terms of population, demographics, geography, crime rates, priorities, beliefs and attitudes, constraints, resources, caseloads, and assumptions about how to best deal with crime, among many other differences. Then there is variation in all of those factors across states, plus differences in laws and policies.

There is plenty of inertia keeping current policies going forward. Without doubt, there are considerable financial interests focusing on keeping correctional control the centerpiece of U.S. criminal justice. The economies of many smaller, local communities in the United States are heavily dependent on prisons as economic drivers. There are several publicly traded corrections companies in the United States that depend on the size of the criminal justice system. Their presence is no doubt felt in our legislative hallways.

While the challenges are considerable, so are the potential benefits. I am talking about a sea change in how we go about the business of criminal justice in the United States. I am talking about changing how we think about crime and its origins, how we think about behavior change, and how we effectively and cost-effectively spend public resources. We are moving toward removing emotion from the decision-making process and replacing it with rational, research-based practices and principles. This is in effect a culture change in U.S. criminal justice, along with structural, statutory, and funding changes. We are on a path of reducing crime and its consequences, of reducing victimization, and of saving hundreds of billions of dollars in direct criminal justice expenditures, as well as additional hundreds of billions more in the collateral costs of crime, such as economic loss, physical harm and its costs, and social costs like fear.

CHAPTER 5

Diversion and Problem-Solving Courts

ONE OF THE PRIMARY RESEARCH findings of the past twenty years or so, and much more conclusively in the past six to seven years, is the efficacy of diversion from traditional criminal prosecution, adjudication, sentencing, and punishment. Diversion is one of the most important recidivism reduction strategies currently known. When diversion programs are properly scaled, implemented, and operated/managed, they can have remarkable impacts on recidivism. The purpose of this chapter is to discuss what an optimal, balanced diversion court component of justice policy should look like based on what the scientific evidence indicates. I will address the diversion of offenders to probation in chapter 6.

Diversion courts come in a wide variety of types and designs. They are intended to address a range of criminogenic needs. Some are preindictment and others are postindictment and postadjudication. They vary in terms of eligibility criteria, the types and length of therapeutic interventions, and how they respond to rule infractions.

Drug courts are the most common (there are over 2,400 in the United States in 2014). Additionally, there are 1,200 or so other types of diversion courts, including mental health courts, community courts, domestic violence courts, homeless courts, truancy courts, veteran courts, sex offender courts, and reentry courts, among others. Most are therapeutic in design and practice. There are also accountability or sanction courts, which focus on sanctioning for noncompliance (although accountability and sanctioning are an important component of the therapeutic courts as well).

Unfortunately, most diversion courts amount to a largely token effort (for example, drug diversion courts are quite popular today, but their capacity is inconsequential compared to the need or demand). Others are inadequately designed, implemented, managed, and/or funded.

PROBLEM SOLVING IN PROBLEM-SOLVING COURTS

Diversion courts are generally based on the concept of therapeutic jurisprudence, typically understood as a balance between intervention and treatment on the one hand and accountability and responsibility on the other. Well-designed and operated diversion courts are premised on the principle of proactive problem solving. The concept of problem solving in criminal justice and especially in the criminal court system began to gain national traction in 1999 when New York State's chief judge Judith Kaye published an article in *Newsweek* on the benefits of problem solving as an overarching principle in criminal courts. Problem solving as a judicial concept has a number of defining characteristics, including greater, more accurate information, enhanced expertise, community engagement, collaboration with a variety of stakeholders, a focus on the individual and the individual case, and accountability. In principle, these components of problem-solving diversion make perfect sense, and their practice is clearly supported by scientific research. In practice, they present some significant challenges.

Enhanced, Accurate Information and Expertise

As I discussed earlier, one of the major problems facing the U.S. criminal justice system is the historical inability to make good, informed decisions regarding matters such as sentencing. Absent accurate, predictive data and staff trained to interpret such data and formulate well-considered recommendations, the diversion process will flounder and its outcomes will be compromised. Obviously, the success of diversion programs depends on a number of factors, including who gets in the front door. Thus, it is vital that upfront decision making is as informed as possible, including who should be diverted, what they need if diverted, and what risks they pose if diverted. To that end, current-generation, actuarial, static, and dynamic needs and risk assessments should be commonplace. These assessments should be scientifically validated and administered by trained professionals.

A recent screening, assessment, and treatment focus, spearheaded by the Substance Abuse Mental Health Services Administration (SAMHSA), focuses on trauma. Trauma-informed care is a particular emphasis on measuring the presence of childhood and adult trauma in order to better understand and treat the needs of offenders. Results from the Adverse Childhood Experiences Study (ACE) indicate that 64 percent of the population has had at lease one adverse childhood experience and 13 percent have had four or more (Centers for Disease Control and Prevention, Data and Statistics, Prevalence of Individual Adverse Childhood Experiences). These trauma events range from emotional, physical, and sexual abuse, to emotional and physical neglect, to violence, substance abuse, mental illness, and/or marital disruption in the household, as well as incarceration of a household member. The most common ACE is physical abuse (28 percent), followed by household substance abuse (27 percent) and marital disruption (23 percent).

The ACE research has clearly linked the experience of adverse childhood events to a wide variety of behavioral and health outcomes, including alcohol and substance abuse and dependence, depression and other mental health conditions, neurocognitive impairments, engaging in a variety of risky behaviors, and a number of physical health consequences. Several studies have also explicitly linked childhood abuse and neglect with subsequent criminal offending (for example, Currie and Tekin 2006; Rebellon and Van Gundy 2005; Siegel and Williams 2003; Swantson et al. 2003; Widom 2000).

The importance of understanding the presence of trauma experiences is the likely impact they have had or potentially will have on criminal behavior. As such, trauma experiences are both risk factors and dynamic (treatable) criminogenic needs. One of the leading researchers of the ACE study (Anda 2007) stated:

> The vast array of problems that arise from ACEs calls for an integrated view of the origins of health and social problems throughout the lifespan. Our approach to growing up with ACEs and to the consequences of exposure to them—in effect, making the invisible engine visible—may unify and improve society's understanding of many seemingly unrelated health and social problems that tend to be identified and treated as separate issues. Development of more integrated approaches will likely contribute to more meaningful diagnoses, improved treatment of at-risk and affected persons,

and better integration of research priorities, preventive and social services, and legal venues

The National Leadership Forum on Behavioral Health/Criminal Justice Services (2009) reports nearly universal histories of trauma among mentally ill individuals with justice involvement. Ninety-three percent of mentally ill men and women in samples of jail diversion programs reported a history of at least one incident of physical or sexual abuse. Sixty-one percent reported physical or sexual abuse in the past twelve months. Even with such extraordinarily high prevalence of trauma, few community-based or institutional programs offer trauma-informed or trauma-specific programming.

Individuals assisting in the referral to diversion should have the clinical expertise to interpret diagnostic data regarding common criminogenic circumstances such as substance abuse and mental illness. In some instances, such as pretrial diversion or preindictment diversion, those referrals will likely originate from the prosecutor's office. In such instances, it is important that prosecutors have accurate information and the experts to interpret it. In the case of postadjudication diversion, the court will require the same information and expertise.

It is also important to have the expertise and resources to assess neurocognitive and neurodevelopmental deficits and impairments. Risk factors include trauma, poverty, head injury, and neglect and abuse, among others. Such deficits are relevant to treatment planning as well as responsivity considerations.

Individual offenders typically present with a variety of criminogenic needs or deficits. Thus, whether diversion originates from the prosecutor or the court, it is necessary that the advisory staff have expertise in a variety of need areas. For example, if a prosecutor understands substance abuse but is not well informed on the intricacies of mental illness or neurodevelopmental deficits, a decision to refer to substance abuse treatment may result in a poor outcome if the mental illness and other problems remain untreated. Staff involved in diversion should possess expertise in a variety of criminogenic need areas, including mental health, neurocognitive, substance abuse, physical health, education, employment, homelessness, and legal issues, among others, as well as supervision/risk and case management.

The question of accurate assessment and the expertise to appropriately interpret, diagnose, develop proper interventions, and actually carry out such treatment has become much more complex than focusing on remedial education and job training. As discussed previously, recognizing and understanding the presence and consequences of trauma is no simple matter. Identifying the neurocognitive deficits associated with poverty (inhibited self-control, impulse regulation, lower IQ, poor language skills, poor working memory function, impaired attention control and focus) and designing appropriate interventions for offenders with co-occurring disorders require expertise and skills that likely exceed those of the traditional justice setting. The accumulation of knowledge about the factors that underlie criminal offending requires much enhanced reliance on an increasing diversification of expertise in order to properly address the circumstances of crime and offending.

Community Engagement

Public safety is a public good that has for most of our history been the nearly exclusive responsibility of the government. Diversion, by definition, involves the community, in the sense that the community has a stake in and a responsibility for public safety.

Engaging the community in the judicial and rehabilitative process helps establish a community role in problem solving. Citizen engagement also enhances public trust in the justice system. Public trust and other forms of social capital are fundamental in rebalancing or redistributing some of the responsibility for public safety to a shared government-community effort. Community engagement is also quite important in terms of securing the appropriate community-based resources for intervention, as discussed in the next section.

Collaboration

Accomplishing public safety through mechanisms other than punishment and control requires a wide variety of assets, many of which are local, NGO, community-based resources. These include substance abuse treatment facilities, mental health and psychiatric treatment facilities, sustainable, supportive housing providers, employment training, medical clinics, and adult education, among others. Collaboration and public-private partnerships have characterized many local initiatives designed to address any number of circumstances. It is no different when it comes to criminal justice, diversion, and rehabilitation. We should not expect and probably should not prefer that government maintain the programs and services needed to address the variety of offenders' criminogenic needs. Instead, diversion courts and diversion programs should establish relationships with local providers and rely on them to provide needed services. However, as I discuss below, this is not just a matter of having local vendors to provide services. There must be serious consideration given to quality of services provided.

Individualized Justice

Sentencing and corrections have amounted to putting convicted offenders into a limited number of categories and all or most in each category get the same sanction or intervention. Assaultive offenders get anger management classes. Substance abusers get six-week outpatient classes or are ordered to attend AA meetings. First-time DWI offenders get alcohol awareness classes. The same applies for punishment. States with determinate sentencing do this more deliberately: those with offense level X and criminal history category Y get Z years of incarceration. States with indeterminate sentencing get to the same place more slowly by considering aggravating and mitigating circumstances, but in reality the sentencing outcomes become fairly standard for categories of offenders with similar characteristics, although there are many exceptions.

The point is an obvious one. Offenders come into the criminal justice system with some shared circumstances, but at the same time, they exhibit considerable differentiation in circumstances. Why would we expect an anger management class to work the same way and have the same impact for offenders that may share a small number of things in common (age, gender, aggressive behavior), but may differ greatly in terms of substance use, psychiatric well-being, employment status, income, marital status, cognitive abilities, intellectual capability, and so on.

Diversion programs are designed to provide the opportunity to identify and consider individual circumstances and in turn to tailor programs to particular individual needs and abilities. Offenders' needs vary in terms of severity. Some with substance problems may perform well with outpatient services, others may need thirty-day residential treatment, and still others may require six months of inpatient treatment. We need to get serious about identifying the particular needs and circumstances of individual offenders and stop trying to make one size fit all. It does not work, it is a waste of resources, and it compromises public safety.

Multiple Criminogenic Needs

Properly matching programming to offender needs and capabilities is one important aspect of individualized justice. This is the responsivity principle discussed in chapter 3. However, there is an often-neglected aspect of diversion and problem solving that has far greater consequences for the effectiveness of intervention. Offenders typically enter the justice process with a variety of criminogenic circumstances. We often identify the more obvious one or the one for which a diversion program exists. We usually do not have much clinical assistance in determining which need (if any) is addressed and how. The other needs remain unaddressed.

We need to get serious about identifying the multitude of needs of individual offenders, effectively triage those identified needs, and develop a program to address the most serious needs first in an appropriate sequence. This will require clinical expertise, case management, and a variety of resources. Absent these efforts, we will continue to see suboptimal outcomes from correctional intervention.

Offender Accountability

The jurisprudence component of therapeutic jurisprudence involves holding the offender accountable and responsible. This is accomplished by regular appearances in court, client monitoring, and drug testing, among others, and then having appropriate sanctions in place for failure to comply. Evidence indicates that swift and certain consequences or sanctions are effective in encouraging compliance (Office of Justice Programs, National Institute of Justice, 2012). The sanction court concept, modeled after the Hawaii HOPE Court, provides an evidence-based approach to enhance compliance and perceptions of fairness. At the beginning of the diversion process, participants are subject to a warning hearing or orientation hearing in which the judge explains the ground rules, what is expected from participants, what participants can expect from the court, and what types of sanctions are involved. When a participant is in noncompliance, the court then swiftly imposes the sanction. The research indicates dramatic increases in compliance and completion as well as significantly lower revocation rates.

GETTING SERIOUS ABOUT DRUG DIVERSION

Drug law violations constitute the most common type of criminal offense (Glaze and Bonczar 2009) and prevalence studies estimate that over 50 percent of state and federal prison inmates meet the Diagnostic and Statistical Manual for Mental Disorders criteria for drug abuse or dependence (Bureau of Justice Statistics). Yet fewer than 15 percent receive *any* drug treatment while incarcerated (Karberg and James 2005; Karberg and Mumola 2006).

Substance abuse, addiction, and dependence are the most common criminogenic factors in the U.S. criminal justice system. Substantial research has established the variety of drug-crime linkages, including the psychopharmacologic effects of drug or alcohol use on the propensity to commit crimes, the economic incentive to commit crime in order to buy substances, the victimization of drug users, and the violence associated with the drug trade, multiplied many-fold due to the Mexican cartels' activities on both sides of the border. Research clearly demonstrates that as the frequency and intensity of drug use increases, so does criminal offending (Anglin, Longshore, and Turner 1999; Anglin and Maugh 1992; Anglin and Perrochet 1998; Ball, Shaffer, and Nurco 1983; Bhati and Roman 2010; Boyum and Kleiman 2002; Brownstein et al. 1992; Chaiken and Chaiken 1990; Condon and Smith 2003; Dawkins 1997; DeLeon 1988a, 1988b; Goldstein 1985; Harrison and Gfroerer 1992; Inciardi et al. 1996; Inciardi 1992; Inciardi and Pottieger 1994; Johnson et al. 1985; MacCoun and Reuter 2001; Miller and Gold 1994; Mocan and Tekin 2004; MacCoun, Kilmer, and Reuter 2003; Stewart et al. 2000; Vito 1989). There is also a wealth of research that indicates that drug and alcohol treatment for the offender population is effective in reducing drug/alcohol use and abuse and reducing the associated offending and victimization.

In short, alcohol and drugs are a key criminogenic problem and treatment can reduce use and recidivism. Moreover, research indicates that treatment is more cost-effective than incarceration (Caulkins and Reuter 1997; Lipsey and Cullen 2007; MacKenzie 2006).

One of the principles of effective correctional intervention (discussed in chapter 3) is the administration of treatment in a community setting, rather than in a custodial setting such as prison or jail. Diversion through a drug court is an increasingly popular mechanism for delivering treatment designed to reduce substance use and recidivism. I now turn to the effectiveness and cost-effectiveness of drug diversion courts.

Drug diversion courts have been the subject of a substantial amount of research and evaluation. The volume of research that has been conducted permits several clear conclusions (Aos, Miller, and Drake 2006a; Belenko, Patapis, and French 2005; Bhati, Roman, and Chalfin 2008; Carey et al. 2006; Barnoski and Aos 2003; Caulkins and Reuter 1997; Finigan, Carey, and Cox 2007; GAO 2005; Gottfredson et al. 2005, 2006; Lipsey and Cullen 2007; Logan et al. 2004; Loman 2004; Lowenkamp, Holsinger, and Latessa 2005; MacKenzie 2006; Rossman et al. 2011a; Shaffer 2006; Turner et al. 1999; Wilson, Mitchell, and Mackenzie 2006).

Drug court diversion significantly reduces recidivism on average by 26 percent. The best drug courts reduce recidivism by as much as 35 to 40 percent, and the magnitude of the recidivism outcome depends on the particular court. Drug court diversion significantly reduces drug relapse, and drug court participants are significantly less likely to test positive for drug and alcohol use, and less likely to use "serious" drugs when they relapse. Relapses are also less frequent and shorter than for comparisons. The reduction in drug/alcohol use and recidivism appears to persist over time after drug court graduation. Drug court diversion has higher treatment retention rates compared to drug/alcohol treatment in the general population. Drug court diversion is associated with other positive psychosocial outcomes such as a significantly reduced need for employment, educational, and financial services. Economic studies have found that drug/alcohol treatment is more cost-effective than incarceration.

While drug courts require greater upfront investment than "business as usual" in services like addiction/abuse treatment, mental health treatment, housing assistance, case management, and drug tests, among others, the research clearly demonstrates substantial longer-term cost savings through reduced involvement in the justice system. The estimates range from $2.21 in direct justice system benefits for every $1 invested in drug courts. When targeting more serious, high-risk offenders, the net benefit is $3.36 for every $1 invested. Furthermore, there is evidence that the indirect, collateral savings to the broader community range between $3,000 and $13,000 per court participant.

The takeaway from the drug court research and evaluation literature is that drug courts are effective and cost-effective. I now turn to a discussion of the key components of drug courts. The Multi-Site Adult Drug Court Evaluation (MADCE) (Rossman et al. 2011a and b) provides a detailed look of not only the effectiveness and cost-effectiveness of drug courts, but it also demonstrates which drug court components are more important in producing positive outcomes.

The *judge* is *critical* for outcome success. The role of the judge in a problem-solving court and in particular in a drug court is pivotal in enhancing the perception of fairness, respect, and a genuine interest in clients' well-being. Participants who have a more positive attitude toward the judge have better outcomes (Rossman et al. 2011a and b). This finding holds regardless of participant demographics and socioeconomic status (SES). Additional research on drug court judges found that judges who are perceived to be fair, respectful, attentive, consistent, enthusiastic, caring, and knowledgeable presided over courts with better outcomes, compared to drug courts in which the judge was not so perceived. Careful selection of the judge is critical to the success of the program.

Judicial status hearings are an essential component of drug court operation (Carey, Finigan, and Pukstas 2008; Festinger et al. 2002; Marlowe, Festinger, and Lee 2004a, 2004b; Marlowe et al. 2006, 2007). One of the primary beneficial components of frequent judicial hearing is that it increases the interaction between participants and the judge (clearly this is beneficial if the judge is perceived as fair, respectful, and interested in participants' well-being). The frequency of such status hearings is phase dependent and specific to individuals' progress and maintenance of sobriety.

Consistent point of entry into the court is important for therapeutic success. While the MADCE results indicate that the desistence effects of drug court participation did not vary by offender type, there is evidence that courts that limit admission to either preadjudication or postadjudication (but not both) had better outcomes. Whatever the reason, the MADCE results indicate that courts that permit multiple points of entry should consider limiting entry to individuals at the same point in judicial processing.

Progressive sanctions and incentives play a key role in motivating positive behavioral change (Farole and Cissner 2007; Goldcamp et al. 2002;

Hawken and Kleiman 2009; Lindquist, Krebs, and Lattimore 2006). *Predictable* imposition of gradually escalating sanctions, including short intervals of jail incarceration, have been shown to significantly enhance outcomes as long as the sanctions are perceived to be sufficiently severe by participants. Judicial praise is a very important incentive.

Drug testing is also essential in holding participants accountable and keeping them motivated. Frequency of UA testing is phase- and progress-dependent (Carey, Finigan, and Pukstas 2008). Drug testing is more effective if it is truly random.

Not all *substance abuse treatment* programs are designed and operated the same. The research clearly indicates that evidence-based treatment programs provide better outcomes. Evidence-based treatment programs are characterized by being highly structured and clearly documented, applying behavioral-cognitive interventions, being tailored to individual needs including length of treatment, and being culturally sensitive. The MADCE research indicates that treatment dosage between thirty-five and sixty-five days is optimal (referring to inpatient and outpatient treatment and counseling). The point is that the treatment plan must be tailored to the needs of the individual participant in terms of type of treatment and dosage.

Case management is an important component for reducing recidivism. The MADCE findings show that frequency of contact with a case manager is an important predictor of reduced relapse and reduced reoffending.

A *multidisciplinary team approach*, which includes cooperation and collaboration by the judge, the prosecutor, defense counsel, treatment providers, law enforcement, court clinicians, and case managers, is essential. Evidence indicates that if any of these professional disciplines is regularly absent from court staffing and judicial status hearings, the effectiveness of the court is dramatically reduced (Carey, Finigan, and Pukstas 2008; Carey et al. 2011).

Many jurisdictions have implemented drug diversion courts over the past twenty or so years. However, one thing that is safe to conclude that most share in common is that their capacity is well below need or demand. Estimates vary, but the consensus is that less than 5 percent of the potentially eligible defendant population ever participates in drug diversion court (Bhati and Roman 2010; Pollack, Reuter, and Sevigny 2011). The message is clear that in most jurisdictions, diversion through specialized courts is the exception, not the rule, in terms of numbers of offenders.

There are two primary reasons for the limited caseloads in drug courts: restricted eligibility criteria and limited capacity. As Pollack, Reuter, and Sevigny (2011) note, the limited capacity of current drug courts and their restrictive eligibility criteria, focusing on relatively low-risk offenders, render drug courts as currently configured and operated unable to significantly impact crime rates and prison populations.

The scientific evidence clearly indicates that drug diversion courts work for a wide variety of offenders, that they significantly reduce relapse and recidivism, and that they are cost-effective. It is time to consider the possibility of a substantial expansion of eligibility criteria and a dramatic scaling up of capacity.

There were over 2,450 drug and alcohol courts in the United States in 2009 (this includes drug courts, DWI courts, juvenile and family drug courts, tribal, federal, and veteran drug courts [Huddleston and Marlowe 2011]). Roughly 1,400 of these are adult drug courts in the United States. A recent drug court survey (Rossman et al. 2011a) indicates that most courts have relatively small numbers of participants. Forty-six percent have fewer than fifty participants; two-thirds of the drug courts in the United States have fewer than seventy-five participants. Case flow statistics show an average of eighty-nine new admissions annually (median of forty-one), and an average of forty-two program graduates (median of seventeen). Slightly over one-half of the courts in the survey reported that there are more individuals eligible to participate than there is available capacity.

Eligibility criteria for the vast majority of the courts (96 percent) limit participation based on criminal history. Nearly all courts limit entry to individuals with no prior violent convictions. Interestingly, most courts do not exclude defendants based on the number of prior convictions. Eligibility is also based on the nature of substance use. Slightly over one-third (38 percent) of the courts require that participants be diagnosed as addicted or dependent. Another third require that participants are frequent or regular users, as well as diagnosed as addicted. Surprisingly, 29 percent admit anyone who used illegal drugs, regardless of whether they are diagnosed as addicted or dependent.

The vast majority of drug courts have exclusion criteria in addition to the instant offense and violent priors. The most typical is a refusal by a defendant to participate (86 percent of courts), a suspicion a defendant is a major drug trafficker (79 percent), a defendant is a sex offender (72 percent), the presence of a co-occurring mental disorder (70 percent), and prosecutor discretion (57 percent).

Ironically, many drug courts are designed to exclude longer-term cocaine, heroin, and methamphetamine users. Research indicates (Hser et al. 2001; Hser 2007; Hser et al. 2007) that longer-term cocaine and heroin users tend to have extensive criminal histories for violent crimes and tend to have co-occurring disorders. It is these higher-risk offenders for whom the drug court impact is more substantial. Moreover, targeting high risk is one of the principles of effective correctional intervention discussed in chapter 3.

The MADCE research results lead to several significant recommendations for drug court policy and procedure. One of the most important involves the eligibility criteria for participants (Rossman et al. 2011a: 260):

> A pressing question for the drug court field has been "for whom drug courts work." A critically important finding emerging from the MADCE study is that drug courts work equally well in reducing crime and drug use for nearly all client subgroup populations, and the mechanism through which these reductions result—positive attitudes towards the judge—is the same across subgroups, even when accounting for client demographics, drug use and criminal histories, and mental health. One positive exception to this is that for offenders with violent criminal histories, drug court had a greater positive impact on reducing crime.

The MADCE researchers thus recommend expanding drug court eligibility criteria in order to include a greater variety of criminal histories, drugs of choice, and particular mental health problems. Moreover, the research findings indicate that violent offenders perform equally well in drug courts in terms of relapse reduction and are helped even more than typical drug court participants in terms of crime reduction. The MADCE research found no evidence to support the practice of "creaming," which is limiting admission to low-risk offenders for whom the probability of success is perceived to be high. This practice is directly contrary to the risk principle.

Recent research by Bhati and Roman (2010) provides estimates of the benefits of taking drug courts up to scale by changing eligibility criteria and expanding capacity. Bhati and Roman present national estimates of the number of participants admitted and the number of crimes averted under

different scenarios, including expanding capacity to treat all currently eligible offenders and expansion of eligibility criteria by relaxing instant offense
restrictions (including the violence restriction). Under current eligibility criteria and capacity limitations, Bhati and Roman estimate that drug
courts avert approximately 34 million drug crimes and 170,000 nondrug
crimes. By expanding capacity to admit all currently eligible offenders, they
estimate that drug courts would avert 65 million drug crimes and 342,000
nondrug crimes.

Clearly, these benefits to expansion of drug court caseloads are
impressive. But what is missing from the analyses is the cost side, as well
as more refined assumptions about treatment effects, retention, and so
on. However, the simulations produced by Bhati and Roman indicate
that there is good reason to seriously consider a substantial expansion of
drug court capacity and substantial modification to eligibility criteria.
The research clearly demonstrates that drug courts are equally effective
with higher-risk offenders and that the benefits are greater than with
low-risk offenders.

A related concept is diversion to probation without verdict (also known
as deferred adjudication or deferred prosecution). This type of diversion
is designed to place drug offenders in community-based treatment while
under probation supervision. The leverage is that such dispositions typically require a plea of guilty or nolo contendere, which means that if a
participant fails to meet the conditions imposed, they can be immediately
sentenced. If they succeed, the plea is vacated and the individual may also
be able to expunge the arrest. California expanded probation without verdict for drug offenders in 2000 (Proposition 36), allowing this disposition
for a large segment of the drug offender population. Research shows that
the outcomes of this diversion are mixed. The lower-risk segment of the
population of drug offenders (those with relatively limited criminal backgrounds) perform relatively well and benefit from treatment. Higher-risk
offenders had lower treatment compliance and higher rearrest rates. One
takeaway from this research is to improve the identification of candidates
for probation without verdict. Another consideration, discussed in greater
detail in subsequent chapters, is a supervision and sanction protocol (the
HOPE Court model) that emphasizes swift and certain sanctioning for
noncompliance but not revocation, unless there are clear and compelling
reasons for incarceration.

GETTING SERIOUS ABOUT MENTAL HEALTH DIVERSION

On December 13, 2012, a lone gunman entered Sandy Hook Elementary School in Newtown, Connecticut, and summarily murdered twenty children and eight adults. Two primary findings quickly emerged: he used an assault rifle, among other weapons, and there was evidence that he was mentally ill. All too often, the combination of dangerous weapons and mental illness produce horrific results.

The issue of gun control has been debated for decades. In 1994, the federal government banned some types of assault weapons. The federal law prohibited the manufacturing of eighteen specific models of semiautomatic weapons, along with the manufacturing of high-capacity ammunition magazines that could carry more than ten rounds. The ban was allowed to expire during the Bush administration. The current response from the gun lobby is that the problem is not assault weapons, but mental illness. Wayne LaPierre, the executive vice president of the National Rifle Association (NRA), stated just days after the Newtown shooting that "We have a mental health system in this country that has completely and totally collapsed." It is interesting that this situation has resulted in the NRA serving as an advocate for mental health treatment.

One of the most troubling trends in the U.S. criminal justice is the phenomenal growth in the prevalence of mentally ill individuals in the justice system. This trend closely follows the trends in crime control policies, sentencing reform, and the incarceration boom.

It is an often-recounted story. Public mental health treatment in the United States has a long history of "public neglect and penny pinching." That characterization from a 1946 *Life Magazine* exposé of the state of the psychiatric hospital system went on to describe widespread abuse and hazardous living conditions, including inadequate staffing, substandard treatment, inappropriate use of restraints, and providing little more than simple custodial care (National Leadership Forum on Behavioral Health/Criminal Justice Services 2009). The *Life Magazine* article concluded that state psychiatric hospitals were "costly monuments to the States' betrayal of the duty they have assumed to their most helpless wards."

The familiar story of deinstitutionalization involves the dismantling of the psychiatric hospital system in the United States and the "replacement" of that system with local, community-based treatment centers. Reasonable concept, but very poor execution. For the most part, the capacity for inpatient treatment lost with the dismantling of the old system was never replaced, leading to extraordinarily limited public inpatient treatment. The National Leadership Forum (2009) experts note that the failure to provide adequate capacity for inpatient mental health treatment and substantial restriction of eligibility and access to public behavioral health services, combined with changes in sentencing laws and procedures, and a focus on quality of life offenses, has led to approximately 300,000 to 400,000 mentally ill prison and jail inmates and 500,000 mentally ill individuals on community control (probation, parole, deferred adjudication, and other forms of diversion). There are two key factors that present significant barriers to accessing mental health care: lack of insurance or sufficient behavioral health coverage for those with insurance, and lack of adequate capacity for treatment.

The President's New Freedom Commission on Mental Health (2003) sent its final report to President George W. Bush. The Commission reported the following:

> Mental health delivery system is fragmented and in disarray . . . lead[ing] to unnecessary and costly disability, homelessness, school failure and incarceration. . . . In many communities, access to quality care is poor, resulting in wasted resources and lost opportunities for recovery. More individuals could recover from even the most serious mental illnesses if they had access in their communities to treatment and supports that are tailored to their needs.

The Congressional Research Service (CRS) (2009) reported the current state of access to mental health treatment in the United States in quite dismal terms. Despite substantial advances in the understanding and effective treatment of mental illness, access is extraordinarily limited. The CRS estimates that over 17 percent of the U.S. population lacks health insurance, and there is a substantial amount of underinsurance for mental health treatment for individuals who have health insurance. Limited access is also a function of lack of available treatment providers, especially in rural areas. In 2008, two-thirds of the Health Professional Shortage Areas (HPSAs) were in rural areas. All told, there were over 3,000 HSPAs in the United States in 2008, potentially affecting 77 million individuals living in those areas.

The Substance Abuse and Mental Health Services Administration (SAMHSA), through the National Survey on Drug Use and Health, reports that only 13.4 percent of the U.S. population received any mental health services in 2008. This is well below the estimated 26 percent of the U.S. population who experience mental illness in a given year. Moreover, in a recent study, while 3 million individuals in the United States aged twelve and over received treatment for a substance abuse disorder, 18 million reported abusing or being dependent on alcohol, illicit drugs, or prescription drugs. Kessler and colleagues (2005) report that only 41 percent of adults aged between eighteen and fifty-four who met a definition of serious mental illness received *any* treatment for that problem (saying nothing about the quality, duration, or effectiveness of that treatment). Data from a survey conducted by the National Alliance for Mental Illness (NAMI 2005) shows significant variation by state in terms of public funding for mental health treatment. On average, NAMI reports that state mental health agencies are funded to serve just 28 percent of individuals with serious mental illness, from a low of 15 percent in Vermont to a high of 55 percent in New York.

One of the more significant consequences of the shift in the treatment model is the critical lack of nonforensic inpatient treatment beds for longer-term, structured care for the seriously mentally ill. In 1955, there were 339 psychiatric inpatient treatment beds per 100,000 Americans. In 2014, there are just 22. And many of those beds are filled with court-ordered forensic and competency cases. The availability of treatment beds varies significantly by state. For example, in California, there are just 2 nonforensic inpatient treatment beds per 100,000 people (Lamb and Weinberger 2005). Recent research recommends 50 per 100,000.

Recent statistics for Texas reflect the situation in a state with serious limitations on access to public mental health care (NAMI 2009). In 2010, only 33 percent of the estimated number of Texas adults with a serious, persistent mental illness received *any* services or treatment from the public mental health system. Only 29 percent of Texas children with a severe emotional disturbance received *any* services or treatment. While there are many reasons for these deficits, one of the primary ones is lack of adequate capacity to treat individuals with mental illness. It is not at all unusual in Texas for the public mental health treatment facilities to have extensive waiting lists and delays of months to get an appointment.

Another issue involves the quality of mental health care when it is provided. Significant departures from evidence-based treatment practices have been repeatedly reported in a variety of studies (cited in Board of Health

Care Services 2006). In a landmark study of the quality of mental health care for a limited number of conditions in the United States, McGlynn and colleagues (2003) found that individuals diagnosed with depression received evidence-based treatment 58 percent of the time. Individuals diagnosed with alcohol dependence received evidence-based care 11 percent of the time.

Anecdotal evidence reported by Board of Health Care Services (2006: 6) may not necessarily be generalizable, but nevertheless is particularly troubling:

> Poor care has serious consequences for the people seeking treatment, especially the most severely ill. One review of the charts of 31 randomly selected patients in a state psychiatric hospital detected 2,194 medication errors during the patients' collective 1,448 inpatient days. Of those errors, 58 percent were judged to have the potential to cause severe harm (Grasso et al. 2003). The use of seclusion and restraints in inpatient mental health facilities is estimated to cause 150 deaths in the United States each year (SAMHSA 2004b). Moreover, a continuing failure of the health care system in some cases to provide any treatment for M/SU illness has been documented (Kessler et al. 2005), even when people are receiving other types of health care and have financial and geographic access to treatment (Jaycox et al. 2003; SAMHSA 2004a; Watkins et al. 2001). Diagnostic failures and failures to treat can be lethal; M/SU illnesses are leading risk factors for suicide (Maris 2002).

Thus, it comes as no surprise that the criminal justice system has become the system that cannot say no. To that point, 40 percent of individuals with mental illness have been or will be in prison and/or jail at some point in their lives. This is not to imply that mental illness causes crime. Instead, mental illness is a correlate or criminogenic risk factor. Untreated mental illness can produce symptoms that are fear invoking, threatening, disorderly, and sometimes violent. In many of these situations, it is the justice system that responds.

In addition, a recent study in the Los Angeles County jail found that 75 percent of individuals with severe mental illness (defined in this study as schizophrenia, schizoaffective disorder, bipolar disorder, and major depressive disorder with psychotic features) had at least one prior arrest for a violent offense (Lamb et al. 2007). The Bureau of Justice Statistics (BJS) estimates that in 2005, over half of the inmates in U.S. prisons and jails had a mental health problem (Bureau of Justice Statistics 2006). The 2005 estimates are the most recent that have been published by BJS. The definition of mental illness used for this study was a clinical diagnosis or treatment by a mental health professional and/or exhibition of symptoms within the past twelve months. Symptoms of a mental health disorder were based on the Diagnostic and Statistical Manual of Mental Disorders, fourth edition (DSM-IV). Granted, this is a liberal definition of mental illness (MI) and there is tremendous variation in severity, need for treatment, and type of treatment. Nevertheless, the prevalence of MI in state prisons was estimated at 56 percent; for federal prisons it was 45 percent, and for local jails it was 64 percent. While definitions and measurements of mental illness differ from study to study, it cannot be denied that the prevalence of MI in the nation's prisons and jails is two to three times the prevalence in the general population. Today, there are over three times as many seriously mentally ill persons in prisons and jails than in inpatient psychiatric treatment hospitals (Torrey et al. 2010).

Serious mental illness (SMI) is usually defined as schizophrenia, bipolar disorder, and major depression. Research shows that the prevalence of SMI in U.S. prisons and jails is two to three times that of the general public. Estimates show that approximately 16 percent of state prison inmates suffer from SMI, up from 6.4 percent in 1983. Steadman and colleagues (2009) estimate that nearly 15 percent of male jail inmates and 31 percent of female jail inmates have a current serious mental illness. When PTSD is included (as is recommended under the trauma-informed care protocol), the estimates rise to 17 percent for males and 34 percent for females.

Co-morbidity (the presence of more than one mental health problem) is common. The BJS research referenced above reports that 42 percent of state prison inmates were found to have both a mental health problem and a substance abuse problem. The BJS data indicate that 49 percent of jail inmates have a co-occurring mental health problem and a substance abuse problem. Co-morbidity also takes the form of multiple, nonsubstance-involved psychiatric diagnoses.

Research has demonstrated that mentally ill individuals who also abuse drugs and alcohol have a higher likelihood of ending up in the justice system on drug charges and intoxication charges (Lurigio 2004, 2011; Swartz and Lurigio 1999). Moreover, mentally ill individuals who use illicit drugs are more likely to be violent, and are again at higher risk of arrest and prosecution for that reason compared to mentally ill persons who do not abuse illicit drugs (Clear, Byrne, and Dvoskin 1993; Harris and Lurigio 2007; Swanson et al. 1997; Swartz et al. 1998). This accounts in part for the presence of seriously mentally ill individuals in prison. As Lurigio (2011) and Lurigio and Swartz (2000) indicate, the absence of treatment for co-morbid disorders and, when it does exist, the fragmentation of the mental health and substance abuse treatment systems, further aggravates the problem and serves to heighten the likelihood of criminal justice intervention rather than treatment intervention.

It is also well established that significant numbers of individuals with SMI share many of the other criminogenic circumstances as the rest of the criminally involved who are not seriously mentally ill—unemployment, poverty, lack of education, and substance use (Lurigio 2011; Fisher, Silver, and Wolf 2006). Moreover, there is a strong link between mental illness and homelessness. Is has been estimated that approximately one-third of the nation's homeless suffer from schizophrenia or bipolar disorder. At any moment, there are more mentally ill persons living on the streets than are receiving care in hospitals (Mental Illness Policy Organization).

Neurocognitive impairments and deficits are common among individuals with substance abuse problems, mental health problems, the homeless, individuals living in poverty, and individuals exposed to trauma, abuse, and neglect. Failure to screen and assess neurocognitive problems dramatically reduces the likelihood of successful outcomes.

No matter how it is measured, mentally ill individuals are substantially overrepresented in prisons and jails. Thus the label "the asylum of last resort." Unfortunately, everything we know about mental health treatment and incarceration clearly indicates that prisons and jails are not appropriate venues for mental health treatment, even if (and this is decidedly not the case) sufficient treatment resources were available to inmates.

A well-researched report on the state of mental health treatment in U.S. prisons (Human Rights Watch 2003: 3–4) paints a fairly bleak picture:

> Mentally ill offenders face mistreatment and neglect in many U.S. prisons. One in six U.S. prisoners is mentally ill. Many of them suffer from serious illnesses such as schizophrenia, bipolar disorder, and major depression. There are three times as many men and women with mental illness in U.S. prisons as in mental health hospitals. The rate of mental illness in the prison

population is three times higher than in the general population. Other prisoners victimize and exploit them. Prison staff often punish mentally ill offenders for symptoms of their illness, such as being noisy or refusing orders, or even self-mutilation and attempted suicide. Mentally ill prisoners are more likely than others to end up housed in especially harsh conditions, such as isolation, that can push them over the edge into acute psychosis. Woefully deficient mental health services in many prisons leave prisoners undertreated, or not treated at all. Across the country, prisoners cannot get appropriate care because of a shortage of qualified staff, lack of facilities, and prison rules that interfere with treatment.

The National Leadership Forum on Behavioral Health/Criminal Justice Services (2009: 3) reported an overview from studies of mental health treatment and services in incarceration settings. The irony is telling: "Equally reminiscent of the past, among the more pervasive findings from these investigations are severely inadequate staffing, substandard treatment, inappropriate use of restraints and provision of little more than custodial care."

A more balanced and effective approach to dealing with mentally ill individuals coming into contact with the justice system is a more concentrated focus on diversion. Clearly, some mentally ill offenders should be adjudicated and sentenced in criminal courts. Mental illness should not be an excuse for criminal behavior. However, mental illness is often a mitigating circumstance that should be considered from the very first point of contact with the justice system. I now turn the discussion to diversion.

It is important to get our expectations clear. Treating mental illness alone may have no direct impact on recidivism (Lurigio 2011). Serious mental illness does not often in itself lead individuals to engage in crime. However, there is every reason to believe and expect that there are indirect effects of treating mental illness on recidivism and crime. As I discussed previously, mental illness is related to a variety of criminogenic factors, situations, and deficits for which there is clear scientific evidence indicating that they facilitate or cause crime. Poverty is a key component of crime and mental illness; thus, a mentally ill individual may engage in crime more because of poverty than mental illness (Fischer, Silver and Wolf 2006; GAINS Center 2010; Lurigio 2011).

Research has demonstrated that high-risk scores for the "central eight" risk factors (Andrews, Bonta, and Wormith 2006) are often present for individuals with mental illness. The "central eight" include: criminal history, antisocial personality disorder, antisocial cognition, antisocial peers, family/marital discord, poor school/work performance, few leisure activities, and substance abuse. Thus, what may appear as criminal offending as a consequence of MI in reality is a consequence of associated criminogenic circumstances. As Lurigio (2011: 17) concludes:

> Treating mental illness could have an indirect effect on recidivism. In other words, relieving symptoms could help PSMI [persons with serious mental illness] become sober and employed, find and retain stable housing, develop better self-control, return to school, mend relationships with family, and follow the designated rules of supervision, thereby avoiding probation and parole violations. Further, relieving the symptoms of major mental illness can make PSMI more amenable to interventions that will have a positive effect on crime, such as cognitive behavioral therapy that can change criminal thinking (Bonta et al. 1998).

On the other hand, there are instances in which mental illness is the crime, cases of what has been labeled criminalization of mental illness. In those instances, appropriate treatment of MI will likely have a direct impact on reducing contacts with the justice system.

The primary policy argument in favor of diversion and treatment is not necessarily that there is a direct effect of mental illness on crime, and thus, when the mental illness is treated, we can expect a reduction in recidivism as a direct result of that treatment. It is more complex than that. But the evidence indicates that treating mental illness is a necessary step toward reducing recidivism.

Jail diversion for individuals with serious mental illness and/or co-occurring disorders who have contact with the criminal justice system redirects or diverts selected individuals from jail to community-based treatment resources. The initial impact is avoidance of or dramatic reduction in jail time.

Jail diversion involves two broad processes, depending on when and how the diversion works. First, diversion requires the identification of appropriate candidates and redirection from criminal justice processing to treatment. Second, diversion requires appropriate community-based mental health, substance abuse, housing, employment, and other services.

Prebooking Diversion

The usual first point of contact that a mentally ill person has with the justice system is law enforcement, typically local police or sheriff. The authority to intervene in a psychiatric emergency derives from the power the law provides the police to transport an individual for psychiatric evaluation and treatment if there is probable cause to believe the individual is at risk of harming themselves or others. On the other hand, if an individual has engaged in a criminal act, law enforcement has the responsibility to determine if psychiatric intervention is required or if the criminal act is the primary concern. As such, law enforcement serves as the gatekeeper for who enters the criminal justice system and, in that context, who enters the mental health system. That is a very important responsibility as it determines not only the short-term disposition of the situation, but such decisions can determine the longer-term trajectory of mentally ill individuals in terms of continually cycling in and out of the justice system, potentially interrupting that cycle, or preventing it from starting in the first place.

The responsibility of law enforcement to serve as the front line in mental health cases poses a significant challenge in terms of use of resources. Law enforcement contacts with mentally ill individuals (Reuland, Schwarzfeld, and Draper 2009) typically involve three things: subjects engaged in low-level misdemeanor crimes; repeated contacts with a small subset of individuals; and significantly more officer time, depending on disposition (the most time-consuming event is transport to an emergency psychiatric facility and then waiting to be seen).

One of the more significant challenges to law enforcement's mental health triage role is lack of training in dealing with mentally ill individuals. Many observers believe that law enforcement decisions to more readily opt for the criminal justice path when dealing with the mentally ill has led to the increasing criminalization of mental illness (Lamb, Weinberger, and DeCuir 2002). In some situations, a police officer may not recognize that the behavior exhibited by a mentally ill individual is a symptom of mental illness. For example, mental illness may be mistaken for intoxication. Or, in the confusion of subduing an individual, the symptoms go unnoticed. Research has shown that in encounters in which the individual is violent, the likelihood of being arrested is heightened. There may also be an inclination to arrest and book a mentally ill person, especially for a misdemeanor, if it is perceived that there are no other viable alternatives at the moment and that the individual will be assessed and treated in jail. In many jurisdictions, the perception of lack of viable alternatives is quite realistic. Even where there are public mental health treatment services available, the wait to obtain services may render that option untenable. Whatever the reason, one result of taking the criminal justice path is the criminalization of mental illness. Once a mentally ill person enters the justice system, it becomes more likely that he or she will go down that same path the next time and the next time and the next time. However, some have cautioned against overstating the extent and effects of criminalization of mental illness (Junginger et al. 2006).

Many communities have developed strategies to more effectively address encounters with mentally ill individuals. Mobile crisis teams, also known as crisis intervention teams (CITs), mental health units, or mental health response teams generally operate under similar principles (Lamb, Weinberger, and DeCuir 2002; Lamb, Weinberger, and Gross 2004; Steadman et al. 2001). These typically take the form of specially trained police officers that respond to mental health situations. Other prebooking diversion programs have formal liaisons between the police and mental health professionals (referred to as police-based specialized mental health response). Some use mental health consultants to provide expertise in the field when requested by police.

The estimates vary, but a recent survey indicates that there are over 1,000 communities in the United States that have some form of law enforcement, mental health crisis intervention strategy (Reuland, Schwarzfeld, and Draper 2009). Successful prebooking programs have specialized training for police officers, and triage/treatment facilities available twenty-four hours per day with a no refusal policy for individuals who are brought by the police.

These prebooking intervention teams have been found to increase resolution of mental health situations at the scene, increase transport to emergency psychiatric facilities, increase acceptance rates at hospitals, reduce subsequent contacts with police for those referred to mental health treatment, decrease arrests and increase diversion from the criminal justice system, reduce the number of injuries to officers, and reduce certain law enforcement costs associated with things like SWAT callouts. In short, these strategies have helped decrease criminal prosecution of individuals with mental illness, although how much is yet to be determined (Deane et al. 1999; Dupont and Cochran 2000; Lamb et al. 1995; Lamb, Weinberger, and Gross 2004; Lamb, Weinberger, and DeCuir 2002; Reuland, Schwarzfeld, and Draper 2009; Steadman et al. 2000; Wolff 1998).

As the responsibility for dealing with increasing numbers of mentally ill individuals falls on police, it is important that all police, not just members of the mobile crisis teams or CITs, are better trained on a variety of matters relevant for dealing with mentally ill individuals. Research demonstrates that not only is law enforcement not sufficiently trained on such matters, it shows a desire on the part of police to receive such training (Bean 1999; Borum 2000; Lamb, Weinberger, and Decuir 2002; Steadman et al. 2000). Police officers want to learn how to recognize mental illness, how to handle violent and psychotic behavior, how to intervene when someone is threatening suicide, and when to call the mobile crisis unit (Bean 1999; Borum 2000; Lamb, Weinberger, and DeCuir 2002). At a minimum, police training should focus on familiarity with the general classification of mental disorders, learning how to manage individuals with mental illness in crisis, how to access resources in the community, understanding the laws governing mentally ill individuals, as well as de-escalation strategies for situations that could lead to the use of lethal force (Borum 2000; Lamb, Weinberger, and DeCuir 2002).

Postbooking Jail Diversion

Postbooking jail diversion programs divert individuals after arrest or booking into jail. There are two major forms of postbooking diversion: those that divert individuals at the arraignment court to treatment, and those that divert out of specialty courts or regular trial courts to treatment. One thing both types have in common is some form of monitoring of compliance with treatment (CMHS National GAINS Center 2007).

Jail-based postbooking diversion programs are typically operated by pretrial services or specially trained jail staff. The idea is to identify (screen and assess) appropriate candidates, negotiate an arrangement with the prosecutor, judge, and defense counsel for referral to community-based treatment, and link these individuals to the appropriate services (Lattimore et al. 2003).

Court-based postbooking diversion can occur in criminal courts in which diversion staff work in several courts, or diversion may occur in a specialty court. Trial courts that rely on deferred adjudication or conditional release are able to include a broad array of mentally ill defendants, including those with more serious charges and criminal histories that involve some violent behavior (Bush 2002).

Research on jail diversion has produced a short list of the key elements for successful diversion programs (CMHS National GAINS Center 2007):

1. Interagency collaboration, including agencies providing mental health and substance abuse treatment (inpatient and outpatient), physical health, housing, education, veterans services, Medicaid, workforce development, local corrections, and other social services agencies; collaboration assumes formal agreements among agencies when/where required or necessary; there is of course an assumption of an appropriate level of capacity and access.

2. Strong, effective leadership in order to bring the various agencies together and maintain active, collaborative relationships.

3. Big picture staff whose experience and expertise cross traditional boundaries of health, mental health, criminal justice, and substance abuse services.

4. Early screening and assessment for mental health needs and determination of whether detainees meet eligibility criteria for diversion.

5. Specialized, intensive case management; one of the most important components of successful diversion is the direct, active involvement of specialized case management that is sufficiently flexible to provide the level of intensity required by each client; case managers should adopt problem-solving strategies and should be familiar and experienced in various substantive areas, including criminal justice, mental health, substance abuse, housing, health, Medicaid and veterans benefits, among others; issues as routine as transportation are critical for successful diversion.

Bexar County, Texas, the county in which San Antonio is located, has one of the older and demonstrably effective and cost-efficient jail diversion programs in the nation. An obvious necessity for a jail diversion program is somewhere to divert individuals. Bexar County initially focused on mentally ill individuals and developed a venue designed for crisis stabilization. Relatively quickly, officials there recognized a bigger need:

"Initially, the focus of our jail diversion efforts was in the area of the mentally ill," explains Gilbert Gonzales, Diversion Program Director. "But we soon found that the real question—the real problem for police—is, 'What is the most appropriate place for this detainee, based on the seriousness of the offense?'" Because hundreds of detainees per month were mentally ill, public intoxicants, or homeless, the cycle of arrest, incarceration, and medical care posed a huge drain on police, hospital, magistrate, and jail resources. (Grantham 2011)

Local officials collaborated with local behavioral health providers, law enforcement, and a variety of community organizations to develop, fund, and resource the Crisis Care Center. The Crisis Care Center is designed to address and provide treatment for mental health, physical health, and substance abuse problems. It is staffed by medical, psychiatric, and social work professionals, and has capacity for sobering, detox, medical attention, and mental health assessment and intervention, as well as transfer to long-term residential treatment for mental illness and substance abuse. This effort has saved Bexar County and the city of San Antonio over $15 million in a two-year period, put more police on the street (rather than the business as usual approach of requiring officers to book individuals in jail or transport individuals to the ER or a state mental health facility). This program has saved money, reduced recidivism, and freed up jail capacity and law enforcement time.

Mental Health Courts

A recent count indicates that there are over 300 mental health courts in the United States (Justice Center, Council on State Governments 2011). Mental health courts were developed in response to the dramatic increase in the prevalence of mental illness in prisons and jails, the inability of the correctional system to effectively and cost-effectively respond to offenders with mental illness, and the extraordinary costs of housing inmates with mental illness.

Mental health courts have been somewhat loosely modeled after drug courts, with the exception that while drug possession is a criminal offense, being mentally ill is not. Therapeutic jurisprudence is still the basis for mental health courts, but in reality, as Steadman and colleagues (2001) note, they operate rather idiosyncratically, with no single, definitive model. Accordingly, there does not appear to be consensus regarding the definition of a mental health court (Christy et al. 2005).

Mental health courts can have a separate docket for selected offenders with mental health problems, they can have a mixed docket with expertise in the courtroom to address mental health cases, or they can be stand-alone courts with a dedicated judge and court staff. The courts determine the appropriate criminal and mental health criteria for eligibility for referral to the court. Some courts limit participation to misdemeanants and individuals with criminal histories of low-level offending; however, in recent years, courts are increasingly admitting more serious felony offenders. Courts that admit offenders with more serious charges often require that they enter a plea and be supervised by criminal justice personnel. These courts are also more likely to use jail time as a method to leverage compliance (CMHS National GAINS Center 2007).

The majority of participants in mental health courts suffer from significant mental illness, including schizophrenia, schizoaffective disorders, bipolar disorder, serious depression, and anxiety disorders. Moreover, approximately 75 percent of mentally ill individuals who have criminal justice involvement also have a co-occurring substance abuse disorder. Thus, one significant challenge for mental health courts is addressing mental illness and substance abuse in a comprehensive and integrated manner.

While there is no consistent model, it appears that most mental health courts share several elements in common (Council on State Governments Justice Center, Criminal Justice/Mental Health Consensus Project 2007, vii). First is a specialized court docket, which employs a problem-solving approach to court processing. Second are judicially supervised, community-based treatment plans for each defendant participating in the court, which a team of court staff and mental health professionals design and implement. Third are regular status hearings at which treatment plans and other conditions are periodically reviewed for appropriateness, incentives are offered to reward adherence to court conditions, and sanctions are imposed on participants who do not adhere to the conditions of participation. Fourth are criteria defining a participant's completion of the program.

Other essential elements identified by the Consensus Project and others (for example, Mental Health America; NAMI 2008; Ryan et al. 2010) include screening, assessing, qualifying, and admitting to the court as quickly as possible, individual treatment plans developed by clinical staff, timely linkage of clients to evidence-based community treatment resources, monitoring progress, rewarding success and sanctioning noncompliance, and case management, including intensive case management when needed.

The most recent round of evaluation research (CMHS National GAINS Center 2010; Ryan et al. 2010; Sarteschi et al. 2011; Steadman et al. 2010) shows a variety of significant positive outcomes from jail diversion programs. The major findings indicate the clearest impacts on drug and alcohol use, daily functioning, reduced psychiatric symptoms, recidivism, jail days, and timely linkage to social and clinical services. Specifically, short-term (six- and twelve-month) declines in drug and alcohol use as well as use to intoxication were evident for the diverted samples with co-morbidity. Daily functioning, independent living, well-being, and symptom reduction improved for those diverted. Public safety benefits include significant reduction in rearrests for both misdemeanants and felons, as well as reductions in days of detention in jail. On balance, the data demonstrate improved mental health outcomes, enhanced functioning and mitigation of symptoms, reduced rearrests, lower charges for those rearrested, and fewer days in jail (CMHS National GAINS Center 2010).

Mental health courts have been evaluated a fair amount in recent years, although nothing like drug court evaluations. A multisite study reported by Steadman and colleagues (2010) indicates that mental health courts produce measurable public safety benefits, including reduced arrests and reduced days of incarceration. A meta-analysis by Sarteschi et al. (2011) indicates that mental health courts are effective at linking individual participants with local, community-based mental health treatment services compared to individuals in traditional criminal court and traditional jail systems. Sarteschi et al. also report reductions in rearrests and reconvictions for mental health court participants compared to treatment as usual, as well as increased time to rearrest for those who did experience a subsequent arrest.

Sarteschi et al. conclude that the meta-analytic effect size for mental health courts render them "moderately effective" for reducing recidivism. Moreover, they report that mental health courts appear to improve general functioning and reduce psychiatric emergency room visits. Finally, the data indicate that the clinical and justice outcomes are consistently better for those who finish or graduate from mental health court compared to those who drop out or are involuntarily terminated (see also Cosden et al. 2005; Dirks-Linhorst and Linhorst 2012; Herinckx et al. 2005; Hiday and Ray 2010; McNiel and Binder 2007; Moore and Hiday 2006). Some limited research indicates that mental health courts may be cost-effective (Almquist and Dodd 2009; Boothroyd et al. 2003; Council of State Governments Justice Center 2008; Kaplan 2007).

Criminal justice system benefits of mental health courts include quicker disposition of cases compared to traditional criminal adjudication, enhanced communication and collaboration between criminal justice and mental health agencies, and successful targeting of appropriately diagnosed mentally ill offenders (Council of State Governments Justice Center 2008).

There is a pivotal role in mental health diversion for the prosecutor. Referral to a mental health court will often originate in the prosecutor's office, as will other forms of postbooking jail diversion. This requires that prosecutors are familiar with therapeutic jurisprudence, evidence-based interventions, and the longer-term effectiveness and cost- effectiveness of treatment/intervention. In some cases, this will require a cultural shift as some prosecutors move away from a nearly universal reliance on punishment.

LOW-LEVEL MISDEMEANOR DIVERSION:
COMMUNITY COURTS

Diversion programs have also been developed for individuals who are at the lowest end of crime severity. Public order or quality of life offenses have increasingly been the focus of attention in recent years. The argument is that where the physical environment is allowed to deteriorate and public order crime is tolerated and flourishes, land use and commerce can be negatively affected and more serious crimes will likely follow. This is the familiar "broken windows" theory of crime. Public order crimes often have profound economic impacts in terms of reducing land value and retail trade. Probably all large metropolitan areas in the United States deal with quality of life crimes and the revolving door of the municipal justice systems. Substantial portions of individuals who are often involved in petty offending (for example, loitering, aggressive panhandling, sleeping in public, public intoxication, disorderly conduct) are mentally ill, chronically homeless, unemployed, and addicted to or abusing drugs/alcohol.

The first community court was launched in midtown Manhattan in 1993 in response to the order maintenance initiatives that were underway in the subway system, Times Square, and other areas of midtown. It become readily apparent that relying on the municipal justice system for adjudicating and sanctioning petty offenders arrested in the order maintenance initiative was not productive. Behavior was not changed and the revolving door just continued to spin.

Community courts vary substantially in design and operation. However, typical components include screening and assessment, collaboration with local service providers, intervention/treatment, case management, individualized justice, community engagement, restorative justice/community service, and accountability. Typical goals of community courts, as articulated in a survey administered in 2008 (Karafin 2008) include: to help offenders with their problems, reduce crime and reoffending, address community needs, improve public perception of the court and the justice system, increase offender accountability, and renew a focus on quality of life crime. Today, there are sixty community courts in operation globally, thirty-three of which are in the United States (Henry and Kralstein 2011).

The concept underlying community courts is the same as other problem-solving courts: therapeutic jurisprudence. However, community justice has a dual focus of repairing the harm done to the community by low-level crimes and rehabilitating the offender in an effort to reduce recidivism and crime. The restorative focus typically involves community service. The recidivism and crime-reduction component involves both individualized intervention and treatment, as well as bringing the community together in developing strategies for reducing crime and witnessing the justice system at work.

One of the primary mechanisms for accomplishing the goals of assisting offenders with underlying problems and reducing crime and recidivism is an individualized focus, including extensive use of alternative sanctions, and referring/linking offenders to individually tailored community-based social services, such as mental health treatment, drug/alcohol treatment, job training, life skills, counseling, and permanent supportive housing, among others. The use of alternative sanctions and dispositions has a net impact of reducing jail time and providing services designed to address criminogenic circumstances and behavior change. Effective screening and assessment is essential, as is tiered case management for the lower-functioning segment of community court populations.

Community courts serve as the portal to social services for many individuals. Because the criminal involvement of the participants is relatively less serious, community courts have a bit more flexibility in terms of focusing more on treatment and services, and a bit less on risk management and public safety. As such, many seriously disadvantaged individuals can enter the social service network through community courts.

Because of the severity of some participants' condition and the length of time they have been mentally ill and homeless, they often present at community court with little interest in services. While the offenders who are the primary focus of these courts do not typically have extensive histories of serious crime, there are segments of this population that are very challenging and service resistant. Most metropolitan areas have a portion of the population that is chronically homeless, unemployed, mentally ill, physically unhealthy, and abusing drugs/alcohol, among other circumstances. For example, the Downtown Austin Community Court in Austin, Texas, is currently focusing a substantial amount of court and community rehabilitation resources on approximately 300 repeat offenders (twenty-five or more cases in the court). Many are chronically homeless: 50 percent have been identified as having mental health problems and over 90 percent have substance abuse or dependence problems. The challenge with this chronic population for community courts is that they lack much leverage to motivate participation. Another significant challenge is the lack of sufficient local social service resources. We have already discussed some of the problems associated with access to mental health services and substance abuse treatment. Those constraints are just as critical for community court participants.

The jury is still out in terms of the effectiveness of community courts. Few studies have been completed to date. As of 2011, nineteen evaluations, some outcome, some process, have been completed. The key finding from the process evaluations is that community courts have been able to successfully implement problem-solving strategies. Process evaluations also reported positive perceptions about the courts and about community safety. Community court impact studies have documented changes in sentencing practices, specifically reductions in jail sentences and time served, and increases in sentences of community service and referrals to social services. Some community courts also significantly reduce case processing time and have greater offender compliance with alternative sentences.

Community courts also appear to garner community support, including, in two instances, citizens' willingness to pay more in taxes to support community courts (Midtown Community Court, Hennepin County Community Justice Project, Minneapolis). Positive attitudes about community courts appear to spill over into enhanced perceptions about the justice system and community safety (The Red Hook Community Justice Center, Bronx, New York).

Evidence on crime and recidivism reduction is limited and the research that does focus on crime reduction and lower recidivism is mixed. The midtown court may play a part in reductions in arrests for prostitution and illegal vending, along with economic development and citywide quality of life initiatives (Henry and Kralstein 2011). Other studies focusing on recidivism either lack valid control groups or report statistically nonsignificant effects. While there is evidence of increased referrals and linkages to community social service resources (Henry and Kralstein 2011), little is known about clinical outcomes of participants.

ADDITIONAL CONSIDERATIONS

As I discussed previously, while drug courts have an impressive track record in terms of their presence across the country and in terms of recidivism reduction, our expectations about broader public safety impacts should be tempered due to limited scale. As of 2009, there were 3,650 problem-solving courts in the United States. With a few exceptions, these courts could have their capacity expanded significantly and maintain full caseloads (Huddleston and Marlowe 2011). A primary factor preventing expansion is lack of funding. Until evidence-based diversion courts are taken to appropriate scale, we shall see little *aggregate* impact on prison and jail diversion, recidivism and victimization reduction, and public safety.

Individuals with serious mental illness and/or substance abuse also typically exhibit many of the criminogenic circumstances and deficits as non-mentally ill offenders (Bonta, Law, and Hanson 1998; Skeem et al. 2008). Additionally, individuals participating in pre- and postbooking jail diversion, entering drug courts and community courts, and participating in other types of diversion programs typically exhibit multiple criminogenic circumstances or needs. Just addressing mental illness, just addressing substance abuse, or just addressing the primary criminogenic circumstance is likely to be inadequate in successfully reducing criminality, recidivism, and victimization in the longer term. Typically, the situation is more complex, involving multiple primary criminogenic needs and multiple secondary needs, including neurocognitive and neurodevelopmental deficits and impairments, all of which probably affect the likelihood of criminality. As discussed in chapter 3, the scientific evidence clearly demonstrates that effectively addressing appropriate multiple criminogenic needs substantially decreases the likelihood of reoffending (Carey 2011).

Supportive housing is a critical criminogenic need among the offender population (National Reentry Resource Center). Research indicates that other treatment outcomes are significantly enhanced for individuals who are housed versus those who are chronically homeless or periodically homeless (Buchholz et al. 2010; Burt and Anderson 2005; Milby et al. 2005; Toros and Moreno 2012). And this makes intuitive sense. Participation in treatment programs is enhanced when individuals are housed. Treatment retention is enhanced, as is treatment success. Thus, the research indicates that housing should be a priority in the array of interventions for criminogenic needs.

Another very important consideration is the significant limitation of local, community-based treatment resources. As crime control and the incarceration boom took both energy and resources away from correctional rehabilitation, state- and local-level funding shifted considerably in the direction of correctional budgets and away from matters such as public mental health treatment, public substance abuse treatment, permanent supportive housing, and employment training, among others. As a result, one of the serious challenges that diversion programs face is the lack of community-based treatment capacity. It should be unacceptable that a local, public mental health facility has a six-month waiting list and is restricted to serving those diagnosed with bipolar disorder, major depression, or schizophrenia. Or that a local public substance abuse treatment facility has a capacity of ten beds (for an area with a population of over 1.5 million). This is anecdotal evidence, but it is characteristic of too many jurisdictions to be the exception.

The point is a simple one in principle, but extraordinarily difficult to implement. Diversion and treatment of many criminal offenders is much more cost-effective than business as usual. Even considering that correctional treatment has high failure rates does not change the conclusion. Every time an offender reenters the justice system, the costs begin anew—costs associated with law enforcement, jail, the prosecutor, pretrial services, the court, a public defender or appointed counsel, and then corrections. Every time this offender reenters the justice system and he or she gets business as usual, we are enhancing the likelihood of a return visit and are simply providing oil for the revolving door.

Policymakers should begin considering the longer-term consequences of funding decisions. Much more is known about the primary criminogenic needs that drive much of criminal offending, and we have the tools to effectively interrupt the cycle of reoffending. What we lack are many state and local governments that are willing to provide adequate financial resources to the social, economic, and medical services that over the long term would provide dramatic cost savings to the criminal justice system and significantly reduce recidivism and crime—in short, an effective and cost-effective path to public safety.

The basic diversion court model is appropriate for application in a variety of other problem areas in the justice system, including veterans, domestic violence, reentry from jail and prison, prostitution, sex offending, and many applications for juveniles. Each of these was the product of some form of creative problem solving, by identifying a persistent problem that is not being adequately resolved by traditional criminal justice adjudication and sanctioning and applying the diversion court model and principles to that problem.

A FINAL NOTE ON DIVERSION AND PUBLIC OPINION

The most recent National Center for State Courts sentencing attitudes survey was conducted in 2006 (Princeton Survey Research Associates International 2006). At that time, the clear majority of respondents embraced alternative sentences for nonviolent offenders. For example, 65 percent supported placing nonviolent mentally ill offenders in treatment and counseling rather than prison; 56 percent supported placing drug offenders in treatment and counseling rather than prison; 63 percent supported requiring mandatory education and job training; and 61 percent supported placing youthful offenders (under age twenty-five) in treatment and counseling.

Support for diversion through problem-solving courts is even higher. The vast majority (82 percent) believe that diverting nonviolent mentally ill offenders through mental health courts in which they receive treatment rather than jail or prison is better than traditional adjudication and punishment. Seventy-eight percent believe drug courts are a better way to sentence drug offenders than jail or prison.

More recent sentencing and corrections public opinion surveys (Pew Center on the States 2012) support the overall thrust of the earlier results. While the Pew survey did not focus on diversion or problem-solving courts specifically, it reported that a majority of respondents believe there are too many individuals in prison and that policy changes should be implemented that shift nonviolent offenders out of prison and into (unspecified) alternatives.

To the extent that public attitudes matter in policy decisions, it appears that there is sufficient popular support for reducing prison populations and expanding diversion programs. It is also likely that these attitudes are even more widespread today as states confront the fiscal realities of crime control and huge, expensive prison systems.

CHAPTER 6

Community Supervision

"A recent survey of state chief justices conducted by the National Center for State Courts found . . . that the most frequent complaints from state trial judges hearing felony cases included the high rates of recidivism among felony offenders, the ineffectiveness of traditional probation supervision in reducing recidivism."
—Judge Roger Warren (2007: 4–5)

THERE ARE TWO PRIMARY TYPES of community supervision: probation, which is a sentence of conditional supervision in lieu of incarceration, and parole, which is conditional supervision after a period of incarceration. Probation and parole are both significantly underperforming in terms of adoption of best evidence-based practices and outcomes such as recidivism and revocation (unsuccessful completion of supervision). Approximately 40 percent of prison admissions are parole and probation revocations. I begin with a discussion of probation, and then turn to parole later in this chapter.

PROBATION TODAY

Probation is a postadjudication sentence of diversion from incarceration to conditional, supervised community release. The conditions of probation are imposed by the court and can be modified over time as circumstances warrant. Typical conditions, generally aimed at control over behavior while on community release, include: avoid the use of drugs and alcohol, avoid

This chapter was written in collaboration with Sarah Appleby, MA.

persons and places of disreputable or harmful character, commit no new offenses, attend all scheduled meeting with the probation officer (at the probation office or at home as directed), retain gainful employment and support any dependents, do not change residence without permission, do not leave the county without permission, submit urine and/or breath specimens as directed, pay all court and supervision fees, and keep proper identification on your person at all times. There are also a variety of special conditions that apply at the discretion of the court or the probation office, including electronic monitoring, GPS monitoring, ignition interlock devices, community service restitution, inpatient and outpatient treatment, and special classes for drug and alcohol problems, psychological/psychiatric problems, anger/aggression, intimate partner and family violence, parenting, relapse prevention, sex offender intervention, and so on.

Individuals serving a sentence of probation are subject to revocation upon discovery of violations of the conditions of supervision (a technical violation) or a new offense. The typical path to revocation is the filing of a motion to revoke probation, followed by a court hearing in which a determination is made to revoke to prison (for felony probationers) or jail (for misdemeanor probationers), or continue probation with modifications to the conditions, and/or imposition of a variety of intermediate, graduated sanctions.

Probation was originally designed as an opportunity to allow an offender to remain in the community, and remain employed and supporting his or her family while receiving intervention and treatment to help address the reasons for criminal involvement. Probation is, in theory, designed to accomplish public safety through the three primary functions of surveillance, treatment, and enforcement. These goals went to the wayside as probation populations escalated and caseloads exploded, without commensurate increases in probation budgets. The probation model that emerged from the realities of increasing caseloads was largely supervision and risk management.

While incarceration rates and prison populations are typically what observers point to as the defining characteristic of U.S. crime control policies, in terms of sheer numbers of offenders, the probation population exceeds the prison and jail population by a factor of nearly two. In 2012, there were 4.3 million individuals on probation (both felony and misdemeanor, including formal probation, community-based correctional supervision, and specialized court supervision programs), compared to

2,239,800 individuals in prison and jail. Between 1990 and 2012, the incarcerated population grew 100 percent; however, the probation population increased by a healthy 50 percent over that time period.

As a share of correctional budgets, probation and other forms of community supervision decidedly take a back seat. Between 1982 and 2010, inflation-adjusted total correctional spending increased by 223 percent, totaling $48.5 billion in 2010. Spending for noninstitutional corrections (community corrections, halfway houses, and so on) increased by 160 percent. Most telling is the share of corrections expenditures for community corrections. In 1982, community corrections expenditures constituted 25.3 percent of total correctional spending. By 2010, the share of corrections spending for community corrections had dropped to 20.4 percent (Kyckelhahn 2012). Clearly, expenditures for prison and jail capacity and operations have consumed the vast majority of corrections spending over time, and the share of total outlays for incarceration has increased over time. The conclusion reached by many observers is not just that incarceration expenditures far exceed community corrections, but also that community corrections is seriously underfunded (Petersilia 1998; Pew Center on the States 2009). That conclusion appears to be reasonable: at least in terms of funding, probation is the stepchild of the U.S. criminal justice system, which is ironic because it is responsible for the bulk of criminal offenders in the correctional system.

There have been three very significant changes to probation that have radically affected the ability of probation departments and probation officers to manage the risk of offenders. One trend has been the sheer increase in the probation population, which, when combined with relatively stagnant expenditures over time, has resulted in increasing caseloads for officers. Caseloads for regular probation supervision can be as high as 300 or more. Caseload size for intensive supervision of high-risk offenders can be over 100. Estimates based on incomplete data indicate average caseloads for regular supervision are around 95.

A second trend has been the hardening of the probation population. Historically, sentences of probation were reserved for low-risk offenders who posed little threat to public safety. However, over time, the composition of the probation population has shifted to a much greater proportion of higher-risk offenders. As Taxman, Shepardson, and Byrne (2004) note, the probation population increasingly resembles the prison population. This higher-risk population poses very significant challenges for probation departments and officers. Higher-risk offenders present with a greater number and intensity of criminogenic needs and deficits, requiring greater allocation of time and resources. The obvious problem is that probation funding has not kept up with changes in caseload size and composition.

A third factor complicating the probation picture has been the increasing number of supervision conditions imposed on probationers. Perhaps partly in response to changes in the risk composition of the probation population, and in part an effort to be more punitive and to enhance correctional control, the increase in conditions has had at least two significant consequences: increased workload for probation officers and increased violations of conditions. Increasing conditions can be a reasonable response to higher-risk offenders, but as several experts have noted, often these new conditions are legislatively mandated or imposed by judges with little reference to presentence investigation reports, clinical assessments, and evidence-based practices.

For a variety of reasons, the probation of today little resembles the original intent. It is a system of correctional control, driven by the get tough mantra of the 1980s and 1990s, focused largely on risk management, and operating with substantially limited resources. In essence, probation over the past thirty years or so has functioned as a sorting mechanism, in which offenders self-identify as failures or successes through their behavior with regard to violating the conditions of supervision and/or reoffending.

As discussed earlier in this book, the great U.S. experiment with punishment has been a failure, and probation as currently funded and operated has contributed to that failure and largely been a lost opportunity. The evidence is clear. Probation as currently implemented does not significantly impact recidivism (Aos, Miller, and Drake 2006a; Bonta et al. 2008; Green and Wink 2010; Solomon et al. 2005; Taxman 2002). As Green and Wink simply state: "probation does not alter the probability of recidivism." This conclusion is echoed time and time again in the research and evaluation literature.

These conclusions, reinforced by research comparing the effectiveness (recidivism) of custodial sentences (prison) and noncustodial sentences (community supervision), further underscore the limitations of probation in meeting its intended goals—to enhance behavioral change and ensure accountability. The research indicates that while probation has lower recidivism compared to prison releasees, in part due to risk differences in the two populations, the differences were small and not statistically significant.

Revocation and recidivism statistics tell the story. Across the board, probationers have about a 40 percent failure rate, but that figure is in the 50 percent or higher range in some states and for certain categories of probationers, for example, high risk and substance abuse. This failure rate is a combination of unsuccessful probation termination, violations of conditions, and revocation. Approximately 16 percent of probationers are revoked to incarceration, an additional 11 percent are classified as having an unsatisfactory probation exit, and around 3 percent abscond (Glaze and Bonczar 2011). Studies that track the timing of probation failure indicate that the probability of rearrest and/or reconviction while on probation is frontloaded in the first twelve months. Essentially 50 percent of rearrests and reconvictions occur during the first year of supervision. A very similar pattern exists for probation violations. While there is variation across states and studies, the bottom line is that probation violations are also frontloaded. One report indicates that 50 percent of probation violators commit the first violation within the first twenty months of supervision (Van Pattan and Matney 2004). Another survival analysis shows 30 percent of violations occurring within the first 100 days of supervision (Gray, Fields, and Maxwell 2001). These results are consistent with dozens of other analyses on the timing of supervision failure.

All in all, probation failure rates are troubling. As Judge Warren concludes (2009a: 1):

> Recidivism rates among these felony defendants are at unprecedented levels. Almost 60 percent have been previously convicted and more than 40 percent of those on probation fail to complete probation successfully. The high recidivism rate among felony probation pushes up state crime rates and is one of the principal contributors to our extraordinarily high incarceration rates.

Recidivism postsupervision is as high as 60 to 75 percent for those discharged from probation and followed for up to five years after discharge. One study of Illinois probationers reported that those who did not successfully complete substance abuse treatment while on probation had a 67 percent four-year recidivism rate after probation discharge, compared to 44 percent for nonsubstance-abusing probationers (Huebner 2006). And as

Warren notes above, the majority of probationers have a prior criminal conviction, regardless of whether they had served a prior probation sentence.

Once again, while a successful discharge from probation is counted as a success, subsequent recidivism is a system failure. Obviously, postdischarge recidivism cannot be eliminated. However, through implementation of research-based practices, as well as the other strategies discussed in chapter 3, the evidence indicates that recidivism can be dramatically reduced. I now turn to an assessment of what it is about probation as currently operated that may account for the high supervision failure rate and the relative inability to alter the likelihood of recidivism and to enhance public safety.

There are a number of factors that contribute to the limitations of probation today. While caseloads have increased dramatically over time, one of the troubling consequences is the impact of increasing caseloads on officer workload. The demands on officer time have escalated along with caseloads, and additional requirements for reporting and paperwork have imposed additional constraints on officers' abilities to effectively supervise. Probation officers also report concerns about lack of clarity of goals, limited funding and resources, and difficulties implementing evidence-based practices (DeMichele and Payne 2007; Paparozzi and DeMichele 2008).

The concern about lack of clarity of goals has its origin in the traditional dichotomy of the probation officer role of cop or social worker—enforcer/punisher versus fixer. Historically, probation officers were considered one or the other, without much room for a balance of the two. The problem appears to be a lack of organizational or administrative direction on priorities or not reaching a balance. Is probation basically a game of "gotcha," or should it focus on behavior change through intervention and treatment? Should revocation be considered a success in that someone who is noncompliant is identified? Or should the bulk of the effort be on factors that enhance the success of offenders on probation (that is, addressing criminogenic needs)? Lack of clear direction, combined with limited funding and resources, further complicate agreement on the goals and objectives of the day-to-day business of probation. Lack of funding results in inadequate training for officers and a lack of proper equipment. It is also evident from survey responses that lack of funding renders evidence-based practices just another catchphrase in many departments. As DeMichele and Payne (2007: 6) conclude, "While agencies are interested in evidence-based practices, it appears that the lack of funding for fully implementing such changes fosters a half-hearted attempt."

TABLE 6.1   Programs and Services Available at Community Corrections
            Agencies, 2005

PROGRAM/SERVICE	PERCENTAGE WITH PROGRAM/SERVICE
Drug/alcohol education	53
Substance abuse counseling (up to 4 hrs/week)	47
Substance abuse counseling (5–25 hrs/week)	21
Substance abuse counseling (>26 hrs/week)	2
Therapeutic community	7
Relapse prevention	34
Case management	7
Day reporting	13
ISP	42
Work release	7
Transitional housing	24
Sex offender therapy	57
Vocational training	23
Education	15
Physical health services	13
Mental health assessment	19
Co-occurring disorders assessment	20
Counseling for co-occurring disorders	18
Family therapy/counseling	13
Domestic violence intervention	19
Communication and social skill development	11
Life skills management	17
Anger/stress management	18
Cognitive skills development	17
Job placement and vocational counseling	19

Taxman, Perdoni, and Harrison (2007) conducted a national survey
(in 2005) of correctional agencies to determine the prevalence of various
correctional and treatment services. Table 6.1 summarizes what Taxman and
colleagues discovered in their survey of probation departments. The numbers in table 6.1, which are from Taxman, Perdoni, and Harrison (2007),

refer to services provided by community supervision agencies and do not reflect programs and services that probationers are referred to in the community. What it shows is the limited availability of rehabilitative programming in probation departments across the country. As Taxman (2012: 369) notes, "on any given day, only about 9% of the offenders in a probation department can actually participate in programs." These statistics only refer to whether the program/service is present. There is no indication from these survey results of the quality of this programming (for example, whether therapy/counseling is cognitive behavioral, whether the assessments are based on validated instruments, or whether there is any effort to target higher-risk offenders, prioritize criminogenic needs, and implement responsivity principles).

The reality is that contemporary probation is seriously under-resourced in terms of screening and assessment and treatment and rehabilitation programming. In part, this reflects resource limitations. It also reflects the relative focus on control and surveillance versus behavioral change. The bottom line is that the availability (or lack thereof) of correctional and rehabilitative programming speaks much louder than any administrative declaration of the goals and objectives of the agency. Spending drives policy, not words or phrases. Probation departments may very well wish to have a more balanced approach to community supervision and implement evidence-based practices, an approach clearly supported by science. However, absent the necessary resources and a concerted cultural shift in how probation accomplishes public safety, the day-to-day activities of the officers on the ground will still be largely focused on enforcement, rather than behavior change.

Much like community policing was for local law enforcement in the 1990s, evidence-based practices (EBPs) appear to be an often-discussed focus for probation. EBPs have been demonstrated to significantly and substantially reduce recidivism. However, it is necessary to look closely at whether and how well EBPs are being implemented.

The day-to-day operations of probation departments, the large caseloads, the continued impact of crime control with a culture that supports surveillance and control, uncertain and limited funding, and the lack of in-house and local community-based treatment and rehabilitation resources all present barriers to institutional and cultural change. Research on California's adult probation system with responsibility for supervising 350,000 probationers found that "many county probation departments are not operating

TABLE 6.2   Use of EBPs in Community Corrections, 2005

EVIDENCE-BASED PRACTICES	PERCENTAGE OF AGENCIES IMPLEMENTING
Use of standardized, validated substance abuse treatment	44
Use of standardized, validated risk assessment	34
Use of methods to increase treatment motivation	22
Use of evidence-based treatment modalities	12
Address multiple criminogenic needs	85
Address co-occurring mental health and substance abuse with integrated models	25
Use of treatment programs that are a minimum of 90 days	40
Continuing care	41
Use of graduated sanctions for negative behavior	37
Use of appropriate incentives for positive behavior	53

Average number of EBPs implemented: 5.0

according to the best practices identified by experts and are underperforming in key outcome measures (such as percentage of probationers successfully completing probation)" (LAO 2009). The data in table 6.2 represent the best national snapshot currently available on the implementation of EBPs in probation. The 2005 results of the survey of the National Criminal Justice Treatment Practices (Taxman et al. 2007) indicate limited implementation and wide variation in which practices are implemented. The limitations are that these results say nothing about how extensively and how well these practices are implemented.

The data in table 6.2, again from Taxman, Perdoni, and Harrison (2007), indicate a general lack of implementing evidence-based practices. Fewer than half used validated risk and needs assessments, so the extent to which they were accurately able to target higher-risk offenders and identify relevant criminogenic needs, let alone obtain clinical diagnoses, is questionable. Moreover, research shows that even when risk and needs are determined, probation officers are not utilizing that information in the supervision of offenders (Bonta et al. 2004; Lowenkamp, Latessa, and Holsinger 2006). It appears reasonable to conclude that there has not been much effort to assess treatment readiness or identify stages of change because less than 25 percent of the agencies report that they engage in any treatment motivation enhancement like motivational interviewing. The vast majority of agencies do not use evidence-based treatment modalities such as cognitive-behavioral, therapeutic communities, or behavioral modification treatment. Surprisingly, 85 percent of the agencies indicate that they address multiple criminogenic needs of offenders, although it is unclear how those needs are identified. Research indicates that substance abuse is widespread in the criminal justice population and that a very typical co-morbid diagnosis is mental illness and substance abuse. However, only 25 percent of the agencies in the sample indicated that they address this co-morbidity with an integrated treatment model. Treatment dosage is problematic in the majority of agencies because 40 percent use treatment programs that are at least ninety days in duration. Research also clearly indicates that treatment effects are usually quickly lost if the individual does not engage in ongoing aftercare. The minority of probation agencies (41 percent) offer continuing care. Roughly half use appropriate incentives to reinforce positive behavior. Only one-third have a graduated sanctions system. Finally, the agencies indicated that on average they have implemented five EBPs.

The survey results indicate some significant effort in the direction of implementing EBPs. Because the survey results are for 2005, it is reasonable to assume that implementation is greater today. However, we know very little about how extensive these practices are, how frequently they are used, for how many individuals, and how faithfully or well they have been implemented. As I discussed in chapter 3, reducing recidivism, crime, and victimization through engaging in meaningful behavioral change requires extraordinary commitment, not simply token efforts with limited capacity, inappropriate modalities and dosage, unreliable risk and needs assessments, and lack of aftercare, among others. Again, there is little systematic evidence that speaks to the fidelity of implementation.

Additional research has assessed the recidivism impact of implementing EBPs (without regard necessarily to fidelity, capacity, and so on). Andrews and Bonta (2010) focused on the risk, need, and responsivity (RNR) components of the effective principles of correctional intervention. The risk principle is accurately assessing risk with standardized, validated assessments and then targeting higher-risk offenders. The need principle also involves accurately and comprehensively assessing criminogenic needs with standardized and validated needs assessments and then targeting treatment resources on those needs. Responsivity refers to the use of cognitive-behavioral modalities, and tailoring the interventions to the motivation, learning style, abilities, and strengths of the participants. Adherence to these basic principles greatly reduces probation recidivism. When all three are implemented, the effect size from the meta-analysis is 0.26. When only two are implemented, the effect size is 0.18. When only one of the principles is implemented, it is 0.1. Implementation of none results in a modest increase in probation recidivism. Translated into a more meaningful metric, the implementation of all three principles results in a reduction of probation recidivism of roughly 16 to 18 percent.

A PATH FORWARD FOR PROBATION

Implementation of the evidence-based practices and policies for probation can result in recidivism reductions as high as 50 percent (Andrews and Bonta 2006; Aos, Miller, and Drake 2006a; Paparozzi and DeMichele 2008). However, as discussed in chapter 3, evidence-based practices are necessary, but not sufficient to maximize recidivism reduction. In this section, I first discuss those EBPs, or principles of effective correctional intervention, as they apply to probation. I then turn to what else should accompany these practices and principles.

One of the problems with probation as implemented in recent decades is that recidivism is a fact of life in which supervision failure is viewed as a public safety success—the surveillance/control system succeeded in detecting a violation or a new offense and took the appropriate action of revocation. In another important sense, probation violations are failures, largely because many are preventable if the probation system functioned with the primary goals of reintegration, behavioral change, and accountability; if it had appropriate, effective sanctions and rehabilitative interventions; and if it had sufficient funding and the proper cultural orientation. There needs to be an ultimate sanction like incarceration. However, revoking a probationer to prison does nothing to enhance behavioral change in a positive direction and further heightens the probability of recidivism upon release. The probation model going forward is one in which much more effort is focused on shared responsibility for success and failure, behavioral change, and reducing recidivism. In turn, failure on probation is a failure for which revocation is a last resort.

The Basics—Evidence-Based Practices for Probation

The research-based practices for effective probation have been articulated in a variety of relatively recent publications (Andrews and Bonta 2006; Aos, Miller, and Drake 2006a; Bonta et al. 2008 2010; Colorado Division of Probation Services 2010; Lutze et al. 2012; Solomon et al. 2008; Taxman et al. 2006; among many others). Here are the essential elements of these practices.

1. CLARIFY THAT THE GOALS OF PROBATION ARE SUCCESSFUL COMPLETION OF SUPERVISION, REINTEGRATION INTO THE COMMUNITY, AND RECIDIVISM REDUCTION

Identify these outcomes as the primary performance measures, measure them, and hold probation staff accountable for achieving these goals. The traditional focus on measuring outputs such as office visits and field visits is not performance measurement. Clarify that the model going forward is a balance between risk management and accountability on the one hand, and behavioral change and successful reintegration on the other. Minimize the traditional dichotomy of law enforcement and social work and instill the risk management–behavioral change balance into the culture of probation agencies.

It is also critical that supervision officers understand that the goals of successful completion of supervision, reintegration into the community, and recidivism reduction are not just the responsibility of the offender. This is not a situation of giving an offender a chance to prove he or she can make it, and if not, yanking him or her off probation. It is a situation of collective responsibility for accomplishing these goals. That needs to be ingrained in the culture of the agency. Evaluations also need to be conducted to determine outcomes, and the relationship between outcomes and supervision and program attributes.

2. ADHERE TO THE PRINCIPLE OF RESPONSIVITY

—Use cognitive-behavioral intervention modalities and tailor supervision conditions to the needs and risk of offenders. Conditions should be realistic, relevant, and based on research, not the typical laundry list of generic conditions that too often characterize the judicial imposition of conditions and can lead to inappropriate oversupervision. Conditions should focus on those that reduce the likelihood of violations and reoffending and enhance behavioral change. At the end of the day, this practice involves greater thought and consideration of the individual circumstances of the offenders and requires engaging in greater problem solving when imposing conditions of supervision.

3. ADHERE TO THE RISK PRINCIPLE

—Devote the bulk of supervision and intervention resources to higher-risk offenders. Research consistently shows that allocating resources to higher-risk offenders is much more productive in terms of positive longer-term outcomes than devoting resources to lower-risk offenders.

4. FRONTLOAD SUPERVISION RESOURCES

It is known from numerous survival analyses of probation failure patterns that the first six to twelve months of probation supervision are higher risk than subsequent time periods of supervision. This information is quite actionable and should lead to frontloading supervision and intervention resources. Clearly, this is not an across-the-board pattern, so thoughtful assessment of individual offenders should determine frontloading for whom.

5. PROBLEM SOLVING

Whether we like it or not, many probationers need case management, assistance, and problem solving. While part of the point of probation is accountability and accepting responsibility, some offenders are not as well prepared or equipped to effectively deal with compliance with supervision conditions. One of the key roles for probation officers is problem solving—working with probationers to overcome barriers or problems. Part of the process is to teach problem-solving skills so those who are not good at it can improve. It is unfortunate that this is the situation, but it just is. No one wins if we simply put someone on probation and then wait for them to violate.

6. IDENTIFY DYNAMIC CRIMINAL RISK AND CRIMINOGENIC NEEDS/ DEFICITS, AND TARGET BEHAVIORAL CHANGE INTERVENTIONS AND TREATMENT TO ALL PRIORITY CRIMINOGENIC NEEDS/DEFICITS

All of the discussions of evidence-based practices or the principles of effective correctional intervention indicate that assessing risk and needs is the key starting point to the entire process. They also advocate the use of standardized, validated risk and needs assessments for determining the risk level posed by the offender and the criminogenic needs that may require intervention. Moreover, risk is dynamic, reflecting real-time events. Thus, risk prediction must be dynamic, utilizing changeable factors as well as static ones (Connolly 2003; VanBenschoten 2008). Risk is also a driver of level of intervention and dosage of treatment. One size does not fit all, not only because it is wasteful, but because it is ineffective and counterproductive. Intensity or dosage must be tied to level of risk, and intensity of needs and assessments must be able to accurately measure intensity. The variety of interventions must be tied to the variety of criminogenic needs. Correctional intervention cannot continue just focusing on the primary or most obvious criminogenic problem. I have emphasized throughout that many criminal offenders come to the justice system with multiple problems and deficits. Perhaps one compelling explanation for recidivism (surely not the only one) is that the interventions provided did not sufficiently address all of the key, priority criminogenic needs.

The success of any interventions, services, or rehabilitation efforts is dependent on, among other factors, what is identified for intervention. Standardized assessments are fine for what they are. They are designed to discover or identify a limited range of needs or deficits. They can identify what they are designed to identify. They miss a wide range of circumstances, conditions, and deficits that are relevant to the intervention process. For example, few if any are designed to identify trauma and its consequences. There is little discussion of assessing cognitive or learning deficits and neurocognitive impairments, which clearly have consequences for an individual's ability to learn. Structured assessments are fine, but they preclude deviating from the structured topics of the assessments. Clinical judgments and diagnosis are appropriate when there is evidence of such impairments and deficits.

Taxman and colleagues (2006: 5) describe the assessment and intervention plan as follows:

> Under the behavioral management model, this phase [assessment and case planning to engage the offender in the change process] consists of four chief tasks: 1) identify or assess offenders' criminogenic traits and triggers; 2) diagnose the typology of offender (drug, alcohol, dissociated, violent, domestic violence, sexual predator, etc.); 3) develop a supervision plan for changing offenders' behavior that the offender and supervision staff

mutually consent; and 4) implement the agreed upon plan through a behavioral contract that facilitates change.

What is described is a structured process of classification typically engaged in by probation staff. Understandably having probation staff do this is more efficient and cost conserving. However, it is at the same time rather limiting in terms of obtaining a comprehensive picture of an individual's circumstances and situation. One element that is often missing in the assessment process is a true clinical diagnosis conducted by experts in mental or behavioral health.

Consensus indicates the following are the eight primary factors that are correlated or related to the propensity to engage in crime: a history of antisocial behavior; antisocial personality; antisocial values and attitudes; criminal peers; substance abuse; dysfunctional family relations; school/work failure; and lack of prosocial recreational and leisure activities. This consensus is good news because it allows probation staff to focus resources on these primary factors. This consensus is bad news because it allows probation staff to focus resources on only these primary factors. The point is that while these eight factors appear often as correlates or precursors to criminal activity, they are not the only factors that may require focus and resources. The "big eight" create the propensity to classify offenders into one or more of these eight categories. The point is that these eight may blind practitioners from the bigger picture, and create the tendency to think of offenders as categories or types rather than individuals.

In some respects, the process depicted by these discussions of assessment and classification is similar to the processes physicians use for diagnoses. Research has shown that many physicians make their minds up about a diagnosis on fairly limited information. Unsurprisingly, physicians are trained to look for certain things, and if they are specialists, which most are, they look within a fairly narrow range. The more limited the perspective, the more likely the diagnosis will miss potentially important information.

6. SUPERVISION SHOULD OCCUR IN THE COMMUNITY

The traditional office-based supervision is inadequate for understanding an offender's circumstances and risk of reoffending. Places are criminogenic and research indicates that probationers tend to be geographically concentrated, living in a relatively small number of resource-poor, higher-risk neighborhoods. Place-based supervision appreciates the importance of geography and puts supervision officers in communities where they can better observe, establish relationships with family and friends, and become familiar with community resources and high-risk areas and people. In turn, much like the community policing model, place-based supervision puts officers in a position to be better informed and connected with local communities.

7. ENGAGE INFORMAL SOCIAL CONTROL

Research consistently shows that informal social control is more effective than formal legal sanctioning in fostering behavioral change and reducing recidivism. One of the advantages of community- or place-based supervision is the ability to leverage family, employers, friends, and community residents in engaging informal social control.

8. EMPLOY INCENTIVES AND REWARDS

Traditional supervision has relied primarily on sanctions and punishments for controlling and attempting to change behavior. While sanctions are important, exclusive use of punishment is ineffective in reducing recidivism. Positive reinforcement is a very important element in the process of behavior change, and the evidence indicates that positive reinforcement has persistent effects, while the effect of punishment quickly erodes. Incentives and rewards motivate compliance and progress and encourage positive responses. For example, reduction in supervision fees and earned discharge can motivate and reinforce compliance and progress. Incentives and rewards should be delivered swiftly, consistently, predictably, and with certainty for maximum impact. Incentives and rewards that are delayed or arbitrary are generally less effective.

Key to the big picture of behavioral change and supervision compliance is a balance between rewards and incentives on the one hand, and punishment and sanctions on the other. I now turn to the use of sanctions.

9. RESPOND WITH SWIFT AND CERTAIN GRADUATED SANCTIONS FOR VIOLATIONS OR INAPPROPRIATE BEHAVIORS

Recidivism reduction, not revocation, should be the goal of probation. Revocation should be a last resort, after appropriate graduated sanctions or intermediate sanctions (supervisory and administrative hearings) and behavioral change interventions have been exhausted.

Punishment or sanctioning is relevant in the context of correctional control, risk management, and behavioral change. However, it is swift, certain, proportional, and graduated sanctioning that has been shown to be effective in supervision compliance and behavioral change. Again, sanctioning is effective in the context of a balance of rewards and sanctions.

In 2004, Judge Steven Alm responded to the frustration of high levels of probation violations by drug offenders by developing a new, specialized sanction court called Hawaii's Opportunity Probation with Enforcement (HOPE). The principle was simple: enhance compliance and accountability by invoking the two dimensions of punishment that do deter negative behavior—swift and certain punishment. The model has caught on, with variations of the HOPE Court in several jurisdictions, including Anchorage, Alaska; Maricopa County, Arizona; Fort Worth, Texas; and Austin, Texas, as well as in states such as Oregon, Washington, Massachusetts, and Arkansas.

The HOPE model is based on swift, certain, predictable, consistent, and proportional sanctions, which typically take the form of graduated stays in jail. The procedure involves a warning hearing in which the expectations for performance and the consequences for noncompliance are made clear. The theory is that revocation to prison is overkill and ineffective in many instances of probation violation and does nothing to change behavior. Deferred and low-probability threats of more severe punishment are not terribly effective. Instead, swift, certain, modest, and proportional sanctions (immediate, high-probability threats) may motivate compliance and progress on probation, largely based on the idea that immediate, proportional punishment is a more realistic threat.

The evidence indicates that the theory is on target. Evaluations by Hawken and Kleiman (2009) show substantial increases in supervision compliance and reductions in revocations in the Hawaii HOPE Court. Positive drug test results dropped dramatically as did no-shows for probation appointments in the HOPE sample. HOPE probationers, compared to the control group of probation as usual probationers, were 55 percent less likely to be arrested for a new crime, 72 percent less likely to use drugs, 61 percent less likely to skip appointments, and 53 percent less likely to have probation revoked. These results were found across probation offices, officers, and judges. An assessment regarding whether or not the effects persist is currently underway. The recent results indicate that the longer-term recidivism impacts of the HOPE Court are maintained (personal communication with Angela Hawken). The research evidence also indicates that where there is some erosion of the recidivism impact, it is a result of a drift from implementation fidelity of the HOPE model.

10. COMMUNITY SUPERVISION SHOULD CONSIST OF A BALANCE OF SUPERVISION, SURVEILLANCE, AND RISK MANAGEMENT ON THE ONE HAND, AND BEHAVIORAL CHANGE TREATMENT AND INTERVENTION ON THE OTHER

Probation is part risk management and part recidivism reduction. Risk management involves elements of surveillance and officer-offender contact, efforts that are aimed at restraint and control. However, surveillance and control have limited impacts on recidivism. Longer-term recidivism reduction requires behavioral change, such as drug and alcohol treatment, cognitive restructuring, employment training, mental health treatment, education, and so on. It is also important to engage offenders in the development of treatment and supervision plans. Offender participation in the process and agreement to the plan increases commitment, compliance, and motivation.

11. ENGAGE COMMUNITY EXPERTISE AND RESOURCES

A report for the Crime and Justice Institute and the National Institute of Corrections (Scott 2008: ix) provides a very realistic picture of the challenges faced by corrections personnel:

> Corrections professionals must manage and supervise offenders who present with high-risk behaviors and complex, overlapping problems, including addiction, chronic mental health challenges, domestic violence, and sex offending behaviors. The complexity of the multi-problem offender necessitates that, in order to be effective in their work and to reduce recidivism, corrections professionals must work collaboratively with professionals in other fields, particularly those who provide behavioral healthcare. Correctional treatment, as defined here, is multidisciplinary.

Criminal offenders often have multiple, complex criminogenic deficits, circumstances, and needs. Identifying, prioritizing, and addressing these needs is not a simple matter and requires a variety of resources and expertise that many probation agencies do not possess. Establishing relationships with local community agencies and organizations is critical for providing appropriate behavioral change interventions, treatment, and rehabilitation.

There is a tendency for the government bid process to favor the low-cost provider for treatment and rehabilitation services, with less consideration given to differences in qualifications and expertise. Common sense would suggest that we get what we pay for, and using inexpensive treatment providers may save money up front, but the longer-term costs due to recidivism (police, jail, prosecutor, court, corrections) quickly obliterate those cost savings many times over. If we are going to get serious about behavior change and recidivism reduction, we need to get serious about quality of services. A reasonable approach to achieving enhanced quality of services is performance-based contracting, whereby providers are required to engage evidence-based practices with fidelity and sufficient flexibility for implementing the most effective interventions science provides. Performance-based contracts should be tied to outcomes, not outputs. Typical outcomes are successful completion of treatment, evidence of changes in reassessed risk and needs, and reductions in recidivism.

There is evidence that the incentives for achieving these outcomes are greater in the private and nonprofit sector, compared to government providers. Enhanced use of private and nonprofit providers may increase competition and, in turn, the quality of services, level of innovation, and cost-effectiveness. This is the strategy followed in the United Kingdom. As the chief executive of the National Offender Management System describes the logic (Terry 2006: 13):

> We want to get a wider range of partners involved in managing offenders and cutting re-offending. Therefore, we will legislate to open up probation to other providers, and will only award contracts to those who can prove they will deliver reductions in re-offending, and keep the public safe. We need to bring in expertise from the private and voluntary sectors to drive up the quality and performance of community punishments.

These are the basic evidence-based practices that experts recommend probation agencies should implement. We know from the Taxman and colleagues (2007) national survey that as of the mid-2000s, use of these practices does not appear to be the norm. Again, the survey results just report use (yes, no) and not how much or how well. There is considerable work to be done in getting probation agencies to embrace the use of EBPs, accurately and appropriately implementing them, and monitoring their use. There is a substantial difference between doing it and doing it well.

The implementation of EBPs requires a significant reengineering of probation, which involves changing probation structures, policies and practices, roles and responsibilities, the culture of the organization, and funding. As Bourgon and colleagues (2010b: 2) conclude: "Translating empirical knowledge into system-wide everyday practice has proven difficult." Obviously, integrity of implementation is critical and barriers can range from top-level administration not understanding the big picture of EBPs, to inadequate funding for treatment and intervention, to a lingering culture of probation as mainly enforcement, surveillance, and control, to line officers who do not engage the basics of the risk-need-responsivity (RNR) principles.

Caseload Size

Research indicates that simply reducing caseload size does not reduce recidivism (Jalbert et al. 2011). However, reduced caseloads in combination with surveillance/control and EBP treatment and rehabilitation services can reduce recidivism. Determining the appropriate caseload size going forward should be driven by consideration of the new role of probation officers. As the roles and responsibilities of probation staff are expanded, caseload size should shift to accommodate that expansion. It would obviously be inappropriate and counterproductive to implement the changes discussed herein but require probation staff to maintain caseloads that prevent effective interaction with offenders and the optimal balance of supervision and behavioral change efforts. Lutze and colleagues (2012) suggest a caseload upper limit of fifty for probation staff who are implementing the expanded roles and responsibilities.

ADDITIONAL CONSIDERATIONS FOR EFFECTIVE
COMMUNITY SUPERVISION INTERVENTION

The implementation of evidence-based practices and reinvention of the role of the supervision officer are important and essential changes to community supervision. However, they are just the starting point. The time has come for community corrections agencies to reject the idea that failure is an acceptable outcome of supervision. Failure is largely avoidable and preventable. The task now is to outline factors in addition to EBPs that are essential to reducing supervision failure.

One of the primary considerations is creating a role for clinical assessment and clinical expertise in the process of identifying and diagnosing not only criminogenic needs, but also cognitive and behavioral impairments such as low intellectual functioning, as well as developmental, behavioral, and psychosocial problems. It is known from clinical research that such functional impairments affect an individual's ability to effectively participate in treatment, as well as adhere to supervision requirements. As I noted earlier, these cognitive impairments are often important in predicting treatment retention and success, and should provide critical guidance for adhering to the responsivity principle of matching treatment/intervention programs and modalities to the abilities of the offender. We know that cognitive and behavioral impairments can affect understanding, comprehension, memory, intellectual functioning, inappropriate responses to stress, poor judgment and coping skills, among others.

An obvious question is: Why does the justice system, in this case community supervision, have to ramp up implementation of EBPs, as well as screening, assessment, diagnosis, treatment planning, and structuring of treatment, to a level that rivals the evidence-based practices of clinical psychology in the private sector? The answer is simple: if the justice system does not come to the table and engage what it takes to effectively sustain behavioral change, no one else will, and the taxpayers will continue to pay time and time again for these failures. Each time an offender recidivates, the cash register rings and someone is needlessly victimized, incurring physical, financial, psychological, or emotional harm.

Reinventing the Role of the Probation Officer

A 2008 review of fifteen studies of recidivism among probationers (Bonta et al. 2008) found only a two percentage point reduction in recidivism associated with offenders on community supervision compared to alternative criminal sanctions. There was no reduction in violent recidivism. Such results raise important questions, especially when compared to the research on offender rehabilitation, which routinely finds substantial recidivism reductions associated with implementation of the Risk-Need-Responsivity (RNR) model (Bourgon, Gutierrez, and Ashton 2012). A concerted focus on offender–probation officer interactions has led researchers to a better understanding of how typical probation officers fall short in the implementation of the RNR model, in establishing a therapeutic relationship, in the extent to which the offender-officer interactions focus on behavioral change, and in the efficacy of officers in promoting offender change (Bourgon et al. 2009; Bourgon, Gutierrez, and Ashton 2012; Gleicher, Manchak, and Cullen 2013).

In response to the research findings that probation officers do not sufficiently or effectively promote behavioral change, Canadian researchers developed an officer training program that focuses on enhancing the quality of the offender-officer relationship, concrete RNR-based intervention skills, prosocial modeling, effective use of disapproval and reinforcement, collaborative problem solving, and building trust between the officer and the offender. The Strategic Training Initiative in Community Supervision (STICS) is a training program built on research-based core correctional principles (Bonta et al. 2010b; Bourgon et al. 2010a; Bourgon et al. 2010b). STICS is based on the premise that criminal behavior is learned just as any other behavior is learned, and is subject to the laws of social learning and operant conditioning. It is based on changing officer behavior, which can lead to behavior change in offenders when the skills officers have learned are applied in officer-offender interactions. The STICS training protocol includes a three-day training session, followed by monthly skill maintenance meetings in which officers discuss and practice the skills they have learned. STICS also includes ongoing clinical support and a one-year follow up refresher course consisting of a day-long training.

Evaluation results indicate that STICS is important. Random assignment to STICS training and a no-training control showed that STICS-trained officers substantially improved their interactions with offenders in terms of engaging RNR-based skills and techniques, and at a two-year follow-up, the probationers supervised by STICS-trained officers had a recidivism rate of 25 percent compared to 41 percent for the control group. The STICS initiative has encouraged others to develop similar training programs for community supervision officers, including Staff Training Aimed at Reducing Rearrest (STARR) (Robinson et al. 2012) and Effective Practices in Community Supervision Settings (EPICS) (Thompson and Lovins 2012; Smith et al. 2012).

STARR, similar to STICS and EPICS, is an RNR-based training program that includes skill enhancement in active listening, role clarification, effective use of authority, effective disapproval and reinforcement, problem solving, and application of the cognitive model. Evaluation of the impact of STARR indicates the training substantially improves the strategies used by supervision officers and in turn significantly lowers recidivism (Robinson et al. 2012). The EPICS training applies the RNR model to supervision, trains officers on the core correctional practices, and coaches officers to intervene and to be proactive in offender decision making. It is designed to teach supervision officers to increase the dosage for higher-risk offenders, target criminogenic needs, and to use cognitive-behavioral and social learning skills and approaches with offenders in the context of supervision meetings. Officers are trained to intervene in offender situations, as well as trained in thinking, feelings, actions, and consequences. Core skills include cognitive restructuring and problem solving, among others. Evaluation results indicate that EPICS-trained officers used core correctional practices more consistently and became more proficient in the use of these skills.

The goal of all of these officer training programs (STICS, STARR, and EPICS) is to transition the role of the community supervision officer from case manager and law enforcement agent to a more balanced role of supervision officer and change agent. Bourgon, Gutierrez, and Ashton (2012: 6) describe it as follows:

> It is the recent work of STICS . . . and other similar new training initiatives [that] suggests community supervision officers take on a more active and direct role in [order for] the change process to be more effective. A closer look at these training programs illustrates how community supervision officers are being encouraged to take on the "change agent" role. At the heart of these training courses are fundamental therapeutic concepts, cognitive-behavioural intervention techniques, and structuring skills. Officers are taught to take on a "change agent" role where the dominant task is to actively engage in the therapeutic change process with the client while traditional case management work is viewed as supplementary. This is a new demand on community supervision officers, challenging them to work with clients in a therapeutic manner and to employ skills and techniques that are firmly rooted in RNR principles so that they can directly facilitate personal, attitudinal, and behavioural change.

The point is simple and clear. Supervision as usual is not enough. Case management, while important, is insufficient in many cases for recidivism reduction. Accountability, compliance, and control are important but insufficient in many cases. It is time that community supervision recognizes that research and development have transformed the role of the community supervision officer in very important, research-based ways. There are significant challenges in making such transitions. For many, the new role of change agent requires substantially different ways of thinking, understanding new concepts, and applying them in day-to-day activities. This transition is not just a matter of training, although the training for STICS, STARR, or EPICS is obviously critical. It is a cultural shift, a repositioning toward a more balanced approach, which incorporates a substantial behavioral change role and responsibility for the officer in addition to case management, compliance, supervision, and accountability responsibilities.

However, it is important to caution that this new role for supervision officers does not and should not substitute for clinical therapy, counseling, and treatment. It is not the intent that the officer is the therapist/counselor and that clinical expertise is no longer needed. That may be sufficient in some cases, but it is a clinical decision whether an offender needs expert therapy or counseling.

The Question of Funding

It is important to be realistic with regard to funding—what is proposed herein for community supervision is not cheap. It will require more extensive screening and assessment; participation by clinical experts on a more consistent basis; substantially increased utilization of treatment and rehabilitation programming; higher standards for treatment and rehabilitation reflecting evidence-based practices of psychology, psychiatry, social work, and others; enhanced training for supervision officers; reduced caseloads, resulting in the need for more officers; and greater use of evaluation of effectiveness, among others.

At the same time that costs substantially increase, program retention and successful completion of supervision will increase, and violations, revocations, and recidivism, both short term and long term, will decline. There will be significantly reduced cycling of offenders in and out of the justice system and victimization will decline. Probation is an opportunity to keep offenders out of prison and jail, the outcomes for which are much grimmer. Probation is an opportunity to hold offenders accountable, supervise them, and require compliance with thoughtfully considered, individualized conditions of supervision. It is also an opportunity to address the reasons for criminal involvement in a setting that is much more conducive to behavior change. It is an opportunity to reverse past failures, both institutional and individual. Many criminal offenders are a product of failed public institutions, and many are a product of poor individual choices and self-imposed circumstances. So why should the justice system have to pick up the pieces and fix these failures and mistakes? Because no one else will. If the justice system does not engage in behavior change and recidivism reduction, the burden and the cost will continue to fall on the justice system, as the revolving door of the past forty years continues spinning.

Current funding models encourage probation as usual, a system whereby problem offenders are revoked off of probation caseloads and sent to prison. This approach is encouraged because probation is either funded primarily at the county level, or when funded by the state, the supervision budgets are separate from prison. Thus, there is a presumably unintended incentive to revoke probationers and pass the cost on to the state or to the state prison budget (LAO 2009 describes the revocation incentive as a primary problem with California probation). As funding for probation declined over the past several decades as funds were appropriated to prison construction and operation, those incentives likely increased. As the Justice Center, at the Council of State Governments (2011) notes:

> Inadequate funding of community corrections agencies puts incredible strain on these organizations, which has significant, unintended consequences. There is little incentive for officers to keep individuals on caseloads instead of returning them to jail or prison at the first opportunity. In fact, helping people comply with conditions of release will result in an officer's caseload remaining high or even swelling, even while reducing revocation rates. States and localities can re-align their fiscal relationship by sharing the savings from avoided prison costs with successful probation and parole agencies.

Going forward, the funding formula for probation must change. The performance incentive funding (PIF) or the performance-based funding model is advocated by a number of policy organizations, including the Council of State Governments, the Pew Center on the States, Public Safety Performance Project, and the Vera Institute. As of November 2012, eight states have implemented some form of performance-based community supervision funding. California was an early adopter of this model.

California has been operating a prison system at approximately 200 percent capacity, and nearly 40 percent of new prison admissions in 2009 were probation revocations. Moreover, California probationers had a successful completion rate about 10 percent lower than most other states. This led to the development in California of a performance-based funding model (SB 678, The Community Corrections Performance Incentives Act) that reduces the probation revocation incentive and provides enhanced funding for probation to implement best practices and engage behavior change strategies and recidivism reduction. The model is simple. A portion of the avoided incarceration costs due to the reduction of probation revocations (approximately 40 to 45 percent) are allocated to probation agencies in counties that reduced revocations; the funds are intended for implementation of enhanced probation services. For counties that already had low revocation rates, the California legislation provides for High Performance Grant awards that allocate funding for counties that were already reducing revocations. As probation improves and revocation and recidivism decline, prison costs are reduced, probation budgets increase, and public safety is enhanced. A 2011 assessment of SB 678 in California shows a 32 percent reduction in probation revocations in 2011 (two years after the legislation was in place), resulting in a savings of $278 million in prison costs. More than $136 million was distributed to local probation departments in 2012 and 2013. Moreover, forty-seven of California's fifty-eight counties reduced their revocation rates, and fourteen counties qualified for High Performance Grants of $87.5 million in 2011. Use of revocation reduction funding and High Performance Grant funds is tied to implementation of evidence-based practices.

California's 2013–2014 budget proposes a reduction of $139 million in performance incentive funding for local probation departments. The proposed total PIF funding is $35 million. This is based in part on the observation that California probation departments have successfully reduced revocation to prison. However, it is unclear how and if probation will be able to sustain these reductions in the face of funding cuts.

Other states that have some version of performance incentive funding for probation include Arkansas (2011), Illinois (2009), Kansas (2008), Kentucky (2011), Ohio (2011), South Carolina (2010), and Texas (2011). One lesson learned is to define multiple performance measures so that funding is not simply tied to revocation reductions. This will help enhance probation performance in a variety of areas such as assessment, rehabilitation and treatment services, training for supervision officers, and successful supervision completion. In turn, these performance improvements, tied to evidence-based practices, will enhance public safety.

Public Opinion About Probation

The public is clearly on board regarding diverting nonviolent offenders from incarceration to a more effective community supervision alternative (Pew Center on the States 2012). Nearly 85 percent of survey respondents believe that some of the money being spent on incarceration of low-risk, nonviolent offenders should be shifted to strengthening community corrections. Although respondents were not asked about California's performance incentive funding, the opinion results indicate compelling public support for such initiatives.

PAROLE AND SUPERVISED RELEASE TODAY

Parole is conditional, supervised early release from prison (the terms parole, early release, supervised release, and conditional supervision are all used interchangeably in this section). Depending on the jurisdiction and therefore the laws that govern release from prison, an individual is eligible to be considered for discretionary early release after he or she has served the requisite percentage (25 percent, 33 percent, 50 percent, 85 percent, and so on, depending on the offense and the jurisdiction) of the sentence imposed. The requisite percentage of the sentence served is generally set by the state legislature. Discretionary parole was originally designed as a component of correctional rehabilitation, and was coupled with indeterminate sentencing, in which offenders were incarcerated for an indeterminate period of time. The point was that inmates progress or get better at different rates, therefore the decision regarding when they were ready for release was up to the parole board. The concept was in theory tailored to the circumstances and progress of individual offenders. Parole was designed as an incentive for good behavior and cooperation in whatever programming was required while incarcerated, and as a safety net, providing supervision and control over releasees to reduce the risk of reoffending. Parole was also designed as a way to assist or facilitate successful reintegration or reentry into the community. In the event that an individual violates the conditions of release, with probable cause, the parole authority may initiate a revocation process whereby the parole board will determine whether the individual shall be revoked back to prison, or allowed to remain on parole, perhaps with modified conditions.

Mandatory release is automatic (not discretionary), and is dictated by prevailing law in a particular jurisdiction. Mandatory release may or may not involve conditional supervision. For example, in Virginia, mandatory parole occurs when an inmate is six months from completing a sentence. In Texas, it is when the calendar time served plus any good conduct credits equal the sentence imposed.

The balance of prison releases that are discretionary parole decisions versus mandatory releases has shifted dramatically over the past forty years. In 1976, two-thirds of inmates released from prison were discretionary parole releases. In 2014, over three-quarters are mandatory releases. There is substantial variation across states regarding the use of discretionary release. For example, California, Illinois, New Mexico, Indiana, and New Hampshire have essentially abandoned discretionary parole and rely on mandatory release. On the other hand, Alabama, Pennsylvania, Oklahoma, and Florida rely nearly exclusively on discretionary release decisions by parole boards or commissions.

A key element in the shift away from discretionary release is truth in sentencing and the impact it has had on early release and mandatory release laws. Truth in sentencing is the term that applies to the gap between sentence imposed and actual time served under traditional indeterminate sentencing schemes. The effects of truth in sentencing on parole and mandatory release vary by jurisdiction. The federal government eliminated parole all together. Several other states eliminated discretionary parole. The majority of states adopted the federal truth in sentencing standard of requiring inmates convicted of violent felonies (typically murder, attempted murder, rape, sexual assault, aggravated assault, robbery) to serve 85 percent of the sentence imposed before they are eligible for release.

There are fifty-two different state parole agencies in the United States, consisting of nearly 2,300 parole offices, and an estimated 14,000 full-time parole officers responsible for supervising active parolees. With around 850,000 parolees in the United States in 2012, the average caseload per officer is around seventy parolees, about twice the caseload that experts recommend (Baer et al. 2006). The majority of these parolees are on active supervision, meaning they must meet with their parole officer on a regular basis as a condition of their parole—generally at least once a month.

For the past two decades or so, approximately 600,000 to 700,000 inmates have been released from the nation's prisons each year, and the vast majority (80 percent) have been on conditional, supervised release. There is some reason to suspect that this flood of prison releases beginning in the mid-1990s may not have been fully anticipated. Crime control has focused on maximizing punishment—lock 'em up and throw away the key. Despite our efforts to increase the length of sentences imposed and time served, the reality is that the vast majority do come home. The question is: What happens once they are released? How well do our community supervision systems manage this flood of inmates who are released from prisons, many of whom receive little or no programming or rehabilitative services, and for whom the prison experience is criminogenic? How well do we manage the public safety risk posed by these individuals? Are we able to effectively assist in successful reintegration into the community? Reentry into the community after a period of incarceration is often neither smooth nor successful. Two-thirds are rearrested and nearly 50 percent of offenders end up reincarcerated within three years following their release from prison (Pew Center on the States 2001; Visher and Travis 2011). The recidivism rate varies widely based on the individual policies and practices of each state, from a low of 24 percent in Oklahoma to a high of 66 percent in Utah. The notable variation in these rates can partially be accounted for by the unique parole revocation policies employed by each state. Despite overall decreases in crime across the United States, the recidivism rate among those released from prison has instead increased almost 12 percent between 1999 and 2004. Former prison inmates account for 15 to 20 percent of all adult arrests, so individuals we have punished and released account for substantial amounts of prison admissions, crimes, arrests, and victimizations. Parole revocations and new offenses by parolees account for 35 percent of prison admissions nationally.

The Urban Institute took the lead in the early 2000s in a nationwide assessment of prison release and reentry—a report card of sorts. The results are essentially consistent with what we already know about how well the justice system works: the prison release, parole, and supervised release picture is pretty bleak. This is a product of several collaborating factors: unmanageable supervision caseloads, inadequate programming and rehabilitation services in prison, inadequate programming and rehabilitation services while on supervision, a clear lack of funding for programs and services for supervision populations, a primary emphasis on risk management rather than successful reintegration, and lack of community-based resources, among others.

Research by Glaze and Bonczar (2011), Harlow (2003), James and Glaze (2006), MacLellan (2005), and the National Research Council (2007) provides a profile of the characteristics of individuals released from U.S. prisons. The vast majority are male (88 percent). Race and ethnicity are varied, with 42 percent categorized as white, 39 percent black, and 18 percent Hispanic. Drug offenses tend to be the most common crime for which releasees find themselves originally incarcerated (35 percent), followed by violent offenses (27 percent), property offenses (25 percent), and sex offenses (8 percent) (Glaze and Bonczar 2011). Forty percent of state prisoners have never completed high school or received a GED, and around half are functionally illiterate (Harlow 2003; MacLellan 2005). Mental and physical illnesses also tend to be widespread across this population. Over half of all state inmates suffer from a mental health problem (James and Glaze 2006). Inmates also exhibit higher rates of health problems than the general population, particularly chronic illnesses such as HIV and AIDS, hepatitis C, and tuberculosis (Roman and Travis 2004). Substance abuse issues are similarly prevalent. An estimated 60 to 80 percent of all prisoners are drug dependent or abusers and require extensive treatment and follow-up after release from prison (National Center on Addiction and Substance Abuse 1998; National Research Council 2007).

The Returning Home research conducted by the Urban Institute (Baer et al. 2006) profiles the needs of returning inmates, the services and programming received while they were in prison, and the services and programming they receive while on supervised release in the community. The research also looks at the impacts on families, communities, and public safety. Here is what we know from this substantial undertaking:

Gainful employment is a tremendous challenge for releasees. The majority stated they needed assistance finding a job, but very few received any in-prison employment training. Twenty percent stated they had a job lined up upon release, while well under 50 percent worked at all eight months after release; 24 percent were employed full time. Transportation appeared as a significant barrier to employment.

Significant health and mental health problems are common. Thirty to forty percent have been diagnosed with a chronic physical or mental health condition; only a small fraction (10 to 15 percent) receives any in-prison treatment. Corrections agencies tend to lack discharge planning and referral provisions, dramatically impacting access to care. The vast majority of releases lack health insurance; incarceration disqualifies inmates from Medicaid, and it takes several months postrelease to reinstate it, denying access to care and medication.

Housing is a substantial problem; while a majority of releasees live with family or intimate partners upon release, for many it is temporary. Seventy percent of releasees report that they would need assistance securing housing upon return; there is little evidence they receive any help. There are obvious barriers to former prison inmates finding housing, including lack of affordable housing, legal barriers, and eligibility requirements. Estimates vary, but it appears that at least 10 to 15 percent of prison releasees are homeless soon after release for some period of time; the estimates of homelessness are dramatically higher for releasees who are mentally ill and/or have substance abuse problems (Roman and Travis 2004). Research shows that the likelihood of parole revocation is considerably higher for parolees who are homeless; it should be obvious that complying with supervision conditions is more difficult when someone is homeless.

Substance abuse (addiction, dependence, or abuse) is the most common criminogenic condition among prison inmates. Research indicates that from 60 to over 80 percent of state prison inmates have substance abuse problems, yet only 15 to 25 percent receive any treatment while incarcerated; in some states, it is considerably lower. For those who receive treatment, there is a critical discontinuity upon release because provisions for aftercare are essentially absent. There is an obvious heightened probability of recidivism and revocation for those with untreated or undertreated substance abuse problems.

Inmates released from prison tend to have extensive criminal histories and the majority are revoked or recidivate early in their release period. Research indicates that half of those arrested were on probation, parole, or pretrial release at the time of their arrest (Pew Center on the States 2011): 60 percent of all felony-level arrests in 2000 were committed by individuals on parole (Rainville and Reaves 2003). There is a clear pattern to parolee recidivism; the Returning Home findings, as well as research by Ekland-Olson and Kelly (1993) and the National Research Council (2007), among others, have documented the transition curve, which shows that the first nine to twelve months are the period of greatest risk of recidivism.

Surveys of inmates who were soon to be released reveal a variety of self-reported needs. These reflect potential criminogenic needs as well as factors that simply could enhance the likelihood of successful reintegration. These needs constitute areas in which the prison system, the parole agencies, and local community agencies could assist. The key services in which the percent of males state they need assistance include: education (94 percent), driver's license (83 percent), job training (82 percent), employment (80 percent), transportation (72 percent), changing criminal attitudes (64 percent), a mentor (60 percent), access to clothing and food (60 percent), medical treatment (56 percent), and housing (49 percent). Females report greater need for services than males, including education (95 percent), employment (83 percent), a mentor (83 percent), a driver's license (82 percent), access to food and clothing (76 percent), and mental health treatment (55 percent).

Research conducted by the Returning Home project indicates that only half of releasees report that their parole officer was helpful in the transition from prison to the community. The number of prison releasees has increased substantially in the past ten to fifteen years, caseloads have risen to unmanageable levels, resources are extremely limited, and the characteristics of inmates (criminogenic deficits or problems) are associated with a higher likelihood of recidivism or revocation. Taking all of this into consideration, I ask three broad questions. First, is parole supervision or supervised release effective in terms of enhancing public safety or improving reentry transitions? The research indicates that it is not. An Urban Institute study (Solomon, Kachnowski, and Bhati 2005) of fourteen states leads to the conclusion that parole supervision has little effect on rearrest rates. This conclusion is supported by research reported by the Washington State Institute of Public Policy, which indicates that parole supervision without treatment does not produce reductions in recidivism (Aos, Miller, and Drake 2006a). These are not surprising findings given the phenomenal challenges faced by both offenders and parole systems. Parole is largely focused on supervision, control, and risk management. Such tactics can control some offending, but at the end of the day, there is not much in place that serves to change behavior. In turn, there is not much in place to reduce recidivism. As Bogue and colleagues (2004:1) state, "the conventional approach to supervision in this country emphasizes individual accountability from offenders and their supervising officers without consistently providing either with the skills, tools and resources that science indicates are necessary to accomplish risk and recidivism reduction."

The second question is: What do we expect? We release hundreds of thousands of prisoners each year who are generally worse off than when they went into prison. We have documented the criminogenic problems of offenders, the inability or unwillingness of prison systems to engage much behavioral change intervention or treatment, the difficulties releasees face in the community, the inability or unwillingness of parole agencies and officers to effectively assist in the transition from prison to community, and the restrictions the law places on what ex-offenders may and may not lawfully do in the free world, among many others. We continue to punish offenders well after they have "paid for their crimes." For example, states impose a wide variety of restrictions on licensing for hundreds of occupations; there are significant restrictions on ex-felons obtaining government education grants and aid, on serving in the military, obtaining veterans' benefits, food stamps, and Temporary Assistance for Needy Families (TANF) benefits, and doing business with the government. Other benefits (such as Medicare and Medicaid) are curtailed while an individual is incarcerated and require reapplication upon release, a task that is often challenging for homeless, substance abusing, and/or mentally ill individuals, as well as those without those challenges. This is just a very brief sampling of the restrictions and limitations placed on offenders. Not that these restrictions are always necessarily wrong, but they make successful reentry and reintegration more difficult.

When viewed through this lens of circumstances, it becomes clear—the odds of an offender turning it around when released from prison are quite limited. The question is not what would we like to happen, but realistically, what do we expect offenders to do when released from prison? Prison (revocation) should not be the remedy for a failed prison and community supervision system.

I had a conversation about fifteen years ago with the head of the parole division of a state criminal justice agency. In the course of the discussion, this person stated that the purpose or function of parole is as a sorting mechanism: those who can make it do, and those who can't, get revoked. This person further indicated that the success of parole is the effective identification of those who can't make it—the revocation rate. That way of thinking speaks volumes.

The third question is: Where do we go from here? There are two versions of the answer, one for near- to medium-term supervised release and one for the longer term. The difference is one of scale and composition of the release population. In the near to medium term, supervised release will be at or near the current level of 500,000 to 600,000 releasees per year, with substantial demands on supervision agencies and officers. In the near term, incarceration will continue to be used as it has been for the past few decades and individuals will be released at current rates. During this period, the supervised release systems will need to balance supervision, accountability, and community-based intervention and treatment for numbers of releasees at or near current levels. Intermediate sanctions or graduated sanctions are effective strategies for holding offenders accountable, providing need-based interventions (such as substance abuse treatment), and reducing revocations to prison. The use of intermediate sanctions in a number of states (for example, Arkansas, Texas, Kentucky, Georgia, North Carolina, South Carolina, Louisiana, Kansas, and Pennsylvania, among others) has resulted in significant reductions in recidivism and revocations (Urban Institute 2013).

It is critical that supervised release transition into a system for providing the balance of risk management, accountability, and compliance on the one hand, and the resources for effective behavior change on the other. One of the keys to going forward is substantially reducing the flow of revoked parolees back to prison. The only evidence-based way of doing that is through effective behavioral change.

As justice systems transition to a substantially greater reliance on rehabilitative diversion through mechanisms such as problem-solving courts, probation, and deferred adjudication (combined with rehabilitation), and in turn as the prison population changes in size and composition, the volume of prison releases will decline. At the same time, we will see the composition of the prison population and the release population change to higher risk as more serious offenders are incarcerated for longer sentences and greater time served, and lower-risk property and drug offenders are diverted from incarceration. As those changes come about, by necessity, the roles and responsibilities of supervised release will change, focusing more on risk management, accountability, and supervision for the high-risk violent offender segment, the habitual offender segment, and the segment of offenders identified as untreatable. Supervised release will also have to focus on risk reduction through intervention and rehabilitation, although for a uniformly more challenging population than now is the case. The end game here is to transition the prison systems to nearly exclusively focusing on incapacitating a relatively smaller but high-risk offender population, balanced against an increasingly rehabilitation-focused diversion from prison for nonviolent, property, and drug offenders, who are not habitual offenders or untreatable.

EFFECTIVE STRATEGIES FOR PAROLE
AND SUPERVISED RELEASE

The near- to medium-term policies governing supervised release from prison must adopt research-based programs and strategies to reduce recidivism and victimization, and enhance successful reentry and reintegration. Because prisoner reentry has been a neglected policy area, there is not nearly as much research on best practices as in other criminal justice areas. Some research has been conducted on what is effective with parole, and there are several state-level initiatives that are instructive for developing a path forward. In addition, evidence-based practices used for probation supervision can apply well in the parole setting.

In 2004, the Bush administration announced its commitment to a multiyear federal reentry initiative. In April of 2008, the administration signed the Second Chance Act, legislation that supports the implementation of a variety of reentry efforts. The 2010 budget for the Second Chance Act was $100 million, followed by $83 million in 2011, $63 million in 2012, $64 million in 2013, and the Obama administration's proposed $119 million for

2014. Federal leadership in this reentry initiative has dramatically focused attention on the issues and remedies and has provided funding to local jurisdictions for program implementation. Some experts mark the passage of the Second Chance Act as a "turning point in U.S. history in terms of justice policy" (Travis, Crayton, and Makamal 2010).

The current emphasis of the reauthorized Second Chance Act is in seven "purpose areas," which are the priorities for funding:

1. Educational, literacy, vocational, and job placement services.
2. Substance abuse treatment and services, including programs that start in placement and continue through the community.
3. Comprehensive supervision and services in the community, including programs that provide housing assistance and mental and physical health services.
4. Family integration during and after placement for both offenders and their families.
5. Mentoring programs that start in placement and continue into the community.
6. Victim-appropriate services, including those that promote the timely payment of restitution by offenders and those that offer services (such as security or counseling) to victims when offenders are released.
7. Protection of communities from dangerous offenders, including developing and implementing the use of risk assessment tools to determine when offenders should be released from prison.

The U.S. Justice Department launched a major initiative to implement and evaluate reentry services for prisoners and releasees, particularly high-risk, violent offenders. The Serious and Violent Offender Reentry Initiative (SVORI) began in 2003. SVORI attempted to measure how five major elements of reentry—criminal justice outcomes, housing, education, health, and employment—were affected by the creation of prerelease treatment plans and accessible services postrelease for eligible offenders. Substance abuse treatment, cognitive-based programs, and, in particular, educational programming proved to have modest yet positive effects on housing, education, health, and employment outcomes. Interestingly, programs with a focus on "practical needs"—employment, drug use, life skills, and reentry preparation—did not prove beneficial to ex-offenders and even negatively affected nonrecidivism outcomes in some cases. Recidivism outcomes were modest at best. The mixed results from the SVORI initiative are likely due to less than full implementation of the interventions, insufficient program dosage (amount or intensity of the intervention provided), and the fact that interventions were most intense while offenders were incarcerated, and tailed off after release (Visher and Travis 2011).

A number of states have placed a priority on tackling the issues surrounding prisoner reentry in the community. Below are short summaries of the actions taken by a number of states. While tactics among the states differ, a number of trends shine through. First and foremost is acknowledging the interconnectedness of reentry with the entirety of the criminal justice system.

Successful reentry into the community is closely tied to correctional and sentencing policies. A number of states have recognized the importance of this relationship and made crucial, comprehensive reforms across their criminal justice systems. One such state is Oregon, which features the lowest recidivism rate in the United States, and places a large emphasis on implementing evidence-based practices in its criminal justice system. Oregon's SB 267, passed in 2003, requires all corrections programs receiving money from the state to be evidence-based in both design and actual implementation, including regular evaluations. Additionally, in an effort to target the reentry process, prisoners in Oregon receive a risk and needs assessment at the time of intake into prison. These assessments serve as a basis for case management and the transition plan for the offender's release from prison, beginning six months prior to his or her release. Once on parole, offenders face graduated sanctions for violations of community supervision, including short-term stays in jail. As a result, only 3.3 percent of Oregon's offenders released from prison in 2004 returned to prison within three years due to a technical violation. Oregon's overall recidivism rate among released prisoners is 22.8 percent—vastly better than the national average (Pew Center on the States 2011).

Michigan emphasized improving reentry outcomes among offenders through the Michigan Prisoner Reentry Initiative (MPRI). Born initially out of a budget crisis, the MPRI was expanded statewide in 2008 after positive results at a local level. Under MPRI, offenders receive a risk, needs, and strength assessment at prison intake, which is used to create a case management plan. Prior to release, inmates transfer to a facility specifically tailored to those about to reenter society, where a transition plan is created to address the necessities of postrelease life. This is done in close conjunction with community service providers. The results are impressive: offenders involved in MPRI are one-third less likely to return to prison than those who do not participate. Additionally, due to greater confidence in the ability of parole to reduce recidivism, parole boards are approving more offenders for parole, relieving some of the stress on Michigan's prisons (Pew Center on the States 2011).

Missouri has addressed reentry issues at both the incarceration stage and the postrelease stage. While an offender is incarcerated, the Missouri Department of Corrections uses an assessment of the offender to create a Transition Accountability Plan, which is shared with the parole board and the parole agency responsible for the offender following his release from prison (Council of State Governments 2005). Missouri has also targeted its historically high levels of parole revocations due to technical violations. Recognizing the strain placed on its criminal justice system (and the inevitable costs that accompany such a heavy reliance on incarceration), Missouri created a comprehensive plan to reduce the number of technical violations. This approach took the form of an "inter-agency team that drafted a vision and set goals, continued through a pilot project and ultimately took flight through new policies and procedures, coupled with extensive parole and probation staff training, in 2006" (Pew Center on the States 2011: 23). Postprison supervision is now referred to as "e-driven supervision," an evidence-based supervision using risk assessment tools and a variety of graduated sanctions that do not include prison time. Since implementing "e-driven supervision," Missouri's prison population has leveled out and the two-year recidivism rate among offenders dropped from 46 percent in 2004 to 36.4 percent in 2009 (Pew Center on the States 2011: 23).

The Urban Institute convened a wide variety of national practitioner and academic experts on parole supervision to identify strategies to enhance reentry outcomes. The experts identified thirteen strategies for which there was consensus (Solomon et al. n.d.). Two primary approaches were utilized: (a) research evidence on parole strategies; and (b) because of the relative scarcity of such research, "best thinking" or the combination of expert and practitioner experience, knowledge, and theory was also used. The thirteen strategies are as follows:

1. Define success as recidivism reduction and measure performance (focus on outcomes, such as recidivism reduction, rather that outputs, like contact standards).
2. Tailor conditions of supervision to the individual (responsivity).
3. Focus resources on moderate- and high-risk parolees.
4. Frontload supervision resources.
5. Implement earned discharge.
6. Implement place-based supervision based on GIS assessment of the location of parolees.
7. Engage partners to expand intervention capacities.
8. Assess criminogenic risk and need factors.
9. Develop and implement supervision case plans that balance surveillance and treatment.
10. Involve parolees to enhance their engagement in assessment, case planning, and supervision.
11. Engage informal social controls to facilitate community reintegration .
12. Incorporate incentives and rewards into the supervision process.
13. Employ graduated, problem-solving responses to violations of parole conditions in a swift and certain manner.

Moreover, Petersilia (2004) indicated that the evidence also supports beginning treatment in prison and providing continuity in the community by continuing treatment and/or aftercare, and providing intensive interventions for at least six months. These strategies are standard evidence-based practices that overlap nearly completely with what I discussed earlier in this chapter regarding probation. As I discussed there, these evidence-based practices, faithfully and fully implemented, are the starting point. Meta-analyses of particular reentry programs have used ratings of the quality of evaluations to determine which are more rigorous than others. The use of these methodological and statistical criteria allows readers to have added confidence regarding what has been demonstrated to be effective. Programs that have been shown to work in prisoner reentry include employment, in the form of vocational and work programs that improve job readiness; drug treatment, including intensive treatment in prison, followed by integrated aftercare after release; and transitional housing, often in the form of halfway houses. Research shows that participation improves employment, self-sufficiency, self-support, and participation in other improvement programming (James 2011; Seiter and Kadela 2003).

ADDITIONAL CONSIDERATIONS FOR PAROLE
AND SUPERVISED RELEASE

Several states have begun reducing their prison populations, as well as expanding probation caseloads. This is largely a response to tight budgets as a consequence of the recession that began in 2008. While reducing the prison population and increasing reliance on probation are moves in the right direction, absent many essential elements, these efforts may very well jeopardize public safety. Releasing inmates from prison without the resources in place to manage risk, reduce recidivism and enhance successful reentry is incautious.

As I discussed earlier, parole, like probation, must ramp up efforts to assess, diagnose, and treat a variety of criminogenic deficits, including the array of neurocognitive impairments that often are found among criminal offenders. We need to get better at assessing trauma and its effects. Substance abuse is a quite prevalent criminogenic factor, but efforts at intervention pale in comparison to the need. Absent housing, employment, and mental health, successful reentry is problematic. Supervised release needs to achieve a balance between risk management, control, and accountability on the one hand, and rehabilitation on the other. Individual offenders should be considered individuals, not categories. Furthermore, supervision agencies should not rely on prisons engaging in much more treatment or release preparation than they currently do. There needs to be the realistic presumption that the bulk of the assessment, planning, treatment, and aftercare will be the responsibility of community corrections.

Culture Change

The bigger picture is a cultural change in how we think about supervised release and recidivism, and how we think about, develop, and implement the tools, tactics, training, and funding needed to effectively reduce risk, recidivism, and victimization. Failure on parole (revocation) is not a success. It should not be a sorting device, driven by the strategy of "tail 'em, nail 'em, and jail 'em." Failure is in many cases avoidable and preventable if we are willing to do what it takes, especially for the near- and medium-term timeline for supervised release. The challenges are substantial. This is a higher-risk population than probation and higher risk still due to the criminogenic effects of prison, as well as the barriers we continue to impose on releasees during the supervision period and after they are discharged from parole.

Caseloads

Caseload size, which translates into workload demand, must be reduced if we are serious about risk management and recidivism reduction. Parolees present complex constellations of problems, deficits, and circumstances, and they are high risk and reoffend quickly and often. Supervision is not enough, but if it was, current caseloads do not permit effective supervision, let alone accommodating what parole should look like going forward.

Role of the Supervision Officer

As is the case with probation, the role of the parole officer needs substantial revision. It is clear that the case manager and law enforcement role is insufficient for reducing recidivism. Once again, the goal is to strike a balance between supervision and control and change agent. This is a new perspective and requires a cultural change and training and retraining in approaches such as problem solving. The STICS, STARR, and EPICS programs are appropriate for training parole officers in this new role. The Center for Effective Public Policy, the Urban Institute, and the Carey Group have developed a series of coaching packets as part of the Bureau of Justice Assistance's Prisoner Reentry Initiative (Domurad and Carey 2010). These provide technical assistance to local jurisdictions regarding strategic planning for reentry initiatives, implementing evidence-based practices, case management, behavioral change, and so on. Much of the material in these coaching packets is relevant to supervision staff and supervision officers as well as administrators.

A Promising Risk-Assessment Strategy

Risk assessment has improved significantly in the past ten years, but there is still considerable room for improvement. This is a critical issue because the efficacy of intervention efforts depends on our ability to identify for whom interventions are appropriate and potentially productive. Recent research on "signaling" provides an opportunity to incorporate and test the role of signals that inmates or parolees send regarding their willingness to engage in activities and programs that are prosocial. The example used in the research is employment training (Bushway and Apel 2012). The fact that an inmate participates in employment training or other voluntary activities while incarcerated, activities that require significant effort, may indicate they are a good candidate for intervention or successful reentry. Such signals may also be used postrelease to tap likelihood of reoffending and reentry outcomes. The fact that these kinds of measures are potentially fluid and can be assessed in real time makes them appealing. It is certainly worth investigating their relevance in the bigger picture of risk and recidivism reduction (Mears and Mestra 2012).

Collaboration with Key Stakeholders

The initiatives discussed here require more than establishing partnerships with local community-based resources. Clearly that is necessary as capacity for rehabilitative programming is extremely limited. In addition, however, the cooperation and collaboration of a variety of other justice agencies are required. These include law enforcement, prosecutors, judges, parole authorities, legislators, and the executive branch (Vera Institute of Justice 2013). But it is not just soliciting cooperation. Instead, this effort requires selling the benefits of these new initiatives to individuals who have been practicing in an environment of crime control and punishment. The rebalancing of risk management/control on the one hand, and rehabilitation and behavioral change on the other, is not a "no brainer" for all key players in the justice system.

Setting Appropriate Expectations

I am talking about an evolutionary process, one that requires many moving parts to act in concert. Changing minds, changing policy, changing procedure and practice, changing law, and changing funding will take time.

Leadership

Effective, visionary, bold leadership is essential to guide this process, motivate cooperation and compliance, and implement the necessary changes.

It is not just a matter of having the language down. Being familiar with evidence-based practices is not the same as directing the faithful, full implementation of evidence-based practices. It requires that the leadership "gets it," which places added pressure on making the right choices in the selection process, but it is absolutely essential.

Funding

What is proposed here, as in the case with probation, is a substantial ramping up of efforts and resources, and in turn funding. Current funding models will not support the level and scope of implementation required to reduce recidivism and enhance successful reentry. A reasonable approach for parole funding going forward is the performance incentive funding model developed and utilized in California, Illinois, and several other states (Vera Institute of Justice 2013)

In order for this performance incentive funding model to work, parole agencies will need to be tied to specific geographic areas. Probation agencies are typically at the county level. Parole may or may not be so geographically specific. That way, performance is assessed at a local level and funding is allocated to a local area.

Reentry Courts

The alternative, problem-solving court model has evolved into a variety of different types, including one of the more recent versions, the reentry court. The premise is quite similar to drug courts, mental health courts, or community courts. The model is based on therapeutic jurisprudence or judicial oversight to assure accountability and enhance public safety, and programming and services to facilitate behavioral change. The primary difference is that while the other versions are diversion courts, the reentry court deals with the population of offenders who have been released from prison. The key strategy is the adaptation of the principles of problem solving, community-based services, and judicial oversight to manage the transition from prison to community.

The rationale for reentry courts centers on several observations. First, prison releasees are high risk and high needs and therefore require a coordinated, powerful intervention or set of interventions to facilitate behavioral change. Moreover, because of their high risk and high needs, a highly structured environment is preferable to leaving a highly structured environment (prison) and moving to a much less structured environment. Third, the judge, as a significant authority figure, can serve as a powerful change agent who takes an interest in individuals' welfare and progress, who hands out incentives and sanctions, and who problem solves and provides links with necessary social services (clearly with the assistance of expert court staff). Finally, the court can help hold collaborating local community agencies to a necessary standard of care and accountability, and can hold the offender and all other participants in the process to a high level of accountability and performance.

Today there are over twenty-five reentry courts across the nation. While they share a similar basic premise, they differ somewhat in design, implementation, and operation. Here is what is known about the key components of a reentry court, based on research conducted by the Center for Court Innovation and the Bureau of Justice Assistance (Hamilton 2010; Lindquist et al. 2013; Wolf 2011). They include psychosocial screening and assessment to determine criminogenic needs and services required; collaborative case planning involving the judge, case manager, parole officer, and clinical experts; active oversight by the judge, parole officer, and case manager, involving formal court appearances and supervision; management of support services involving court monitoring of social services; intensive case management as needed; accountability to the community by payment of fees and restitution; collaboration with victims' groups; graduated and parsimonious sanctions in lieu of revocation; swift and certain sanctions in which revocation is a last resort; and rewards and incentives for success and progress, including public praise and other types of incentives.

A focus on procedural justice keeps the proceedings open and public, and enhances the perception of fairness, which in turn is important for offender participation and cooperation. It may be beneficial to incorporate the HOPE Court model of a warning hearing up front that clarifies roles, responsibilities, expectations, and consequences. As is the case in other problem-solving courts, judicial authority is collaborative (with the parole officer and clinical staff, among others) and the judge is involved with issues such as case planning, case management, and supervision, as well as incentives and sanctions. Ideally, it should be the same court that monitors the parolee in the reentry process as sentenced him or her originally. As Judge Jeffrey Tauber of Reentry Court Solutions notes:

> This is perhaps the most promising reentry drug court hybrid developed to date. The court maintains jurisdiction and authority over the felon and a well-structured program beginning (optimally) at the time of plea or probation violation, provides a seamless process, with the same personnel working with the participant over the course of the program. Future programs may see the value of interim progress reports and the opportunity for negative incentives while in prison.

Reentry courts tend to frontload supervision, rehabilitative, and training resources during the first six months or so after release from prison. Caseloads for parole officers tend to be lower than the average of seventy for standard parole, typically around forty per officer. This permits closer supervision and more attention to social services and problem-solving activities.

The reentry court model is a preferable approach for a variety of reasons. First, the preliminary evaluation research shows that reentry courts reduce recidivism (rearrest and reconviction). There is some evidence that revocation increases in reentry courts, but this is at least in part a supervision effect, that is, lower caseloads lead to greater supervision, which can lead to more frequent discovery of violations. Moreover, parole, like probation, is local. Individuals released from prison are released to a local jurisdiction. It makes less sense to have administrative decisions like supervision standards, conditions of supervision, and disciplinary and revocation decisions made by some state or regional office. A reentry court judge is usually in a better position, in collaboration with the parole officer, clinical staff, and program providers, among others, to make decisions about treatment and rehabilitation, sanctions, and incentives. It is also quite likely that a reentry court will have greater assessment, case management, planning, and rehabilitation resources compared to parole as usual.

CHAPTER 7

Recalibrating Drug Control Policy

I found a quote on the drug war that I want to share with you in closing. "The war against drugs provides politicians with something to say that offends nobody, requires them to do nothing difficult, allows them to postpone, perhaps indefinitely, the more urgent questions about the state of the nation's schools, housing, employment opportunities for young black men, the condition to which drug addiction speaks as a symptom not a cause. They remain safe in the knowledge that they might as well be denouncing Satan and so they can direct the voices of prerecorded blame at metaphors and apparitions, wars and battles." The war on drugs becomes a perfect war for people who would rather not fight. A war on which politicians who stand fearlessly on the side of the good, the true, and the beautiful need do nothing else but strike noble poses as protectors of the people and defenders of the public trust. We can't let that continue.

— Judge Nancy Gertner, United States District Court, Boston, Massachusetts

IN THIS CHAPTER, I FOCUS on drug crime. The reason for discussing drug crime in a separate chapter is because of the many unique and far-reaching consequences drug use and drug crimes have for the U.S. criminal justice system, criminal justice policy, economic and social costs, and public health.

Drug control and the "War on Drugs" have played a fundamental role in U.S. criminal justice policy over the past forty years. The statistical evidence is clear: absent the War on Drugs, the incarceration boom would have been considerably smaller in scale (Caplow and Simon 1999) and U.S.

prisons would be incarcerating nearly 500,000 fewer prison inmates today. Approximately 25 percent of all inmates incarcerated in state prisons are drug offenders (over 350,500 inmates) and 65 percent of federal prison inmates are drug offenders (over 136,300 federal inmates). Moreover, drugs contribute substantially to overall crime problems. Research (Caulkins, Rydell, Schwabe, and Chiesa 1997) estimates that 25 percent of crime in the United States is directly drug caused (not just drug related). Add drug-related crime to drug-caused crime and it is close to 50 percent of crimes, if not higher. A 1996 study found that between 50 and 80 percent of individuals arrested for a nondrug crime tested positive for drugs at the time of their arrest (Freeman 1996).

In 2014, somewhere between 60 and 80 percent of inmates in U.S. prisons and jails met the standard diagnostic criteria in the DSM-IV for alcohol and/or drug dependence or abuse. Because rehabilitative programming is essentially nonexistent in prisons and jails, at best 15 percent of those in need of substance abuse treatment receive *any* intervention, let alone treatment that realistically meets their needs. Extrapolating the numbers amounts to somewhere between 1,100,000 and 1,540,000 prison and jail inmates in need of substance abuse treatment. Between 165,000 and 231,000 receive any treatment while under correctional control.

The National Institute on Drug Abuse estimates that 5 million of the 7 million individuals under correctional control in the United States (prison, jail, probation, and parole) would benefit from substance abuse treatment (that is, 71 percent, a figure that has repeatedly been replicated as a reasonable estimate of the percent of the criminal justice population that is abusing, dependent, or addicted to substances).

Of the approximately 600,000 to 700,000 inmates released each year, approximately 400,000 of those in need of substance abuse treatment leave prison and jail untreated. Over a ten-year period, these are numbers rivaling the entire population of Los Angeles, the second-largest city in the United States, or the populations of Chicago and Indianapolis combined.

The connection between substance abuse and crime is well established, as is the failure of punishment to reduce the likelihood of substance use, let alone substitute for treatment. The cycle continues as addicted and substance-abusing individuals repeatedly reenter the justice system, causing the expenditure of police, jail, prosecutor, court, and corrections resources each time they cycle through.

There is a clear relationship between substance abuse and homelessness. The National Institute on Drug Abuse estimates that 31 percent of homeless Americans suffer from drug or alcohol abuse. Whether cause or effect, the result is that both addiction and homelessness are criminogenic circumstances (National Coalition for the Homeless 2009). The problems with addiction and homelessness are particularly acute among individuals released from prison and jail. Survey data from several states indicate that anywhere from 10 to 30 percent of individuals released from prison are homeless (Bureau of Justice Assistance 2006; Rodriguez and Brown 2003). When mental illness is added to the mix, the criminogenic situation becomes dramatically exacerbated.

Drug and alcohol abuse take a tremendous toll on U.S. public health and have extraordinary fiscal impacts such as lost productivity, physical and mental health consequences, and crime. The Substance Abuse and Mental Health Services Administration (SAMHSA), a federal agency that sponsors research and provides funding for direct services, reports that in 2009, there were nearly 2.3 million hospital emergency department visits for health issues associated with drug abuse. A recent study by the National Institutes of Health (Caldwell et al. 2013) estimates that the median cost of an emergency department visit is $1,233. Extrapolating the number of drug-related visits indicates a cost of those 2.3 million visits of around $2,835,900,000. It is also estimated that every year, there are approximately 30,000 drug-related deaths in the United States. The Johns Hopkins University estimates that the total economic impact of substance abuse, including lost productivity and health- and crime-related costs, exceeds $600 billion annually. By way of comparison, in 2011, the fifty states combined had budget expenditures from state general funds of $637 billion. Moreover, cancer costs society $172 billion annually, and diabetes costs $132 billion annually.

The National Center on Addiction and Substance Abuse at Columbia University reports that in 2005, state and federal governments combined spent over $467 billion on substance abuse and addiction. Only 1.9 percent of those funds were spent on treating and preventing addiction. As noted in their 2009 report "Shoveling It Up: The Impact of Substance Abuse on Federal, State and Local Budgets" (2):

A staggering 71.1 percent of total federal and state spending on the burden of addiction is in two areas: health and justice. Almost three-fifths (58.0 percent) of federal and state spending on the burden of substance abuse and addiction (74.1 percent of the federal burden) is in the area of health care where untreated addiction causes or contributes to over 70 other diseases requiring hospitalization. The second largest area of substance-related federal and state burden spending is the justice system (13.1 percent).

The title of the National Center's report—"Shoveling It Up"—is a reflection of the nearly exclusive focus of federal and state spending on the consequences of substance abuse and addiction, rather than on treatment and prevention. As noted in the report, for every dollar that federal and state governments spend on prevention and treatment of substance abuse and addiction, they spend nearly $60 on shoveling up the consequences, primarily in terms of public health, crime, and criminal justice consequences. In 2005, federal and state governments spent over $207 billion on the health consequences of substance abuse and addiction. Nearly 10 percent of the federal budget, 16 percent of state budgets, and 9 percent of local budgets are spent on the consequences of addiction and substance abuse.

SAMHSA estimates that, in 2011, there were 21.6 million individuals in the United States in need of alcohol and/or drug treatment; 2.3 million received treatment at a specialty facility. Nearly 20 million individuals in need of treatment did not receive it. The primary reasons for not receiving treatment are lack of health care coverage and inability to pay for treatment out of pocket.

There appears to be clear agreement that the consequences of substance abuse and addiction have substantial fiscal impacts, particularly with regard to health care and criminal justice. Moreover, there is scientific consensus that substance abuse and addiction treatment is effective and cost-effective. The National Institute on Drug Abuse estimates that the return on investment of drug/alcohol treatment may exceed 12:1, meaning that for every dollar invested in treatment, there is an expected savings of $12 in drug-related health care and criminal justice costs.

The U.S. demand for drugs—some call it our insatiable appetite—has consequences that reach well beyond our own borders. That demand has resulted in one-half to two-thirds of the marijuana in the United States originating in Mexico; 95 percent of the cocaine that enters the United States travels through Mexico; Mexico is also a major supplier of heroin and methamphetamine to the United States. It is estimated that between $19 and $29 billion are being put into the coffers of the cartels annually by

U.S. drug users. It is further estimated that the drug trade makes up approximately 10 percent of the Mexican economy. By way of comparison, the entire manufacturing sector of the U.S. economy constituted 11.7 percent of total gross domestic product in 2010.

In 2006, Filipe Calderon initiated a massive crackdown on the Mexican drug cartels. In the time since that initiative was launched, over 50,000 people have been killed in drug-related violence. Included in this figure are over 3,000 Mexican soldiers and police. Beginning in 2010, the targeting of the cartel-initiated violence began to shift to elected officials in Mexico, including nineteen sitting mayors and numerous other elected officials. Moreover, the Mexican government is experiencing substantial and widespread corruption and economic hardship, leading many observers (for example, Stratfor, a private firm that provides strategic intelligence on economic, security, and geopolitical affairs) to predict that Mexico is on a path to becoming a failed state. At the heart of all of this is the U.S. demand for illicit drugs.

U.S. DRUG CONTROL POLICY

In 1970, President Richard Nixon declared war on drugs in signing the Comprehensive Drug Abuse Prevention and Control Act. Nixon declared "the nation faces a major crisis in terms of the increasing use of drugs, particularly among our young people." The next year Nixon ramped up the language: "Public enemy No. 1 in the United States is drug abuse. In order to fight and defeat this enemy, it is necessary to wage a new, all-out offensive."

Nixon also brought drug control policy into the executive branch of the federal government by creating the Drug Enforcement Administration (DEA). Control of drug policy over time continued to be concentrated in the White House. The Reagan administration shifted focus from heroin as the drug of primary concern to cocaine. Obviously, the concern over cocaine was greatly fueled by the crack epidemic, which began in 1984 on the west coast of the United States and quickly spread east. The conversion of powder cocaine to crack was a business decision by the drug cartels. Faced with an oversupply of powder cocaine and consequently falling prices, the cartels launched crack, which was sold in smaller quantities, was easy to use, and was profitable. By 1987, crack was available essentially throughout the urban areas of the United States.

A significant amount of violence accompanied the introduction of crack in U.S. cities. While the conventional wisdom at the time largely viewed the violence as a pharmacological effect of crack, the reality was that it was due to the "negotiations" of street gangs for the new, profitable crack markets. That violence added an accelerated level of fear to the drug problem.

The Reagan administration took a hard, punitive line regarding drug control policy, implementing mandatory minimum sentences for federal drug law violations in 1986, ramping up the punishment for drug crimes in the Federal Sentencing Guidelines in 1987, taking a zero-tolerance stand on drug law violations, and positioning the drug problem as a national security threat. Nancy Reagan's "Just Say No" campaign reinforced the idea that drug use and addiction are willful acts, presumably due to a weakness of character. The solution: just don't do it. That logic fits well with a primarily punitive approach to drug use. Punishment should be an effective remedy to a conscious, willful decision.

The National Drug Abuse Act of 1988 created the Office of National Drug Control Policy (ONDCP). It was signed into law in 1988 by then-president Reagan. The War on Drugs metaphor was extended by the designation of the director of the ONDCP as the Drug Czar. The first Drug Czar, under President George H. W. Bush, was William Bennett, a conservative on a variety of social issues, who expanded the arsenal of the War on Drugs to the Department of Defense. The drug control efforts were further expanded under the Clinton administration, in part as a consequence of the Republican Contract with America initiative, as well as a shift in the political equity associated with crime control policies, that is, the Clinton administration's tough on crime stance.

The aftermath of September 11, 2001, led to framing the War on Drugs as a part of the war on terror. As President George W. Bush put it: "If you quit drugs, you join the fight against terrorism." The Bush administration dramatically expanded U.S. interdiction in Columbia and Afghanistan, aimed at reducing production of cocaine and heroin, and interdiction in Mexico (the Merida Initiative), targeting drug trafficking activities in Mexico, Central America, and parts of the Caribbean.

For most of its forty-plus-year existence, the bulk of the federal effort and the funding for the War on Drugs have focused on controlling supply. Trends in the budget for the Office of National Drug Control Policy show an increasing emphasis on supply reduction, compared to demand reduction. In 2002, 27 percent of the federal drug control budget was for drug treatment and 54 percent was for supply reduction (domestic law enforcement, interdiction, and international activities). By 2006, the treatment budget fell to 23 percent compared to the supply reduction increase to over 62 percent. In 2011, the drug treatment budget was at 25 percent, but supply control rose to 64 percent. The 2012 budget significantly increased allocations for treatment (34 percent) and supply control was reduced somewhat to 59 percent. The 2013 budget was quite similar (36 percent for treatment and 59 percent for supply control). In addition to that funding stream, asset forfeiture laws helped provide a built-in incentive to keep drug control efforts focused on supply reduction. Local law enforcement and prosecutors are able to lawfully retain assets seized in the course of drug arrests and prosecutions. These assets include money, property, and real estate, among other things, and they provide a significant, generally unaudited revenue stream to operating budgets

Over the past decade, the federal government has spent nearly $100 billion on efforts to control the supply of illegal drugs in the United States. The obvious question is whether and to what extent this approach has been successful.

There are two readily available metrics regarding the impact of the U.S. drug control strategy: the street-level cost of illicit drugs and usage rates of illicit drugs. The drug cost metric is a simple reflection of supply and demand. Assuming demand is constant, if supply control efforts are sufficiently successful in reducing supply, there should be some evidence of that on the street in higher prices. Use rates of illicit drugs should go down over time if efforts to reduce supply (and deter drug use) are successful.

To be fair, these are "wholesale" metrics that focus on drug prices and drug use rates for the United States as a whole. It is quite possible that these aggregate statistics mask local variation that reflect greater or lesser impacts of drug control policy. However, our question is whether on balance, U.S. policies have had the desired impacts and outcomes.

Street-level drug price data for the period from 1980 to 2009 indicate that while there is some year-to-year fluctuation, the general trend for cocaine, crack, heroin, and methamphetamine has been downward. There was a dramatic reduction in price that began in the early to mid-1980s and continued through the early to mid-1990s. Prices essentially stabilized through the early 2000s. Marijuana follows a slightly different trend, actually increasing in price through the early 1990s, declining through the rest of the 1990s, and then essentially stabilizing through the early 2000s (Office of National Drug Control Policy 2011).

The data on illicit drug use over the period from 1979 to 2010 for the population twelve years of age and older reflects a significant drop in "current use of any illicit drug" from 1979 to 1988, followed by a period of stabilization from 1990 to 2000, then an increase between 2001 and 2010. Much of the trend is driven by marijuana use because it is the most common drug in the category "any illicit drug."

About 22.6 million U.S. residents used any illicit drug in 2010. The majority, 17.4 million, used marijuana; 7 million used psychotherapeutics (stimulants, pain relievers, tranquilizers, and sedatives); 1.5 million used cocaine (including crack); 1.2 million used hallucinogens; 0.7 million used inhalants; and 0.2 million used heroin.

The expectations, if U.S. drug policies were working, would be noticeable increases in drug prices and noticeable declines in drug use. The evidence indicates, at least according to these metrics, that U.S. drug policy does not seem to be working.

In 1990, the journal *Science* noted that the United States was "still flying blind in the war on drugs." Little has changed. There continues to be substantial discussion (but much less debate) about the effectiveness of the U.S. supply control efforts. The conclusions are approaching unanimity. The War on Drugs as it has been waged has not worked. There is no shortage of commentary declaring at least a ceasefire, if not an all-out surrender, with regard to the supply control effort. Every major (and many more minor) media outlet has reported the growing consensus:

"'War on drugs' has failed, say Latin American leaders," *The Guardian*, April 2012

"It's time to end dismally failed 'war on drugs,'" *Chicago Sun-Times*, June 2011

"It's time to end the failed war on drugs," *The Telegraph*, November 2012

"Commentary: 40 years of War on Drugs Failure: Rethink the warfighting model," *The Palm Beach Post*, June 2011

"The Drug Czar's Report Card: F," *New York Times*, October 2008

"Kofi Annan, George Shultz say drug war a failure," *Christian Science Monitor*, June 2011

> "The War on Drugs is a Failure so Give Drug Policy Back to the States,"
> *Forbes*, July 2011
>   "U.S. Drug war has met none of its goals," *NBC News*, May 2010
>   "War on Drugs a Trillion-Dollar Failure," *CNN*, December 2012
>   "Let's Be Blunt: It's Time to End the Drug War," *Forbes*, April 2012
>   "U.S. can't justify its drug war spending, reports say," *Los Angeles Times*,
> June 2011
>   "Numbers Tell of Failure in Drug War," *New York Times*, July 2012
>   "Obama should have the 'audacity' to end the war on drugs," *Daytona*
> *Times*, May 2013
>   "Chicago's Top Cop Calls U.S. War on Drugs 'Wholesale Failure,'"
> *Huffington Post*

Gil Kerlikowske, the Obama administration's director of National Drug Control Policy until March 2014, conceded the strategy hasn't worked. "In the grand scheme, it has not been successful," Kerlikowske told the *Associated Press*. "Forty years later, the concern about drugs and drug problems is, if anything, magnified, intensified."

Former president Jimmy Carter wrote in the *New York Times* (June 2011) a plea to "Call Off the Global War on Drugs." He stated:

> In a message to Congress in 1977, I said the country should decriminalize the possession of less than an ounce of marijuana, with a full program of treatment for addicts. I also cautioned against filling our prisons with young people who were no threat to society, and summarized by saying: "Penalties against possession of a drug should not be more damaging to an individual than the use of the drug itself." These ideas were widely accepted at the time. But in the 1980s President Ronald Reagan and Congress began to shift from balanced drug policies, including the treatment and rehabilitation of addicts, toward futile efforts to control drug imports from foreign countries.

In June of 2011, the Global Commission on Drug Policy issued a report that articulated the failure of the U.S. supply side drug control effort. The Commission, consisting of former presidents and prime ministers of five nations, a former United Nations secretary general, as well as George Schultz (former Secretary of the Treasury and Labor under President

Nixon and Secretary of State under President Reagan) and Paul Volcker (former chair of the Federal Reserve under Presidents Carter and Reagan), concluded that the "global war on drugs has failed with devastating consequences to individuals and societies around the world." The Commission's conclusions are an extraordinary indictment of U.S. (and other nations') drug policies.

> Vast expenditures on criminalization and repressive measures directed at producers, traffickers and consumers of illegal drugs have clearly failed to effectively curtail supply or consumption. Apparent victories in eliminating one source or trafficking organization are negated almost instantly by the emergence of other sources and traffickers. Repressive efforts directed at consumers impede public health measures to reduce HIV/AIDS, overdose fatalities and other harmful consequences of drug use. Government expenditures on futile supply reduction strategies and incarceration displace more cost-effective and evidence-based investments in demand and harm reduction.

The U.K. Drug Policy Commission concluded back in 2007 that the drug control policies of the United Kingdom, the United States, or other nations do not influence the number of drug users in that country, nor the proportion of drug users who are dependent, abusing, or addicted (Reuter and Stevens 2007). That conclusion led the Commission to recommend that the area in which national drug control policy can have an effective impact is in terms of harm reduction strategies. A similar conclusion was offered by the Beckley Foundation's global report on cannabis use and policy. They conclude that the principal goal of a government's drug control policy should focus on harm reduction.

Most recently, on August 12, 2013, in a speech before the American Bar Association, Eric Holder, the Attorney General of the United States stated:

> As the so-called "war on drugs" enters its fifth decade, we need to ask whether it, and the approaches that comprise it, have been truly effective—and build on the Administration's efforts, led by the Office of National Drug Control Policy, to usher in a new approach.

Public opinion has shown remarkable consistency over the past ten to fifteen years in Americans' recognition that the drug problem in the United

States has not gotten better, and that the War on Drugs has failed. As far back as the mid-1990s, the public recognized these failures, but ironically they also supported continued expenditure of resources for the drug war (Blendon and Young 1998). At the same time, public opinion is fluid regarding remedies. In 1990, 41 percent responded that convicting and punishing for drug crimes "would do the most to reduce the drug problem in this country." Five years later, only 21 percent thought such a strategy would remedy the problem. A Pew survey found a similar pattern. In 1988, nearly 40 percent believed arresting drug users was a productive strategy. By 2001, that had dropped to 30 percent. Moreover, the 2001 Pew survey found that the majority (52 percent) of respondents believe that drug use should be treated as a disease, rather than as a crime.

Two recent public opinion polls, one conducted in June 2012 and one in November 2012, continue to show that the public believes that the War on Drugs has been a failure. In June 2012 (Angus Reid, June 6, 2012), an online poll found that 66 percent of respondents believe U.S. drug policy has been futile (only 10 percent believe it is a success, and the rest do not know). The November 2012 telephone poll (Rasmussen, November 13, 2012) found that 82 percent of respondents believe the war on drugs has been a failure. In addition, only 23 percent of respondents in the Rasmussen poll believe that the United States should spend more on the War on Drugs, although it is not clear from the survey whether these respondents think that U.S. drug policy would be effective if more money were spent. Moreover, two thirds of the nation's chiefs of police believe the War on Drugs has been a failure.

The consensus of the evidence is that supply strategies have not worked. Crop eradication and border control efforts have not had any truly noticeable impact on the supply of illicit drugs in the United States. Nor has punishment and its threat had significant effects on distribution/dealing and drug use in the United States.

Research first conducted two decades ago confirms the failure of control strategies to produce positive outcomes and the fact that supply control efforts are a waste of public funds. An important cost benefit study conducted by The RAND Corporation in the 1990s revealed the relative and sizable disparity in the cost-effectiveness of supply versus demand approaches. RAND found that $1 invested in control tactics produces a cost savings of 15 cents if used for source country control efforts, 32 cents if used for interdiction strategies, and 52 cents if used for domestic (U.S.) enforcement strategies. They also found that $1 used for drug treatment produces a societal cost savings of $7.48.

U.S drug policies have not been effective, in simple terms, because demand is high and generally inelastic. There is so much money to be made and international drug distribution cartels have become extraordinarily sophisticated, adopting organizational strategies of successful large-scale corporations, but also relying on ruthless violence. High demand combined with highly efficient and effective distribution channels result in ample supply entering the United States.

While popular perception may suggest that U.S. prisons are filled up with low-level drug users, the reality is that the target of much of domestic drug intervention has been those involved at some level in distribution (Sevigny and Caulkins 2004). There are relatively few low-level drug users and relatively few high-level drug distribution kingpins incarcerated in U.S. prisons. The majority of incarcerated drug offenders are lower- to midlevel dealers. Most lower-level drug users occupy the nation's jails and probation caseloads. Significant numbers of them eventually graduate to prison upon conviction for more serious offenses.

Punishment does not significantly inhibit distribution of drugs (distribution within the United States) largely because of relatively high demand. The key reason that law enforcement efforts and incarceration do not impact drug dealing to any significant extent is because of the replacement effect. Arresting and incarcerating a dealer removes that individual from the street but does not remove the drug dealing. The removal of the dealer simply provides the opportunity for another individual to fill the vacancy. Economists have provided the evidence and the rationale for the replacement explanation (Bushway and Reuter 2011).

Punishment does not work for drug abusers and addicts because it does not change behavior. Recreational drug use may be affected by threats of punishment, but recreational use is not the primary concern. Chronic drug use—abuse, dependence, and addiction—have extraordinary consequences for public health, productivity, collateral crime, family integrity, and more. It is precisely these drug users, those who are abusing, dependent, and addicted, for whom punishment has no effect.

Those collateral consequences and costs of drug abuse are not mitigated by a national and local drug control policy that focuses largely on supply reduction and punishment. Absent a focus on demand reduction, abuse of drugs and alcohol will continue unabated at or near current levels and the costs and consequences will continue as well, requiring enormous expenditure of public resources.

The supply control efforts to date have had, as I have shown, little consistent, long-term impacts on street-level prices of drugs. Thus, an obvious question is: How much supply control is sufficient to trigger a price elasticity of demand effect, meaning that prices are high enough to dissuade users from purchasing drugs? Economists have shown that there is some evidence that initiation of use (not addiction, but recreational use) is price elastic (Rhodes et al. 2000). As prices increase, use levels decline. This is not particularly strong evidence, but it is suggestive. Thus, the argument is if we could sufficiently reduce supply to the point at which the price elasticity effect kicks in, we could in theory reduce at least initiation or recreational drug use. On the other hand, economists have demonstrated that demand for drugs among hardcore users (abusers, those dependent and addicted) is generally price inelastic—addiction trumps price.

ILLICIT DRUG USE AS A PUBLIC HEALTH ISSUE

Public opinion lags behind the scientific community's findings that drug abuse and drug addiction are clinical conditions. For example, a 2005 Ohio survey found that 72 percent of respondents believe drug users are to blame for their substance abuse problem. Forty percent of New Jersey survey respondents in a recent poll stated that substance abuse and addiction are a moral failing. Depending on the survey and question wording, roughly one-half of respondents state that they believe that substance abuse should be treated as a disease. Another survey found that the majority of Americans believe that drug abuse, dependence, and addiction are medical conditions and should be addressed that way (Pew Center on the States 2001). Somewhere between one-third and one-half believe it is a crime and is the business of the criminal justice system.

Substance abuse and dependence are diagnoses in the Diagnostic and Statistical Manual of Mental Disorders (DSM). The American Psychiatric Association, which produces the DSM, has announced significant revisions regarding substance abuse disorders, including expanding the number of recognized symptoms for drug and alcohol addiction and reducing the number of criteria required for a substance abuse diagnosis. The Surgeon General identified substance abuse and dependence as a disease years ago. The American Medical Association, the American Psychiatric Association, and the American Psychology Association have all recognized the disease model of substance abuse and addiction. The National Institute on Drug Abuse (NIDA) defines addiction and substance abuse as a chronic, often-relapsing brain disease that causes compulsive drug use, in spite of substantial harmful consequences to the addicted individual and to those around him or her. NIDA also notes that while the initial decision to take drugs is willful or voluntary, the changes to the brain caused by chronic substance use inhibit the ability to resist impulses to take drugs. One would be hard pressed to find a public health, medical, or mental health professional who denies the scientific evidence regarding the fact that substance abuse and addiction are a disease.

Physicians and Lawyers for National Drug Policy (PLNDP) is a partnership of physicians, lawyers, judges, medical organizations, and bar associations that has been in existence since 2004. Its purpose is to advocate for an evidence-based public health approach to national drug policy. PLNDP's policy priorities include removing barriers and increasing access to drug and alcohol treatment, using alcohol and drug screening as a clinical and public health tool, making substance abuse treatment available throughout the criminal justice system, and providing policymakers with research-based evidence for informed decision making.

In 2010, the Obama administration announced that it was shifting focus regarding illegal drug use. The new approach was a more comprehensive, balanced strategy, which included an enhanced emphasis on drug prevention and drug treatment, through a focus on evidence-based practices. Gil Kerlikowske, Obama's Drug Czar, stated "We've never worked the drug problem holistically. We'll arrest the drug dealer, but we leave the addiction." Kerlikowske said the new policy focus "changes the whole discussion about ending the war on drugs and recognizes that we have a responsibility to reduce our own drug use in this country." Kerlikowske criticized past drug strategies for measuring success by counting the number of children and teens who have not tried marijuana. At the same time, he said, the number of deaths from illegal and prescription drug overdoses was rising. "Putting treatment into the primary health care discussion is critical."

Thus, the new policy emphasizes treating drug use more as a public health issue, resulting in an enhanced focus on treatment and prevention. "By boosting community-based prevention, expanding treatment, strengthening law enforcement and working collaboratively with our global partners, we will reduce drug use and the great damage it causes in our communities," President Obama said. "I am confident that when we take the steps outlined in this strategy, we will make our country stronger and our people healthier and safer." The Obama administration's national drug control policy signaled a significant rebalancing of efforts.

On June 11, 2012, Kerlikowske clarified the Obama administration's position on drug and alcohol abuse and addiction. Kerlikowske stated: "Drug addiction is not a moral failing on the part of the individual, but a chronic disease of the brain that can be treated." Kerlikowske declared that the paradigmatic shift in policy is necessary because an emphasis primarily on incarceration and the criminal status of drug users fails to effectively address the problem by disregarding prevention, treatment, and recovery. In launching the Obama administration's 2012 National Drug Control Policy, labeled the 21st Century Drug Policy, Kerlikowske stated:

> Outdated policies like the mass incarceration of nonviolent drug offenders are relics of the past that ignore the need for a balanced public health and safety approach to our drug problem. The policy alternatives contained in our new Strategy support mainstream reforms based on the proven facts that drug addiction is a disease of the brain that can be prevented and treat-ed and that we cannot simply arrest our way out of the drug problem.

The rhetoric of the Obama administration indicates a more balanced approach, and the reality shows significant movement in that direction. Perhaps the most compelling evidence of that is the provision in the Affordable Care Act, passed in 2010, that requires, by 2014, insurers to cover substance abuse treatment just as they cover treatment for any other chronic disease (discussed in greater detail later in this chapter). The Obama administration has also revised some of the more punitive federal laws regarding punishment of drug offenders under the Federal Sentencing Guidelines and there are likely more revisions to mandatory drug sentences underway as part of General Holder's Smart on Crime initiative.

At the same time, while the 2011, 2012, and 2013 national drug control budgets reflect a trend toward modest increases in treatment and prevention resources, the clear majority of funds are still allocated to supply control efforts, essentially 60/40 supply reduction versus demand reduction. And the relative allocation of demand reduction and supply reduction resources has not changed in any significant ways since at least the early 2000s.

DEMAND REDUCTION

The primary reasons that punitive supply control strategies have failed are: (a) substance abuse, dependence, and addiction are disorders of the brain and punishment is not a clinical intervention that can change that behavior; and (b) arresting and incarcerating drug distributors does not remove the drug dealing—the replacement effect.

Demand reduction has two primary components: prevention and treatment. The scientific evidence is reasonably compelling with regard to prevention and very compelling regarding treatment.

Prevention

Most of the scientific evaluation of prevention focuses on child, adolescent, and teenage prevention programs. Babor and colleagues (2010) reviewed the drug abuse prevention literature and concluded that the effects of youth prevention efforts are modest and variable. One limitation is that most of the research has focused on delaying initiation of marijuana use, rather than harder drugs. Another limitation is the inability to address whether delaying initiation of marijuana use translates into lower lifetime use rates of marijuana and other drugs. Others observe that the gap between best practice and implementation is substantial and that many school-based programs are poorly implemented, especially those with higher-risk populations. With these (and other) limitations in mind, the authors concluded that such prevention programs are probably worthwhile (in terms of relatively low cost and modest benefit) regarding delaying initiation of drug use.

The research suggests that programs that are effective provide early intervention in the relevant environments of school and family and that focus on social and behavioral development. It has also been observed that effective school-based prevention programming may be less about a specific curriculum and more about the creation of an atmosphere of appropriate attitudes and expectations (Manski, Pepper, and Petrie 2001). Research shows that factors that predict the onset of a drug problem are the same as those that predict school failure, social isolation, aggression, and other behavioral problems. Thus, programs that address these root causes and that promote a more favorable developmental environment are more productive than those that simply provide drug information including the harms of drug use. And this makes intuitive sense as well. Programs that provide alternatives to drug use and reduce the motivation or need to use drugs are more productive than programs such as "just say no." Much of the prevention approaches in the United States have simply focused on the obvious problem: drugs and drug use. Programs (like DARE) that primarily provide drug-related information are not effective because they do not address the underlying causes or precipitants of drug use.

One of the key policy issues with such prevention programs is whether simply delayed initiation of marijuana (or other drugs) use is of sufficient benefit to warrant supporting these initiatives. At this point, the research is not dispositive regarding lifetime use effects as well as longer-term health, mental health, economic, social, and criminal justice consequences. However, the relatively low cost, as well as the other potential collateral benefits associated with engaging these programs (enhanced academic success, social development, reduction in aggression, and so on), indicate that they are worthwhile (Manski, Pepper, and Petrie 2001; Caulkins et al. 2002).

Treatment

One of the key concerns from a policy perspective is how to prevent individuals from entering the justice system on a drug-related incident in the first place and, for those who have entered, how to reduce the likelihood that they will return. The scientific evidence indicates that a key component of the solution to both is effective substance abuse treatment. Treatment not only reduces drug use, it also reduces the risk of intoxication-related crimes, the urgent need for money for drugs and therefore the need to take immediate risks, and it puts distance between the treated individual and the subculture of users and dealers.

Substance abuse treatment in the free world has been shown to be quite effective in reducing substance use when the treatment protocol follows evidence-based practices and is followed by long-term aftercare or maintenance, typically in the form of twelve-step programs like Alcoholics Anonymous and Narcotics Anonymous. Dr. Nora Volkow, the director of the National Institute of Drug Abuse, stated in 2004:

> In fact, recovery from addiction is an established reality, achieved through a variety of treatment modalities when they are matched for the needs of individual patients. Numerous studies have shown that addiction treatments are comparable in effectiveness to treatments for other chronic illnesses.

The evidence clearly indicates that drug addiction treatment fails for reasons quite similar to why treatment for other chronic diseases like asthma, diabetes, and hypertension fail (McLellan et al. 2000). The key appears to be long-term adherence to treatment and behavioral change. In the *Journal of the American Medical Association* analysis by McLellan and colleagues, treatment compliance, drop-out rates, and relapse rates were similar for drug/alcohol addiction, diabetes, hypertension, and asthma.

Substance abuse treatment in the free world is more effective than treatment in the corrections system. There are many reasons for that, including the fact that individuals in the free world likely have fewer criminogenic needs, may be more motivated to engage in treatment, are engaging in treatment in a more therapeutic environment compared to prison and jail, and have fewer of the challenges and limitations associated with the justice system. It is also likely that substance abuse treatment in the free world is more appropriate in terms of matching the intensity of treatment to the assessed need, implementing cognitive behavioral modalities, having well-trained treatment staff, and addressing co-occurring disorders, among others.

Historically, substance abuse treatment has been a stand-alone specialty, set apart from the general medical environment. Most treatment facilities are small, offering mainly outpatient services. Only about 25 percent of providers offer inpatient residential treatment. Treatment often does not employ current generation medications such as buprenorphine for opiate addiction. Moreover, evidence indicates that many treatment facilities are staffed by individuals with limited professional training (Buck 2011).

One of the major challenges in obtaining substance abuse treatment outside of the justice system has been cost—lack of personal resources and lack of proper insurance coverage for behavioral health treatment. The Affordable Care Act of 2010 will implement significant changes to the substance abuse treatment landscape, resulting in significantly enhanced access to treatment that is better integrated with general health care, and increased treatment capacity. The Affordable Care Act will expand the coverage in health plans for substance abuse treatment, and will dramatically expand the number of insured individuals with substance abuse disorders by a substantial increase in Medicaid eligibility. As Buck (2011: 1408–1409) concludes:

> Transforming the public substance abuse treatment system was never one of the explicit goals of health reform. But policies expanding health insurance coverage and providing substance abuse treatment benefits at parity with medical and surgical benefits are likely to have that effect. The result will be a different system of treatment, with a greater variety of larger providers in the mainstream of general health care. This will be a more ambulatory-based, medically oriented, and physician-directed system. . . . Although not originally designed to do so, health reform's changes offer the potential to address some of the concerns associated with the current system of public substance abuse care. These include limited funding and access to services, and the failure to develop and implement plans of care that effectively treat those with both substance abuse and physical health conditions. If health reform even partially addresses these problems, the result will be a system of care that greatly improves the treatment of substance abuse disorders in the United States.

In addition to the cost barriers to treatment, there is also the issue of denial of the problem and resistance to treatment. Adding to that difficulty is the fact that because substance abuse treatment has historically been segregated from general medical care, there are not that many entry points or portals into treatment.

Screening, Brief Intervention, and Referral to Treatment (SBIRT)

Every year, there are 7.6 million admissions to the nation's emergency rooms. Forty percent of those admitted have a positive blood alcohol concentration (BAC). Adding to that those on drugs results in 60 percent of ER admissions under the influence of drugs or alcohol. The Substance Abuse and Mental Health Services Administration (SAMHSA) has championed an integrated, comprehensive public health approach to early substance abuse intervention that was developed twenty-five years ago. The SAMHSA Screening, Brief Intervention and Referral to Treatment (SBIRT) model is a substance abuse early intervention strategy that makes imminent sense. Primary care offices, hospital emergency rooms, college and university health clinics, trauma centers, and community health centers are the intercept or contact points for engaging patients who have a substance abuse problem or are at risk of developing a disorder.

SBIRT consists of four components. First is universal screening during routine medical and dental visits, using a validated, standardized screening instrument, which assesses substance use and identifies people with substance use problems; the modal time for the screen is three to six minutes; SBIRT can be implemented by a wide variety of health professionals such as physicians, nurses, social workers, health educators, and paraprofessionals. Second, the brief intervention utilizes motivational interviewing techniques designed to enhance patients' awareness of substance use and its consequences, and motivate them toward positive behavioral change. Third, the therapy portion of the intervention may continue for those requiring more than the brief intervention mentioned above; this may involve additional motivational interviewing, further assessment, education, problem solving, coping mechanisms, and creating a supportive environment. Fourth, for individuals assessed as high risk, the SBIRT model provides referral to specialty substance abuse treatment.

One of the determinants of the success of SBIRT is the existence of well-established specialty care referral networks. It is also important that transitions from screening and assessment to brief interventions to referral to treatment be as seamless as possible. Simply referring individuals to treatment is insufficient. Efforts must also include follow-up to determine compliance, engagement, and participation.

SBIRT is designed to integrate and coordinate screening, intervention, prevention, and treatment into a comprehensive system of care. An essential characteristic is linking community health care and social service agencies with appropriate specialty substance abuse treatment. The goal is identifying risky and harmful use of substances, with the objective of securing treatment for those who are high risk and to reduce the number of people who are on the path to addiction through prevention, education, and treatment.

SBIRT is a unique, proactive community health initiative that places substance use, abuse, and addiction squarely in the arena of public health. That is an important step in what appears to be the right direction. The next question is: What do we know about how it works and whether it is effective?

The Columbia University National Center on Addiction and Substance Abuse has published (November 2012) an overview addressing the population that SBIRT is targeting, how SBIRT works across various settings, and whether it is effective. Their overall conclusion is that brief, targeted, opportunistic interventions are effective in helping at-risk individuals change their behavior. A summary of the results of fifteen systematic analyses and meta-analysis reveal the following (National Center on Addiction and Substance Abuse 2012: 4–5):

1. Most people with substance use problems do not seek formal treatment.
2. While risky substance users are often reluctant to seek specialist addiction treatment, about two-thirds do visit their general practitioner each year.
3. Substance use problems are overrepresented in populations seeking medical care, but screening and brief interventions for substance use are rarely performed in primary care.
4. SBIRT—even a five-minute intervention reduces risky substance use.
5. SBIRT in medical settings reduces health-related diseases and consequences related to risky substance use (for example, emergency room visits).
6. Screening and brief interventions work across settings, though the effects are more powerful in some than in others (primary care has very good outcomes).
7. Screening and brief interventions work across populations (for example, pregnant women, college students).
8. Simple feedback on risky substance use based on a brief screening is one of the most important factors in why people change.

The short answer to does SBIRT work is yes. Research demonstrates significant short-term (six-month) abstinence from alcohol and drug use as well as reductions in heavy use of alcohol and drugs, improvements in quality of life including education, employment, housing stability, reduced criminal justice involvement, and reductions in risky behaviors (Madras et al. 2009; Insight Project Research Group 2009; SAMHSA 2009, 2011). The evidence indicates there are also irrefutable improvements in short-term health and mental health and indications of substantial long-term benefits (Babor et al. 2007). There are demonstrated significant cost savings associated with SBIRT as well (SAMHSA 2009, 2011), including significantly reduced hospital admissions, traumas and injuries, and a conservative health-related cost benefit of 1:4, meaning for every $1 invested in SBIRT, there is a $4 savings in health-related costs.

Results from SAMHSA's initial SBIRT Cohort 1 Cross Site Evaluation indicate that 118 sites screened 658,000 patients between 2005 and 2009. The evaluation results demonstrate that SBIRT is associated with significant reductions in drug and alcohol use, up to a 27 percent reduction among high-risk individuals, as well as a reduction in the harms associated with substance use. The evaluation also indicates that SBIRT is economically viable and sustainable (SAMHSA n.d.: 33).

It is not clear how extensively SBIRT is implemented and how its implementation is distributed across different public health contact points (ERs/EDs, primary care clinics, school/college clinics, behavioral health settings, and employee assistance offices). At best probably fewer than 10 percent of those eligible for or in need of substance abuse intervention receive any SBIRT services.

The research evidence regarding the short-term prevention and treatment effects/benefits from alcohol and drug screening indicate it is a valuable and worthwhile intervention strategy. The current Office of National Drug Control Policy has as one of its action items increasing the adoption of and reimbursement for implementation of SBIRT. In announcing a funding enhancement to SBIRT in July 2012, the Obama administration acknowledged the importance of the public health approach of screening and intervention (ONDCP July 25, 2012).

"This program saves lives, saves money, and can reduce the significant burden our drug problem places on both health care and criminal justice systems," said Director Kerlikowske. "SBIRT represents the future of drug policy in America and I commend our partners in the medical community for working with us to implement smart approaches in health settings to reduce our Nation's challenges with substance use.

SAMHSA has recently issued a technical assistance guide for implementing SBIRT in a variety of settings (SAMHSA n.d.: 33).

Treatment in the Justice System

Substance abuse treatment among the incarcerated population is relatively absent. Research shows that approximately 80 to 85 percent of prison inmates in need of drug treatment do not receive it (Chandler, Fletcher, and Volkow 2009). Despite the challenges and limitations, treatment in an incarceration setting can be successful, though less so than community-based justice treatment programs. The therapeutic community (TC) model has been shown to be the most successful approach for the incarcerated population in terms of reducing both relapse and reoffending (Mitchell, Wilson, and MacKenzie 2007). The TC approach has existed for nearly forty years. It is a residential treatment model that incorporates stages of treatment that reflect increased levels of personal and social responsibility. It is at its core a peer-based approach that through a variety of group processes helps individuals acquire and assimilate social norms and social skills. The primary difference between TCs and other treatment approaches is the use of the community or peers as the key agents of change. TC members and staff interact to influence attitudes, perceptions, and behaviors associated with drug use. The concept of mutual self-help, also a core component of TCs, places partial responsibility for recovery on peers in the community.

There are many barriers to adequate treatment in the justice system. One of the ironies is that among policymakers and legislators, drug and alcohol abuse and addiction tend not to be recognized as medical conditions. Thus, there is no constitutional right to treatment as there is under the Eighth Amendment for medical conditions. Other barriers include lack of funding and resources (the priority by far under crime control has been control and punishment, at the expense of programming) and lack of infrastructure and trained treatment staff. For those who do receive treatment while incarcerated, the continuity of care postrelease is often missing, so loss of the treatment effect dramatically increases the likelihood of relapse and recidivism.

The scientific community is quite clear regarding what works in correctional substance abuse treatment. What is missing for both the incarcerated population and the community supervision population of offenders is the widespread institutional recognition and acceptance that treatment is essential for longer-term crime and recidivism reduction, not to mention the broader social, economic, and public health benefits. Moreover, there often seems to be an institutional disregard for doing what needs to be done to enhance the likelihood of longer-term success.

There is commonly a significant gap between what the evidence indicates is effective (evidence-based practices) and what the interventions look like in practice (when they exist at all). A survey of the integration of evidence-based practices into day-to-day correctional treatment programming (Taxman et al. 2007) uncovered the overall failure of the justice system to adopt best practices. Findings include: less than one-third of correctional agencies use a standardized risk assessment tool; less than 20 percent of the agencies report using cognitive-behavioral modalities in their clinical interventions and fewer yet use a manualized (that is, documented) treatment curriculum; only 30 percent report having substance abuse treatment programs of ninety days or more in duration; medications for substance abuse are rarely used (for example, methadone and other medications play a fundamental part in the treatment of opiate addiction and alcohol addiction); and a majority of agencies use passive referral methods to assist offenders in obtaining access to community-based resources. The evidence clearly indicates that an active approach is much more effective.

On balance, it is clear that correctional substance abuse treatment is hit and miss in terms of even adopting the basics of best practices. The *quality* of care is another matter. Research by the Urban Institute and the Council of State Governments Justice Center indicates that individuals in the justice system who do receive treatment services likely do not receive the appropriate level or intensity of treatment. The most common forms of intervention are self-help groups like Alcoholics Anonymous and Narcotics Anonymous, and alcohol and drug education classes. The lack of appropriate, high-quality drug and alcohol treatment in the justice system, particularly in prison, has been well documented (Belenko and Peugh 2005; National Center on Addiction and Substance Abuse 2004; Mumola and Karberg 2006).

The evidence is clear about the individual-level effects of drug and alcohol treatment. The proper dosage of treatment, with sustained aftercare, dramatically reduces relapse and criminal justice involvement. However, what does the evidence indicate about aggregate effects of treatment? Does treatment reduce crime and recidivism in the aggregate? Does drug treatment improve public health? In effect, is treatment a viable, effective, and cost-effective policy for larger-scale criminal justice benefits, public health benefits, and social and economic benefits?

The Efficacy of Substance Abuse Treatment

The scientific evidence is conclusive regarding the effects of drug and alcohol treatment. Treatment reduces drug use. Reducing drug use also reduces many of the collateral consequences, for example morbidity, mortality, economic, social, and familial impacts, as well as their economic and social costs. Treatment reduces crime and incarceration, reduces the public health consequences of abuse and addiction (including HIV and hepatitis B and C, as well as reducing ER and hospital visits), increases economic productivity and employment, improves family functioning, and enhances mental health.

Various sources document the statistical impacts of drug treatment. The National Treatment Improvement Evaluation Study (1997) found that treatment reduces rearrest by 64 percent, drug use by 50 percent, and criminal activity by 80 percent. The National Institute on Drug Abuse conducted extensive research on the effects of drug treatment (the Drug Abuse Treatment Outcome Studies or DATOS) and has compiled an impressive portfolio of evidence showing a variety of positive outcomes. These include consistent behavioral and psychological improvements, reductions in criminality and recidivism, enhanced social performance, psychological functioning, and full-time employment. The DATOS research also showed that the effects are generally sustained five years after completion of treatment (Hubbard, Craddock and Anderson 2003; Simpson and Flynn 2008).

The director of the National Institute on Drug Abuse, National Institutes of Health makes a very powerful case for the large-scale adoption of drug treatment for reducing drug abuse, dependence, and addiction, and their collateral social, economic, public health, familial, and criminal justice consequences. Director Lesher notes that research from the National Institutes of Health, Columbia University, University of Pennsylvania, and many other prestigious institutions have demonstrated that drug treatment reduces drug use by 50 to 60 percent, reduces arrests and therefore criminal justice involvement by 40 percent or more, increases employment by 60 to 80 percent, reduces cases of HIV, and provides many other public health benefits.

While Reuter and Pollack (2006) acknowledge that drug treatment is effective and cost saving, they caution that it is still imperfect, often not eliminating drug and alcohol use completely for those who have gone through treatment. They note that countries like The Netherlands, and other democracies that have liberal treatment availability, have not been able to treat their way out of a drug problem. What this demonstrates is what I mentioned earlier: substance abuse is a chronic disease, and just like other chronic diseases, it requires certain behavioral changes, a maintenance regime, and sometimes medication, especially for opiate addiction. Thus, relapse is a real possibility.

The research is clear on the economics or cost/benefit of treatment. The calculable economic benefits of drug treatment significantly and substantially exceed the costs, whether it is in-prison treatment or treatment provided under community supervision. While the cost-benefit results vary across settings and assumptions, they all indicate that economic benefits exceed costs of treatment by a substantial margin. McCollister and French (2003) reviewed the results of eleven economic studies of the cost-benefit of drug and alcohol treatment. They estimate that the annual economic benefit accrued in the domains of avoided crimes, employment, avoided health service utilization, employment income, and money not spent on substances was $42,905 greater than the cost of treatment. The vast majority, $42,151, was due to avoided criminal activity. Other reviews of the economic analyses of the costs and benefits of treatment (for example, Cartwright 2000) and analyses in other countries (for example, Godfrey, Stewart, and Gossop 2004) report similar findings.

Dr. Nora Volkow, the director of the National Institute of Drug Abuse in 2006, stated:

> Recent studies show it is actually less expensive for communities to treat drug-abusing offenders than to let them sit in jail or prison. It is estimated that every dollar invested in addiction treatment programs yields a return of $4 to $7 in reduced drug-related crimes. Savings for some outpatient programs can exceed costs by a ratio of 12 to 1.

The economic benefits of drug treatment are consistent and robust. It is safe to suggest that the estimates are conservative in that they generally do not consider the lifetime economic benefits of interrupting the cycle of criminal offending.

The National Institute on Drug Abuse (2006) has developed thirteen principles of effective treatment of addiction for criminal justice populations:

1. Drug addiction is a brain disease that affects behavior.
2. Recovery from drug addiction requires effective treatment, followed by management of the problem over time.
3. Treatment must last long enough to produce stable behavioral changes.
4. Assessment is the first step in treatment.
5. Tailoring services to fit the needs of the individual is an important part of effective drug abuse treatment for criminal justice populations.
6. Drug use during treatment should be carefully monitored.
7. Treatment should target factors that are associated with criminal behavior.
8. Criminal justice supervision should incorporate treatment planning for drug abusing offenders, and treatment providers should be aware of correctional supervision requirements.
9. Continuity of care is essential for drug abusers reentering the community.
10. A balance of rewards and sanctions encourages prosocial behavior and treatment participation.
11. Offenders with co-occurring drug abuse and mental health problems often require an integrated treatment approach.
12. Medications are an important part of treatment for many drug abusing offenders.
13. Treatment planning for drug abusing offenders who are living in or reentering the community should include strategies to prevent and treat serious, chronic medical conditions, such as HIV/AIDS, hepatitis B and C, and tuberculosis.

Research evidence indicates several additional elements should be incorporated into the treatment protocol. Not all individuals entering treatment are equally motivated to change (Prochaska and DiClemente 1992).

Treatment amenability or readiness can be determined by using assessment instruments that measure stages of change. Five stages of change have been identified: precontemplation, contemplation, preparation, action, and maintenance. Treatment motivation or readiness for change is easily assessed using validated assessment instruments such as the University of Rhode Island Change Assessment (URICA) and the Stages of Change Readiness and Treatment Eagerness Scale (SOCRATES) instruments. When an individual is in the precontemplation or contemplation stage, motivational interviewing (MI) can be used to enhance internal motivation (Rubak et al. 2005) and sanctions can be used to apply external pressure (Nace et al. 2007). MI is successfully used in a variety of clinical settings and has been found to be very effective in moving individuals to the proper stage to begin intervention. Justice pressure is also effective in motivating individuals to begin treatment. Court-ordered treatment has been shown to result in higher treatment retention rates, increased number of days abstinent, and decreases in criminal offending.

Research also indicates that there are two effective therapeutic modalities for substance abuse treatment: behavioral therapies and pharmacological treatment, although these are not mutually exclusive. When indicated, medication can help reduce craving and withdrawal symptoms and also serve as an effective therapy for opiate addiction. However, behavioral therapy should be used in conjunction with any pharmacological intervention. Behavioral therapies include cognitive-behavioral, contingency management, motivational interviewing, and multisystemic therapy, among others.

There are two factors that are worth reemphasizing. One, criminal offenders with a substance abuse problem are likely to have additional criminogenic circumstances. The NIDA framework mentions co-occurring mental health problems. There are often several more that co-exist with substance abuse and it is important that justice agencies identify these and address the more critical problems in a holistic manner. Only addressing the substance abuse problem may not reduce criminal involvement. This is a point that cannot be overemphasized.

Second, aftercare is one the components of substance abuse treatment that is often neglected. Research indicates that absent aftercare (maintenance), the necessary behavioral changes associated with the treatment effect are likely lost. Again, this is not that different from patterns evident in other chronic diseases.

HARM REDUCTION

Supply reduction and demand reduction both share the common goal of reduction of use. Harm reduction on the other hand acknowledges that no matter how successful supply and demand strategies are, drug use and problem drug use will always be a fact of life. Supply control is ineffective and treatment in the United States for substance abuse is currently limited and high threshold. Treatment is limited in terms of capacity and public funding and because of cost barriers to access (lack of insurance coverage, affordability). It is high threshold because it generally requires total abstinence. Add to the treatment challenges the fact that some level of motivation for treatment is required. In many cases, that motivation is absent. Again, even in the best-case scenario, drug use and problem drug use are realities. Harm reduction is a complementary strategy that can be implemented to help mitigate the harms associated with substance use and abuse.

Most of the efforts at harm reduction have focused on the harms to the user, such as health, economic, and social/familial consequences. The most prominent harm reduction strategies have primarily targeted user health: needle exchange programs and heroin substitution. The research evidence clearly supports the effectiveness and cost-effectiveness of these two strategies. Needle exchange programs have repeatedly been shown to significantly and substantially reduce the incidence of HIV, hepatitis, and other blood-borne diseases. In 1998, the U.S. Surgeon General concluded that "there is conclusive scientific evidence that [these needle exchange programs], as part of a comprehensive HIV prevention strategy, are an effective public health intervention that reduces transmission of HIV and does not encourage the illicit use of drugs." It is worth repeating: there is a large body of research that shows that needle exchange programs do not increase illicit drug use. The Surgeon General's report also noted that needle exchange programs have spillover effects in that they provide an opportunity to identify and refer individuals to treatment.

Heroin substitution, typically in the form of methadone or buprenorphine, is a safe, effective way to manage heroin addiction. Methadone does not have the euphoria associated with heroin and does not compromise cognitive functioning and employability. It serves essentially as a method for addressing the withdrawal symptoms of heroin. Heroin substitution has been shown to be effective and cost-effective, saving $4 to $7 dollars in social and health costs for every $1 dollar invested in these programs. Moreover, because methadone reduces needle use, it can also reduce the transmission of HIV, hepatitis, and other diseases. Heroin substitution is also associated with lower criminality and enhanced health, social functioning, mental health, and productivity.

A federal ban on needle exchange programs was put into effect in 1988. That ban survived through the George H. W. Bush, Clinton, and George W. Bush administrations. The ban was lifted by the Obama administration in 2009. Heroin substitution has been in effect for decades and has been generally supported by various administrations' drug control policies. It is still the case, however, that only a fraction of heroin addicts receive methadone treatment, in part because of barriers to access.

Drug use as well as drug manufacture and distribution have significant negative consequences for communities and neighborhoods, as well as cities, states, and the nation. One of the greatest concerns is violence. Drug-related violence has little to do with the actual ingestion of controlled substances. Instead, the violence associated with drugs is largely a consequence of prohibition. The U.S. Department of Justice conducted an assessment of the research and concluded in 1994 that alcohol is the only substance that often increases aggression and that the violence that is commonly attributed to the consumption of drugs is a product of their prohibition and distribution. The Drug Policy Task Force, convened by the New York County Lawyers Association, reached a similar conclusion (NYCLA 1996: 17):

> it appears that the overwhelming causes of violent crimes, which often find categorization under the heading "drug related" are caused by various factors unrelated to actual pharmacological effects of controlled substances upon human behavior. Rather, much of the violent crime can be said to be "drug prohibition-related," insofar as it results from the high costs and huge profits and great stakes involved in the world of drug commerce as it is carried out in the cities, states and nations of the world.

The Mexican cartels pose significant and real threats to the well-being of individuals in communities on both sides of the Mexican border. They also pose real threats to communities throughout the United States as their distribution channels are highly sophisticated, well resourced, and have high potential for violence. Even absent the cartel threat, drug distribution at the local level has tremendous impacts on public safety and public well-being. Much local gang activity is driven by drug distribution and it is a reality that in many areas of many cities in the United States, gang activity is a prevalent feature with substantial consequences for public safety, public health, and quality of life.

Caulkins and Reuter (2009), two of the nation's leading experts on drug control policy, expand the idea of harm reduction beyond the harm to the user and consider how drug manufacture and distribution harm communities and, in turn, how law enforcement can help reduce some of that harm. Once again, I invoke the principle of problem solving. In this case, it is recognizing the broader harm that drug use and drug distribution cause in communities and developing strategies to help mitigate some of that harm. For example, one of the consequences of drug use is the harm that intoxicated individuals can cause others, harm as a result of neglect and abuse of dependents, or the harm from engaging in dangerous, disorderly, or threatening activity. Thus law enforcement's intoxication control interventions should be expanded to help reduce these impacts of drug use on others.

Drug dealing can cause serious harm when rival gangs engage in violence to establish markets, or when a dealer or buyer is robbed. Dealing can also perpetrate more subtle, chronic harm in the deterioration of quality of life in a neighborhood (a "broken windows" effect). Police intelligence and tactics can be used to contain or relocate drug distribution markets, and reduce distribution-related violence. Much distribution-related harm can be minimized by simply relocating a drug market away from a school or a residential neighborhood. The goal in such a strategy may not be use reduction, but simply moving transactions to a less vulnerable place. Local law enforcement can also develop strategies to minimize violence associated with dealing. For example, informing gangs that the priority is the reduction in violence and that violence will be met with a very repressive response that will interfere with their business may cause them to think differently about using violence.

The point is that by employing problem-solving principles in combination with a focus on harm reduction, local law enforcement has the potential to significantly impact harm in a broader context.

DECRIMINALIZATION AND LEGALIZATION

There has been some confusion over the meaning of decriminalization, legalization, and harm reduction. It seems that some have lumped them together in an effort to derail efforts at harm reduction. Let's be clear here. For my purposes, decriminalization and legalization are different from harm reduction. Harm reduction involves working within the law to reduce harms. Legalization and decriminalization may impact harm, but they require statutory changes, as well as changes in policy and procedure.

The other thing to clarify before I discuss these issues is that drug use and addiction should not be reduced to an emotional, moralistic judgment. Labeling drug use and addiction as a character flaw or a weakness has not gotten us out of the drug problem. Those are unproductive arguments that are also counter to the scientific evidence. The American Medical Association (AMA) defined addiction as a disease in 1956. In 1991, the AMA endorsed the dual classification of addiction as a medical and psychiatric disorder. It really should not be a matter of right and wrong. The United States has made it clear that drug use is wrong, both in principle and in the law. Making it wrong, however, has not been terribly effective in reducing use and the problems and harms associated with its use, manufacture, and distribution.

Three 2012 surveys indicate significant support for legalizing marijuana. According to Gallup, 16 percent of respondents favored legalization of marijuana in 1970. All of the recent surveys indicate it is now more than 50 percent. The headlines from nearly any newspaper after the November 2012 election reported (in addition to Obama's reelection) that two states had legalized possession of "personal" quantities of marijuana. The *New York Times* reported:

> DENVER—For supporters of legalizing marijuana it was a historic moment, one that drew comparisons to the end of Prohibition: On Tuesday, voters in Colorado and Washington State made it legal to smoke pot recreationally, without any prescription or medical excuse.

There is a federal interest in this issue because it is still a violation of federal law to possess marijuana. However, the Obama administration has signaled (December 2012) that it will not make possession of personal amounts of marijuana a federal priority. In addition, statements by U.S. Attorney General Eric Holder (August 14, 2013) indicate that the Obama administration is questioning the efficacy of our traditional drug policy. In the 2012 Rasmussen poll cited earlier, 60 percent believe that legalization of marijuana is a state, not a federal, issue. And on August 29, 2013, the U.S. Attorney General indicated that the federal government will not attempt to block the Colorado and Washington laws.

In May 2013, the Vermont legislature passed legislation that decriminalizes possession of a limited amount of marijuana. Vermont is the seventeenth state to reduce the sanction for possession of a personal quantity of marijuana. Because the legalization in Colorado and Washington has opened the door on the issue, it may be time and smart policy to consider expanding the legalization of possession of marijuana to all states and at the federal level. Here are some of the reasons why this may be a prudent path. First, individuals will use marijuana regardless of whether it is legal. Second, between 1990 and 2002, drug arrests in the United States increased by 450,000. Eighty-two percent of that growth in arrests was for marijuana and the vast majority (79 percent) of that was for simple possession of marijuana. In 2010, the FBI reported that there were nearly 854,000 arrests in the United States for marijuana-related offenses; 88 percent of those were possession only. Marijuana arrests now comprise over one-half of all drug arrests and 46 percent of all drug arrests in the United States are for possession of marijuana. It is estimated that $4 billion annually is spent on the arrest, prosecution, and incarceration of marijuana offenders.

The impact of the criminal justice response on marijuana possession and use has been trivial to nonexistent. The price of marijuana has declined or remained stable since 1992 and the potency has increased by over 50 percent (King and Mauer 2006). Current use rate levels by high school seniors are what they were in 1975, thus ramping up the justice response does not appear to have had substantial impacts on reducing use of marijuana.

Moreover, the scientific evidence provides little support for the idea that legalization or decriminalization would encourage or substantially increase use. Nor is there conclusive evidence to support the assertion that marijuana is a gateway to more serious drugs (Caulkins et al. 2012), although there is at least anecdotal evidence to that effect.

On the other hand, there are serious concerns associated with marijuana use and abuse. There are significant health and mental health consequences that cannot be ignored. For example, chronic, heavy smoking of marijuana can cause respiratory and pulmonary damage. Chronic use can cause neurocognitive impairment as well. The mental health consequences include potential dependence and addiction, and increased rates of anxiety, depression, and schizophrenia.

Clearly, the benefits of legalization of possession of marijuana need to be balanced against these risks. Perhaps one of the key questions to consider is the impact of legalization on initiation of use and frequency of use. Will legalization lead to increased rates of initiation and will it increase the frequency of use? If not, then from a use perspective, we are in the same position with or without legalization.

Research in other countries, especially in Portugal and Holland, indicates little impact of decriminalization on use rates. Research published in *Scientific American* and the *British Journal of Criminology* both confirm that decriminalization resulted in declines in use rates of illicit drugs, especially among problematic users and adolescents. A 2004 comparative study in The Netherlands found no support for the prediction that decriminalization of marijuana leads to increases in use, or changes in negative patterns of use such as earlier age of onset and increased frequency of use. Moreover, The Netherlands' research disconfirmed assertions that marijuana is a gateway drug to harder, more dangerous illicit substances (Reinarman, Cohen, and Kaal 2004).

The Dutch and Portuguese drug policies are both decriminalization, not legalization policies. Both focus on harm reduction in that they are designed to encourage treatment for problem users, although in different ways. The Portuguese model decriminalizes personal possession of all illicit drugs (manufacture and distribution are still serious crimes, punishable by incarceration). The Dutch model decriminalized marijuana possession and use of small quantities. Possession of harder drugs as well as manufacture and distribution are prosecuted and punished.

The evidence for Portugal and The Netherlands is consistent and compelling. There is no necessary relationship between decriminalization of marijuana and increases in use rates, age at onset of use, and frequency of use. The Global Cannabis Commission Report "Cannabis Policy: Moving Beyond Stalemate" (2010) concludes that lessening of penalties and decriminalization of marijuana in a number of jurisdictions has not been followed by upsurges in use. A May 2013 report issued by the Organization of American States (OAS) went on the record discussing the potential benefits of legalizing marijuana, eventually leading to the reallocation of resources away from controlling drugs and drug users, to preventing and treating problematic use and shrinking criminal markets and criminal enterprises involved in drug manufacture and distribution (OAS 2013).

Uruguay's lower house voted to legalize marijuana (August 1, 2013), rendering Uruguay the first South American nation to legally regulate production, distribution, and sale of marijuana. It is estimated that marijuana is a $40 million dollar commodity on the illegal market in Uruguay. The senate passed the bill and the president of Uruguay signed the legislation in December of 2013.

Let's be clear. Marijuana is not a public good. It does have potentially harmful effects. But there are many substances that have potentially harmful effects. There are many activities that have potentially harmful effects. These substances and activities are not illegal or banned outright. Many are regulated. If the evidence indicates that under proper management, legalization or decriminalization of marijuana use does not lead to increased frequency of use, increases in numbers using, and/or an earlier age at onset of use, the advantages in terms of justice system savings and avoiding criminalizing users are quite significant benefits.

The cost of keeping marijuana possession illegal is substantial, especially with regard to the criminal justice system. A 2010 report by the Cato Institute (Miron and Waldock 2010) estimates that legalization of marijuana could save $8.7 billion per year in criminal justice costs. They also estimate that legalization of marijuana could net $8.7 billion in tax revenue per year if marijuana was taxed at rates similar to those of alcohol and tobacco.

The illegality of marijuana possession also has personal consequences that are not necessarily trivial. Conviction of possession of marijuana can have a variety of consequences, some short term and some longer term. For example, in Texas the least severe charge for possession of marijuana is a Class B misdemeanor. A conviction of possession of marijuana may have any and all of the following consequences:

- Up to 180 days in jail
- Up to a $2,000 fine
- Up to two years on probation
- An adult driver's license suspension of 180 days

- A minor's driver's license suspension of one year
- Disqualification from obtaining a concealed weapon license if charged within five years prior to the application
- Prohibition to ship, transport, or receive a firearm or ammunition
- Expulsion from school if the student is on or within 500 feet of school property or attending a school-sponsored or school-related event
- Denial of a permit to sell alcoholic beverages

Also, those who have obtained or want to obtain a professional license from the state of Texas (such as doctors, lawyers, CPA, dentist, nurse, physician's assistant, electrician, cosmetologist, air conditioning technician, and many others), may face other consequences. Those include suspending or revoking the license or denying a person the opportunity to take the licensing exam. Moreover, the licensing authority may consider a person convicted even if the case is dismissed. Access to rental housing may also be affected, depending on the criminal background criteria of landlords. In Florida, the consequences may include a three-year ban on public housing for any misdemeanor or felony conviction, a lifetime ban on the right to possess a firearm, ineligibility for state financial aid, ineligibility for public employment, ineligibility for certain permits, state licenses, or certifications, and a five-year ban on the eligibility to adopt a child or become a foster parent.

One of the results of entering and being processed through the U.S. criminal justice system is the criminalization of the offender. Incarceration is criminogenic, meaning that when individuals are released from prison they have a higher likelihood of reoffending, net of other risk factors. The mere fact of arrest, indictment, conviction, and punishment can be criminogenic as well. The question at this point is whether *on balance* it is wise, prudent, and useful to continue to criminalize marijuana possession and to continue to punish marijuana offenders well after they have been discharged from the criminal justice system.

The advantage we have today is that we can conduct a natural experiment on legalization of possession of marijuana. We can study the experiences of Colorado and Washington State, learn from those experiences in terms of the consequences of legalization, the particulars of administering legalization, amount of revenue generated from taxes and regulatory fees, and how to improve policies and procedures going forward.

The manufacture and distribution of marijuana will need to be regulated just as tobacco, alcohol, and prescription medication are regulated. This will require state regulation, and federal regulation where federal jurisdiction is involved, such as transportation across state lines or national boundaries. States will also have to develop statutes and procedures for manufacture, distribution, and use. Just as is the case with alcohol, there will need to be laws governing any potential public harms that come from use of marijuana, such as public use, intoxication, and so on. How it will be distributed will need to be addressed as well as enforcement of age requirements for purchase. Revenue from taxation could be used to pay for regulation and will likely provide states with additional income, some of which could be used to fund public substance abuse treatment. If legalization moves forward, Congress will need to draft federal law that is broad enough to accommodate anticipated variation in state statutes and procedures.

While there is a growing political will to legalize (or at least substantially decriminalize) possession of marijuana in the United States, the political reality is quite different for other illicit drugs such as cocaine, crack, methamphetamine, heroin, and a variety of other drugs. The political climate in the United States is currently not conducive to a discussion of legalization of possession of "harder" drugs. There is probably merit to these concerns. Research indicates that the potential harm from these harder drugs is significantly greater than from marijuana. There is greater risk for addiction, as well as implications for physical health, social functioning, and economic productivity. Moreover, there is little current public support for legalization of these other drugs.

At the same time, a very compelling argument can be made for the negative consequences of the criminalization of drug use and the failure of supply side strategies to reduce available quantities, increase prices, and in turn reduce use rates. So what is the path forward regarding possession and use of more serious drugs?

Decriminalization of possession of personal amounts of more serious drugs can provide an important new opportunity, which is that arrest for possession can serve as a portal into a system that treats drug users differently than in the past. Decriminalization can potentially: (a) reduce the criminalizing effects of arrest and conviction; (b) provide an opportunity and the leverage to channel appropriate individuals into treatment; and

(c) allow a more problem-solving approach to addressing the needs of individuals, including harm reduction, education, and medical attention, among others.

For simplicity, let's assume that there are just two types of drug users: occasional, recreational users, and problem, dependent, abusing, addicted users. All of those in the latter category likely started as occasional, recreational users. There is little evidence that legal sanctions had much of an impact on preventing recreational users from becoming problem users. In fact, research indicates that across a variety of circumstances and environments, decriminalization does not lead to increases in use (for example, Rosmarin and Eastwood 2012). Thus, continuing to criminalize occasional, recreational use seems of little value, either in the short term or long term, and can have substantially negative consequences for those arrested and prosecuted as well as for the criminal justice system.

However, differentiating between the occasional, recreational user and the problem user requires that we get much smarter about sorting offenders once they come into the system. Arrest should be considered an opportunity to intervene, not punish. Arrest should serve as the entry point to comprehensive screening and assessment, clinical decision making, and development of appropriate interventions, not "you're busted" case making and punitive consequences. Once again, it is useful to reiterate that drug use is first and foremost a public health problem.

It is also a global issue. The U.S. demand for drugs, which is a consequence of many factors, has profound effects not only on the United States, but on the international community. The production and distribution of drugs have global consequences and impact many nations in addition to the United States. The consequences for Mexico are fairly obvious, even to the casual observer. Manufacture and distribution of drugs present significant problems in Central America, the Caribbean, South America, Southwest Asia (Pakistan and Afghanistan), and Southeast Asia (Burma/Myanmar and Laos). Distribution involves quite sophisticated criminal organizations that accrue tremendous amounts of money, are able to evade detection by government agents, compromise legitimate social, economic, and political structures through violence, intimidation, corruption, and extortion, and challenge the authority of local and national governments. In short, drug trade organizations compromise political, economic, and social stability in many of the nations through which they channel drugs.

When U.S. policymakers do confront the international consequences of the U.S. demand for drugs, it is nearly exclusively in the form of supply control strategies such as international drug interdiction, crop eradication, and so on. The point is a simple one: while the United States is legitimately concerned about the impact the U.S. drug demand has on this country, it is not alone in the consequences of the drug trade. Once again, we are faced with reducing the financial incentives of the drug trade by effectively reducing demand and legalizing or decriminalizing the possession of marijuana and potentially other substances.

The Cato report mentioned earlier also estimates the revenue savings and revenue gains due to the legalization of all controlled substances. Legalization of all illicit drugs would save approximately $41.3 billion per year in enforcement and prohibition costs. The bulk of it, $25.7 billion, would accrue to state and local governments, and $15.6 billion per year would accrue to the federal government. Tax revenue from the sale of drugs would generate $46.7 billion annually. These are just estimates. Obviously, there would be costs associated with the administration and management of the sale of drugs as well as tax collection. Assuming no major increases in drug use and drug abuse, there would still be the social and economic costs associated with use and abuse, including drug-related crimes, medical and mental health consequences, and lost productivity, as well as others.

Perhaps a reasonable first step is to focus on legalization of marijuana. Again, Colorado and Washington State can serve as the test cases for this, and policymakers across the nation can learn valuable lessons about how and how not to go about such legalization.

THE DRUG PROBLEM GOING FORWARD

The United States has been on a concerted supply reduction path for forty-plus years. Most informed observers as well as most of the general public have concluded that these efforts have not been effective. There is little evidence of significant reductions in supply and reductions in drug use because of that. Fifteen years ago, the vast majority of the public (70 percent) reported that U.S. drug policy was a failure. That failure to reduce prevalence does not mean that supply reduction initiatives (and, specifically, law enforcement) are having no impact on drug markets. It is widely—and reasonably—argued that supply reduction contains the expansion of drug markets, even if it fails to reduce markets and overall supply.

Drug use has been a highly emotional, politicized issue. Drug use, and in particular, abuse, dependence, and addiction, have been viewed as a moral failing. For example, the Obama administration's Drug Czar Gil Kerlikowske recently admitted that during his thirty-seven-year law enforcement career, prior to becoming the director of national drug policy, he held the belief that drug abuse was a moral problem.

At least for the past ten to fifteen years, the vast majority of Americans indicate that they believe drug abuse is a disease. Moreover, a 2000 Harvard School of Public Health survey indicates that drug abuse was mentioned as a "very serious public health problem" by 82 percent of respondents, more than mentioned any other public health problem, including cancer, heart disease, HIV/AIDS, smoking, and obesity, among others. The public understands that drug abuse is a disease and a very serious public health issue.

There is considerable public support for addressing the drug abuse problem in this country. In 2002, three-quarters of respondents to a national survey supported mandatory treatment for those arrested for possession and for selling small amounts of illicit drugs. Large majorities in other surveys indicate that they support drug treatment for those incarcerated as well as after release.

The public no longer believes that a nearly exclusive punishment-focused approach to the drug problem is appropriate. Public opinion is clear: punishment is not doing the job. It does not address drug abuse and addiction.

What does this mean for drug control policy? It means a dramatically ramped-up effort at drug demand reduction, primarily though not exclusively focused on treatment. Some prevention/education and some supply control are warranted. But as the title of this chapter implies, it is time to significantly recalibrate or rebalance drug policy. It means continuing supply control efforts, although at reduced levels than has been the case. It means addressing drug abuse and addiction for the justice-involved population as well as those outside of the justice system, many of whom are at risk of becoming justice involved.

For the justice involved, it means treatment in diversion settings (such as diversion court, probation, deferred adjudication, and deferred prosecution) as well as treatment for those incarcerated in jail and prison, and those released on parole or some form of mandatory supervision. But not just treatment. Instead, treatment that conforms to what the research indicates is the most effective for the needs of each individual case.

For the nonjustice involved, it means access to affordable substance abuse treatment, either through adequate insurance coverage for those with insurance or access to public treatment. It simply makes sense that we should keep as many individuals out of the justice system as possible. The primary path for accomplishing that is access to substance abuse treatment.

It is troubling that we knew at least fifteen years ago what we know today about what works and does not work in terms of drug abuse, justice responses to illicit drugs, and public opinion regarding what should and should not be done to address the drug issue. It is pretty clear that elected officials and policymakers have failed taxpayers, those with drug problems, and the criminal justice system. It is time to rectify that.

Probably the most important change that will dramatically increase access to public substance abuse treatment is the Affordable Care Act of 2010 (ACA). The ACA will fundamentally expand insurance coverage for substance abuse and transform the nature of substance abuse treatment. The U.S. Department of Health and Human Services reports that in 2014, approximately 5.1 million individuals with health insurance lack access to substance abuse treatment. In addition, 27 million individuals lack any health insurance coverage at all. In total, the ACA will expand access to substance abuse treatment to 32.1 million under- and uninsured individuals. The ACA also has a parity provision that requires insurers who provide limited substance abuse coverage to expand that coverage to be comparable to the federal standard. This will affect an additional 30.4 million Americans.

Historically, substance abuse treatment has been a separate, typically nonmedical system of treatment facilities. Treatment has generally been focused on counseling and education. Research (Buck 2011) shows that substance abuse treatment facilities that rely mainly on public funding typically offer counseling and education by individuals who have limited professional training. Fewer than half employ Master's-level counselors; one-third do not have a physician on staff or under contract; and three-quarters of the directors of these facilities have a bachelor's degree or less.

It is anticipated that this situation will also change dramatically under the ACA. In addition to expanding coverage, the ACA will also elevate substance abuse treatment to the level of other chronic diseases. This means that substance abuse will be considered a medically "essential service."

Substance abuse treatment will be "medicalized," meaning it will be integrated into the primary practice of medicine, with much greater involvement and participation by physicians, psychologists, nurse practitioners, and other health professionals. Treatment will typically be physician directed because that is generally a requirement for Medicaid reimbursement. Thus, the ACA requirements and Medicaid reimbursement requirements will lead to significant improvements in the substance abuse treatment model, service delivery, staffing of facilities, and overall quality of treatment. The ACA will also likely result in consolidation of the substance abuse treatment industry, leading to a number of larger, better-managed and resourced treatment providers in the market. While expansion of access and the transformation of substance abuse treatment were not the primary goals of the ACA, these are important collateral consequences. As Buck (2011: 1408) concludes:

> The result [of the ACA] will be a different system of treatment, with a greater variety of larger providers in the mainstream of general health care. This will be a more ambulatory-based, medically oriented and physician-directed system . . . health reform's changes offer the potential to address some of the concerns associated with the current system of public substance abuse care. . . . If health reform even partially addresses these problems, the result will be a system of care that greatly improves the treatment of substance abuse disorders in the United States.

The ACA will provide the framework within which to effectively and cost-effectively address the most common criminogenic need among the correctional population in the United States. It is a problem for which 23 million Americans are in need of treatment, but do not receive it, largely because of barriers to access. This represents a sea change in substance abuse treatment and a tremendous opportunity for addressing one of the most important public health problems in the nation. That is good news, especially for those states that have opted to participate in Medicaid expansion (as of November 2014, twenty-eight states have elected to participate). Twenty states have declared that they will not participate in the Medicaid expansion under the ACA and three are still considering it. Rick Perry, the governor of Texas, by far the largest state to opt out and the state with the largest Medicaid qualifying population, seems to be basing his decision not to participate on mainly political grounds. On April 1, 2013, Perry was quoted by Reuters as saying:

> Seems to me April Fool's Day is the perfect day to discuss something as foolish as Medicaid expansion, and to remind everyone that Texas will not be held hostage by the Obama administration's attempt to force us into the fool's errand of adding more than a million Texans to a broken system.

Perry has failed to offer what will be done for the health needs, or any mental health and substance abuse needs, of those 1.5 million Texans. For those states that have decided not to participate in Medicaid expansion, there are still benefits from the ACA, however, absent an alternative, significant segments of the population will remain uninsured.

Moving in the direction of smart policy regarding substance abuse treatment will require leadership. While the consequences of substance abuse are local and efforts to remedy the problem will occur locally, it makes sense that the process begins with leadership at the national level. After all, crime control, sentencing reform, and the corrections explosion all originated as national initiatives, with financial assistance and technical assistance from the federal government. The advantage is that a national focus will span state-level agendas and provide some continuity and consistency of policy. A national focus will also be more visible, especially a coordinated effort involving Health and Human Services, the Department of Justice, the Surgeon General, and others forging a strategic initiative funded largely by federal resources under the ACA.

Another very important component of recalibrated drug policy is a problem-solving focus on harm reduction. There are obvious, effective, and cost-effective harm reduction policies such as needle exchange, heroin substitution, and use reduction.

In addition to harm reduction, demand reduction, supply control, and prevention/education, there seems to be significant evidence supporting legalization of possession of marijuana. Research indicates that contrary to some expectations, legalization seems to not result in increased usage or increased problem usage. There is also public support; a Pew survey conducted in March 2013 indicates that 52 percent of the public favor legalization of marijuana and over 60 percent believe marijuana use is either morally acceptable or is not a moral issue. Moreover, nearly three-quarters believe that government efforts to enforce marijuana laws cost more than they are worth.

Tokenism is not going to accomplish the task. Just as is the case with drug diversion programs, limited funding and capacity are not going to noticeably impact crime. What is envisioned in this effort to address the drug problem in the United States and get the U.S. criminal justice system out of the business of punishing drug possession offenders to no productive end is a proactive, concerted, national drug policy that is based on what is effective and cost-effective—and appropriately funded. This will involve substantial changes to sentencing laws (the U.S. Attorney General is taking the lead in initiating changes to federal drug sentencing laws), including the elimination of mandatory and mandatory minimum sentences, providing the statutory ability to divert nonviolent drug offenders, and the elimination of asset forfeiture laws that provide incentives for law enforcement and prosecutors to seek traditional criminal justice responses to drug cases. Once again, it is a properly balanced set of initiatives that includes first and foremost dramatically expanded demand reduction (public substance abuse treatment, diversion to treatment, prevention and education), as well as harm reduction, supply control, and federal and state legalization of possession of marijuana.

Most importantly, any drug policy initiatives must be considered in the context of drug use as a public health problem. Thus, tax revenues generated from legalization and regulation of marijuana should be invested in public substance abuse treatment. If the climate becomes amenable to decriminalization of additional substances, cost savings to the justice system should be directed to expansion of treatment.

CHAPTER 8

Cost-Effectiveness

FEDERAL, STATE, AND LOCAL GOVERNMENTS collectively spend over $260 billion annually for criminal justice, an expenditure that has increased by 210 percent since 1982. Much of the financial burden falls on local government. In 2010, city and county governments contributed over 50 percent of total direct criminal justice expenditures. The bulk of law enforcement spending originates at the local level (67 percent): nearly 40 percent of judicial/legal expenditures and one-third of corrections expenditures are local. State government contributes under one-third (30.5 percent) of total justice expenditures and 57 percent of corrections costs.

While state-level corrections costs constitute approximately 2.5 to 3 percent of total state expenditures, the relative burden at the local level is much higher. Jurisdictions differ in terms of how much of local criminal justice activities are funded by city, county, or state revenue. Overall, law enforcement (police) is paid out of municipal budgets. Sheriff's agencies and the courts are typically funded by counties, as is local corrections (jail, pretrial, and probation). Local police generally consume a minimum of one-third of municipal budgets. Courts and other judicial services require between 35 and 50 percent of county budgets.

Regardless of the perspective—federal, state or local—the United States spends an extraordinary amount of public tax revenue on the administration of criminal justice. The $260 billion annual expenditure is higher than the gross domestic product of 80 percent of the nations in the world.

The question prudent policymakers, elected officials, and taxpayers should ask is: What is the return on investment. Has this been a cost-effective use of public resources? Can we develop a more cost-effective strategy going forward? But first, an example.

I have served several times as a consulting expert for inmates being considered for discretionary parole release. One case in particular illustrates many things about the justice system that are problematic, including lack of informed decision making, poor judgment, and wasteful expenditure of public resources. This case involves a sex offender (call him Mr. Davis) who in the 1970s abducted a teenage boy and sexually assaulted him. He was convicted and sentenced to prison. Davis served ten years and was released on parole supervision. Two years into his parole, he abducted another boy and molested him. Davis was convicted on the new charge and sentenced to twenty-five years in prison. I got involved in this case when Davis was completing year twenty-two of the twenty-five-year sentence. At this time, Davis was seventy-three years old, impudent, arthritic, and in poor health. He had been airlifted from the prison to a hospital on several occasions for life-threatening medical emergencies. His parole plan had him moving to another state to live on a farm with his nephew, who was a retired U.S. Marshall and an active deputy sheriff. His psych exam indicated no major concerns and he acknowledged responsibility and remorse for his crimes. While it is clear that Mr. Davis committed some bad crimes, it was clear to me that he had aged out of crime. My estimate of his risk was essentially zero. The risk assessment used by the parole board was a static assessment and, among other problems, only considered age in terms of whether the applicant is under or over age twenty-five. In essence, an offender in this system would have the same assessed risk at age ninety-six as at age twenty-six. The parole board showed no appreciation for how this assessment is inappropriate. Needless to say, Mr. Davis was denied parole release. This example illustrates tough on crime decision making gone haywire. Davis posed no threat to the public, but the parole board wanted to be tough on crime. In addition, they relied on a faulty assessment instrument and ignored dispositive contrary information. Unfortunately, this case is not the exception. The primary point here is that the individuals responsible for the decision to keep Davis in prison have no accountability for the financial cost of their decision.

THE COST OF CRIME

I start by assessing the financial impact of crime. Table 8.1 presents average estimates of the criminal justice cost of selected offenses. These criminal justice cost estimates were developed by McCollister, French, and Hai (2010), based upon an extensive review and analysis of a variety of crime costing methods and unit costing studies that generate estimates for particular types of crimes. The criminal justice costs associated with each of the thirteen offenses included in the McCollister, French, and Hai research reflect a law enforcement component, a legal and adjudication component, and a corrections component. Keeping in mind that there are several assumptions that are employed in the estimation procedure, these are estimates, and as such there is error, I can cautiously extrapolate the overall criminal justice costs. Since the legal/adjudication and corrections costs are postoffense, I use 2010 arrest data from the Uniform Crime Reports (UCR) for 2010 to determine the number of arrests for each

TABLE 8.1 The Direct Criminal Justice Cost of Crime

OFFENSE	CJS COST	2010 ARRESTS	TOTAL
Murder	$392,350	11,201	$4,400,000,000
Rape/sexual assault	$26,480	20,088	$532,000,000
Aggravated assault	$8,640	408,488	$3,500,000,000
Robbery	$13,830	112,300	$1,553,000,000
Motor vehicle theft	$3,870	71,487	$277,000,000
Arson	$4,390	11,296	$49,590,000
Burglary	$4,130	289,769	$1,200,000,000
Larceny/theft	$2,880	1,271,410	$3,660,000,000
Stolen property	$6,842	94,802	$649,000,000
Vandalism	$4,160	252,753	$1,051,000,000
Forgery/counterfeit	$4,605	78,101	$360,000,000
Embezzlement	$4,820	16,616	$80,000,000
Fraud	$4,372	187,887	$821,400,000
Annual total:			**$18,132,990,000**

TABLE 8.2 The Tangible and Intangible Costs of Crime

OFFENSE	TOTAL TANGIBLE COST	TOTAL INTANGIBLE COST	TOTAL
Murder	$14,400,000,000	N/A	$14,400,000,000
Rape/sexual assault	$829,000,000	$48,700,000,000	$49,529,000,000
Aggravated assault	$7,954,000,000	$99,971,000,000	$107,925,000,000
Robbery	$2,400,000,000	$12,570,000,000	$14,970,000,000
Motor vehicle theft	$753,000,000	$165,000,000	$918,000,000
Arson	$186,000,000	N/A	$186,000,000
Burglary	$1,800,000,000	$1,160,000,000	$2,960,000,000
Larceny/theft	$4,480,000,000	$120,825,000	$4,600,825,000
Stolen property	$758,400,000	N/A	$758,400,000
Vandalism	$1,228,000,000	N/A	$1,228,000,000
Forgery/counterfeit	$411,000,000	N/A	$411,000,000
Embezzlement	$91,000,000	N/A	$91,000,000
Fraud	$945,000,000	N/A	$945,000,000
Annual total:			**$198,922,225,000**

crime type. Multiplying the cost per offense by the number of arrests provides the aggregate criminal justice cost estimate. These thirteen offenses, which constituted only 21 percent of all 2010 arrests reported in the UCR, cost federal, state, and local governments over $18 billion in 2010. Eighteen billion dollars is quite a sum of money, but pales in comparison to the $260 billion in total annual criminal justice expenditures.

Table 8.2 provides estimates (from McCollister, French, and Hai 2010) associated with tangible crime costs and intangible crime costs for the selected thirteen offenses. Tangible cost estimates are based on the criminal justice costs, victim costs, and loss of productivity of perpetrators committing the crimes. The intangible costs include pain and suffering (McCollister, French, and Hai 2010). The total tangible costs for each offense are based on 2010 arrests. The total intangible costs (victim costs, among others) are based on National Crime Victimization Survey estimates of crimes committed in 2010. Taking this broader view of the cost of crime is rather sobering. These estimates indicate that the overall financial impact of these thirteen crimes is nearly $200 billion annually. Seeing the financial impact on victims in terms of direct costs as well as the intangibles of the emotional and physical harm raises the stakes in seeking more effective and cost-effective crime solutions. Again, if the criminal justice system more effectively reduced recidivism, many victimizations and much of the cost of victimization could be avoided.

Criminal Careers

While the cost of crime analysis is quite illuminating, it is even more compelling when we consider that the majority of offenders are repeat offenders. In effect, each time we investigate and arrest a suspect, place him or her in custody, pass the case to the prosecutor's office, hold a preliminary hearing or magistration, engage pretrial services, detain some in jail pretrial, provide legal counsel (for roughly 80 percent of felony defendants), indict the case, dispose of the case in court at a plea hearing, hold a sentencing hearing, and then transfer the offender to corrections, costs are incurred. A felony arrest may cost $150 to $200, taking into consideration transportation of the suspect, police time booking the individual, and preparation of the incident/ arrest report. Typical booking costs $175. Detention in jail costs $45 per day (booking and detention data are for Travis County [Austin] Texas).

What most of the cost analyses and cost-benefit studies fail to incorporate into their models is the impact of lifetime offending and desistence. There is good reason for this omission because the assumptions required produce a considerable amount of error in the forecasts. We do not have very precise data on aggregate criminal career trajectories. Clearly, the amount of repeat offending depends on a wide variety of factors, including age, gender, type of offenses (violent, property, drug), education, marital status, employment, among others. However, we can generate a reasonable, informed estimate of what this looks like in the aggregate. The following is based on a personal correspondence with Al Blumstein at Carnegie Mellon University. Best estimates indicate the following. Assume a cohort of 100 individuals who were arrested in 1990. Within an approximate two-year window, 60 percent of them have been rearrested. There is clearly an important role here for the efficiency of law enforcement; this procedure is silent regarding crimes committed that are either unknown to law enforcement or known but not leading to an arrest. The remaining 40 percent stay arrest free into the future. Of the 60 percent who were arrested a second time, approximately 70 percent of them (42 of the original 100) are arrested for a third time within twenty or twenty-one months. The next round involves roughly 80 percent of those with a third arrest (33 of the original 100) who are arrested again within nineteen to twenty months of the prior arrest. The pattern then persists with around 80 percent of each prior arrest group (26 of the original 100) being rearrested in a slowly diminishing time window. A minority of offenders commit the majority of crimes. Moreover, this smaller group of high-risk, high-criminogenic-need habitual offenders is responsible for most of the tangible and intangible costs of crime. The point is simple. Our failures to interrupt the cycle of reoffending that is all too typical of criminal offenders causes the needless expenditure of phenomenal amounts of public funds.

Costs and Benefits Over Time

The costs and benefits of policies and programs weigh heavily in the policy development process. Unfortunately, in the majority of states, policymakers and elected officials are not properly informed of the fiscal impacts of policy changes. Poorly performed cost-benefit or cost-impact analyses fail to provide the true financial effects of criminal justice reforms over the long term. Research conducted by the Center on Budget and Policy Priorities and the American Civil Liberties Union (Leachman, Chettiar, and Geare 2012) reveals a substantial lack of proper financial analysis of proposed criminal justice legislation. The ACLU study examined the fiscal notes for over 600 legislative bills on sentencing and corrections in forty-nine states that were enacted in 2009, 2010, and 2011. Fiscal notes are the financial assessments of pending legislation.

Leachman, Chettiar, and Geare (2012) report that for about 40 percent of the 600 bills, the states did not even prepare fiscal notes, thus they lacked an official certification regarding the fiscal impact of the legislation. Moreover, for those states that did prepare fiscal notes, the majority of the analyses of fiscal impact failed to assess that impact beyond two years. Without an assessment of the longer-term financial impacts, legislators are unable to appreciate the longer-term fiscal benefits of such reforms. Many criminal justice reforms that target recidivism will, by design, require time to realize their impact. Failure to provide a financial analysis, or focusing the financial analysis on just one to two years, is clearly inappropriate for capturing a realistic, longer-term economic impact. Leachman, Chettiar, and Geare (2012: 2) conclude:

> the vast majority of states do not accurately perform these fiscal notes in a way that is useful to legislators. . . . By following these best practices, states can calculate both short- and long-term costs and cost savings for criminal justice bills and easily provide that information to legislators, who can then know the true fiscal implications of reform proposals before voting on them. . . . Improved fiscal notes will illuminate the short- and long-term benefits of ending our dependence on incarceration, bolster reforms that will reduce prison spending and save states millions that they can spend on other vital services.

THE COSTS AND BENEFITS OF INCARCERATION

Incarceration is the most expensive form of corrections. The per-inmate costs vary from $22,000 to $50,000 and more depending on jurisdiction, custody level, and other circumstances, such as physical health and age. On top of that, most states have funding obligations that figure into the cost of prison that are routinely not reported in their corrections budgets. On average, an additional 14 percent of prison costs excluded from reported corrections costs are due to obligations for employee benefits, pension contributions, retiree healthcare contributions, capital costs, legal judgments and claims, and hospital care for inmates, among others. Illinois leads the nation in prison costs excluded from the corrections budget (33 percent), followed by Iowa (26 percent) and Texas (24 percent).

It should be a fairly safe conclusion that given the relatively high cost of incarceration, high recidivism rates, and the marginal impact of incarceration on crime rates, incarceration alone as a correctional strategy is generally cost ineffective. Let's look at the evidence.

A study conducted by the Pew Center on the States (2012) focuses on the cost- effectiveness of increased punishment severity over the past two decades, measured as increased time served. The research is based on release cohorts from Michigan, Florida, and Maryland. Since 1990, the growth in time served was relatively consistent by type of crime: drug crimes (36 percent increase), property crimes (up 24 percent), and violent crimes (up 37 percent). The question posed in the Pew study is: What was the cost and impact on public safety of these increases? Based on a risk analysis of individuals released from prisons in the three states included in the research, they found that 14 percent of releasees in the Florida cohort, 18 percent of the releasees in Maryland, and 24 percent in Michigan could have been released between three months and twenty-four months earlier without any negative impact on public safety. The extra sentence length cost $54 million in Florida, $30 million in Maryland, and $92 million in Michigan.

There has been a fair amount of attention in recent years on the marginal utility of incarceration. Diminishing returns of incarceration refers to the public safety benefit of continuing to imprison larger numbers of offenders. The logic is clear: locking up the most dangerous and highest-risk offenders can have a significant public safety impact; however, as larger and larger numbers of offenders are incarcerated, increasingly lower-level offenders who are lower risk enter the inmate pool, thus in turn, the public safety payoff diminishes. Washington State research shows the effect: in 1980, the number of crimes committed by the average inmate was sixty-two; it dropped to thirty-seven in 1990 and to eighteen in 2001. As noted in Pew Center on the States (2009: 18):

Back in 1980, state researchers found, each prison bed represented a positive benefit-to-cost ratio. But during the 1990s and the first part of this decade, prison expansion captured less and less harmful offenders, leading to a dilution of impact. Put simply, after 20 years, locking up more drug and property offenders in Washington began to cost more than it was worth.

Nearly all of the cost-benefit research conducted on corrections focuses on alternatives to incarceration. There is very little directly on incarceration. One exception is Aos and colleagues (2001), who computed cost-benefit ratios for incarceration in Washington State. The 2001 ratios range from 0.37 for drug offenders to 2.84 for property offenders and 2.74 for violent offenders. These cost-benefit ratios declined dramatically since 1980, a reflection of the earlier discussion on the diminishing public safety returns of incarceration. A similar analysis of incarceration in North Carolina shows comparable reductions in the cost-benefit ratios over time (Yearwood et al. 2007).

COST-BENEFIT ANALYSES OF IN-PRISON
INTERVENTION PROGRAMS

Whatever the computed cost-benefit ratios for incarceration, the question is whether alternative correctional strategies pay greater dividends per dollar invested than simple punishment. The answer is that there are many, many alternatives that do precisely that. What follows is not an exhaustive inventory of cost-benefit analyses. Instead, the research discussed here is illustrative of the cost-effectiveness potential of prison-based alternatives that provide more than just loss of liberty.

The research shows that prison-based treatment and intervention can produce substantial returns. For example, estimates from Washington and Iowa (respectively) show the cost-benefit ratio for in-prison cognitive behavioral programs is $49.55 and $37.70; in-prison drug treatment is $8.25 and $3.69; vocational education is $12.43 and $4.12; and correctional education is $18.11 and $2.91. These are just examples from two states. Returns on investment are a function of many factors. However, these results show that there is substantial potential to engage much more cost-efficient strategies than simply punishment.

The state of Connecticut implemented a multitier in-prison substance abuse treatment program. Eighteen-month postrelease rearrest was used as a measure of the impact of the program compared to similar inmates who did not receive the treatment. The substance abuse program, especially the more intensive tiers, significantly reduced postrelease recidivism and was cost-effective. The cost-benefit ratios, which measured the cost impact of reincarceration avoided, ranged from 1.8 to 5.7, depending on the tier of treatment (Daley et al. 2004).

New Jersey also implemented prison-based substance abuse treatment for inmates nearing their release date. Like the programming in Connecticut, the New Jersey in-prison substance abuse treatment was determined to be effective in reducing postrelease recidivism one year after release compared to similar controls that did not receive treatment. The net economic benefits were estimated to be between $4,307 and $6,209 per participant (French, Fang, and Fretz 2010).

The Washington State legislature passed the Drug Offender Sentencing Alternative (DOSA) in 1999. DOSA provides for judicial discretion in sentencing drug-involved felony offenders providing they are not sex offenders or violent offenders and if their instant offense involved a limited amount of a controlled substance. DOSA gives the court the option to impose the alternative of a split prison and community release sentence, providing the offender agrees to participate and complete drug treatment while confined. There are two primary groups of offenders sentenced under DOSA: drug offenders and drug-involved property offenders. Cost-benefit research conducted by the Washington State Institute for Public Policy shows a cost-benefit ratio range of $7.25 to $9.94 for the drug-involved offenders, and $0.93 for drug-involved property offenders. The alternative sentence and treatment is very cost-effective for drug offenders and neutral for drug-involved property offenders.

COST-BENEFIT ANALYSES OF ALTERNATIVE CORRECTIONAL INTERVENTION PROGRAMS

There is a growing body of cost-benefit research that indicates that correctional treatment in general is cost-effective. Even absent cost-benefit analyses, if such alternatives reduce recidivism and are cheaper than incarceration, they are likely to be a cost-efficient strategy compared to incarceration alone.

Some of the early work, summarized by Welsh and Farrington (2000), shows favorable cost-benefit ratios (ranging from $1.13 to $7.14, meaning that for every dollar invested, the benefits range from $1.13 to $7.14 depending on the intervention). The programs evaluated are largely community based and include pretrial diversion, employment training, and substance abuse treatment. The Washington State Institute for Public Policy (WSIPP) reviewed and meta-analyzed over 570 evaluations of adult correctional programs, juvenile correctional programs, and community-based crime-prevention programs. The WSIPP (2011) provides an extensive menu of the costs and benefits of intervention and treatment programs that have a low risk of failure. These include juvenile justice interventions (for example, Multisystemic Therapy, Aggression Replacement Training, Functional Family Therapy, Multidimensional Treatment Foster Care) and adult justice interventions (Dangerously Mentally Ill Offenders, Electronic Monitoring, Correctional Education, CBT, Work Release, and Vocational Education among others). They also include a wide variety of community-based crime prevention programs for children and families, community mental health programs, public health, and substance abuse treatment, and others. For example, Aos and colleagues (2001) report that on average, intensive supervision treatment-oriented programs can produce a nearly 17 percent reduction in recidivism and an $11,500 net economic benefit per offender. Community-based drug treatment can produce an average 9 percent reduction in recidivism and a $10,000 net economic benefit per offender. In-prison vocational education can reduce recidivism by 9 percent and provide a nearly $14,000 net benefit. On the other hand, the evidence confirms some of the conventional wisdom about ineffective programs. For example, adult boot camps have a zero recidivism return and a zero economic benefit, as do most domestic violence education programs and life skills education.

In a similar vein, the Iowa Department of Corrections conducted a comparable assessment of correctional interventions in that state. They found substantial cost-benefit ratios for both institutional programs and community-based programs for parolees and probationers.

Yearwood and colleagues (2007) estimated the cost-benefit ratios associated with community supervision in North Carolina. This analysis is simply the supervision costs, with no provision for added services targeting behavioral change. The results, comparing the cost benefit for community supervision to that for incarceration is as follows: violent ($22.58 versus $4.04 for incarceration), property ($47.89 versus $8.56), and drug ($6.29 versus $1.13). Again, there is little provision in these estimates for enhanced programming to mitigate public safety risk. Nevertheless, the analysis does decisively show the relative costs and benefits of community corrections compared to incarceration.

Diversion and Community-Based Alternatives

Community supervision is much less expensive than incarceration. Prison (in 2008) costs on average $79 dollars per day (nearly $29,000 per year); average probation cost is $3.42 per day ($1,250 per year), and parole is $7.47 per day ($2,750 per year). With careful screening for risk and provision of known recidivism-reducing strategies and interventions, public safety can be enhanced with considerable cost savings.

Diversion from incarceration, whether probation, deferred adjudication, jail diversion, and drug court, among others, has a quite favorable cost-benefit track record. The WSIPP and Iowa Department of Corrections research indicates that several community-based correctional programs analyzed are cost-effective. Examples, with their cost-benefit ratios, include: drug treatment ($5.11 to $7.35), cognitive-behavioral therapy in the community ($19.46 to $35.70), intensive supervision probation with treatment ($2.28 to $2.78), and community employment training and job assistance ($2.88 to $35.13). Community-based drug treatment utilizing a therapeutic community model (often in the context of a work release facility) yields an average cost-benefit ratio of $8.87 (Aos et al. 2001).

Jail diversion for individuals with co-occurring mental illness and substance use disorders is recognized as an effective way to divert offenders to necessary treatment services. Cowell, Broner, and Dupont (2004) assessed the effectiveness and cost- effectiveness of diversion of mentally ill, substance abusing individuals with justice system involvement. The diversion is either pre- or postbooking. Eligible individuals presented with bipolar disorder, depression, or schizophrenia and co-occurring substance abuse or dependence disorders. This assessment occurred at four different sites: Memphis, Tennessee; Lane County, Oregon; New York City; and Tucson, Arizona. There was variation in outcomes across the four sites, due to factors such as prebooking diversion versus diversion sometime subsequent to booking, as well as the type and intensity of treatment. The primary cost saving was due to diversion from jail. At the same time, when diversion leads to linking individuals to treatment, those costs can be quite high, depending on what treatments are involved (for example, inpatient mental health treatment). At two of the sites (Memphis and Tucson), the diversion resulted in psychiatric improvement. At the others, there was no significant increase in alcohol and drug use and rearrest, a modestly positive outcome in light of the characteristics of the population served. Due to a variety of research limitations, Memphis was the only site for which a cost-effectiveness estimate was derived. The finding is that for each one-point improvement in the Colorado Symptom Index (a measure of mental health functioning), the jail diversion program spent $1,236. It is important to keep a few things in mind. First, this is a challenging population of individuals who have a wide variety of significant criminogenic needs. Second, individuals with co-occurring disorders tend to be more service resistant than others, making intervention more difficult. Moreover, the primary cost saving is averted jail days and the primary expenses are for mental health, substance abuse, and physical health treatments. To the extent that jail diversion programs like these can even partially address the psychiatric problems of this population and interrupt the cycle of justice system involvement, future cost savings can be significant as mental health costs stabilize and diminish and jail days continue to be averted. This can be substantial in the long term as this population has historically cycled in and out of the justice system over a considerably long period of time. The point is that these cost-effectiveness studies are essentially static in time, without statistical and fiscal consideration for longer-term effects (that is, ten, twenty, or thirty years out).

Mental health courts are a relatively new diversion approach to addressing the needs of mentally ill individuals with justice system involvement. They are limited in number in part because of the high cost associated with treating individuals with mental health disorders and often co-occurring substance abuse disorders. We also know little about their effectiveness and cost-effectiveness, especially compared to diversion programs like drug courts. Ridgley et al. (2007) assessed the cost-effectiveness of the Allegheny County, Pennsylvania, Mental Health Court. The analysis included one- and two-year follow-up comparisons for similar individuals who were not diverted to community-based treatment. The evaluation indicates that the Allegheny County court experience is one of essentially offsetting jail and treatment costs for the first year of follow-up. The evidence also indicates that over a longer period (two years) the program may actually save public resources. In short, it was successful at diverting nonviolent offenders with serious mental illnesses out of traditional criminal adjudication and punishment and into community-based mental health treatment and other supportive services. It appears that this program does so without incurring substantial incremental costs.

California's Proposition 36, passed in 2000, provides for selected California drug offenders to be diverted from incarceration to probation with drug treatment. The Substance Abuse and Crime Prevention Act (SACPA) was a substantial change to criminal justice policy. SACPA not only provides for diversion for nonviolent drug offenders with no serious or violent prior felonies or misdemeanors, it also provides that probationers and parolees who committed nonviolent drug offenses and who violate drug-related conditions of supervision can elect drug treatment rather than revocation. The law generally allows three opportunities to reenter drug treatment for violations. An assessment of the impacts of SACPA (Anglin et al. 2013) shows an economic benefit of $2,317 per offender. While a true cost-benefit ratio was beyond the scope of the research, the authors project a $97 million net savings from the first year of the program. Anglin and colleagues (2013: 1100) conclude:

> Thus, moving offenders from the correctional system and into the treatment system, where they are exposed to rehabilitative efforts, should provide long-term savings through reduction in the overall incarcerated population, or at least an attenuation of its historical growth rate.

In 2009, New York State passed reforms to the Rockefeller drug laws, infamously some of the most punitive drug laws in the nation. The reform eliminated mandatory prison sentences for most felony drug offenders and provided for judicial diversion for many drug and drug-involved property offenders to drug treatment (Center for Court Innovation 2013). The cost difference between diversion to treatment and prereform comparison cases (including case disposition and the sentence) is $5,564. Taking recidivism into consideration, the net cost savings per diverted offender is $5,144 or a cost-benefit ratio of $2. Including victimization costs changes the ratio to $3.56. The aggregate cost savings to the state amounts to over $7 million per year.

A third example of diversion comes from the District of Columbia, which estimates the cost benefit of electronic monitoring while on probation. The comparison is regular probation. Roman et al. (2012) estimate an 80 percent probability that the electronic monitoring program will be cost-effective and determine the cost benefit due to recidivism reduction to be approximately $4,600. Another cost-benefit analysis by Yeh (2010) shows a cost-benefit ratio of $12.70 for the combination of home detention and electronic monitoring for probationers and parolees. The benefit includes justice system savings as well as broader social benefits.

The Juneau County Diversion Program diverts nonviolent misdemeanor offenders from traditional criminal adjudication and punishment in an effort to reduce the costs of processing these low-level offenders. The program matches offenders with mentors, participants attend life skills workshops, complete a minimum of twenty hours of community service, and pay full restitution. Upon successful completion, the charges are dropped. Analysis by Bong and colleagues (2012) shows the average annual net present value of the program is $25,734, based on four components of savings: the criminal justice system, the jail, community service, and enhanced employability and earnings for program completers.

The Program for Offenders, Inc. (TPFO), located in Pittsburgh, is a nonprofit community-based corrections facility that provides residential jail services to offenders diverted from prison. Participants are assessed for criminogenic needs and are provided a variety of services, including case management, inpatient substance abuse treatment, counseling, employment assistance, life skills training, education, and referrals for intensive outpatient substance abuse treatment, mental health treatment, housing and other services not directly provided by TPFO. The estimated cost-benefit ratio is approximately $4.09 (Yamatani 2012).

The Pima County Arizona Drug Treatment Alternative to Prison (DTAP) program is probation-based drug treatment that provides enhanced recovery support services for selected nonviolent drug offenders with at least two prior narcotics offenses who are diverted from prison to residential, community-based treatment. A cost-benefit analysis conducted by Herman and Poindexter (2012) reports that the Pima County diversion program, compared to a matched control group, saves the state of Arizona an average of $8,807 per offender compared to incarceration.

A similar drug offender diversion program was implemented in King's County (Brooklyn), New York, in the 1990s. It was designed to divert nonviolent felony drug offenders to community-based drug treatment. A six-year follow-up showed that, compared to incarceration, the recidivism results of the diversion program with treatment had a cost-benefit ratio of $2.17.

Zarkin et al. (2012) conducted a simulation analysis of the lifetime costs and benefits of diversion of drug offenders from incarceration to community-based drug treatment. The authors develop two different scenarios and compare long-term outcomes (recidivism) with the no-diversion baseline data. The scenarios differ with regard to a 10 percent probability of diversion and a 40 percent probability of diversion, so scenario two is more aggressively scaled up. The results indicate in the 10 percent scenario, in which 44,200 offenders are diverted, the lifetime net benefit to the criminal justice system is $4.8 billion. The 40 percent scenario, in which 118,300 are diverted, the criminal justice cost saving is $12.9 billion. Estimation of the broader societal economic impact of diversion (which includes victimization costs, criminal justice costs of arrest, courts, incarceration, and health care costs) ramps up the net economic benefits to $8.5 billion for the 10 percent scenario and $22.5 billion for the 40 percent scenario.

The most commonly evaluated justice alternative is probably drug court. It is also the justice program for which the most cost-benefit research has been conducted. Drug courts can produce substantial reductions in recidivism and relapse (as discussed in chapter 5). At eighteen months after completion, drug court participants are less likely to need employment, educational, and financial services. These results are generally evident across a variety of offender types. Cost-benefit analyses have been conducted in drug courts across the country including, but not limited to, Washington, Oregon, Ohio, Vermont, California, Maryland, Michigan, Florida, Georgia, Illinois, Pennsylvania, South Carolina, Texas, and New York (Carey, Finigan, and Pukstas 2008; Carey and Waller 2011; Finigan, Carey, and Cox 2007; NPC Research 2009; Rossman et al. 2011a; Shaffer, Bechtel, and Latessa 2005; Washington State Institute for Public Policy 2003). Cost impacts and cost-benefit ratios all indicate favorable cost-effectiveness across the board. Cost-benefit ratios range from $1.74 to $9.43. Per participant net (of comparison group costs) cost savings due to recidivism reductions include $1,362 (St. Louis City Adult Drug Court), $1,982 (Maryland Drug Treatment Court Program), $3,451 (Baltimore City Drug Court), $4,133 (St. Joseph County Indiana Drug Court), $4,251 (Vigo County Indiana Drug Court), $4,600 (Howard County, Maryland), $4,896 (Montgomery County, Maryland), $5,809 (Vermont Drug Courts), $6,744 (Multnomah County, Portland, Oregon), $7,040 (Monroe County Indiana Drug Treatment Court), and $11,366 (Prince George's County, Maryland). In those cases, for example Ohio, in which the cost-benefit ratio is relatively low or the cost-effectiveness is marginal, the analysts indicate that they were unable to control for offender risk. They suggest that had the risk principle been faithfully implemented so that higher-risk offenders populated drug courts, the cost results would be more favorable.

John Roman, an expert on drug courts, estimates that if drug courts were taken to scale to accommodate the roughly 1.5 million drug-involved offenders in need of substance abuse treatment, it would cost more than $13 billion annually. However, that investment would return more than $40 billion annually in benefits. Roman's testimony before a House of

Representatives subcommittee included the prediction that drug court effectiveness could be enhanced and cost controlled by utilizing a HOPE Court accountability model in conjunction with drug courts. This would allow the use of accountability/sanction courts for those who do not need drug treatment in order to desist from offending and therefore reserving the more expensive drug court model for those who cannot desist without substance abuse treatment.

Reentry

Despite the recent national focus on reentry spearheaded by the Urban Institute, there has been relatively little cost-effectiveness or cost-benefit analysis of reentry programs. Here is what is known. Welsh (2004) poses the question of whether there is a compelling economic argument for correctional treatment for offenders leaving prison. Welsh reports the cost-benefit results of a review of fourteen fairly early studies (most from the 1970s, 1980s, and 1990s) that focus on community-based correctional treatment. Most exhibited a favorable cost-benefit ratio, ranging from $1.13 to $2.82 to $7.14 to $53.73 to $270.00. Some of the studies monetized the recidivism effects and others monetized other outcomes such as substance use, education, and employment. Welsh (2004: 5) concludes

> Offender reentry programs are crucial in an effort to reduce recidivism rates. But it may be that what comes before this end stage—in the form of correctional treatment programs—is equally, if not more, important. From the cost-benefit studies reviewed here, it would seem that a case can be made for increasing treatment resources for offenders, and this may improve offenders' chances for a successful return to the community.

The Iowa Department of Corrections conducted a cost-benefit analysis of some of their reentry programs. Their analysis was modeled after the analytic approach developed by a partnership between the Pew Center on the States and the Washington State Institute for Public Policy. The Iowa Department of Corrections analysis determined the following reentry programs provided significant cost benefit: cognitive-behavioral programs ($34.30), drug treatment ($8.98), intensive supervision based on the risk-need-responsivity principle ($7.18), electronic monitoring ($6.43), employment training and job assistance ($5.02), and intensive supervision with treatment ($5.01).

McCollister and colleagues (2004) assessed the longer-term costs and benefits of in-prison substance abuse treatment in California (the Amity in-prison therapeutic community) and subsequent community-based aftercare postrelease from prison (the Vista aftercare programs). While substance abuse treatment required an average investment of $7,041 per participant over a five-year follow-up period (including primary treatment and after-care), the averted incarceration days attributed to the program produced a cost-benefit ratio of $65. The additional investment of $5,311 in treatment yielded eighty-one fewer incarceration days (13 percent) among Amity participants relative to controls—a cost-effectiveness ratio of $65. When considering the average daily cost of incarceration in California ($72), these results suggest that offering treatment in prison and then directing offenders into community-based aftercare treatment is a cost-effective policy.

The State of Oregon's Criminal Justice Commission (Officer, Bajpai, and Wilson 2011) conducted a cost-benefit analysis of an offender reentry program for releasees who received substance abuse treatment while incarcerated. The reentry program is designed to continue substance abuse programming once released, as well as provide assessment of the need for community-based services including mental health, employment counseling, career development, housing, and GED completion. The goal is to increase self-sufficiency and reduce recidivism. The evaluation research shows that the treatment group had significantly fewer rearrests (both felony and misdemeanor) than the control group. The cost-benefit analysis reveals a positive economic impact ($6.73 return for every dollar invested in the reentry programming).

The Maryland Reentry Partnership Initiative (MRPI) was established in 1999. It is a partnership of service providers that coordinate services for releasees returning to particular Baltimore neighborhoods. The goal is to provide coordinated and comprehensive reentry services including housing, substance abuse treatment, mental health treatment and counseling, education, and employment and vocational training, among others. The program is designed to identify inmates prior to release, provide prerelease planning and preparation, and then assist the transition by assessing service needs and providing community-based services. The evaluation indicated lower recidivism for the MRPI group compared to the controls. The total net economic benefit per participant is estimated to be $21,500. The cost benefit is estimated to be $3.00 (Roman et al. 2007). The greatest benefit from the program, in terms of cost and crime, is the reduction in serious crime. This finding of reduction in more serious crimes has been reported by other evaluators of reentry programs.

The Ready, Willing and Able program, based in New York City and Philadelphia, assists individuals recently released from prison by providing transitional housing, employment, and other support services. The goal is for releasees to independently maintain housing, employment, and sobriety. Cost-benefit analysis indicates the program benefits exceed the costs by approximately 20 percent.

The Nebraska Department of Correctional Services implemented a serious and violent offender reentry program in 2003. The intent was to target particularly dangerous and high-risk offenders and facilitate reentry. The first phase of the program was designed to provide substance abuse and mental health treatment, education, and life skills training while still incarcerated. Phase one also provided for the creation of transition teams responsible for developing individualized reentry plans for each releasee. Phase two was the transition to the community while receiving services from the state and private treatment providers. They also were on electronic monitoring until they demonstrated the ability to function without it. Phase three continued treatment services, but essentially no correctional control. The evaluation indicated a lower recidivism for program participants, compared to controls. The cost-benefit analysis resulted in an estimated net annual cost savings to the justice system of $5,849 per participant. When victimization costs are included, the total annual savings amount to $10,637 per program participant (Sample and Spohn 2008).

Dangerous mentally ill inmates who are released from prison present a particular risk to public safety. Odds are that they receive little effective mental health treatment while incarcerated and likely experience the criminogenic impact of incarceration. Postrelease supervision and control are important, however absent effectively addressing the mental health problems, that public safety risk persists. The Dangerous Mentally Ill Offender Program (DMIO) is designed to assess and intervene with more effective treatment for dangerous, mentally ill prison releasees. This is a postrelease program in Washington State for mentally ill releasees who are assessed to be a danger to themselves or others. The DMIO program begins while offenders are still incarcerated. Once identified as a dangerous mentally ill offender, they will be assigned to a treatment provider and will receive pre-engagement services during the three to four months prior to release, as well as treatment and transitioning planning. Upon release and up to five years out, DMIO participants receive community-based services including mental health and substance abuse treatment, housing assistance, medical care, and other support services. Mayfield (2009) reports that the four-year follow-up evaluation shows significant reductions in felony recidivism for program participants. The cost savings to the justice system as well as savings to potential crime victims average about $21,600 per participant. After four years, the cost-benefit ratio is $1.64 returned for every $1 spent on this program. A three-year follow-up reports a cost-benefit ratio of $1.24 of benefits to the justice system and crime victims (Mayfield and Lovell 2008).

Zhang, Roberts, and Callanan (2006) conducted a cost-benefit analysis of a statewide parole program in California. The California Preventing Parolee Failure Program (PPFP) was developed in response to record high recidivism rates of prison releasees. A California Department of Corrections analysis identified several factors that were related to parole failure: substance abuse, unemployment, illiteracy, and homelessness. The PPFP provided education, training, treatment, and assistance designed to mitigate these criminogenic circumstances. Initial positive findings of recidivism reduction and cost savings led to expanded funding and a new name, the Preventing Parole Crime Program (PPCP). The budget tripled in 1998. The 2006 evaluation results indicated that the PPCP reduced returns to prison among paroles who received services under the program, compared to controls. The reduction in reincarcerations led to aggregate cost savings of $21 million during the study period. The cost-benefit analysis resulted in an estimated net return on investment of 47 percent, or a 47 percent net return for every $1 invested in the PPCP.

Roman and Chafin (2006) assessed the economic impact of reentry initiatives for jail inmates. The initiatives included services such as provision of life skills and substance abuse counseling, employment and education services, and healthcare, among other services designed to assist with reentry. The economic analysis compared the reentry program participants' outcomes to business as usual processing in the justice system without reentry services. The analysis indicated that under different conditions of program cost, it only requires modest reductions in offender recidivism to render jail-based reentry programs cost-effective. They conclude that the case for implementing jail-based reentry programs is strong based on cost-effectiveness analyses.

The Washington State Institute for Public Policy in conjunction with the Pew Center on the States has developed a cost benefit tool, as has the Vera Institute (Cost Benefit Knowledge Bank). These tools are easily available for practitioners to use to assess cost-effectiveness and estimate cost-benefit ratios.

The end game here is to reduce recidivism and crime. I have discussed a variety of evidence-based strategies that have demonstrable track records for being effective and cost-efficient. The financial impacts on the criminal justice system of engaging proven practices and implementing them in effective, appropriate ways are substantial. These impacts include reductions in incarceration costs, the cost of law enforcement and the courts, as well as victimization costs. Shapiro and Hassett (2012) have taken these economic impacts and extrapolated the effects to particular U.S. cities. For example, they estimate that a 10 percent reduction in violent crime in Boston will produce a $5 million savings to local government and $73 million in intangible losses to victims. A 25 percent reduction in violent crime would result in a $12 million annual savings, reduce the direct costs to victims by $18 million, and the intangible victim costs by $180 million. They estimate that a 10 percent reduction in homicide in the Boston area would boost the value of residential real estate by $4.4 billion. A 10 percent reduction in violent crime in Chicago translates into a $24 million savings to local government, a $43 million savings in direct costs to victims, and $420 million in victim intangibles. Residential real estate value is expected to increase by $2.2 billion with a 10 percent reduction in murder in Chicago. The scenario for Houston is a $17 million annual savings in direct costs to local government, $27 million for victim direct costs, and $265 million in victim intangible costs. The impacts are equally impressive for Dallas, Jacksonville, Milwaukee, Philadelphia, and Seattle.

The takeaway from the Shapiro and Hassett analysis and forecasting is that the economic impact of crime reduction affects the expense side as well as the revenue side of government. The expense side is in terms of the criminal justice cost savings; the revenue side is in terms of things such as increases in property values, which in turn translate into higher property tax revenue. Some of the savings to victims may translate into increased consumer spending, resulting in increases in sales tax revenues. Such revenue increases could in part be used to fund or increase funding for initiatives that have been demonstrated to be effective crime prevention programs; for example, programs identified by the Washington State Institute for Public Policy as having quite favorable cost-benefit ratios, including a variety of early childhood education programs such as Nurse-Family Partnerships, parent training, children's mental health interventions, and youth mentoring programs.

WHAT DOES THE COST-BENEFIT RESEARCH TELL US ABOUT THE RECOMMENDED PATH FORWARD?

This section provides a brief summary of what is known about the cost benefit of the recommendations made in prior chapters. At the outset, the evidence is clear that since incarceration alone does not effectively reduce recidivism and is extraordinarily expensive, it is reasonable to conclude that alternatives that are demonstrated to be effective at reducing recidivism and cost less are, by definition, more cost-efficient than incarceration. However, the incapacitation function of incarceration going forward is necessary. It is important, however, that the justice system transition the use of incarceration for serious violent offenders, truly habitual offenders, and those for whom there is clear, compelling evidence that rehabilitation is not possible. At the same time, incarceration should not be void of programming. The vast majority of the offenders that are incarcerated in the future will be released and will have significant risk when released. Some of that risk can be mitigated by implementing programing while incarcerated. The evidence indicates that in-prison substance abuse treatment as well as cognitive-behavioral interventions targeting other criminogenic deficits are cost-effective.

Many of the recommendations I have discussed are not programs per se and thus are not as amenable to cost-benefit analysis. For example, problem-solving prosecution and collaborative sentencing are statutory, procedural, and cultural changes that facilitate the goals of recidivism reduction, targeted incarceration, and behavioral change. Others are too new to have cost-benefit analyses. For example, targeting neurocognitive deficits and impairments and swift and certain sanctioning are relatively new initiatives with evaluation research speaking to effectiveness, however, the specific economic analyses are yet to be conducted.

The primary focus of what this book is recommending is a concerted and dramatically expanded effort at behavioral change. On balance, the evaluation research and the cost-benefit analyses indicate that is a prudent and profitable path.

First, the research indicates that diversion is a wise investment. Whether probation, deferred adjudication, jail diversion, diversion courts, and others, the research indicates that when properly implemented, these treatment-based alternatives to incarceration have substantial economic benefits, including cost savings to the criminal justice system, local government, communities, and victims. Moreover, the cost-benefit research supports efforts to take many of these initiatives to scale. The evidence regarding the effectiveness of drug diversion is so compelling and the cost-benefit impacts are so favorable that the economics clearly support expansion of capacity. The cost-benefit results are also compelling for programs that address a variety of other criminogenic deficits and impairments. Programs that are designed to assist with educational deficits, employment, vocational training, mental health, and housing, among others, when implemented in community-based settings, are not only effective in helping to reduce recidivism, they are also cost-effective.

The evidence regarding probation is especially important. Probation is a critical opportunity to advance the goals of behavioral change, reduce recidivism, reduce victimizations, and enhance cost-effectiveness. There is tremendous potential there and the research indicates that additional investment in probation is clearly warranted and fiscally prudent. Again, community-based substance abuse treatment, cognitive-behavioral therapy, employment and job training, and intensive supervision with treatment are a few of the probation-based interventions that provide positive ROIs.

Reentry is another clear opportunity for improvement and the research indicates that reentry programming can be cost-effective. Substance abuse treatment and aftercare, cognitive-behavioral interventions, employment, housing, job assistance, electronic monitoring, mental health treatment, and education programming, as well as prerelease planning and preparation, can be cost beneficial.

The results of the cost-benefit research can be helpful in transitioning our thinking away from the tough rhetoric of crime control and seeming disregard for scientific evidence to policymaking that is informed by an emphasis on what is effective and financially prudent. There is clear guidance provided by the cost-benefit research regarding where to invest wisely in the future.

SUMMARY

The goal of this chapter has been to provide policymakers with information regarding the potential for alternatives to incarceration to be not only effective, but cost-efficient as well. Much of our effort over the past forty years and much of the money spent on that effort has not provided a reasonable return on investment. Let's be fair. Policy development and implementation is a result of many factors, some of which concern whether certain initiatives are effective and whether they are cost-efficient.

In the course of the discussions in chapters 3 through 7, I have provided alternatives and options that are grounded in scientific evidence and for which the scientific community has demonstrated effectiveness. The inventory of effective practices and programs is quite impressive and provide policymakers with a wide variety of viable options. Moreover, I have also shown in this chapter that engaging in actual behavioral change, which is the goal of most of these alternatives to incarceration and control, can be cost-effective. The evidence indicates that for the programs for which cost-benefit analyses have been conducted, most return more financial benefit to the justice system and society at large (potential victims, property values) than the upfront investment.

The brevity of this chapter serves to illustrate that the assessment and evaluation of the financial impacts of correctional alternatives has not kept pace with the evaluation of program effectiveness. We are just recently beginning to learn that evidence-based practices are reasonable choices, not only because they effectively change behavior and reduce recidivism and crime, but also because many do so by returning more fiscal benefit relative to the cost incurred. Moreover, the dividends from these programs are likely significantly understated as they ignore the longer-term financial impacts of desistence from crime of career offenders—breaking the cycle of repeat offending, reductions in crime, reductions in justice system contacts, and reductions in victimizations.

Much of what is recommended in the preceding pages is based on prioritizing and addressing in a meaningful sequence or cluster the primary criminogenic needs of offenders. What is missing in the cost research are estimates of the fiscal benefits of targeting multiple criminogenic needs, that is, the cumulative, marginal effect.

While cost-benefit research has not yet provided the full picture of return on investment of the variety of alternatives discussed in the preceding pages, at the end of the day, we know that incarceration is quite expensive and has limited effectiveness. If the prison population declines, the marginal utility of incarceration may, all else equal, improve. However, the fact that alternatives are effective and in most instances cost less is assurance that the path outlined in this book is fiscally prudent.

Conclusions

CRIME CONTROL EMERGED IN THE United States in an era of unprecedented turmoil and disorder. Historically high crime rates, massive and frequent race riots, and protests over the war in Vietnam provided much of the provocation for a profound shift in the U.S criminal justice system. That sea change in crime policy included the construction of the world's largest prison system, extensive changes to criminal laws and sentencing statutes, and the redirection of extraordinary amounts of public funds. For nearly four decades, tough on crime has been the centerpiece of U.S. criminal justice policy and has played a prominent role in U.S. politics. It has been the one size that we have tried to fit all. It is based on a very simple premise that is embedded in the Protestant ethic and Judeo–Christian theology: punishment is the appropriate response to wrongdoing. The appeal of punishment is intuitive and understandable. Its political importance is clearly evident at all levels of government—few have lost elections by being tough on crime. It has been the rally for elected officials, policymakers, law enforcement, prosecutors, judges, and corrections officials. Tough on crime is how we have thought about crime and justice and how we have largely done the business of criminal justice. And punishment's inability to effectively reduce crime and recidivism is undeniable.

At the outset, I stated that while this is in part a book about a policy failure of remarkable scale and scope, it is mainly an effort to forge a new path forward, a path informed by evidence, not intuition. The title of the book is intended to convey the opportunity that is currently available to engage real change. That opportunity is a product of three significant factors: (1) compelling scientific evidence indicating that punishment does not work and is a poor return on investment; (2) a wealth of scientific evidence demonstrating the effectiveness of a wide variety of interventions, programs, and policies that successfully change behavior, reduce recidivism and victimization, and save money; and (3) a nationwide recession that caused state, local, and federal elected officials and policymakers to pause and take a hard look at the cost of crime control and initiate discussion of alternatives. We find ourselves at a crossroads today, an opportunity to move in a direction of informed policy and practice, rather than basing how we deal with crime on instinct, anger, or gut feelings.

It is irresponsible to continue down the current path of crime control policies. It is irresponsible to put individuals and communities in jeopardy of avoidably being victimized. It is irresponsible in terms of offenders as it is a waste of human capital. And it is fiscally irresponsible. Twenty-five years ago, we could have legitimately pleaded ignorance because we did not have the scientific evidence available today regarding effective alternatives to punishment. In 2015, we have the tools to be smart on crime, save tremendous amounts of money (both in the short term and long term), and enhance public safety.

CHALLENGES GOING FORWARD

My personal experiences developing and evaluating justice programs, as well as observing, interacting and consulting with judges, prosecutors, court administrators, justice planning officials, law enforcement officials, prison and jail administrators, probation administrators and officers, and defense attorneys, has provided me with considerable insight regarding some of the more compelling barriers and challenges to implementing change. The obvious candidates are lack of innovation, vision, and leadership, failure to properly fund and resource a program or policy, failure to access appropriate research regarding program design, implementation and operation, lack of implementation and operational fidelity, failure to evaluate, and political and cultural barriers. I have discussed many of these more obvious difficulties in the preceding chapters. This section details some of my observations about these and other less obvious roadblocks or barriers to successful implementation and performance.

Nearly fifteen years ago, I attended a community-oriented policing conference sponsored by the office of Community Oriented Policing

Services (COPS), a division of the U.S. Department of Justice. The conference hall was filled with about 500 to 600 mainly senior officials from local police departments from all over the United States. The conference began with the moderator asking two questions. First: How many of your departments practice community policing? Every hand in the room was raised. Second question: Who can tell us what community policing is? Three hands went up. I have seen versions of this play out in a variety of situations. Putting a label on a program or a practice is a far cry from actually doing it and doing it well. Simply stating that a department or agency uses some evidence-based practice is not the same as actually understanding what it is and implementing and operating it correctly throughout the organization.

Change is usually hard. It can be threatening, and often impacts roles and responsibilities and ruptures traditional balances of power within an organization. It can impact workloads and require a reorientation of priorities and resources in an agency. Change is typically top-down, originating with senior management, but the day-to-day implementation is up to middle management and line staff. Therein lies one of the more significant barriers to proper implementation and operation. If middle management and/or line staff do not understand and buy in to the relationship between some new initiative (for example, a more balanced accountability and behavior change model) and the goals of the agency (for example, recidivism reduction or public safety), the initiative is in jeopardy. If the dots are not connected, there will likely be pushback. Yes, staff can take direction, but the extent to which they actually embrace their roles and responsibilities depends on many things, including understanding the bigger picture, cultural barriers, personal biases, and so on. How well management actually sells an initiative (versus simply ordering it) is important.

Motivational interviewing (MI) is a relatively recent "go to" approach for encouraging or motivating individuals to engage in criminal justice programming. While probation administrators state that their officers are using MI on a routine basis, when I ask the officers about MI, many brush it off as the "flavor of the month" or state that they really have no idea what it is. Some roll their eyes and say, "it sounds like hug-a-thug to me."

The point is that there is quite a divide between saying it is so and actually understanding and embracing a practice or innovation. Implementation on paper is different than implementation in the field. Probably one of the biggest barriers to effective, comprehensive, faithful implementation of a new innovation is the failure of the senior administration: to properly communicate the rationale and necessity for the policy; to properly motivate middle management and line staff; and to provide incentives for excellence. Simply ordering it is insufficient and is often a recipe for failure.

Even if the rationale for a new policy or a new initiative is explained well and makes sense, the goals are established, and the roles and responsibilities are clarified, there can be a reluctance on the part of line staff and middle management to engage in the change process. Part of this is just inertia against change. Change requires effort. Not everyone is willing to do what is necessary to fully and successfully implement the change. Some are just not motivated to engage in change at the level required to be successful. Yes, they can go through the motions when that is required, but that obviously is not the same.

One of the primary concerns of middle management and line staff is workload. New initiatives often add to current roles and responsibilities, which in turn adds to workload. This is a significant source of staff pushback. In addition to administrators realigning roles, responsibilities, and workload to the demands imposed by the new initiative, it may be useful to focus on the longer-term gain of reduced workload. If the initiative results in reduced recidivism, then workloads should decline over time.

One of the more common barriers to successful implementation and outcomes is the failure to hire the right people for the right positions. Often the scenario is one of simply not understanding the proper roles and responsibilities for a given position and/or trying to fit current staff into new or modified positions. Training clearly helps, but often a philosophical alignment is required, and along with it, the right attitude and the proper level of motivation. I have seen this in all levels of program staffing, from the line staff going through the motions, to administrators and judges just not getting it. I have seen more than one problem-solving court judge who did not understand and did not embrace the principles of the court or the principles of therapeutic jurisprudence. Research and common sense tell us that the role of the judge in problem-solving courts is fundamental to success. If the judge just doesn't get it, the mission is clearly jeopardized.

Then there is turf control. Innovation requires collaboration with others within an agency as well as across agencies and organizations. Turf control can play out in a variety of ways within organizations. Individuals may try to preserve their influence or authority in a variety of unproductive ways, like being excessively "nitpicky" or obstructing or stonewalling others.

I have often seen turf control like this play out in terms of lack of information sharing. A good example of this was the repeated refusal of the administrator of a problem-solving court to provide the advisory board with basic statistical information regarding the operation of the court. The administrator's excuse was that everybody at the court was too busy to provide the information. The backstory was that the court was not functioning properly, and the administrator knew it and did not want that to get out.

Failure to evaluate processes and outcomes leaves administrators in the dark about what is really happening day to day (Are goals being accomplished? What needs to be modified or changed?). Evaluation is typically tied to federal program funding, but is much more problematic in other settings. Even where process and outcome evaluations are conducted, it is not necessarily the case that program managers will use the information to improve those processes and outcomes. Knowing the value of evaluation, properly implementing it (proper design and data collection, use of qualified, experienced external evaluators), and knowing how to use the results and actually implementing corrective actions where necessary are critical to program effectiveness and cost-efficiency. During my years conducting program evaluations, I have often encountered the concern that individuals think I am evaluating them. That can create a situation in which, for example, the individuals being interviewed are not as forthcoming as is necessary for a productive evaluation. I have found that can be mitigated by clarifying the purpose of the evaluation and assuring confidentiality.

Early adopters of innovation can be at a disadvantage because evaluation research is generally more limited. The early drug courts were launched well before we knew much about effectiveness, process efficiencies, and implementation barriers and strategies. In 2015, after some twenty-five years of research, we are in a position to design and implement the most effective drug court model, not to mention many other types of programs and processes. Thus, the situation today is considerably different in terms of the nuts and bolts of behavioral change processes and programming. Those engaged in program development have many well-tested principles, evidence-based practices, and prototypes from which to model new programs.

However, the thousands of existing programs that were developed over the years require not only evaluation, but may also significantly benefit from some renovation or refinement. Aligning current programming with the current evidence base is required if the goal is maximum impact and cost-effectiveness. Once again, we are back to a familiar point: just having a program is not the same as maximizing the impact and minimizing the cost. This is an ongoing process and it seems too often that we settle for less than need be.

EVIDENCE-DRIVEN POLICYMAKING

There is another significant challenge in addition to lack of funding, innovation, leadership, fidelity, cultural barriers, and the more subtle impediments discussed previously. It is the current status of the policy-making process and the divide between producers and consumers of knowledge.

The basis for the recommendations made in this book is the availability of valid, actionable, scientific research, evidence that demonstrates the viability and effectiveness of a variety of policies, procedures, principles, and strategies for effectively and cost-efficiently reducing crime and recidivism. The current evidence base is the starting point. Much more research is required to further clarify, elaborate, modify, expand, and qualify what we currently know, and to explore new strategies and innovations. Obtaining that research can be challenging.

There are a variety of research institutions, both private and public, that have played a critical role in generating the evidence base. These include the Washington State Public Policy Institute, the RAND Corporation, the Urban Institute, the Justice Center at the Council on State Governments, the Center for Court Innovation, the Vera Institute, and the Pew Center on the States, among others. What these organizations produce has played a fundamental role in advancing scientific knowledge about crime and justice. But much social science research comes from research universities. Part of the challenge lies in the culture and reward structures of those institutions. Applied or policy research is not nearly as valued in university settings as is basic research, which is often published in relatively obscure journals that are intended for other academics, not practitioners and policymakers. Academic research is written for other academics in a language and format that is not often accessible to policymakers and practitioners.

Time is not as valued in university environments, thus the production of knowledge is not often driven by the need for timely answers. The questions that much academic research addresses are generally not driven by broader policy interests or needs, but by the interests of the individual or what will advance their academic careers. Borgenschneider and Corbett (2010), in their influential book *Evidence-Based Policymaking*, make the points quite well (2010: 13):

> The very institutions through which knowledge is generated and power is exercised often operate in ways that are counterproductive to evidence-based policymaking. . . . Those who operate within the academic community know what they have to do in order to thrive and advance. They must cater to their peers who more or less do basic research within narrow specializations. Working too closely with the real world bears considerable professional risk.

Borgenschneider and Corbett's research included determining what makes research useful to policymakers. The characteristics of useful research include that it is actionable, definitive, generalizable, objective, relevant, timely, of high quality, and presented in an accessible, understandable manner. Unfortunately, much of the social science research on crime and justice does not conform to many of these criteria.

Working with policymakers and practitioners requires at a minimum understanding the context and environment in which policy decisions are made; the needs, interests, and constraints imposed on policymakers and practitioners; knowing how to communicate with policymakers and practitioners; and being aware of and sensitive to the requirements for translating research evidence into policy and practice. Academic researchers doing basic research do not typically cross these boundaries. Borgenschneider and Corbett conclude that movement in that direction, where academics and policymakers come to better understand and collaborate with each other, can be facilitated by understanding and changing the culture in which much scientific research is produced.

But it doesn't end with researchers providing the evidence. Instead, the collaboration should extend to design and implementation. Helping policymakers and practitioners translate research results into program and policy components is just as important as providing answers regarding what works and what doesn't.

A CAVEAT REGARDING RESEARCH EVIDENCE

On balance, the evidence is clear that alternatives to crime control's punitive policies are more effective. However, it is important to note that the quality of the scientific research evidence varies.

While meta-analyses of evidence-based practices and programs typically screen for reliability and validity of the research, there is variation in the quality of the evidence. Some of the evidence is relatively extensive and strong (for example, drug courts), but many other practices and programs have not received the same level of scientifically valid evaluation (for example, problem-solving prosecution). That reality requires that we adjust our expectations regarding how well particular practices and programs may work. Indeed, even in the presence of the most compelling research evidence, variation in performance is inevitable.

A good example is recent evidence provided by Wright, Sheldon, and Zhang (2012) regarding institutionally blessed evidence-based practices for substance abuse and correctional interventions. Wright et al. conducted an extensive review of the research in the National Registry of Evidence-Based Programs and Practices (NREPP), which is managed by the Substance Abuse and Mental Health Services Administration (SAMHSA). Among the concerns regarding the scientific validity and reliability of the research are the use of small samples, evaluations conducted by the program developers, and a general lack of independent verification of the reported treatment effects. SAMHSA is a quite credible agency. The fact that SAMHSA at least implicitly blesses the programs and practices that are on the NREPP is potentially troubling. As Wright, Sheldon, and Zhang (2012: 955) conclude: "If the NREPP is to fulfill its intended function, a tighter vetting process is needed for programs to be registered so that community agencies and treatment practitioners can consult with confidence."

It is important to note that we need not wait until a program or practice has been examined and vetted to the extent that drug courts have been before we can move forward. Instead, as jurisdictions implement practices, programs, and policies, evaluation research shall continue to accumulate. This is an ongoing process—as we learn more, we can then adjust our implementation and operational strategies and our expectations as we move forward.

BALANCE, BALANCE, BALANCE

Crime control took justice policy and justice funding dramatically out of balance. Much of what the proposed path forward involves is getting crime policy to the middle, where there is a more effective mix of incarceration/control for those who need it and diversion and intervention for the rest.

The research is pretty clear: prison does not effectively reduce recidivism, and in fact, there is mounting evidence that prison is criminogenic, serving to actually increase recidivism (Cullen, Jonson, and Nagin 2011). Thus, the guidance on prison use going forward is to limit incarceration to individuals for whom we have neither the expectation nor the desire to rehabilitate. Instead, the primary purpose of prisons should be incapacitation, either because of the inherent dangerousness of an individual, the characteristics of the particular crime they committed (for example, the level of violence used), and/or a clinical decision that a particular offender cannot be rehabilitated.

There are three aspects of incarceration to consider here: the number of admissions to prison (sentences of incarceration), the length of the sentence imposed, and time served. Because incarceration does not reduce recidivism, a sentence of incarceration should not be imposed lightly. The longer-term consequences should be a significant element in the decision. If incarceration is determined to be the appropriate sentence, it should be clear that the only likely public safety benefit will be incapacitation, and that the effect is small and the broader impact on public safety is clouded by the replacement or substitution effect.

Research indicates the effectiveness of drug diversion. Ramping up drug court capacity to anywhere near the need (estimated at 1.5 million) will result in significant increases in diversion from incarceration. An increase in drug offender diversion of 30 percent (what seems like a fairly conservative number) will reduce drug admissions to prison by over 56,000 per year (all else equal). This estimate is based on total drug offense admissions to prison of 187,200 in 2011 and a number of assumptions, but reflects the likely potential such a policy has.

In 2012, the U.S. Department of Justice reported that the total number of prisoners in state and federal prisons totaled 1,571,013. The state share of that total was 1,353,198. There were 609,800 new admissions to U.S. prisons that year. Twenty-five percent (152,700) of these admissions were parole violators. Felony probation revocations accounted for another 180,000. Over 50 percent of all prison admissions in 2012 were for violations of community supervision.

One very effective way to control prison populations and reduce recidivism is to employ graduated or intermediate sanctions that rely on swift and certain consequences for violations of conditions of supervision and engage behavioral change interventions. The logic is pretty simple. For example, if a parolee or probationer violates the prohibition against drug use, placement in a drug treatment program for those with a clinically determined substance abuse disorder rather than revocation can be an appropriate, effective, cost-saving strategy. For others, a swiftly imposed, brief jail sentence may be all that is necessary for compliance. The next violation may lead to a longer sentence. The point is that typical cases should work through a series of graduated sanctions and interventions, and not just automatically send a problem case to prison. Revocation is a failure of everyone involved and should be a last resort, unless it is clear someone is a significant public safety risk and revocation is the only option. The response to a violation should involve changing behavior, not typically just punishment, tighter supervision or imposing additional condition of supervision. Tighter control may be appropriate, but that alone may not be sufficient to change behavior or enhance compliance. Assuming that is all that is needed is naïve and counter to what the research clearly tells us.

Research indicates that implementation of evidence-based practices and graduated sanctions, often in the form of Justice Reinvestment Initiatives, can significantly reduce probation and parole revocation rates, and in turn reduce prison admissions. The impacts understandably vary depending on what practices states have implemented, how well they have implemented them, and how many individuals are affected. For example, the Travis County (Austin) Texas Adult Probation department reports a 20 percent decline in probation revocations due to the implementation of evidence-based practices and intermediate sanctions. The HOPE Court in Hawaii reports a 50 percent reduction in revocations as a result of swift and certain sanctioning. In Arkansas, probation revocations declined by 15 percent under their Justice Reinvestment Initiative. If we use a percentage reduction between the Arkansas and Travis County numbers and the HOPE Court estimate, say 30 percent, that amounts to a reduction of 60,000 prison admission each year. Assuming an average annual incarceration cost of $25,500 per inmate, this reduction in probation revocations saves $1.53 billion annually just in avoided incarceration costs (it does not reflect all of the other costs avoided due to reductions in recidivism). These estimates are very rough, but may be in the ballpark of reasonable expectation.

Similar initiatives involving the implementation of best practices for parole supervision have had substantial effects in reducing revocation rates. Again, the impacts vary significantly by state: Texas has reduced parole revocation by 25 percent; Michigan has reduced revocation rates by 38 percent; Missouri by 21 percent; and Arkansas by 30 percent. Using a conservative estimate of a 30 percent reduction in parole revocation translates into 61,700 avoided prison admissions. The cost savings amount to $1.573 billion annually just in avoided incarceration costs. A performance incentive funding model would then redirect a portion of the cost savings to enhance community supervision. It is clear that community supervision of the kind envisioned here is expensive. The levels of effort and expertise involved in transitioning community supervision to where the research indicates it needs to be will require appropriate funding.

The Pew Center on the States complied time served data from the states and reported that between 1990 and 2009, length of sentence served increased by 36 percent. This is largely due to mandatory sentences and truth in sentencing laws. This 36 percent increase in time served translates into an additional nine months in prison on average per offender at an annual cost of $10 billion (Pew Center on the States 2012). The distribution of increases in time served was similar across types of crime: time served for drug crimes increased by 36 percent; for property crimes, it increased by 24 percent; and for violent crimes, 37 percent. There are a number of challenges in assessing the crime impact of reduced time served. However, recent, more sophisticated approaches have begun to unravel the consequences of reduced time served and have found that based on the use of valid risk assessments, it is possible to identify individuals who can be released sooner without significant public safety consequences (Pew Center on the States 2012). The Pew research indicates that between 14 percent and 24 percent of release cohorts of nonviolent offenders in Florida, Maryland, and Michigan could have been safely released significantly sooner, and saved $176 million annually. Mississippi recently relaxed its tough truth in sentencing law for nonviolent offenders, allowing parole consideration after serving just 25 percent of the sentence. This policy, based on the use of validated risk assessments for decision making, led to remarkably low recidivism, significantly reduced the prison population, and saved the state $200 million (Clear and Schrantz 2011). There are valid tools and strategies available to implement an informed process for reducing time served for selected inmates without significantly compromising public safety.

A number of states are beginning to address the time served issue with changes to laws and policies. These include: raising the threshold dollar amount on certain property crimes so that more low-level property crimes are no longer classified as felonies; rolling back mandatory minimum sentences; revising drug offense classifications so that the punishment is more proportional to the seriousness of the crimes; and changing eligibility laws for parole consideration. Moreover, states must reduce the use of unconditional release from prison, known as discharge. In 2011, 29 percent (203,000) of all inmates released were unconditional releases (discharged). The reason for an unconditional release is the full discharge of the sentence, meaning the inmate served the entire sentence, which means that there is no legal way to supervise that individual after release. There are obvious concerns with inmates released this way, such as no opportunity for risk management and no assistance in easing the transition into the free world. While requiring inmates to serve the full term imposed may sound tough on crime, it ironically can be a significant threat to public safety.

As diversion from incarceration increases, as community-based programming uses evidence-based practices, the principles of effective correctional intervention, and the other considerations I discussed in these pages, and as the justice system shifts from control and punishment to a more balanced approach of incapacitation and evidence-based behavioral change, recidivism will decline. In a perfect world, recidivism could decline 30 percent. In a realistic world, it is maybe closer to 20 to 25 percent. In either case, the impact on incarceration will be remarkable and cumulative. There were 455,000 admissions to prisons in 2011 that were new court commitments (not parole revocations). How many of those admissions could be avoided due to appropriate, effective interventions? Assume that 70 percent of those admitted to prison had at least one prior conviction, thus subject to, by definition, recidivism reduction through correctional intervention. If we can reduce recidivism by a minimal 20 percent, that translates into nearly 64,000 avoided incarcerations each year. This is just a quick and dirty estimate, but it gives us some picture of what can be accomplished through implementing what research indicates are smart, effective, and fiscally prudent policies.

What can we expect in terms of public safety consequences of downsizing prison populations? First, viewing the totality of the evidence indicates that the incapacitation effect of incarceration is limited and the link between the size of the prison population and public safety is rather weak (Clear and Schrantz 2011). Moreover, incarceration primarily affects the timing of reoffending rather than the overall volume—those who are going to recidivate simply do it sooner if they are released from prison sooner. This in turn indicates that a reduction in the current prison population by accelerated release could result in a short-term increase in crime, and once the prison population stabilizes at a new level, crime will fluctuate independently of the size of the prison population. With the extent to which we are able to address the weaknesses in parole supervision, that short-term increase in crime could be reduced.

The five strategies of (1) reducing and/or eliminating mandatory sentences and mandatory minimums; (2) revision or elimination of truth in sentencing laws; (3) increased diversion of selected drug offenders to treatment, and diversion of property offenders and some low-level violent offenders to indicated and appropriate interventions; (4) reductions in revocations of probationers and parolees through the use of effective evidence-based interventions; and (5) recidivism reductions due to the general implementation of research-based practices, can dramatically assist in reducing the prison populations. In turn, this can result in reducing spending on incarceration, providing performance incentive funding for more effective diversion, treatment, and rehabilitation, avoiding unnecessary criminal victimizations, saving untold social costs associated with crime, and increasing the productivity of once-written-off criminal offenders. As Clear and Schrantz (2011) convincingly argue, no single strategy will significantly reduce prison populations. Instead, taken together, enhancing treatment resources (especially in community settings), accelerating parole releases, substantially upgrading probation and diversion programs, strengthening community-based incentives, changing sentencing laws (especially diverting low-level drug offenders and nonviolent offenders from incarceration), and aggressively focusing on recidivism reduction through evidence-based practices can have substantial, sustainable reductions of prison populations without significant, longer-term increases in crime. The evidence in support of this conclusion is found in the experiences of New York, Michigan, and New Jersey in implementing in limited ways all of these initiatives, with notable reductions in prison populations.

Three major private corrections corporations, GEO (formerly Wackenhut), Corrections Corporation of America, and Management and Training Corp., provide prison management and operations in a number of states. The advocacy group In The Public Interest discovered through an open records request that over two-thirds of the contracts that these companies have with states require quotas of inmates in the institutions they operate. Most of the quota stipulations require that the facilities are at least 90 percent full (In The Public Interest 2013). If the quotas are not met, the state still has to pay the operators for the quota amount. These arrangements make sense from the perspective of the vendor, but are a substantial incentive for states to keep prison beds filled. Clearly, this arrangement is inappropriate, as it significantly limits the ability of states with these contracts to implement strategies that lead to reductions in prison populations. Such contracts should be nullified.

Downsizing prisons clearly requires a very serious effort at reforming diversion and community-based supervision. Probation must become effectively balanced with appropriate provision for surveillance, accountability, and control on the one hand and very concerted, evidence-based behavioral change interventions on the other. In addition, compliance and accountability of offenders in community-based diversion and supervision programs may be enhanced by a swift and certain sanction component, in the form of a HOPE Court model.

As reliance on incarceration is reduced and larger numbers of individuals are diverted to community-based programming, funding for probation and other forms of diversion should shift to a performance incentive model, redirecting resources from incarceration to community-based corrections. That redirection of funds should be dictated by successful recidivism reduction efforts at local probation agencies and diversion programs. The point is to reward success and to incentivize others to improve in terms of recidivism and other outcome metrics.

It is reasonable to expect that the impacts of these initiatives will increase over time. As more and more jurisdictions get on board, as we get better at implementation, as research continues to inform policy and practice, as programs are scaled up to appropriate levels, the public safety and cost benefits should increase significantly over what is indicated here. It is also reasonable to expect cumulative effects over time as these research-based practices are implemented, adapted, added to, evaluated, improved, and expanded. As policy and program development and implementation remain faithful to the evidence-based models, there is good reason to expect substantial, longer-term cumulative benefits, both in terms of reduced crime and recidivism, as well as lower criminal justice costs and lower social costs.

Once the prison population is reduced to acceptable levels and is composed of primarily violent offenders, chronic, habitual offenders and offenders for whom there has been an informed finding that rehabilitation will not work, sentence lengths and time served should reflect the largely incapacitation function incarceration will play. But we also need to assure that incapacitated inmates are not kept beyond the point of minimal risk.

CRIME IS LOCAL

While laws, policies, procedures, and significant amounts of justice funding originate at the state level, crime occurs in communities and in neighborhoods. Much of the response to crime is local as well: law enforcement, jails, prosecutors, the defense bar, the courts, probation, and other diversion programming. At the end of the day, the solutions to crime, recidivism, and victimization are local as well. What we do and how well we do it has less to do with state legislatures and governors and much more to do with local efforts and initiatives.

Counties in the United States serve as the primary venue or geography for arrest, prosecution, sentencing, and much of corrections. There are 3,143 counties or county equivalents in the United States, and while they are subject to the same laws and due process considerations, each has its own problems and priorities, policies and procedures, leadership, culture, politics, beliefs and attitudes, demographics, economies, and funding capacities. Thus, there is plenty of room for variation in how these local governments and communities respond to crime. Counties differ in terms of innovation, resources, abilities, and capacities for implementing diversion and rehabilitative programs, and thus variation in whether and how well various types of justice initiatives are developed, implemented, operated, and funded. In turn, there is significant variation in the outcomes of the local administration of criminal justice. Thus, there will be local successes and local failures as we proceed down this new path.

The point is that while state governments exercise a great amount of influence over local justice administration, we must be able to achieve a balance between state policy development, regulation, and funding on the one hand, and local autonomy on the other. It has been my experience in working with state and local governments in developing policies and programs that there is often a loss of innovation, fidelity, and quality when policies are developed at the state level of government and then dictated to local jurisdictions. Such processes result in policies that are too standardized, too rigidly regulated, and too generic. It often becomes one size fits all, without allowance for local differences, local constraints, and local needs. This is not to say that innovation is reserved for local communities to the exclusion of state or federal government. Instead, when policies, innovations, or programs originate at the state or federal level, there needs to be an appreciation for the need for flexibility, adaption, and tailoring to the circumstances of local jurisdictions.

State regulation and funding should facilitate local implementation, modification, and innovation, while requiring local adherence to standards of fidelity, quality, capacity, and outcomes. There needs to be a priority set for evaluation (both process and outcome evaluations), cost-benefit analysis, and the deliberate and routine use of the evaluation results for identifying what is working, what is not, and how to change and improve.

BIPARTISAN REFORM EFFORTS

In the 1980s, Democrats and Republicans alike embraced sentencing reform, the movement away from indeterminate sentencing to determinate sentencing. While both sides of the political aisle agreed on the remedy of sentencing reform, they did so for different reasons. Once again, criminal justice makes strange bedfellows. In 2014, we may be able to edge closer to bipartisan alignment on criminal justice policy under a similar scenario. Right on Crime is a conservative justice policy organization with signatories that include Jeb Bush, Newt Gingrich, Grover Norquist, Edwin Meese, William Bennett, Asa Hutchinson, David Keene, Erick Erickson, and Ralph Reed, among many others. Their Conservative Case for Reform: Fighting Crime, Prioritizing Victims, and Protecting Taxpayers has identified a multifocused set of recommendations for criminal justice policy reform aimed at reducing recidivism:

> Reducing recidivism should be a central focus of conservative efforts to reform criminal justice. Conservatives understand that reforming offenders is both a moral imperative and a requirement for public safety. Breaking the cycle of crime and turning lawbreakers into law-abiding citizens is a conservative priority because it advances public safety, the rule of law, and minimizes the number of future victims.

Key elements to Right on Crime's proposal include utilization of evidence-based practices, eliminating many mandatory minimum sentences for nonviolent offenders, expanding custodial supervision such as probation and parole for nonviolent offenders, providing substance abuse and mental health treatment for those in need, expanding geriatric release of inmates, and using validated risk assessment instruments to determine who should be released. Parole supervision can be enhanced by the use of GPS for parolees, technology to monitor alcohol use, intermediate sanctions for parole violators (to reduce revocation to prison), and the elimination of civil liability for employers who hire ex-offenders. Right on Crime also calls for the expansion of diversion courts, the expansion of swift and certain sanctioning under a HOPE Court model, drug and mental health treatment for offenders on probation, the use of evidence-based risk assessment for decision making regarding who should be sentenced to probation, and implementation of performance-based funding for probation. While Right on Crime's goals include the reduction of crime, recidivism, and victimization, a primary motive appears to be the excessive cost of the justice system. They have changed the rhetoric a bit by saying that "conservatives are known for being tough on crime, but we must also be tough on criminal justice spending."

On September 18, 2013, Senator Rand Paul, a Tea Party Republican, publically decried the differential impact of mandatory drug laws on minorities. In a public hearing before the Senate Judiciary Committee, Paul criticized mandatory minimum drug laws, and Paul and Patrick Leahy, the democratic chair of the Senate Judiciary Committee, co-authored the Justice Safety Valve Act of 2013, which allows judges in federal sentencing to selectively override mandatory minimum sentences. The Obama administration, through Attorney General Eric Holder, has announced their intention to revise lengthy mandatory sentences for federal drug defendants. In early March of 2014, U.S. Attorney General Eric Holder and conservative Republican (and libertarian) Rand Paul agreed to work together to reduce mandatory minimum sentences for nonviolent federal drug offenders. This is a component of the Attorney General's Smart on Crime initiative that was launched in August of 2013. This is important momentum at the federal level in terms of initiating changes to longstanding sentencing policies.

The result of conservative calls for justice reform is an opportunity to join forces with liberal reformers to develop and implement strategies that recalibrate the U.S. justice system to a more balanced portfolio of incarceration and control for serious, violent offenders, and accountability and behavioral change through intervention for lower-risk, generally nonviolent offenders.

Cost is also a concern for liberals, as is implementing effective policies and practices that reduce recidivism, crime, and victimization. The American Civil Liberties Union, a noted liberal organization, has advocated for criminal justice reform consistently over the years. The ACLU's recommendations for reform are similar to those of other liberal organizations such as the Open Society Institute, Americans for Progress, and the Sentencing Project. Recommendations include eliminating mandatory and mandatory minimum sentences, reducing penalties for drug offenses, decriminalizing drug possession, and use of nonprison sanctions for violations of probation and parole conditions.

Increasingly there are examples of bipartisan efforts to develop and implement limited criminal justice reforms. Georgia instituted a bipartisan commission to pass justice reform and save the state money. In 2012, the governor of Georgia signed legislation that reduces penalties for drug law violations, expands drug courts, expands the use of accountability (swift and certain sanctions) courts, and provides for alternatives to incarceration for nonviolent offenders. Other states are beginning to implement limited justice reform under bipartisan support. The ACLU profiled states' bipartisan initiatives in the report Promising Beginnings: Bipartisan Criminal Justice Reform in Key States. Their analysis included Alabama, Connecticut, Indiana, Kansas, Louisiana, Mississippi, Nebraska, Ohio, South Carolina, Texas, Vermont, and Virginia. While cost was the primary motivator for the initiation of discussions about reform, the preliminary results appear to be smart policies that reduce prison populations and generally focus on diversion from incarceration, enhanced drug and mental health treatment, policies that increase parole releases, and graduated sanctions for parole and probation violations in lieu of incarceration (ACLU 2012). Michigan and New York have also implemented reforms that have significantly reduced their prison populations. New York's bipartisan efforts reduced its prison population by 20 percent by changes to the Rockefeller drug laws, expansion of alternatives to incarceration, enhancements to treatment and drug courts, and policies to expedite parole release. Michigan's bipartisan efforts resulted in a 12 percent reduction of its prison population by eliminating most of its mandatory minimum drug sentences and developing policies and programs such as housing, employment, and treatment to enhance successful reentry from prison.

At the same time, it is important to note that a recent survey (November 2014) of state prison officials reveals projections of increases in state prison populations at least over the next four years. The survey by the Pew Charitable Trusts indicates an average 3 percent increase in the number of prisoners by 2018.

A CULTURAL CHANGE

Crime control has permeated the culture of U.S. criminal justice. It has been the central focus of how we think about crime. It is time to turn that around. It is time for a fundamental change in the culture of crime and justice.

While we may place blame on someone who smoked for forty years and developed lung cancer, would we at the same time deny them health care for treating their cancer? How about someone who is obese and develops heart problems or diabetes? We may think that they are responsible for their situation, but it is doubtful that we would have a policy that would deny them medical care. It seems that we need to try to get to the same place with many criminal offenders—they make bad choices, they do bad things. There are real victims who have suffered real loss. These offenders are, for the most part, blameworthy and culpable for their crimes. At the same time, there likely are a variety of criminogenic deficits, impairments, and problems that are related to their offending. We should not look at these problems and impairment as a means to mitigate culpability. These should be seen not as excuses, but as opportunities for intervention or targets for behavioral change. It makes little sense sitting where we sit today to take the hard line and blame offenders en masse for their crimes and deny them all but punishment. That is counterproductive and it compromises public safety.

So we need to take the emotion out of the calculus. We need to curb our strong need to blame others and to seek wholesale revenge. We need to think differently about the problem of crime and its solutions. We need to take a more pragmatic view, a public health view, of much of the crime we have treated in the past as simply bad behavior in need of punishment. The goal here is not to be soft on crime. In many ways, behavioral change is harder than doing a stretch upstate or being placed on probation. Many offenders are changeable. We have effective tools for changing behavior. We need to appreciate that we benefit when we are able to change an offender's behavior. We win in terms of fewer victimizations, lower recidivism, lower crime, more effective use of resources, and lower criminal justice costs both in the short term and in the long term.

We need to get beyond symbolism. Diversion and rehabilitation should not be window dressing. They should be the primary business of corrections. Diversion courts are a great idea. The evidence indicates that they effectively address the problems for which they are designed. However, having the capacity for just 5 percent of the need is more symbolism than substance. Effective programming designed to enhance success on community supervision should be the rule, not the add on that it seems to be in many jurisdictions. Where we go from here cannot be piecemeal. It is not just fine-tuning. It is a reengineering of the justice system, a reengineering of how prosecutors see their roles and responsibilities, how judges make key sentencing decisions, how corrections agents view the goals of that enterprise and how to achieve them, and how legislatures and local governments shape the priorities, procedures, statutes, and funding that make a wholesale revamping possible. That reengineering also needs to change the justice system from a series of handoffs (police to prosecutors, prosecutors to judges, judges to corrections). It will require everyone involved in the administration of criminal justice to accept responsibility for recidivism, not pass that responsibility down the line. It will require digging deep, avoiding just going through the motions, and engaging a real commitment to change.

The Center for Court Innovation conducted a survey in 2013 of the perceptions of innovation in the criminal justice system (Labriola, Gold, and Kohn 2013). The survey included court administrators, community corrections officials, law enforcement administrators, and prosecutors. Taken together, only about one-third of the respondents believe that the field of criminal justice can be described as innovative. Just over one-half believe that their agency is innovative. Moving toward true innovation and change will require the right individuals at the federal, state, and especially the local level to provide strong, dynamic, innovative leadership. It will also require thoughtful, innovative, courageous legislators, governors, and city and county elected officials and policymakers who "get it" and can be less concerned with the politics of justice policy and more concerned with moving the justice system to where it needs to be in order to accomplish public safety, reduce recidivism and victimization, and do so cost-effectively.

Alexander, J., C. Barton, D. Gordon, J. Grotpeter, K. Hansson, R. Harrison, S. Mears, S. Mihalic, B. Parsons, C. Pugh, S. Schulman, H. Waldron, and T. Sexton. 1998. *Functional Family Therapy: Blueprints for Violence Prevention, Book Three. Blueprints for Violence Prevention Series* (D. S. Elliott, Series. Boulder, CO: Center for the Study and Prevention of Violence, Institute of Behavioral Science, University of Colorado.

Alexander, C. and R. Carroll. 2006. "We're Supposed to Sentence Individuals, Not Crimes: A Survey of Commonwealth of Pennsylvania Court of Common Pleas Judges on Mandatory Minimum Sentencing Statutes." Unpublished report.

Alim T., E. Graves, T. Mellman, N. Aigbogun, E. Gray, W. Lawson, and D. Charney. 2006. "Trauma Exposure, Posttraumatic Stress Disorder and Depression in an African-American Primary Care Population." *Journal of the National Medical Association* 98: 1630–1636.

Almquist, L., and E. Dodd. 2009. "Mental Health Courts: A Guide to Research-Informed Policy and Practice." *Council on State Governments Justice Center*, New York.

Alschuler, A. 1979. "Sentencing Reform and Prosecutorial Power: A Critique of Recent Proposals for Fixed and Presumptive Sentencing." *University of Pennsylvania Law Review* 126: 550–577.

American Civil Liberties Union. 2012. *Promising Beginnings: Bipartisan Criminal Justice Reform in Key States.* New York: Author.

American Psychological Association. 2006. "Evidence-Based Practice in Psychology: APA Presidential Task Force on Evidence-Based Practice." *American Psychologist* 61: 271–285.

Anda, R. 2007. "Presentation at the 2007 Guest House Institute Summer Leadership Conference." Minneapolis, MN.

Andrews, D. 2006. "Enhancing Adherence to Risk-Need-Responsivity: Making Quality A Matter Of Policy." *Criminology and Public Policy* 5: 595–602.

Andrews, D. and J. Bonta. 1994, 2003, 2006. *The Psychology of Criminal Conduct.* Cincinnati, OH: Anderson Publishing.

Andrews, D. and J. Bonta. 2006, 2010. *The Psychology of Criminal Conduct,* 5th ed. New Providence, NJ: LexisNexis Matthew Bender.

Andrews, D. and J. Bonta. 2007. *Risk-Need-Responsivity Model for Offender Assessment and Rehabilitation.* Ottawa, ON: Public Safety Canada.

Andrews, D., J. Bonta, and S. J. Wormith. 2006. "The Recent Past and Near Future of Risk and/or Need Assessment." *Crime and Delinquency* 52: 7–27.

Andrews, D., C. Dowden, and P. Gendreau. 1999. "Clinically Relevant and Psychologically Informed Approaches to Reduced Reoffending: A Meta-Analytic Study of Human Service, Risk, Need, Responsivity, and Other Concerns in Justice Contexts." Unpublished manuscript. Ottawa, ON: Carleton University.

Andrews, D., I. Zinger, R. Hoge, J. Bonta, P. Gendreau, and F. Cullen. 2009. "Does Correctional Treatment Work? A Clinically Relevant and Psychologically Informed Meta Analysis." *Criminology* 28: 369–404.

Anglin, D., B. Nosyk, A. Jaffe, D. Urada, and E. Evans. 2013. "Offender Diversion Into Substance Use Disorder Treatment: The Economic Impact of California's Proposition 36." *American Journal of Public Health* 103 no. 6: 1096–1102.

Anglin, M. D., D. Longshore, and S. Turner. 1999. "Treatment Alternatives to Street Crime: An Evaluation of Five Programs." *Criminal Justice and Behavior* 26: 168–195.

Anglin, M. D., and T. H. I. Maugh. 1992. "Ensuring Success in Interventions with Drug Using Offenders." *Annals AAPSS* 521: 66–90.

Anglin, M. D., and B. Perrochet. 1998. *Drug Use and Crime: A Historical Review of Research Conducted by the UCLA Drug Abuse Research Center.* Los Angeles: UCLA.

Angus Reid Public Opinion. 2012. http://www.angusreidglobal.com/wp-content/uploads/2012/06/2012.06.06_Drugs_USA.pdf.

The Annie E. Casey Foundation. 2013. *The 2013 Kids Count Data Book.* Baltimore, MD: Author.

Aos, S. 2001. "Using Taxpayer Dollars Wisely: The Costs and Benefits of Incarceration and Other Crime Control Policies." Olympia, WA: Washington State Institute for Public Policy.

Aos, S., M. Miller, and E. Drake. 2006a. "Evidence-Based Adult Corrections Programs: What Works and What Does Not." Olympia, WA: Washington State Institute for Public Policy.

Aos, S., M. Miller, and E. Drake. 2006b. "Evidence-Based Public Policy Options to Reduce Future Prison Construction, Criminal Justice Costs, and Crime Rates." Olympia, WA: Washington State Institute for Public Policy.

Aos, S., P. Phipps, R. Barnoski, and R. Lieb. 2001. "The Comparative Costs and Benefits of Programs to Reduce Crime." Vol. 4 (1-05-1201). Olympia, WA: Washington State Institute for Public Policy.

Apel, R. and D. Nagin. 2011. "General Deterrence: A Review of Recent Evidence." In *Crime and Public Policy*, edited by James Q. Wilson and Joan Petersilia. New York: Oxford University Press.

Ardine, V. 2012. "Offending Behavior: The Role of Trauma and PTSD." *European Journal of Psychotraumatology* 3, July 20, 2012.

Ardino, V. 2012. "Offending Behaviour: The Role of Trauma and PTSD." *European Journal of Psychotraumatology* 3: 10.3402/ejpt.v3i0.18968. http://www.ncbi.nlm.nih.gov/pmc/articles/PMC3402156.

Austin, J. 2011. "Making Imprisonment Unprofitable." *Criminology and Public Policy* 10: 629–635.

Babor, T., J. G. Caulkins, B. Edwards, D. Fischer, K. Foxcroft, K. Humphreys, I. Obot, J. Rehm, P. Reuter, R. Room, I. Rossow, and J. Strang. 2010. *Drug Policy and the Public Good*. New York: Oxford University Press.

Babor, T. F. B., B. G. McRee, P. A. Kassebaum, P. L. Grimaldi, K. Ahmed, and J. Bray. 2007. "Screening, Brief Intervention, and Referral to Treatment (SBIRT): Toward a Public Health Approach to the Management of Substance Abuse." *Substance Abuse* 28: 7–30.

Baer, D., A. Bhati, L. Brooks, J. Castro, N. La Vigne, K. Mallik-Kane, R. Naser, J. Osborne, C. Roman, J. Roman, S. Rossman, A. Solomon, C. Visher, and L. Winterfield. 2006. *Understanding the Challenges of Prisoner Reentry: Research Findings from the Urban Institute's Prisoner Reentry Portfolio*. Washington, D.C.: Urban Institute.

Bailey, W. and R. Peterson. 1999. "Capital Punishment, Homicide and Deterrence: An Assessment of Evidence." In *Studying and Preventing Homicide: An Assessment of the Evidence*, edited by M. D. Smith and M. Zahn. Thousand Oaks, CA: Sage.

Bales, W. and A. Piquero. 2012. "Assessing the Impact of Imprisonment on Recidivism." *Journal of Experimental Criminology* 8: 71–101.

Ball, J. C., J. Shaffer, and D. Nurco. 1983. "Day to Day Criminality of Heroin Addicts in Baltimore: A Study in the Continuity of Offense Rates." *Drug and Alcohol Dependence* 12: 19–142.

Barbosa, M. and L. Monteiro. 2008. "Recurrent Criminal Behavior and Executive Dysfunction." *Spanish Journal of Psychology* 11: 259–265.

Barnoski, R. and S. Aos. 2003. "Washington State's Drug Courts for Adult Defendants: Outcome Evaluation and Cost-Benefit Analysis." Olympia, WA: Washington State Institute for Public Policy.

Bean, P. 1999. "The Police and the Mentally Disordered in the Community." In *Mentally Disordered Offenders: Managing People Nobody Owns*, edited by D. Webb, R. Harris, and K. Florence. New York: Routledge.

Beauchaine, T., E. Neuhaus, S. Brenner, and L. Gatzke-Kopp. 2008. "Ten Good Reasons to Consider Biological Variables in Prevention and Intervention Research." *Development and Psychopathology* 20:745–774.

Beaver, K., J. Wright, and M. Delisi. 2007. "Self-Control and Executive Function." *Criminal Justice and Behavior* 34: 1435–1361.

Beckett, K. 1997. *Making Crime Pay: Law and Order in Contemporary American Politics*. New York: Oxford University Press.

Beckett, K. and T. Sasson. 2004. "Crime, Politics and the Public: The Sources of Mass Incarceration in the U.S.A." *The Japanese Journal of Sociological Criminology* 29: 27–49.

Beldon, Russonello and Stewart Research and Communications. 2001. "Optimism, Pessimism and Jailhouse Redemption: American Attitudes on Crime, Punishment and Over-Incarceration." Washington, D.C.: Author.

Belenko, S., N. Patapis, and M. French. 2005. "Economic Benefits of Drug Treatment: A Critical Review of the Evidence for Policy Makers." Missouri Foundation for Health, National Rural Alcohol and Drug Abuse Network.

Belenko, S. and J. Peugh. 2005. "Estimating Drug Treatment Needs Among State Prison Inmates." *Drug and Alcohol Dependence* 77: 269–281.

Berk, R., L. Sherman, G. Barnes, E. Kurtz, and L. Ahlman. 2009. "Forecasting Murder Within a Population of Probationers and Parolees: A High Stakes Application of Statistical Learning." *Journal of the Royal Statistical Society* 172: 191–211.

Berman, G. and A. Gulick. 2003. "Just the (Unwieldy, Hard to Gather but Nonetheless Essential) Facts, Ma'am: What We Know and Don't Know About Problem-Solving Courts." *The Fordham Urban Law Journal* 30: 1027–1053.

Berman, M., J. Tracy, and E. Coccaro. 1997. "The Serotonin Hypothesis of Aggression Revisited." *Clinical Psychology Review* 17:651–665.

Bhati, A. S., J. Roman, and A. Chalfin. 2008. "To Treat or Not to Treat: Evidence on the Prospects of Expanding Treatment to Drug-Involved Offenders." Washington, D.C.: The Urban Institute.

Bhati, S. and J. Roman. 2010. "Simulated Evidence on the Prospects of Treating More Drug-Involved Offenders." *Journal of Experimental Criminology* 6: 1–33.

Blendon, R. and J. Young. 1998. "The Public and the War on Illicit Drugs." *Journal of the American Medical Association* 279: 827–832.

Blumstein, A. 1994. "Prisons." In *Crime*, edited by James Q. Wilson and Joan Petersilia. San Francisco: Institute for Contemporary Studies.

Blumstein, A. 2011. "Approaches to Reducing Both Imprisonment and Crime." *Criminology and Public Policy* 10: 93–101.

Blumstein, A. and A. J. Beck. 1999. "Population Growth in U.S. Prisons, 1980–1996." In *Crime and Justice: A Review of Research*, edited by Michael Tonry and Joan Petersilia. Chicago: University of Chicago Press.

Blumstein, A. and A. J. Beck. 2005. "Reentry as a Transient State Between Liberty and Recommitment." In *Prisoner Reentry and Crime in America,* edited by Jeremy Travis and Christy Visher. New York: Cambridge University Press.

Blumstein, A., J. Cohen, and D. Nagin, eds. 1978. *Deterrence and Incapacitation: Estimating the Effects of Criminal Sanctions on Crime Rates.* Report of the Panel of Deterrence and Incapacitation, Washington D.C.: National Academy of Sciences.

Blumstein, A., J. Cohen, J. Roth, and C. Visher, eds. 1986. *Criminal Careers and "Career Criminals."* Washington, D.C.: National Academy Press.

Board of Health Care Services. 2006. "Improving the Quality of Health Care for Mental and Substance-Use Conditions." *Quality Chase Series.* Washington, D.C.: The National Academies Press.

Bogue, B., N. Campbell, M. Carey, E. Clawson, D. Faust, K. Florio, L. Joplin, G. Keiser, B. Wasson, and W. Woodward. 2004. *Implementing Evidence-Based Practice in Community Corrections: The Principles of Effective Intervention.* Washington, D.C.: National Institute of Corrections. http://www.nicic.org/pubs/2004/019342.pdf.

Bong, Sasha, Peter Braden, Laura Christian, Nayantara Mukherji, and Pamela Ritger. 2012. "Juneau County Diversion Program: A Benefit-Cost Analysis." January 12, 2012, Juneau County, WI.

Bonta, James. 2007. "Offender Risk Assessment and Sentencing." *Canadian Journal of Criminology and Criminal Justice* (October) 49: 519–529.

Bonta, J., G. Bourgon, T. Rugge, T. Scott, A. Yessine, L. Gutierrez, and J. Li. 2010a. *The Strategic Training Initiative in Community Supervision: Risk, Need,*

Responsivity in the Real World. Corrections Research: User Report. Ottawa, ON: Public Safety Canada.

Bonta, James, Guy Bourgon, Tanya Rugge, Terri-Lynne Scott, Annie Yessine, Leticia Gutierrez, and J. Li. 2010b. "The Strategic Training Initiative in Community Supervision: Risk-Need-Responsivity in the Real World." Ottawa, ON: Public Safety Canada.

Bonta, J., M. Law, and C. Hanson. 1998. "The Prediction of Criminal and Violent Recidivism Among Mentally Disordered Offenders: A Meta-Analysis." *Psychological Bulletin* 123: 123–142.

Bonta, James, Tanya Rugge, Terri-Lynne Scott, and Annie Yessine. 2008. "Exploring the Black Box of Community Supervision." *Journal of Offender Rehabilitation* 47: 248–270.

Bonta, J., T. Rugge, S. Sedo, and R. Coles. 2004. "Case Management in Manitoba Probation." Manitoba, Canada: Manitoba Department of Corrections.

Bonta, J., S. Wallace-Capretta, W. Rooney, and K. McAnoy. 2002. "An Outcome Evaluation of a Restorative Justice Alternative to Incarceration." *Justice Review* 5: 319–338.

Boothroyd, N. Poythress, A. McGaha, and J. Petrila. 2003. "The Broward Mental Health Court: Process, Outcomes and Service Utilization." *International Journal of Law and Psychiatry* 26: 55–71

Borduin, Charles, Barton J. Mann, Lynn T. Cone, Scott W. Henggeler, Bethany R. Fucci, David M. Blaske, and Robert A. Williams. 1995. "Multisystemic Treatment of Serious Juvenile Offenders: Long-Term Prevention of Criminality and Violence." *Journal of Consulting and Clinical Psychology* 63: 569–578.

Borgenschneider, Karen, and Thomas Corbett. 2010. *Evidence-Based Policymaking: Insights from Policy-Minded Researchers and Research-Minded Policymakers.* New York: Routledge.

Borum, R. 2000. "Improving High-Risk Encounters Between People with Mental Illness and the Police." *Journal of the American Academy of Psychiatry and the Law* 28: 332–337.

Bosso, C. 1987. *Pesticides and Politics: The Life Cycle of a Public Issue.* Pittsburgh, PA: University of Pittsburgh Press.

Bourgon, G., and B. Armstrong, 2005. "Transferring the Principles of Effective Treatment Into a "Real World" Prison Setting." *Criminal Justice and Behavior* 32: 3–25.

Bourgon, G., J. Bonta, T. Rugge, and L. Gutierrez. 2010. "Technology Transfer: The Importance of On-Going Clinical Supervision" In *Translating 'What*

Works' to Everyday Community Supervision, edited by F. McNeil, P. Raynor, and C. Trotter. Cullompton, UK: Willan.

Bourgon, Guy, James Bonta, Tanya Rugge, Terri-Lynne Scott, and Annie Yessine. 2009. "Translating 'What Works' Into Sustainable Everyday Practice: Program Design, Implementation and Evaluation." Ottawa, ON: Public Safety Canada.

Bourgon, Guy, James Bonta, Tanya Rugge, Terri-Lynne Scott, and Annie Yessine. 2010b. "The Role of Program Design, Implementation, and Evaluation in Evidence-Based 'Real World' Community Supervision." *Federal Probation* 74: 2–15.

Bourgon, Guy, Leticia Gutierrez, and Jennifer Ashton. 2012. "From Case Management to Change Agent: The Evolution of 'What Works' in Community Supervision." *Correctional Research: User Report.* Ottawa, ON: Public Safety Canada.

Boyum, D. A., and M. Kleiman. 2002. "Substance-Abuse Policy from a Crime-Control Perspective." In *Crime: Public Policies for Crime Control,* edited by J. Q. Wilson and J. Petersilia. Oakland, CA: Institute for Contemporary Studies.

Breslau, Naomi, Ronald C. Kessler, Howard D. Chilcoat, Lonni R. Schultz, Glenn C. Davis, and Patricia Andreski. 1998. "Trauma and Posttraumatic Stress Disorder in the Community: The 1996 Detroit Area Survey of Trauma." *Archives of General Psychiatry* 55: 626–632.

Brower, M. C., and B. H. Price. 2001. "Neuropsychiatry of Frontal Lobe Dysfunction in Violent and Criminal Behaviour: A Critical Review." *Advances in Neuropsychiatry* 71: 720–726.

Brownstein, H. H., H. Shiledar Baxi, P. Goldstein, and P. Ryan. 1992. "The Relationship of Drugs, Drug Trafficking, and Drug Traffickers to Homicide." *Journal of Crime and Justice* 15: 25–44.

Buchholz, Jonathan R., Carol A. Malte, Donald A. Calsyn, John S. Baer, Paul Nichol, Daniel R. Kivlahan, Ryan M. Caldeiro, and Andrew J. Saxon. 2010. "Associations of Housing Status with Substance Abuse Treatment and Service Use Outcomes Among Veterans." Washington, D.C.: United States Interagency Council on Homelessness.

Buck, Jeffrey. 2011. "The Looming Expansion and Transformation of Public Substance Abuse Treatment Under the Affordable Care Act." *Health Affairs* 30: 1402–1410.

Bufkin, Jana, and Vickie Luttrell. 2005. "Neuroimaging Studies of Aggressive and Violent Behavior: Current Findings and Implications for Criminology and Criminal Justice." *Trauma, Violence and Abuse* 6: 176–191.

Burt, Martha R., and Jacquelyn Anderson. 2005. "AB2034 Program Experiences in Housing Homeless People with Serious Mental Illness." Washington, D.C.: Corporation for Supportive Housing.

Bureau of Justice Assistance. 2006. "Homelessness and Prisoner Reentry, Strategies for Addressing Housing Needs and Risks in Prisoner Re-Entry." Washington, D.C.: U.S. Department of Justice.

Bureau of Justice Statistics. 1984. "Census of State Adult Correctional Facilities, 1984." Washington, D.C.: United States Department of Justice.

Bureau of Justice Statistics. 1988. "Historical Statistics on Prisoners in State and Federal Institutions, Yearend 1925–1986." Washington, D.C.: United States Department of Justice.

Bureau of Justice Statistics. 1990. "Census of State and Federal Correctional Facilities, 1990." Washington, D.C.: United States Department of Justice.

Bureau of Justice Statistics. 1995. "Census of State and Federal Correctional Facilities, 1995." Washington, D.C.: United States Department of Justice.

Bureau of Justice Statistics. 2000. "Census of State and Federal Correctional Facilities, 2000." Washington, D.C.: United States Department of Justice.

Bureau of Justice Statistics. 2002. "Prisoners in 2001." Washington, D.C.: United States Department of Justice.

Bureau of Justice Statistics. 2005. "Census of State and Federal Correctional Facilities, 2005." Washington, D.C.: United States Department of Justice.

Bureau of Justice Statistics. 2006. "Mental Health Problems of Prison and Jail Inmate." Washington, D.C.: United States Department of Justice.

Bureau of Justice Statistics. June 2010. "Prison Inmates at Midyear 2009—Statistical Tables." Washington, D.C.: United States Department of Justice.

Bureau of Justice Statistics. 2010. *Sourcebook of Criminal Justice Statistics.* Washington, D.C.: United States Department of Justice.

Bureau of Justice Statistics. 2013. "Correctional Populations in the United States, in 2012." Washington, D.C.: United States Department of Justice.

Bureau of Justice Statistics. 2013. "Prisoners in 2012—Advanced Counts." Washington, D.C.: United States Department of Justice.

Bureau of Justice Assistance. n.d. "What Have We Learned from Evaluations of Mental Health Courts." Center for Program Evaluation and Performance Measurement. Washington, D.C.: Office of Justice Programs, United States Department of Justice.

Bush, S. C. 2002. Using Conditional Release as a Strategy for Effective Linkage to Community Mental Health Services: The Memphis Public Defenders Office Model." *Community Mental Health Report* 2: 81.

Bushway, Shawn, and Robert Apel. 2012. "A Signaling Perspective on Employment Based Reentry Programming: Training Completion as a Desistence Signal." *Criminology and Public Policy* 11: 21–50.

Bushway, Shawn, and Peter Reuter. 2011. "Deterrence, Economics and the Context of Drug Markets." *Criminology and Public Policy* 10: 183–194.

Calder, James. 1982. "Presidents and Crime Control: Kennedy, Johnson and Nixon and the Influences of Ideology." *Presidential Studies Quarterly* 12: 574–589.

Caldwell, Nolan, Tanja Srebotnjak, Tiffany Wang, and Renee Hsia. 2013. "How Much Will I Get Charged for This? Patient Charges for Top Ten Diagnoses in the Emergency Department." *PLOS ONE* 8 no. 2.

Canadian Sentencing Commission. 1987. "Sentencing Reform: A Canadian Approach." Ottawa, ON: Canadian Government Publishing Centre.

Caplow, T. and J. Simon. 1999. "Understanding Prison Policy and Population Trends." In *Crime and Justice*, Vol. 26. Chicago: University of Chicago Press.

Carey, Mark. 2011. "Probation." In *Handbook of Evidence-Based Substance Abuse Treatment*, edited by C. Leukefeld, M. Guilotta, and J. Gregrich. New York: Springer-Verlag.

Carey, S. M., M. Finigan, D. Crumpton, and M. Waller. 2006. "California Drug Courts: Outcomes, Costs and Promising Practices: An Overview of Phase II in a Statewide Study." *Journal of Psychoactive Drugs.* SARC supplement 3: 345–356.

Carey, S. M., M. Finigan, and K. Pukstas. 2008. "Exploring the Key Components of Drug Courts: A Comparative Study of 18 Adult Drug Courts on Practices, Outcomes and Costs." Portland, OR: NPC Research.

Carey, Shannon, and Mark Waller. 2011. "Oregon Drug Court Cost Study: Statewide Costs and Promising Practices." Portland, OR: NPC Research.

Carey S. M., M. Waller, and J. Weller. 2011. "California Drug Court Cost Study— Phase III: Statewide Costs and Promising Practices." Final Report. Portland, OR: NPC Research.

Carson, A. E. and Golinelli, D. 2012. *Prisoners in 2012. Bureau of Justice Statistics.* Washington, D.C.: U.S. Department of Justice.

Cartwright, William. 2000. "Cost-Benefit Analysis of Drug Treatment Services: Review of the Literature." *The Journal of Mental Health Policy and Economics* 3: 11–26.

Casey, Pamela, Roger Warren, and Jennifer Elek. 2011. "Using Offender Risk and Needs Assessment Information at Sentencing: Guidance for Courts from a National Working Group." Williamsburg, VA: National Center for State Courts.

Caulkins, Jonathan, Angela Hawken, Beau Kilmer, and Mark Kleiman. 2012. *Marijuana Legalization: What Everyone Needs to Know*. New York: Oxford University Press.

Caulkins, J., R. Pacula, S. Paddock, and J. Chiesa. 2002. "School Based Drug Prevention: What Kind of Drug Use Does It Prevent?" Santa Monica, CA: RAND.

Caulkins, J. P., and P. Reuter. 1997. "Setting Goals for Drug Policy: Harm Reduction or Use Reduction?" *Addiction* 92: 1143–1150.

Caulkins, J. and P. Reuter. 2009. "Towards a Harm-Reduction Approach to Enforcement." *Safer Communities* 8: 9–23.

Caulkins, J., C. Rydell, W. Schwabe, and J. Chiesa. 1997. "Mandatory Minimum Drug Sentences: Throwing Away the Key or the Taxpayers' Money?" Santa Monica, CA: RAND.

Castonguay, L., and L. Beutler, 2006. "Common and Unique Principles of Therapeutic Change That Work: What Do We Know and What Do We Need To Know." In *Principles of Therapeutic Change That Work*, edited by L. Castonguay and L. Beutler. New York: Oxford University Press.

Center for Court Innovation. 2007. *Expanding the Use of Problem Solving the U.S. Department of Justice's Community-Based Problem-Solving Criminal Justice Initiative.* New York: Author.

Center for Court Innovation. 2013. "Testing Cost Savings of Judicial Diversion." New York: Center for Court Innovation.

Center for Substance Abuse and Treatment. 1997. http://www.health.org/nties97/crime.htm.

Chaiken, J. M., and M. Chaiken. 1990. "Drugs and Predatory Crime." *Crime and Justice* 13: 203–239.

Chandler, Redonna, Bennett Fletcher, and Nora Volkow. 2009. "Treating Drug Abuse and Addiction in the Criminal Justice System: Improving Public Health and Safety." *Journal of the American Medical Association* 301: 183–190.

Christy, A., N. Poythress, R. Boothroyd, J. Petrila, and S. Mehra. 2005. "Evaluating the Efficiency and Community Safety Goals of the Broward County Mental Health Court." *Behavioral Sciences and the Law* 23: 227–243.

Cissner, Amanda, and Michael Rempel. 2005. "The State of Drug Court Research." New York: Center for Court Innovation.

CMHS National GAINS Center. 2007. "Practical Advice on Jail Diversion: Ten Years of Learnings on Jail Diversion." Delmar, NY: CMHS National GAINS Center.

CMHS National GAINS Center. 2010. "Getting Inside the Black Box: Understanding How Jail Diversion Works." Delmar, NY: CMHS National GAINS Center.

Clear, Todd. 1981. "Objectives Based Case Planning." Longmont, CO: National Institute of Corrections Monograph.

Clear, T., J. Byrne, and J. Dvoskin. 1993. "The Transition from Being an Inmate: Discharge Planning, Parole and Community-Based Services for Offenders with Mental Illness." In *Mental Illness in America's Prisons*, edited by H. J. Steadman and J.J. Cocozza. Seattle, WA: National Coalition for the Mentally Ill in the Criminal Justice System.

Clear, Todd, and Dessis Schrantz. 2011. "Strategies for Reducing Prison Populations." *The Prison Journal* 9: 138–159.

Clear T., and M. Sumner. 2002. "Prisoners, Prison and Religion: Religion and Adjustment to Prison." *Journal of Offender Rehabilitation* 35: 127–159.

Cohen, J. E. 1995. "Presidential Rhetoric and the Public Agenda." *American Journal of Political Science* 39: 87–107.

Cohen, J., and Michael Tonry. 1983. "Sentencing Reforms and Their Impacts." In *Research on Sentencing: The Search for Reform,* edited by A. Blumstein, J. Cohen, S. Martin, and M. Tonry. Washington, D.C.: National Academy Press.

Cole, David, 2002. "Enemy Aliens and American Freedoms." *The Nation.* September 23, 2002.

Collins, W., and R. Margo. 2007. "The Economic Aftermath of the 1960s Riots in American Cities: Evidence from Property Values." *Journal of Economic History* 67: 849–883.

Colorado Division of Probation Services. 2010. *Colorado Probation and Evidence-Based Practices: A Systemic View of the Past, Present and Future of EBP in Colorado Probation.* Denver, CO: Author.

Condon, J., and N. Smith. 2003. "Prevalence of Drug Use: Key Findings from the 2002/2003 British Crime Survey." United Kingdom Home Office.

Congressional Research Service. 2009. "The U.S. Mental Health Delivery System Infrastructure: A Primer." Washington, D.C.: CRS Report for Congress.

Connolly, Michele M. 2003. "A Critical Examination of Actuarial Offender-Based Prediction Assessments: Guidance for the Next Generation of Assessments." Dissertation presented to the faculty of the graduate school of the University of Texas at Austin.

Cornet, M., Catharina H. de Kogel, Henk L. I. Nijman, Adrian Raine, and Peter H. van der Laan. 2013. "Neurobiological Factors as Predictors of Cognitive–Behavioral Therapy Outcome in Individuals with Antisocial Behavior: A Review of the Literature." *International Journal of Offender Therapy and Comparative Criminology,* July 2013.

Cosden M., J. Ellens, J. Schnell, and Y. Yamini-Diouf. 2005. "Efficacy of a Mental Health Treatment Court with Assertive Community Treatment." *Behavioral Science and the Law* 23: 199–214.

Cose, E. 2000. "US: The Prison Paradox." *Newsweek*, November 13, 2000.

Council of State Governments. 2005. "Report of the Re-Entry Policy Council: Charting the Safe and Successful Return of Prisoners to the Community." Council of State Governments, Re-Entry Policy Council. New York: Council on State Governments, Justice Center.

Council on State Governments. 2007. "Criminal Justice/Mental Health Consensus Project, 2007. Improving Responses to People with Mental Illnesses: The Essential Elements of a Mental Health Court." New York: Council on State Governments, Justice Center.

Council of State Governments Justice Center. 2008. "Mental Health Courts: A Primer for Policymakers and Practitioners." New York: Criminal Justice/Mental Health Consensus Project.

Cowell, Alexander J., Nahama Broner, and Randolph Dupont. 2004. "The Cost-Effectiveness Of Criminal Justice Diversion Programs For People with Serious Mental Illness Co-Occurring with Substance Abuse: Four Case Studies." *Journal of Contemporary Criminal Justice* 20: 292–315.

Cullen, F., and Brandon Applegate. 1997. *Offender Rehabilitation: Effective Correctional Intervention*. Hampshire, U.K.: Ashgate Publishing Co.

Cullen, Francis, Bonnie Fisher, and Brandon Applegate. 2000. "Public Opinion About Punishment and Corrections." In *Crime and Justice, A Review of Research*, edited by Michael Tonry. Chicago: University of Chicago Press.

Cullen, F., and P. Gendreau. 2000. "Assessing Correctional Rehabilitation: Policy, Practice and Prospects." In *NIJ Criminal Justice 2000: Policies, Processes and Decisions of the Criminal Justice System*, edited by J. Horney. Washington, D.C.: U.S. Department of Justice.

Cullen, Francis, Cheryl Jonson, and Daniel Nagin. 2011. "Prisons Do Not Reduce Recidivism: The High Cost of Ignoring Science." *The Prison Journal* 91: 48–65.

Currie, Janet, and Erdal Tekin. 2006. "Does Child Abuse Cause Crime?" Andrew Young School of Policy Studies Research Paper Series, Working Paper 06-31, Georgia State University, Atlanta, GA.

Daley, Marilyn, Craig Love, Donald Shepard, Cheryl Petersen, Karen White, Karen and Frank Hall. 2004. "Cost-Effectiveness of Connecticut's In-Prison Substance Abuse Treatment." *Journal of Offender Rehabilitation* 39: 69–92.

Dawkins, M. P. 1997. "Drug Use and Violent Crime among Adolescents." *Adolescence* 32: 395–405.

Deane, M. W., H. Steadman, R. Borum, B. Veysey, and J. Morrissey. 1999. "Emerging Partnerships Between Mental Health and Law Enforcement." *Psychiatric Services* 50: 99–101.

DeLeon, G. 1988a. "Legal Pressure in Therapeutic Communities." *Journal of Drug Issues* 18: 625–640.

DeLeon, G. 1988b. "Legal Pressure in Therapeutic Communities." In *Compulsory Treatment of Drug Abuse: Research and Clinical Practice*, NIDA Research Monograph 86, edited by C. G. Leukfield and F. M. Tims. DHHS Publication No. ADM 88-1578. Rockville, MD: National Institute on Drug Abuse.

DeLeon, G., and N. Jainchill. 1986. "Circumstance, Motivation, Readiness and Suitability as Correlates of Treatment Tenure." *Journal of Psychoactive Drugs* 18: 203–208.

DeMichele, Matthew. 2007. "Probation and Parole's Growing Caseloads and Workload Allocation: Strategies for Managerial Decision-Making." Lexington, KY: The American Probation and Parole Association.

DeMichele, Matthew, and Brian Payne. 2007. "Probation and Parole Officers Speak Out—Caseload and Workload Allocation." *Federal Probation* 71: 30–35.

DiClemente, C. C., and S. Hughes. 1990. "Stages of Change Profiles in Outpatient Alcoholism Treatment." *Journal of Substance Abuse* 2: 217–235.

Dirks-Linhorst, P. and D. Linhorst. 2012. "Recidivism Outcomes for Suburban Mental Health Court Defendants." *American Journal of Criminal Justice* 37: 76–91.

Doble, John. 2002. "Attitudes to Punishment in the US—Punitive and Liberal Opinions." In *Changing Attitudes to Punishment: Public Opinion, Crime and Justice*, edited by J. Roberts and M. Hough. New York: Routledge.

Doble, John, and Josh Klein. 2009. "Punishing Criminals, The Public's View: An Alabama Survey." *Federal Sentencing Reporter* 21: 291–293.

Domurad, S. and M. Carey. 2010. *Coaching Packet: Implementing Evidence-Based Practices*. Silver Spring, MD: Center for Effective Public Policy.

Donley, Sachiko, Leah Habib, Tanja Jovanovic, Asante Kamkwalala, Mark Evces, Glenn Egan, Beka Bradley, and Jerry Ressler. 2012. "Civilian PTSD Symptoms and Risk for Involvement in the Criminal Justice System." *Journal of the American Academy of Psychiatry and the Law* 40: 522–529.

Doob, Anthony, and Cheryl Webster. 2003. "Sentence Severity and Crime: Accepting the Null Hypothesis." In *Crime and Justice: A Review of Research*, edited by Michael Tonry, vol. 30. Chicago: University of Chicago Press.

Dowden, C. 1998. "A Meta-Analytic Examination of the Risk, Need and Responsivity Principles and Their Importance Within the Rehabilitation Debate." Master's thesis, Carleton University, Ottawa, ON.

Dupont R., and S. Cochran. 2000. "Police Response to Mental Health Emergencies: Barriers to Change." *Journal of the American Academy of Psychiatry and the Law* 28: 338–344.

Durlauf, Steven, and Daniel Nagin. 2011. "Imprisonment and Crime: Can Both Be Reduced?" *Criminology and Public Policy* 10: 9–12.

Ekland-Olson, S. and W. Kelly. 1993. *Justice Under Pressure: A Comparison of Recidivism Patterns Among Four Successive Parolee Cohorts.* New York: Springer.

Elikann, Peter. 1996. *The Tough on Crime Myth.* New York: Insight Books.

Engen, Rodney. 2008. "Have Sentencing Reforms Displaced Discretion Over Sentencing from Judges to Prosecutors?" In *The Changing Role of the American Prosecutor*, edited by John L. Worrall and M. Elaine Nugent-Borakove. Albany, NY: State University of New York Press.

Fabian, John. 2009. "Mitigating Murder at Capital Sentencing: An Empirical and Practical Psycho-Legal Strategy." *Journal of Forensic Psychology Practice* 9: 1–34.

Fagan, Jeffrey. 1993. "The Political Economy of Drug Dealing among Urban Gangs." In *Drugs and the Community*, edited by Robert C. Davis, Arthur J. Lurigio, and Dennis P. Rosenbaum. Springfield, IL: Thomas.

Fahey, Jennifer. 2008. "Using Research to Promote Public Safety: A Prosecutor's Primer on Evidence-Based Practice." Boston, MA: Crime and Justice Institute.

Farabee, David. 2005. "Rethinking Rehabilitation: Why Can't We Reform Our Criminals?" Washington, D.C.: American Enterprise Institute Press.

Farah, Martha, David Shera, Jessica Savage, Laura Betancourt, Joan Giannetta, Nancy Brodsky, Elsa Malmud, and Hallam Hurt. 2006. "Childhood Poverty: Specific Associations with Neurocognitive Development." *Brain Research* 1110: 166–174.

Farole, Donald. 2009. "Problem-Solving and the American Bench: A National Survey of Judges." *The Justice System Journal* 30 no. 1.

Farole, D. J., and A. Cissner. 2007. "Seeing Eye to Eye: Participant and Staff Perspectives on Drug Courts." In *Documenting Results: Research on Problem-Solving Justice*, edited by G. Berman, M. Rempel, and R. V. Wolf. New York: Center for Court Innovation.

Farole, Donald, Nora Puffett, Michael Rempel, and Francine Byrne. 2005. "Applying Problem-Solving Principles in Mainstream Courts: Lessons for State Courts." *The Justice System Journal* 26 no. 1.

Ferguson, J. L. 2002. "Putting the What Works Research Into Practice: An Organizational Perspective." *Criminal Justice and Behavior* 29: 472–492.

Fernandez, Kenneth. 2011. "Crime Policy in the New Millennium: The End of the
'Tough on Crime' Era?" Paper presented at the State Politics and Policy Conference, Hanover, NH, June 3–4, 2011.

Festinger, D. S., D. Marlowe, P. Lee, K. Kirby, G. Bovasso, and A. McLellan. 2002.
"Status Hearings in Drug Court: When More Is Less and Less Is More." *Drug
and Alcohol Dependence* 68: 151–157.

Finigan, M., S. M. Carey, A. and Cox. 2007. "The Impact of a Mature Drug Court
Over 10 Years of Operation: Recidivism and Costs." Portland, OR: NPC
Research.

Fishbein, D. H., C. Hyde, D. Eldreth, M. J. Paschall, R. Hubal, A. Das, and B. Yung.
2006. "Neurocognitive Skills Moderate Urban Male Adolescents' Responses to
Preventive Intervention Materials." *Drug and Alcohol Dependence* 1: 47–60.

Fisher, W. H., E. Silver, and N. Wolff. 2006. "Beyond Criminalization: Toward
a Criminologically Informed Mental Health Policy and Services Research."
*Administration and Policy in Mental Health and Mental Health Services
Research* 33: 544–557.

Fitzpatrick, K. M., and J. P. Boldizar. 1993. "The Prevalence and Consequences of
Exposure to Violence Among African American Youth." *Journal of the American Academy of Child and Adolescent Psychiatry* 32: 424–430.

Fixsen, D., S, Naoom, K. Blasé, R. Friedman, and F. Wallace. 2005. "Implementation Research: A Synthesis of the Literature." Tampa, FL: Louis de la Parte
Florida Mental Health Institute.

Fomby, Thomas B., and Vasudha Rangaprasad. 2002. "Divert Court Of Dallas
County Cost-Benefit Analysis." Department Of Economics Southern Method-
ist University, Dallas, Texas.

Forst, Brian, and Shawn Bushway. 2010. "Discretion, Rule of Law, and Rational-
ity." Paper presented at the Symposium on the Past and Future of Empirical
Sentencing. State University of New York at Albany.

Freeman, R. 1996. "Why Do So Many Young American Men Commit Crimes and
What Might We Do About It?" *Journal of Economic Perspectives* 10: 25–42.

Freidman, Matthew. 2000. "Post-Traumatic Stress Disorder." acnp.org/g4
/GN01000111/CH109.html.

French, Michael, Hal Fang, and Ralph Fretz. 2010. "Economic Evaluation of a Prerelease Substance Abuse Treatment Program for Repeat Criminal Offenders."
Journal of Substance Abuse Treatment 38: 141–152.

French, S. A., and P. Gendreau. 2006. "Reducing Prison Misconducts: What Works!" *Criminal Justice and Behavior* 33: 185–218.

Friedmann, Peter, Faye S. Taxman, and Craig E. Henderson. 2007. "Evidence-Based Treatment Practices for Drug-Involved Adults in the Criminal Justice System." *Journal of Substance Abuse Treatment* 32: 267–277.

Gendreau, P. 1996. "The Principles of Effective Intervention with Offenders." In *Choosing Correctional Options that Work: Defining the Demand and Evaluating the Supply*, edited by Alan T. Harland. Thousand Oaks, CA: Sage Publications, Inc.

Gendreau, P., and C. Goggin. 1995. "Principles of Effective Correctional Programming with Offenders." St John, NB: Center for Criminal Justice Studies and Department of Psychology, University of Brunswick.

Gendreau, P., C. Goggin, and F. Cullen. 1999. *The Effects of Prison Sentences on Recidivism*. A Report to the Corrections Research and Development and Aboriginal Policy Branch, Solicitor General of Canada. Ottawa, ON: Public Works & Government Services Canada.

Gendreau, P., T. Little, and C. Goggin. 1996. "A Meta-Analysis of the Predictors of Adult Offender Recidivism: What Works!" *Criminology* 34: 575–607.

Gendreau, P., and M. Paparozzi. 1995. "Examining What Works in Community Corrections." *Corrections Today* 57: 28–31.

Gerstein, G. 2010. "President Obama Backing Off of Strict Crime Policy." http://www.politico.com/news/stories/0910/42004.html.

Gilbertson, M., T. Gurvits, N. Lasko, S. Orr, and R. Pitman. 2001. "Multivariate Assessment of Explicit Memory Function in Combat Veterans with Posttraumatic Stress Disorder." *Journal of Trauma and Stress* 14: 413–432.

Gillespie, C. F., B. Bradley, K. Mercer, A. K. Smith, K. Conneely, M. Gapen, T. Weiss, A. C. Schwartz, J. F. Cubells, and K. J. Ressler. 2010. "Trauma Exposure and Stress-Related Disorders in Inner City Primary Care Patients." *General Hospital Psychiatry* 31: 505–514.

Glaze, Lauren, and Thomas Bonczar. 2009. "Probation and Parole in the United States, 2008." Washington, D.C.: U.S. Department of Justice, Office of Justice Programs, Bureau of Justice Statistics.

Glaze, Lauren, and Thomas Bonczar. 2011. "Probation and Parole in the United States, 2010." Washington, D.C.: U.S. Department of Justice, Office of Justice Programs, Bureau of Justice Statistics.

Gleicher, Lily, Sarah Manchak, and Francis Cullen. 2013. "Creating a Supervision Tool Kit: How to Improve Probation and Parole." *Federal Probation* 77: 22–27.

The Global Cannabis Commission. 2010. *Cannabis Policy: Moving Beyond Stalemate*. Oxford, UK: The Beckley Foundation.

Godfrey, Christine, Duncan Stewart, and Michael Gossop. 2004. "Economic Analysis of Costs and Consequences of the Treatment of Drug Misuse: 2-Year Outcome Data from the National Treatment Outcome Research Study (NTORS)." *Addiction* 99: 697–707.

Goff, A., E. Rose, S. Rose, and D. Purves. 2007. "Does PTSD Occur in Sentenced Prison Populations? A Systematic Literature Review." *Criminal Behaviour and Mental Health* 17: 152–162.

Goldkamp, J. S., M. D. White, and J. B. Robinson. 2002. "An Honest Chance: Perspectives on Drug Courts." *Federal Sentencing Reporter* 6: 369–372.

Goldstein, P. 1985. "The Drug/Violence Nexus: A Tripartite Conceptual Framework." *Journal of Drug Issues* 14: 493–506.

Gottfredson, D. C., B. W. Kearley, S. S. Najaka, and C. M. Rocha. 2005. "The Baltimore City Drug Treatment Court: Three-Year Outcome Study." *Evaluation Review* 29: 42–64.

Gottfredson, D. C., S. S. Najaka, B. W. Kearley, and C. M. Rocha. 2006. "Long-Term Effects of Participation in the Baltimore City Drug Treatment Court: Results from an Experimental Study." *Journal of Experimental Criminology* 2: 67–98.

Government Accountability Office. 2005. *Adult Drug Courts: Evidence Indicates Recidivism Reductions and Mixed Results for Other Outcomes*. Washington D.C.: Author.

Grantham, Dennis. 2011. "Right Place, Right Time, Right Approach: Texans Collaborate to Build a 'Model' Jail Diversion and Crisis Mental Health System." *Behavioral* November 15, 2011, http://www.behavioral.net.

Grasmick, Harold G., and George J. Bryjak, 1980. "The Deterrent Effect of Perceived Severity of Punishment." *Social Forces* 59: 471–491.

Grasso, B. C., R. Genest, C. W. Jordan, and D. W. Bates. 2003. "Use of Chart and Record Reviews to Detect Medication Errors in a State Psychiatric Hospital." *Psychiatric Services* 54: 677–681.

Gray, M. Kevin, Monique Fields, and Sheila Royo Maxwell. 2001. "Examining Probation Violations: Who, What, and When." *Crime and Delinquency* 47: 537–557.

Green, D., and D. Wink. 2010. "Using Random Judge Assignments to Estimate the Effects of Incarceration and Probation on Recidivism Among Drug Offenders." *Federal Probation* 48: 357–387.

Hamilton, Zachary. 2010. "Do Reentry Courts Reduce Recidivism: Results from the Harlem Parole Reentry Court." New York: Center for Court Innovation.

Hancock, M., J. L. Tapscott, and P. N. Hoaken. 2010. "Role of Executive Dysfunction in Predicting Frequency and Severity of Violence." *Aggressive Behavior* 36: 338–349.

Harlow, Caroline Wolf. 2003. "Education and Correctional Populations." Washington, D.C.: U.S. Department of Justice, Office of Justice Programs, Bureau of Justice Statistics.

Harris, A., and A. J. Lurigio. 2007. "The Mentally Ill as Perpetrators of Violence: A Brief Review of Research and Assessment Strategies." *Aggression and Violent Behavior* 12: 542–551.

Harrison, L., and J. Gfroerer. 1992. "The Intersections of Drug Use and Criminal Behavior: Results from the National Household Survey on Drug Abuse." *Crime and Delinquency* 38: 422–443.

Hartney, Christopher, and Susan Marchionne, 2009. "Attitudes of US Voters Toward Nonserious Offenders and Alternatives to Incarceration." Oakland, CA: FOCUS Views from the National Council on Crime and Delinquency.

Hawken, Angela, and Mark Kleiman. 2009. "Managing Drug-Involved Offenders with Swift and Certain Sanctions: Evaluating Hawaii's HOPE." Washington, D.C.: United States Department of Justice, National Institute of Justice.

Hawkins, Keith, and Krista Trobst. 1999. "Frontal Lobe Dysfunction and Aggression: Conceptual Issues and Research Findings." *Aggression and Violent Behavior* 5: 147–157.

Henderson, Craig, Faye Taxman, and Douglas Young. 2008. "A Rasch Model Analysis of Evidence-Based Treatment Practices Used in the Criminal Justice System." *Drug and Alcohol Dependence* 93: 163–175.

Henry, Kelli, and Dana Kralstein. 2011. "Community Courts: The Research Literature." New York: Center for Court Innovation.

Herinckx, H. A., S. C. Swart, S. A. Ama, C. D. Dolezal, and S. King. 2005. "Rearrest And Linkage to Mental Health Services Among Defendants of the Clark County Mental Health Court Program." *Psychiatric Services* 56: 853–857.

Herman, Patricia, and Beth L. Poindexter. 2012. "Cost-Benefit Analysis of Pima County's Drug Treatment Alternative to Prison (DTAP) Program Final Report." Pima County Arizona Attorney's Office.

Heubner, Beth. 2006. "Drug Abuse, Treatment and Probationer Recidivism." http://www.ncjrs.gov/App/Publications/abstract.aspx?ID248312.

Hiday, V., and B. Ray. 2010. "Arrests Two Years After Exiting a Well-Established Mental Health Court." *Psychiatric Services* 61: 463–468.

Hoelter, Herbert. 2009. "Sentencing Alternatives—Back to the Future." *Federal Sentencing Reporter* 22 no. 1.

Hook, Cayce, Gwendolyn Lawson, and Martha Farah. 2013. "Socioeconomic Status and the Development of Executive Function." In *Encyclopedia on Early Childhood Development*, edited by R. E. Tremblay, M. Boivin, and R. D. Peters. Montreal, QC: Centre of Excellence for Early Childhood Development and Strategic Knowledge Cluster on Early Child Development.

Hser, Yih-Ing. 2007. "Predicting Long-Term Stable Recovery from Heroin Addiction: Findings from a 33-Year Follow-Up Study." *Journal of Addictive Diseases* 26: 51–60.

Hser, Yih-Ing, Valerie Hoffman, Christine E. Grella, and M. Douglas Anglin. 2001. "A 33-Year Follow-Up of Narcotics Addicts." *Archives of General Psychiatry* 58: 503–508.

Hser, Yih-Ing, David Huang, Chih-Ping Chou, and M. Douglas Anglin. 2007. "Trajectories of Heroin Addiction: Growth Mixture Modeling Results Based on a 33-Year Follow-Up Study." *Evaluation Review* 31: 548–563.

Hubbard, Robert, S. Gail Craddock, and Jill Anderson. 2003. "Overview of 5-Year Follow Up Outcomes in the Drug Abuse Outcome Studies (DATOS)." *Journal of Substance Abuse Treatment* 25: 125–134.

Huddleston, West, and Douglas Marlowe. 2011. "Painting the Current Picture: A National Report on Drug Courts and Other Problem-Solving Court Program in the United States." Washington, D.C.: National Drug Court Institute, National Association of Drug Court Professionals.

Huebner, B. M. 2006. *Drug Abuse, Treatment, and Probationer Recidivism*. St. Louis: University of Missouri-St. Louis Department of Criminology and Criminal Justice.

Hyatt, Jordan, Mark Bergstrom, and Steven Chanenson. 2011. "Following the Evidence: Integrate Risk Assessment Into Sentencing." *Federal Sentencing Reporter* 23 no. 4.

Human Rights Watch. 2003. "Ill Equipped: U.S. Prisons and Offenders with Mental Illness." New York: Human Rights Watch.

Inciardi, J. A. 1992. *The War on Drugs II: The Continuing Epic of Heroin, Cocaine, Crack, Crime, AIDS, and the Public Policy*. Mountain View: Mayfield Publishing Co.

Inciardi, J. A., S. Martin, C. A. Butzin, R. M. Hooper, and L. D. Harrison. 1996. "An Effective Model of Prison-Based Treatment for Drug-Involved Offenders." *Journal of Drug Issues* 27: 261–278.

Inciardi, J. A., and A. Pottieger. 1994. "Crack Cocaine Use and Street Crime." *Journal of Drug Issues* 24: 273–292.

Insight Project Research Group. 2009. "SBIRT Outcomes in Houston: Final Report on InSight. A Hospital District-Based Program for Patients at Risk for Alcohol and Drug Use Problems." *Alcoholism: Clinical and Experimental Research* 33: 1374–1381.

In the Public Interest. 2013. "Criminal: How Lockup Quotas and 'Low Crime Taxes' Guarantee Profits for Private Prison Corporations." http://www.inthepublicinterest.org/sites/default/files/Criminal%20Lockup%20Quota%20Report.pdf.

Iowa Department of Corrections. 2012. "Return on Investment: Evidence-Based Options to Improve Outcomes." State of Iowa.

Irwin, J. and J. Austin. 1994. *It's About Time: America's Imprisonment Binge*. Belmont, CA: Wadsworth.

Jalbert, S., W. Rhodes, C. Flygare, and M. Kane. 2010. "Testing Probation Outcomes in an Evidence-Based Practice Setting: Reduced Caseload Size and Intensive Supervision Effectiveness." *Journal of Offender Rehabilitation* 49: 233–253.

Jalbert, S. K., W. Rhodes, M. Kane, E. Clawson, B. Bogue, C. Flygare, R. Kling, and M. Guevara. 2011. "A Multi-Site Evaluation of Reduced Probation Caseload Size in an Evidence-Based Practice Setting." Washington D.C.: U.S. Department of Justice.

James, Doris, and Lauren Glaze. 2006. Mental Health Problems of Prison and Jail Inmates. Washington, D.C.: U.S. Department of Justice, Office of Justice Programs, Bureau of Justice Statistics.

James, Nathan. 2011. "Offender Reentry: Correctional Statistics, Reintegration into the Community, and Recidivism." Washington, D.C.: Congressional Research Service.

Jaycox, L. H., A. R. Morral, and J. Juvonen. 2003. "Mental Health and Medical Problems and Service Use Among Adolescent Substance Users." *Journal of the American Academy of Child and Adolescent Psychiatry* 42: 701–709.

Johnsen, G. and A. Asbjornsen. 2008 "Consistent Impaired Verbal Memory in PTSD: A Meta-Analysis." *Journal of Affective Disorders* 111:74–82.

Johnson, B. D., P. J. Goldstein, E. Preble, J. Schmeidler, D. Lipton, and B. Spunt. 1985. *Taking Care of Business: The Economics of Crime by Heroin Users*. Lanham, MD: Rowman & Littlefield.

Johnson, Bruce D., Terry Williams, Kojo A. Dei, and Harry Sanabria. 1990. "Drug Abuse in the Inner City: Impact on Hard Drug Users and the Community."

In *Drugs and Crime,* edited by Michael Tonry and James Q. Wilson, vol. 13 of *Crime and Justice: A Review of Research.* Chicago: University of Chicago Press.

Jones, P., P. Harris, J. Fader, and L. Grubstein. 2001. "Identifying Chronic Offenders." *Justice Quarterly* 18: 479–508.

Junginger, J., K. Claypoole, R. Laygo, and A. Crisanti. 2006. "Effects of Serious Mental Illness and Substance Abuse on Criminal Offenses." *Psychiatric Services* 57: 879–882.

Justice Center, Council on State Governments. 2011. "Mental Health Courts." consensusproject.org/issueareas/mental-health-courts.

Justice Mapping Center. 2010. "Justice Mapping Center Launches First National Atlas of Criminal Justice Data." http://www.justicemapping.org/archive/28 /justice-mapping-center-launches-first-national-atlas-of-criminal-justice-data.

Kaplan, A. 2007. "Mental Health Courts Reduce Incarceration, Save Money." *Psychiatric News* 24: 1–3.

Karafin, D. 2008. "Community Courts Across the Globe: A Survey of Goals, Performance Measures and Operations." Report submitted to the Open Society Foundation for South Africa, New York. Center for Court Innovation.

Karberg, J., and J. James. 2005. "Substance Dependence, Abuse, and Treatment of Jail Inmates, 2002. Washington, D.C.: U.S. Department of Justice, Office of Justice Programs, Bureau of Justice Statistics.

Karberg, J. C., and C. J. Mumola. 2006. "Drug Use and Dependence, State and Federal Prisoners, 2004." Washington, D.C.: U.S. Department of Justice, Office of Justice Programs, Bureau of Justice Statistics.

Kates, G. 2013. http://www.thecrimereport.org/news/inside-criminal-justice /2013-04-science-in-the-courtroom.

Kaye, Judith. 2004. "Delivering Justice Today: A Problem-Solving Approach." *Yale Law and Policy Review* 22: 125–151.

Kessler, R. C., O. Demler, R. G. Frank. M. Olfson, H. A. Pincus, E. E. Walters, P. Wang, K. B. Wells, and A. M. Zaslavsky. 2005. "Prevalence and Treatment of Mental Disorders, 1990 to 2003." *The New England Journal of Medicine* 352: 2515–2523.

King, Ryan. 2009. "The State of Sentencing 2008: Developments in Policy and Practice." Washington, D.C.: The Sentencing Project.

King, Ryan, and Marc Mauer. 2006. "The War on Marijuana: The Transformation of the War on Drugs in the 1990s." *Harm Reduction Journal* 3: 3–6.

Kingsley, David. 2006. "The Teaching-Family Model and Post-Treatment Recidivism: A Critical Review of the Conventional Wisdom." *International Journal of Behavioral Consultation and Therapy* 2: 481–497.

Kleiman, Mark. 2009. *When Brute Force Fails*. New Haven: Princeton University Press.

Kleiman, Matthew, Brian Ostrom, and Fred Cheesman. 2007. "Using Risk Assessment to Inform Sentencing Decisions for Nonviolent Offenders in Virginia." *Crime and Delinquency* 53: 106–132.

Koenen, K. C., A. Caspi, T. K. Moffitt, F. Rijsdijk, and A. Taylor. 2006. "Genetic Influences on the Overlap Between Low IQ and Antisocial Behavior in Young Children." *Journal of Abnormal Psychology* 115: 787–797.

Kriesberg, Barry, and Susan Marchionne. 2006. "Attitudes of US Voters Toward Prisoner Rehabilitation and Reentry Policies." Oakland, CA: FOCUS Views from the National Council on Crime and Delinquency.

Kyckelhahn, Tracey. 2012. "State Correctional Expenditures, FY 1982–2010." Washington, D.C.: U.S. Department of Justice, Office of Justice Programs, Bureau of Justice Statistics.

Kyckelhahn, Tracy, and T. Cohen. 2008. "Felony Defendants in Large Urban Counties, 2004." Washington, D.C.: U.S. Department of Justice, Office of Justice Programs, Bureau of Justice Statistics.

Labriola, Melissa, Emily Gold, and Julia Kohn. 2013. "Innovation in the Criminal Justice System." New York: Center for Court Innovation.

Lamb, H. Richard, and Linda Weinberger. 2005. "The Shift of Psychiatric Inpatient Care from Hospitals to Jails and Prisons." *Journal of the American Academy of Psychiatry and Law* 33: 529–534.

Lamb, H., and Linda E. Weinberger. 2008. "Mental Health Courts as a Way to Provide Treatment to Violent Persons with Severe Mental Illness." *Journal of the American Medical Association* 300: 722–724.

Lamb, H. Richard, Linda Weinberger, and Walter DeCuir. 2002. "The Police and Mental Health." *Psychiatric Services* 53: 1266–1271.

Lamb, H. Richard, Linda Weinberger, and Bruce Gross. 2004. "Mentally Ill Persons in the Criminal Justice System: Some Perspectives." *Psychiatric Quarterly* 75: 107–126.

Lamb, H., Linda Weinberger, Jeffrey Marsh, and Bruce H. Gross. 2007. "Treatment Prospects for Persons with Severe Mental Illness in an Urban County Jail." *Psychiatric Services* 58: 782–786.

Lamb H. R., R. Shaner, D. M. Elliott, et al. 1995. "Outcome for Psychiatric Emergency Patients Seen by an Outreach Police-Mental Health Team." *Psychiatric Services* 46: 1267–1271.

Landenberger, Nana, and Mark Lipsey. 2005. "The Positive Effects of Cognitive–Behavioral Programs for Offenders: A Meta-Analysis of Factors Associated with Effective Treatment." *Journal of Experimental Criminology* 1: 451–476.

Langan, Patrick, and David Levin. 2002. "Recidivism of Prisoners Released in 1994." Washington, D.C.: U.S. Department of Justice, Office of Justice Programs, Bureau of Justice Statistics.

Latessa, E. n.d. "Improving the Effectiveness of Correctional Programs Through Research." Presentation, Center for Criminal Justice Research, Division of Criminal Justice, University of Cincinnati, Cincinnati, OH.

Latessa, E., F. Cullen, and P. Gendreau. 2002. "Beyond Correctional Quackery—Professionalism and the Possibility of Effective Treatment." *Federal Probation* 66: 43–49.

Latessa, E., and C. Lowencamp. 2006. "What Works in Reducing Recidivism?" *University of St. Thomas Law Journal* 3: 521–535.

Lattimore, P., N. Broner, R. Sherman, L. Frisman, L., and M. S. Shafer. 2003. "A Comparison of Prebooking and Postbooking Diversion Programs for Mentally Ill Substance-Using Individuals with Justice Involvement." *Journal of Contemporary Criminal Justice* 19 1: 30–64.

Lattimore, Pamela K., Danielle M. Steffey, and Christy A. Visher. 2010. "Prisoner Reentry in the First Decade of the Twenty-First Century." *Victims and Offenders* 5: 253–267.

Lawrence, Sarah, and Jeremy Travis. 2004. "The New Landscape of Imprisonment: Mapping America's Prison Expansion." Washington, D.C.: Urban Institute, Justice Policy Center.

Leachman, Michael, Inimai M. Chettiar, and Benjamin Geare. 2012. "Improving Budget Analysis of State Criminal Justice Reforms: A Strategy for Better Outcomes and Saving Money." Center on Budget and Policy Priorities and the American Civil Liberties Union, https://www.aclu.org/files/assets/improvingbudgetanalysis _20120110.pdf.

The Legislative Analyst's Office. 2009. *Achieving Better Outcomes for Adult Probation*. Sacramento: The California Legislatures Nonpartisan Fiscal and Policy Advisor.

Levitt, S. 1996. "The Effect of Prison Population Size on Crime Rates: Evidence from Prison Overcrowding Litigation" *Quarterly Journal of Economics* 111: 319–351.

Levy, Terry, and Michael Orlans. 2000. "Attachment Disorder as an Antecedent to Violence and Antisocial Patterns in Children." In *Handbook of Attachment Intervention*, edited by Terry Levy. Elsevier.

Liedka, R., A. Piehl, and B. Useem, 2006. "The Crime Control Effect of Incarceration: Does Scale Matter?" *Criminology and Public Policy* 5: 245–276.

Life Magazine. 1946. "Most U.S. Mental Hospitals are a Shame and Disgrace."

Lind, Kate. 2009 "Stopping the Revolving Door: Reform of Community Corrections in Wisconsin." *The Wisconsin Policy Research Institute*, 22 no. 5.

Lindquist, Christine, Jenifer Hardison, Michael Rampel, and Sharon Carey. 2013. "The National Institute of Justice's Evaluation of the Second Chance Act Adult Reentry Courts: Program Characteristics and Preliminary Themes from Year 1." Washington D.C.: U.S. Department of Justice, National Institute of Justice.

Lindquist, C. H., C. P. Krebs, and P. Lattimore. 2006. "Sanctions and Rewards in Drug Court Programs: Implementation, Perceived Efficacy, and Decision-Making." *Journal of Drug Issues* 36: 119–146.

Lipsey, M. W. and R. T. Cullen. 2007. "The Effectiveness of Correctional Rehabilitation: A Review of Systematic Reviews." *Annual Review of Law and Social Science* 3: 297–320.

Lipsey, Mark W., Nana A. Landenberger, and Sandra J. Wilson. 2007. "Effects of Cognitive-Behavioral Programs for Criminal Offenders." *Campbell Systematic Reviews*, 2007: 6.

Logan, T. K., W. Hoyt, K. McCollister, M. French, C. Leukefeld, and L. Minton. 2004. "Economic Evaluation of Drug Court: Methodology, Results, and Policy Implications." *Evaluation and Program Planning* 27: 381–396.

Loman, Anthony. 2002. "Cost-Benefit Analysis of the St. Louis City Adult Felony Drug Court." St. Louis, MO: Institute of Applied Research.

Loman, Anthony. 2004. "A Cost-Benefit Analysis of the St. Louis City Adult Felony Drug Court." St. Louis, MO: Institute of Applied Research.

Loo, D., and R. E. Grimes. 2004. "Polls, Politics and Crime: The "Law and Order" Issues of the 1960s." *Western Criminology Review* 5: 50–67.

Loughan, Ashlee, and Robert Perna. 2012. "Neurocognitive Impacts for Children of Poverty and Neglect." *American Psychological Association, CYF News*.

Lowenkamp, C. T., A. Holsinger, and E. Latessa. 2005. "Are Drug Courts Effective? A Meta-Analytic Review." *Journal of Community Corrections*, Fall: 5–28.

Lowenkamp, Christopher, Edward Latessa, and Alexander Holsinger. 2006. "The Risk Principle in Action: What Have We Learned From 13,676 Offenders and 97 Correctional Programs?" *Crime and Delinquency* 52: 77–93.

Lowenkamp, Christopher, Edward Latessa, and Paula Smith. 2006. "Does Correctional Program Quality Really Matter? The Impact of Adhering to the Principles of Effective Intervention." *Criminology and Public Policy* 5: 575–594.

Lurigio, A. J. 2004. "Transinstitutionalization and the Mentally Ill in the Criminal Justice System." Lecture presented at the Corrections and Public Health Task Force Steering Committee Meeting. Cook County Department of Corrections, Chicago, IL.

Lurigio, A. J. 2011. "Examining Prevailing Beliefs About People with Serious Mental Illness in the Criminal Justice System." *Federal Probation* 75: 11–18.

Lurigio, A. and J. Swartz. 2000. "Changing the Contours of the Criminal Justice System to Meet the Needs of Persons with Serious Mental Illness. In *NIJ 2000 Series: Policies, Processes, and Decisions of the Criminal Justice Systems*, Vol. 3, edited by J. Horney. Washington, D.C.: National Institute of Justice.

Lutze, Faith, W. Johnson, T. Clear, E. Latessa, and R. Slate. 2012. "The Future of Community Corrections Is Now: Stop Dreaming and Take Action." *Journal of Contemporary Criminal Justice* 28: 42–57.

Lynch, Michael. 2003. "Consequences of Children's Exposure to Community Violence." *Clinical Child and Family Psychology Review* 6: 265–274.

MacCoun, R. J., B. Kilmer, and P. Reuter. 2003. "Research on Drug-Crime Linkages: The Next Generation." In *Toward a Drugs and Crime Research Agenda for the 21st Century*. Washington, D.C.: National Institute of Justice Special Report, U.S. Department of Justice.

MacCoun, R. J., and P. Reuter. 2001. *Drug War Heresies: Learning from Other Vices, Times, and Places*. New York: Cambridge University Press.

Mackenzie, D. L. 2006. *What Works in Corrections Reducing The Criminal Activities of Offenders And Delinquents*. New York: Cambridge University Press.

MacLellan, Thomas. 2005. "Issue Brief: Improving Prisoner Reentry Through Strategic Policy Innovations." NGA Center for Best Practices.

Madras, B. K., W. M. Compton, D. Avula, T. Stegbauer, J. B. Stein, and H. W. Clark. 2009. "Screening, Brief Interventions, Referral to Treatment (SBIRT) for Illicit Drug and Alcohol Use at Multiple Healthcare Sites: Comparison at Intake and 6 Months Later." *Drug and Alcohol Dependence* 99: 280–295.

Manski, C. F., J. Pepper, and C. Petrie, eds. 2001. *Informing America's Policy on Illegal Drugs: What We Don't Know Keeps Hurting Us*. Washington, D.C.: National Academy Press.

Marcus, Michael. 2003. "Archaic Sentencing Liturgy Sacrifices Public Safety: What's Wrong and How We Can Fix It." *Federal Sentencing Reporter* 16: 76–86.

Marcus, Michael. 2004. "Smarter Sentencing: On the Need to Consider Crime Reduction as a Goal." *Court Review* 40: 16–25.

Marcus, Michael. 2009. "MPC—The Root of the Problem: Just Deserts and Risk Assessment." *Florida Law Review* 61: 751–776.

Marion, N. 1994. "Symbolism and Federal Crime Control Legislation, 1960–1990." *Journal of Crime and Justice* 17: 69–91.

Marion, N. 1997. "Symbolic Policies in Clinton's Crime Control Agenda." *Buffalo Criminal Law Review* 1: 67–108.

Marion, N., and R. Farmer. 2003. "Crime Control in the 2000 Presidential Election: A Symbolic Issue." *American Journal of Criminal Justice* 27: 129–144.

Maris, R. W. 2002. "Suicide." *The Lancet* 360: 319–326.

Marlowe, Douglas. 2009. "Evidence-Based Sentencing for Drug Offenders: An Analysis of Prognostic Risks and Criminogenic Needs." *Chapman Journal of Criminal Justice* 1: 167–201.

Marlowe, Douglas. 2010. "Research Update on Adult Drug Courts." National Association of Drug Court Professionals.

Marlowe, D. B., D. S. Festinger, and P. A. Lee. 2004a. "The Judge Is a Key Component of Drug Court." *Drug Court Review* 4: 1–34.

Marlowe, D. B., D. S. Festinger, and P. A. Lee. 2004b. "The Role of Judicial Status Hearings in Drug Court." In *Treating Addicted Offenders: A Continuum of Effective Practices*, edited by K. Knight and D. Farabee. Kingston, NJ: Civic Research Institute.

Marlowe, D. B., D. S. Festinger, P. Lee, K. L. Dugosh, and K. M. Benasutti. 2006. "Matching Judicial Supervision to Clients' Risk Status in Drug Court." *Crime and Delinquency* 52: 52–76.

Marlowe, D. B., D. S. Festinger, K. L. Dugosh, P. Lee, and K. M. Benasutti. 2007. "Adapting Judicial Supervision to the Risk Level of Drug Offenders: Discharge and Six-Month Outcomes from a Prospective Matching Study." *Drug and Alcohol Dependence* 88: 4–13.

Mascharka, Christopher. 2001. "Mandatory Minimum Sentences: Exemplifying the Law of Unintended Consequences." *Florida State University Law Review* 28: 935–975.

Matthys, Walter, Louk Vanderschuren, Dennis Schutter, and John Lochman. 2012. "Impaired Neurocognitive Functions Affect Social Learning Processes in Oppositional Defiant Disorder and Conduct Disorder: Implications for interventions." *Clinical Child and Family Psychology Review* 15: 234–246.

Mauer, Marc. 2011. "Sentencing Reform Amid Mass Incarcerations—Guarded Optimism." *Criminal Justice* 26 no. 1.

Mayfield, Jim. 2009. "The Dangerous Mentally Ill Offender Program: Four-Year Felony Recidivism and Cost Effectiveness." Olympia, WA: Washington State Institute for Public Policy, Document No. 09-02-1901.

Mayfield, Jim, and D. Lovell. 2008. "The Dangerous Mentally Ill Offender Program: Three-Year Felony Recidivism and Cost Effectiveness." Olympia, WA: Washington State Institute for Public Policy, Document No. 08-02-1901.

McCollister, Kathryn, and Michael French. 2003. "The Relative Contribution of Outcome Domains in the Total Economic Benefit of Addiction Interventions: A Review of First Findings." *Addiction* 89: 1647–1659.

McCollister, Kathryn, Michel French, and Hai Fang. 2010. "The Cost of Crime to Society: New Crime-Specific Estimates for Policy and Program Evaluation." *Drug and Alcohol Dependence* 108: 98–109.

McCollister, Kathryn, Michael French, James Inciardi, Clifford Butzin, Steven Martin, and Robert Hooper. 2003. "Post-Release Substance Abuse Treatment for Criminal Offenders: A Cost-Effectiveness Analysis." *Journal of Quantitative Criminology* 19: 389–407.

McCollister, Kathryn E., Michael French, Michael Prendergast, Elizabeth Hall, and Stanley Sacks. 2004. "Long-Term Cost-Effectiveness of Addiction Treatment for Criminal Offenders." *Justice Quarterly*, September 2004.

McGlynn Elizabeth, Steven M. Asch, John Adams, Joan Keesey, Jennifer Hicks, Alison DeCristofaro, and Eve A. Kerr. 2003. "The Quality of Health Care Delivered to Adults in the United States." *The New England Journal of Medicine* 348: 2635–2645.

McLellan, A. Thomas, David C. Lewis, Charles P. O'Brien, and Herbert D. Kleber. 2000. "Drug Dependence, a Chronic Medical Illness: Implications for Treatment, Insurance and Outcome Evaluation." *Journal of the American Medical Association* 284: 1689–1695.

McNiel, D. E., and R. L. Binder. 2007. "Effectiveness of a Mental Health Court in Reducing Criminal Recidivism and Violence." *American Journal of Psychiatry* 164: 1395–1403.

Mears, Daniel, and Julie Mestra. 2012. "Prisoner Reentry, Employment, Signaling, and the Better Identification of Desisters." *Criminology and Public Policy* 11: 5–15.

Mental Health America. "Position Statement 52: In Support of Maximum Diversion of Persons with Serious Mental Illness from the Criminal Justice System." http://www.mentalhealthamerica.net.

Mental Illness Policy Organization. http://mentalillnesspolicy.org/consequences/homeless-mentally-ill.html.

Miethe, Terance. 1987. "Charging and Plea Bargaining Practices Under Determinate Sentencing: An Investigation of the Hydraulic Dispacement of Discretion." *The Journal of Criminal Law and Criminology* 78: 155–176.

Milby, J., J. Schumacher, D. Wallace, M. Freedman, and R. Vuchinich. 2005. "To House or Not to House: The Effects of Providing Housing to Homeless Substance Abusers in Treatment." *American Journal of Public Health* 95: 1259–1265.

Miller, N. S., and M. S. Gold. 1994. "Criminal Activity and Crack Addiction." *The International Journal of Addictions* 29: 1069–1078.

Miron, Jeffrey, and Katherine Waldock. 2010. "The Budgetary Impact of Ending Drug Prohibition." Washington, D.C.: The Cato Institute.

Mitchell, O., D. Wilson, and D. MacKenzie. 2007. "Does Incarceration-Based Drug Treatment Reduce Recidivism? A Meta-Analytic Synthesis of the Research." *Journal of Experimental Criminology* 3: 353–375.

Mocan, H. N., and E. Tekin. 2004. "Guns, Drugs and Juvenile Crime: Evidence from a Panel of Siblings and Twins." IZA Discussion Paper No. 932.

Moffitt, Terrie. 2006. "Life-Course Persistent Versus Adolescent-Limited Antisocial Behavior." In *Developmental Psychopathology*, vol. 3 *Risk, Disorder and Adaption*, edited D. Cicchetti and D. Cohen. New York: Wiley.

Moore, M. E., and V. A. Hiday. 2006. "Mental Health Court Outcomes: A Comparison of Re-Arrest and Re-Arrest Severity Between Mental Health Court and Treatment Court Participants." *Law and Human Behavior* 30: 659–674.

Moore, T. A. Scarpa, and A. Raine.2002. "A Meta-Analysis of Serotonin Metabolite 5 HIAA and Antisocial Behavior. *Aggressive Behavior* 28 299–316.

Morgan, Alex, and Scott Lilienfeld. 2000. "A Meta-Analytic Review of the Relation Between Antisocial Behavior and Neuropsychological Measures of Executive Function." *Clinical Psychological Review* 20: 113–136.

Mulhausen, D. 2007. "The Death Penalty Deters Crime and Saves Lives." The Heritage Foundation, August 28, 2007.

Mumola, C. and J. Karberg. 2006. *Drug Use and Dependence, State and Federal Prisoners, 2004*. Washington, D.C.: U.S. Department of Justice.

Nace, E. P., F. Birkmayer, M. A. Sullivan, M. Galanter, J. A. Fromson, R. J. Frances, F. R. Levin, C. Lewis, R. T. Suchinsky, J. S. Tamerin, and J. Westermeyer. 2007. "Socially Sanctioned Coercion Mechanisms for Addiction Treatment." *American Journal of Addiction* 16: 15–23.

Nagin, Daniel, Francis Cullen, and Cheryl Jonson. 2009. "Imprisonment and Reoffending." In *Crime and Justice: A Review of Research,* vol. 38, edited by Michael Tonry. Chicago: University of Chicago Press.

NAMI. 2008. "Decriminalizing Mental Illness: Background and Recommendations." A White Paper prepared by the Forensic Task Force of the NAMI Board of Directors, September 2008.

National Alliance for Mental Illness. 2005. *Grading the States: A Report on America's Health Care System for Serious Mental Illnesses*. Arlington, VA: Author.

National Alliance for Mental Illness. 2009. *Grading the States: A Report on America's Health Care System for Serious Mental Illnesses*. Arlington, VA: Author.

National Association of Pre-Trial Services Agencies. 2009. *Promising Practices in Pretrial Diversion*. Washington, D.C.: Author.

National Center on Addiction and Substance Abuse. 1998. *Behind Bars: Substance Abuse and America's Prison Population*. New York: Columbia University.

National Center on Addiction and Substance Abuse. 2004. "Criminal Neglect: Substance Abuse, Juvenile Justice, and the Children Left Behind." New York: National Center on Addiction and Substance Abuse at Columbia University.

National Center on Addiction and Substance Abuse. 2009. *Shoveling Up Ii: The Impact of Substance Abuse on Federal, State and Local Budgets*. New York: Columbia University.

National Coalition for the Homeless. 2009. *Substance Abuse and Homelessness*. Washington, D.C.

National Institute of Justice. 2012. http://www.nij.gov/topics/corrections /community/drug-offenders/Pages/hawaii-hope.aspx.

National Institute on Drug Abuse. 2006. *Principles of Drug Abuse Treatment for Criminal Justice Populations: A Research-Based Guide*. Bethesda, MD: National Institutes of Health, U.S. Department of Health and Human Services.

National Leadership Forum on Behavioral Health/Criminal Justice Services. 2009. "A Call to Action: Ending an American Tragedy: Addressing the Needs of Justice-Involved People with Mental Illness and Co-Occurring Disorders." http://www.gainscenter.samhsa.gov/html/nlf/pdfs/American-Tragedy.pdf.

National Reentry Resource Center. "Reentry Facts." http://nationalreentryre-sourcecenter.org/facts.

National Research Council. 2007. *Parole, Desistance from Crime and Community Reintegration*. Washington, D.C.: National Academy Press.

New York County Lawyers Association. 1996. *Report and Recommendations of the Drug Policy Task Force*. New York: Author.

The New York Times. September 25, 2011. "Sentencing Shift Gives New Leverage to Prosecutors."

Nichols, James, and H. Laurence Ross. 1990. "Effectiveness of Legal Sanctions in Dealing with Drinking Drivers." *Alcohol, Drugs, and Driving* 6: 33–55.

Nobel, Kimberly, M. Frank Norman, and Martha Farah. 2005. "Neurocognitive Correlates of Socioeconomic Status in Kindergarten Children." *Developmental Science* 8: 74–87.

Nolan, James. 2003. "Redefining Criminal Courts: Problem-Solving and the Meaning of Justice." *American Criminal Law Review* 40: 1541–1565.

NPC Research. 2009. "Vermont Drug Courts: Rutland County Adult Drug Court Process, Outcome and Cost Evaluation." Portland, OR: NPC Research.

Nugent-Borakove, M. E. 2007. *Just Look What You've Done: Determining the Effectiveness of Community Prosecution.* Alexandria, VA: American Prosecutors Research Institute.

Nugent, E. 2004. *The Changing Nature of Prosecution: Community Prosecution vs. Traditional Prosecution Approaches.* Alexandria, VA: American Prosecutors Research Institute.

Nugent, E., P. Fanflik, and D. Brominski. 2004. "The Changing Nature of Prosecution: Community Prosecution vs. Traditional Prosecution Approaches." Alexandria, VA: American Prosecutors Research Institute.

O'Connor, T., and M. Perryclear. 2002. "Prison Religion in Action and its Influence on Offender Rehabilitation." *Journal of Offender Rehabilitation* 35: 11–33.

Office of National Drug Control Policy. 2012. "Obama Administration Officials Announce $22 Million Expansion of Innovative Health Program Aimed at Detecting and Intervening in Drug Addiction Early." Washington, D.C.: Author.

Officer, Kelly, Devarshi Bajpai, and Michael Wilson. 2011. "Offender Reentry Programs Preliminary Evaluation." Criminal Justice Commission, State of Oregon.

Oliver, W. 1998. "Presidential Rhetoric on Crime and Public Opinion." *Criminal Justice Review* 23: 139–160.

Oliver, W. 2002. "The Pied Piper of Crime in America: An Analysis of the Presidents' and Public's Agenda on Crime." *Criminal Justice Policy Review* 13: 139–155.

Oliver, W., and N. Marion. 2008. "Political Party Platforms: Symbolic Politics and Criminal Justice Policy." *Criminal Justice Policy Review* 19: 397–413.

Organization of American States. 2013. "Scenarios for the Drug Problem in the Americas 2013–2025." Washington, D.C.: Organization of American States.

Osher, F., and L. Kofoed. 1989. "Treatment of Patients with Psychiatric and Psychoactive Substance Abuse Disorders. *Hospital and Community Psychiatry* 40: 1025–1030.

Padfield, N. D. van Zyl Smit, and F. Dunkel, eds. 2010. *Release from Prison: European Policy and Practice.* London: Routledge.

Padilla, Felix. 1992. *The Gang as an American Enterprise.* New Brunswick, NJ: Rutgers University Press.

Palmer, Ted. 1995. "Programmatic and Non-Programmatic Aspects of Success-ful Intervention: New Directions for Research." *Crime and Delinquency* 41: 100–113.

Paparozzi, Mario, and Matther DeMichele. 2008. "Probation and Parole: Over-worked, Misunderstood and Under-Appreciated; But Why?" *The Howard Journal* 47: 275–296.

Pascal-Leone, Alvaro, Amir Amedi, Felipe Fregni, and Lotfi Merabet. 2005. "The Plastic Human Brain Cortex." *Annual Review of Neuroscience* 28: 377–401.

Paternoster, Raymond. 1989. "Decisions to Participate in and Desist From Four Types of Common Delinquency: Deterrence and the Rational Choice Perspec-tive." *Law and Society Review* 23: 501–534

Peter Hart Research Associates and the Open Society Institute. 2002. "Changing Public Attitudes Toward the Criminal Justice System: Summary of Findings." Peter Hart Research Associates.

Peters, R. H., M. G. Bartoi, and P. B. Sherman. 2008. "Screening and Assess-ment of Co-Occurring Disorders in the Justice System." Delmar, NY: CMHS National GAINS Center.

Petersilia, Joan. 1998. "Probation in the United States." *Perspectives*, Spring 1998. Lexington, KY: American Probation and Parole Association.

Petersilia, Joan. 2004. "What Works in Prisoner Reentry: Reviewing and Ques-tioning the Evidence." *Federal Probation* 68: 4–9.

Pew Center for the Public and the Press. 2001. "Interdiction and Incarceration Still Top Remedies: 74% Say Drug War Being Lost." http://www.people-press.org/2001/03/21/interdiction-and-incarceration-still-top-remedies.

Pew Center on the States. 2009a. "1 in 31 The Long Reach of American Correc-tions." Pew Center on the States, Public Safety Performance Project. Washing-ton, D.C.: The Pew Charitable Trusts.

Pew Center on the States. 2009b. "Study Finds Disparity in Corrections Spend-ing." Pew Center on the States, Public Safety Performance Project. Washing-ton, D.C.: The Pew Charitable Trusts.

Pew Center on the States. 2010a. "National Research of Public Attitudes on Crime and Punishment, Public Opinion Strategies." Pew Center on the States, Public Safety Performance Project. Washington, D.C.: The Pew Charitable Trusts.

Pew Center on the States. 2010b. "Pew Quantifies the Collateral Costs of Incar-ceration on the Economic Mobility of Former Inmates, Their Families, and Their Children." Pew Center on the States, Public Safety Performance Project. Washington, D.C.: The Pew Charitable Trusts.

Pew Center on the States. 2011. "State of Recidivism: The Revolving Door of America's Prisons." Pew Center on the States, Public Safety Performance Project. Washington, D.C.: The Pew Charitable Trusts.

Pew Center on the States. 2012a. "Public Opinion on Sentencing and Corrections Policy in America." Pew Center on the States, Public Safety Performance Project. Washington, D.C.: The Pew Charitable Trusts.

Pew Center on the States. 2012b. "Time Served: The High Cost, Low Return of Longer Prison Terms." Pew Center on the States, Public Safety Performance Project. Washington, D.C.: The Pew Charitable Trusts.

Pew Charitable Trusts. 2014. http://www.pewtrusts.org/en/multimedia/data -visualizations/2014/states-project-3-percent-increase-in-prisoners-by-2018.

Pew Research Center for the People and the Press. January 20, 2011. "Economy Dominates Public's Agenda, Dims Hopes for the Future." http://people-press .org/2011/01/20/section-1-publics-policy-priorities.

Phelan, J. N. and M. D. Schrunk. 2008. "The Future of the Local Prosecutors in America." In *The Changing Role of the American Prosecutor*, edited by J. Worrall and M. Nugent-Borakove. Albany: State University of New York Press.

Piehl, Anne, and Shawn Bushway. 2007. "Measuring and Explaining Charge Bargaining." *Journal of Quantitative Criminology* 23: 105–125.

Polak, Rosaura, Anke Witteveen, Johannes Reitsma, and Miranda Olff. 2012. "The Role of Executive Function in Posttraumatic Stress Disorder: A Systematic Review." *Journal of Affective Disorders* 141: 11–21.

Pollack, Harold, Peter Reuter, and Eric Sevigny. 2011. "If Drug Treatment Works So Well, Why Are So Many Drug Users in Prison?" National Bureau of Economic Research Working Paper Series 16731.

Porter, Nicole. 2010. "The State of Sentencing 2009: Developments in Policy and Practice." Washington, D.C.: The Sentencing Project.

Porter, Nicole. 2011. "The State of Sentencing 2010: Developments in Policy and Practice." Washington, D.C.: The Sentencing Project.

Pratt, Travis C., Francis T. Cullen, Kristie R. Blevins, Leah H. Daigle, and Tamara D. Madensen. 2006. "The Empirical Status of Deterrence Theory: A Meta-Analysis." In *Taking Stock: The Status of Criminological Theory*, edited by Francis T. Cullen, John Paul Wright, and Kristie R. Blevins. New Brunswick, NJ: Transaction.

President's Commission on Law Enforcement and the Administration of Justice. 1967. *The Challenge of Crime in a Free Society*. Washington D.C.: Author.

President's New Freedom Commission on Mental Health. 2003. "Achieving the Promise: Transforming Mental Health Care in America." Washington, D.C.

Princeton Survey Research Associates International. 2006. "The NCSC Sentencing Attitudes Survey: A Report on the Findings." Princeton, NJ.

Prochaska, J. O., and C. C. DiClemente. 1992. "The Transtheoretical Approach." In *Handbook of Psychotherapy Integration*, edited by J. C. Norcross and M. R. Goldfried. New York: Basic Books.

Radelet, Michael, and Ronald Akers. 1996. "Deterrence and the Death Penalty: The Views of Experts." *Journal of Criminal Law and Criminology* 87: 1–16.

Raine, Adrian, Terrie Moffitt, Avshalom Caspi, Rolf Loeber, Magda Stouthamer-Loeber, and Don Lynam. 2005. "Neurocognitive Impairments in Boys on the Life-Course Persistent Antisocial Path." *Journal of Abnormal Psychology* 114: 38–49.

Rainville, Gerard. 2001. "An Analysis of Factors Related to Prosecutor Sentencing Preferences." *Criminal Justice Policy Review* 12: 295–310.

Rainville, G., and B. A. Reaves. 2003. "Felony Defendants in Large Urban Counties." Washington D.C.: Bureau of Justice Statistics.

Raphael, Steven. 2009. "Policy Essay: Explaining the Rise in U.S. Incarceration Rates." *Criminology and Public Policy* 8: 87–95.

Raphael, Steven, and Michael Stoll. 2007. "Why Are So Many Americans in Prison?" Working paper. University of California, Berkeley.

Raphael, Steven, and Michael A. Stoll. 2009. "Why Are So Many Americans in Prison?" In *Do Prisons Make Us Safer?*, edited by Stephen Raphael and Michael A. Stoll. New York: Russell Sage Foundation.

Rasmussen Reports. 2012. http://www.rasmussenreports.com/public_content/lifestyle/general_lifestyle/november_2012/7_think_u_s_is_winning_war_on_drugs.

Rebellon, Cesar J., and Karen Van Gundy. 2005. "Can Control Theory Explain the Link Between Parental and Physical Abuse and Delinquency? A Longitudinal Analysis." *Journal of Research in Crime and Delinquency* 42: 47–274.

Reinarman, Craig, Peter D. A. Cohen, and Hendrien L. Kaal. 2004. "The Limited Relevance of Drug Policy: Cannabis in Amsterdam and in San Francisco." *American Journal of Public Health* 94: 836–842.

Reiss, Albert J. Jr., and Jeffrey A. Roth, eds. 1996. *Understanding and Preventing Violence.* Panel on the Understanding and Control of Violent Behavior. Washington, D.C.: National Academies Press.

Reitz, Kevin. 2011. "Sentencing." In *Crime and Public Policy*, 2nd ed., edited by James Q. Wilson and Joan Petersilia. New York: Oxford University Press.

Reuland, Melissa, Matthew Schwarzfeld, and Laura Draper. 2009. "Law Enforcement Responses to People with Mental Illnesses: A Guide to Research-Informed Policy and Practice." New York: Council on State Governments, Justice Center.

Reuter, P. and H. Pollack. 2006. "How Much Can Treatment Reduce National Drug Problems?" *Addiction* 101: 341–347.

Reuter, Peter, and Alex Stevens. 2007. "Bringing the Evidence and Analysis Together to Inform UK Drug Policy." London: UK Drug Policy Commission.

Rhine, Edward. 1992. "Reclaiming Offender Accountability: Intermediate Sanctions for Probation and Parole Violators." Laurel Lakes, MD: American Correctional Association.

Rhodes, William, Patrick Johnston, Song Han, Quentin McMullen, and Lynne Hozik. 2000. "Illicit Drugs: Price Elasticity of Demand and Supply, Final Report." Washington, D.C.: National Institute of Justice, United States Department of Justice.

Ridgely, Susan, John Engberg, Michael D. Greenberg, Susan Turner, Christine DeMartini, and Jacob W. Dembosky. 2007. "Justice, Treatment, and Cost: An Evaluation of the Fiscal Impact of Allegheny County Mental Health Court." Santa Monica, CA: RAND.

Robertson, Ian, and Jaap Murre. 1999. "Rehabilitation of Brain Damage: Brain Plasticity and Principles of Guided Recovery." *Psychological Bulletin* 125: 544–575.

Roberts, Julian, and Mike Hough. 2002. "Changing Attitudes to Punishment: Public Opinion." In *Crime and Justice*, edited by Julian Roberts and Mike Hough. New York: Routledge.

Robinson, Charles, Scott VanBenschoten, Melissa Alexander, and Christopher Lowenkamp. 2012. "A Random (Almost) Study of Staff Training Aimed at Reducing Re-Arrest (STARR): Reducing Recidivism through Intentional Design." *Federal Probation* 75.

Rodriguez, N., and B. Brown. 2003. "Leaving Prison." New York: Vera Institute.

Rohling, M. L., M. E. Faust, B. Beverly, and G. Demakis. 2009. "Effectiveness of Cognitive Rehabilitation Following Acquired Brain Injury: A Meta-Analytic Re-Examination of Cicerone et al.'s (2000, 2005) Systematic Reviews." *Neuropsychology* 23: 20–39.

Rollnick, H., R. Heather, R. Gold, and W. Hall. 1992. "Development of a Short 'Readiness to Change' Questionnaire for Use in Brief, Opportunistic Interventions Among Excessive Drinkers." *British Journal of Addiction* 87: 743–754.

Roman, Caterina, and Jeremy Travis. 2004. "Taking Stock: Housing, Homelessness, and Prisoner Reentry." Washington, D.C.: Justice Policy Center, the Urban Institute.

Roman, John, and Aaron Chafin. 2006. "Does It Pay to Invest in Reentry Programs for Jail Inmates?" Washington, D.C.: Justice Policy Center, the Urban Institute.

Roman, John, Lisa Brooks, Erica Lagerson, Aaron Chalfin and Bogdan Tereshchenko. 2007. "Impact and Cost-Benefit Analysis of the Maryland Reentry Partnership Initiative." Washington, D.C.: Justice Policy Center, the Urban Institute.

Roman, John, Akiva Liberman, Samuel Taxy, and P. Downey. 2012. "The Costs and Benefits of Electronic Monitoring for Washington DC." Washington, D.C.: Justice Policy Center, the Urban Institute and the Crime Policy Institute.

Rosmarin, Ari, and Niamh Eastwood. 2012. "A Quiet Revolution: Drug Decriminalization Policies in Practice Across the Globe." www.release.org.uk /decriminalization.

Ross, Erin, and Peter Hoaken. 2010. "Correctional Remediation Meets Neuro-psychological Rehabilitation: How Brain Injury and Schizophrenia Research Can Improve Offender Programming." *Criminal Justice and Behavior* 37 no. 6: 656–677.

Rossman, Shelli, Michael Rempel, John Roman, Janine Zweig, Mia Green, P. Mitchell Downey, Jennifer Yahner, Avinash S. Bhati, and Donald J. Farole, Jr. 2011a. "The Multi-Site Adult Drug Court Evaluation: The Impact of Drug Courts, Vol. 4." Washington, D.C.: Justice Policy Center, the Urban Institute.

Rossman, Shelli, John Roman, Janine Zweig, Michael Rempel, and Christine Lindquist. 2011b. "The Multi-Site Adult Drug Court Evaluation." Washington, D.C.: Justice Policy Center, the Urban Institute.

Rottman, David B., et al. 2006. "The Sentencing Context." Washington, D.C.: U.S. Department of Justice, Office of Justice Programs, Bureau of Justice Statistics.

Rubak, S., A. Sandbaek, T. Lauritzen, and B. Christensen. 2005. "Motivational Interviewing: A Systematic Review and Meta-analysis." *British Journal of General Practice* 55: 305–312.

Rudo-Hutt, Anna, Yu Gao, Andrea Glenn, Melissa Peskin, and Yaling Yang. 2011. "Biosocial Interactions and Correlates of Crime." In *The Ashgate Research Companion to Biosocial Theories of Crime,* edited by K. Beaver and A. Walsh. Burlington, VT: Ashgate.

Ryan, S., C. Brown, and S. Watanabe-Galloway. 2010. "Toward Successful Post-booking Diversion: What Are the Next Steps?" *Psychiatric Services* 61: 469–477.

Rydell, C. P., and S. S. Everingham. 1994. "Controlling Cocaine." Santa Monica, CA: Drug Policy Research Center, RAND Corporation.

Sabol, William, Katherine Rosich, Kamala Kane, David Kirk, and Glenn Dubin. 2002. "Influences of Truth in Sentencing Reforms on Changes in States' Sentencing Practices and Prison Populations." Washington, D.C.: U.S. Department of Justice.

Sample, Lisa, and Cassia Spohn. 2008. "Final Report for The Evaluation of Nebraska's Serious and Violent Offender Reentry Program." Omaha, NE: School of Criminology and Criminal Justice, University of Nebraska at Omaha.

Sarteschi, C., M. Vaughn, and K. Kim. 2011. "Assessing the Effectiveness of Mental Health Court: A Qualitative Review." *Journal of Criminal Justice* 39: 12–20.

Savage, Joanne, Stephanie Ellis, and Kathryn Kozey. 2013. "A Selective Review of the Risk Factors for Antisocial Behavior Across the Transition to Adulthood." *Psychology* 4: 1–7.

Scarpa, Angela. 2001. "Community Violence Exposure in a Young Adult Sample: Lifetime Prevalence and Socioemotional Effects." *Journal of Interpersonal Violence* 16: 36–53.

Schaeffer, Cindy M., and Charles M. Borduin. 2005. "Long-Term Follow-Up to a Randomized Clinical Trial of Multisystemic Therapy with Serious and Violent Offenders." *Journal of Consulting and Clinical Psychology* 73: 445–453.

Shaffer, D. 2006. *Reconsidering Drug Court Effectiveness: A Meta-Analytic Review.* Doctoral dissertation. University of Nevada, Las Vegas.

Schiraldi, V., J. Colburn, and E. Lotke. 2004. "An Examination of the Impact of 3-Strike Laws: 10 Years After their Enactment." Washington, D.C.: The Justice Policy Institute.

Scott, Wayne. 2008. "Effective Clinical Practices in Treating Clients in the Criminal Justice System." Washington, D.C.: U.S. Department of Justice, National Institute of Corrections.

Sedlak, A. and D. Broadhurst. 1996. "Third National Incidence Study of Child Abuse and Neglect: Final Report." Washington, D.C.: U.S. Department of Health and Human Services.

Seiter, Richard, and Karen R. Kadela. 2003. "Prisoner Reentry: What Works, What Does Not, and What Is Promising." *Crime and Delinquency* 49: 360–388.

Seligman, D. 2005. "Lock 'Em Up." *Forbes*, May 23, 2005.

Sevigny, Eric, and Jonathan Caulkins. 2004. "Kingpins or Mules: An Analysis of Drug Offenders Incarcerated in Federal and State Prisons." *Criminology and Public Policy* 3: 401–434.

Shaffer, Deborah, Kristin Bechtel, and Edward Latessa. 2005. "Evaluation of Ohio's Drug Courts: A Cost Benefit Analysis." Cincinnati, OH: Center for Criminal Justice Research, University of Cincinnati.

Shapiro, Robert, and Kevin Hassett. 2012. "The Economic Benefits of Reducing Violent Crime." Washington, D.C.: The Center for American Progress.

Sharp, Elaine. 1999. "The Sometime Connection: Public Opinion and Social Policy." Albany: State University of New York.

Shapiro, Carol and Meryl Schwartz. 2001. "Coming Home: Building on Family Connections." *Corrections Management Quarterly* 5: 52–61.

Shermer, Lauren, and Brian Johnson. 2009. "Criminal Prosecutions: Examining Prosecutorial Discretion and Charge Reductions in U.S. Federal District Courts." *Justice Quarterly* 1–37.

Siegel, A. Jane, and Linda M. Williams. 2003. "The Relationship Between Child Sexual Abuse and Female Delinquency." *Journal of Research in Crime and Delinquency* 40: 71–94.

Silver, E., and L. Chow-Martin. 2002. "A Multiple Models Approach to Assessing Recidivism Risk: Implications for Judicial Decision-Making." *Criminal Justice and Behavior* 29: 538–568.

Silver, E., and L. Miller. 2002. "A Cautionary Note on the Use of Actuarial Tools for Social Control." *Crime and Delinquency* 48: 138–161.

Silver, E., W. Smith, and S. Banks. 2000. "Constructing Actuarial Devices for Predicting Recidivism: A Comparison Of Methods." *Criminal Justice and Behavior* 27: 733–764.

Simpson, D. D., and P. M. Flynn. 2008. "Drug Abuse Treatment Outcome Studies (DATOS): A National Evaluation of Treatment Effectiveness." In *The Encyclopedia of Substance Abuse Prevention, Treatment, and Recovery,* edited by G. Fisher and N. Roget. Thousand Oaks, CA: Sage Publishing.

Sirois, Catherine, and Bruce Western. 2010. "An Evaluation of 'Ready, Willing and Able.'" Cambridge, MA: Harvard University.

Skeem, J., J. Eno Louden, S. Manchak, S. Vidal, and E. Haddad. 2008. "Social Networks and Social Control of Probationers with Co-Occurring Mental and Substance Abuse Problems." *Law and Human Behavior* 33: 122–135.

Smith, Paula, Myrinda Schweitzer, Ryan Labrecque, and Edward Latessa. 2012. "Improving Probation Officers' Supervision Skills: An Evaluation of the EPICS Model." *Journal of Crime and Justice* 35: 189–199.

Solomon, A., K. Johnson, J. Travis, and E. McBride. 2004. *From Prison to Work: The Employment Dimensions of Prisoner Reentry*. Washington, D.C.: Urban Institute.

Solomon, A., V. Kachnowski, and A. Bhati. 2005. "Does Parole Work? Analyzing the Impact of Postprison Supervision on Rearrest Outcomes." Washington, D.C.: Justice Policy Center, Urban Institute.

Solomon, A., J. Osborne, L. Winterfield, B. Elderbroom, P. Burke R. Stroker, E. Rhine, and W. Burrell. 2008. *Putting Public Safety First: 13 Parole Supervision Strategies to Enhance Reentry Outcomes.* Washington, D.C.: Urban Institute.

Spelman, William. 2000. "What Recent Studies Do (and Don't) Tell Us About Imprisonment and Crime." In *Crime and Justice: A Review of Research,* vol. 27, edited by Michael Tonry. Chicago: University of Chicago Press.

Spelman, William. 2005. "Jobs or Jails? The Crime Drop in Texas." *Journal of Policy Analysis and Management* 24: 133–165.

Steadman, H. J., S. Davidson, and C. Brown. 2001. "Mental Health Courts: Their Promise and Unanswered Questions." *Psychiatric Services* 52: 457–458.

Steadman, H. J., M. Deane, R. Borum, et al. 2000. "Comparing Outcomes of Major Models of Police Responses to Mental Health Emergencies." *Psychiatric Services* 51: 645–649.

Steadman, H. J., F. C. Osher, P. C. Robbins. 2009. "Prevalence of Serious Mental Illness Among Jail Inmates." *Psychiatric Services* 60:761–765.

Steadman, H., A. Redlich, L. Callahan, P. Robbins, and R. Vesselinov. 2010. "Effect of Mental Health Courts on Arrests and Jail Days: A Multi-Site Study." *Archives of General Psychiatry* 68: 167–172.

Steadman, H., K. Stainbrook, P. Griffin, et al. 2001. "A Specialized Crisis Site as a Core Element of Police-Based Diversion Programs." *Psychiatric Services* 52: 219–222.

Steffensmeier, D., and S. Demuth. 2000. "Ethnicity and Sentencing Outcomes in U.S. Federal Courts: Who Is Punished More Harshly?" *American Sociological Review* 65: 705–729.

Steffensmeier, D., J. Ulmer, and J. Kramer. 1998. "The Interaction of Race, Gender, and Age in Criminal Sentencing: The Punishment Costs of Being Young, Black, And Male." *Criminology* 36: 763–797.

Stein, Bradley, Lisa Jaycox, Sheryl Kataoka, Hilary Rhodes, and Katherine Vestal. 2003. "Prevalence of Child and Adolescent Exposure to Community Violence." *Clinical Child and Family Psychology Review* 6: 247–264.

Stemen, Don. 2007. "Reconsidering Incarceration: New Directions for Reducing Crime." Washington, D.C.: Vera Institute of Justice.

Stemen, Don, Andres Rengifo, and James Wilson. 2006. "Of Fragmentation and Ferment: The Impact of State Sentencing Policies on Incarceration Rates, 1975–2002." Washington, D.C.: National Institute of Justice, U.S. Department of Justice.

Stith, K., and S. Koh. 1993. "The Politics of Sentencing Reform: The Legislative History of the Federal Sentencing Guidelines." *Wake Forest Law Review* 224: 223–289.

Stemen, D. 2007. *Reconsidering Incarceration: New Directions for Reducing Crime.* New York: Vera Institute of Justice.

Stewart, D., M. Gossop, J. Marsden, and A. Rolfe. 2000. "Drug Misuse and Acquisitive Crime among Clients Recruited to the National Treatment Outcome Research Study." *Criminal Behavior and Mental Health* 10: 10–20.

Substance Abuse and Mental Health Services Administration. 2004a. "Results from the 2003 National Survey on Drug Use and Health: National Findings. DHHS Publication Number SMA 04-3964. NSDUH Series H-25." Rockville, MD: Substance Abuse and Mental Services Administration.

Substance Abuse and Mental Health Services Administration 2004b. "SAMHSA Action Plan: Seclusion and Restraint—Fiscal Years 2004 and 2005." http://www.samhsa.gov/Matrix/SAP_seclusion.aspx.

Substance Abuse and Mental Health Services Administration. 2009. "Screening, Brief Intervention and Referral To Treatment." *SAMHSA News* 17: http://www.samhsa.gov/prevention/sbirt.

Substance Abuse and Mental Health Services Administration. 2011. "Screening, Brief Intervention and Referral to Treatment." In *Behavioral Health Care.* http://www.samhsa.gov/prevention/sbirt.

Substance Abuse and Mental Health Services Administration. n.d. "Systems-Level Implementation of Screening, Brief Intervention and Referral to Treatment. Technical Assistance Publication 33." Rockville, MD: Author.

Substance Abuse and Mental Health Services Administration. 2011. *Trauma-Specific Interventions for Justice-Involved Individual.* New York: The National GAINS Center.

Swanson, J., S. Estroff, M. Swartz, R. Borum, W. Lachicotte, C. Zimmer, and R. Wagner. 1997. "Violence and Severe Mental Disorder in Clinical and Community Populations: The Effects of Psychotic Symptoms, Comorbidity, and Lack of Treatment." *Psychiatry* 60: 1–22.

Swanson, Y. Heather, Patrick N. Parkinson, Brian O'Toole, Angela M. Plunkett, Sandra Shrimpton, and R. Kim Oates. 2003. "Juvenile Crime, Aggression and Delinquency After Sexual Abuse: A Longitudinal Study." *British Journal of Criminology* 43: 729–749.

Swartz, J. A., and A. Lurigio. 1999. "Psychiatric Illness and Comorbidity Among Adult Male Jail Detainees in Drug Treatment." *Psychiatric Services* 50: 1628–1630.

Swartz, M. S., J. Swanson, V. Hiday, R. Borum, R. Wagner, and B. Burns. 1998. "Violence and Severe Mental Illness: The Effects of Substance Abuse and Nonadherence to Medication." *American Journal of Psychiatry* 155: 226–231.

Tanner, R. 2007. "Studies Say Death Penalty Deters Crime." *Associated Press*, June 11, 2007.

Tauber, J. n.d. http://www.reentrycourtsolutions.com.

Taxman, Faye. 2012. "Probation, Intermediate Sanctions, and Community-Based Corrections." In *The Oxford Handbook of Sentencing and Corrections,* edited by J. Petersilia and K. Reitz. New York: Oxford.

Taxman, Faye. 2002. "Supervision—Exploring the Dimensions of Effectiveness." *Federal Probation* 66: 14–27.

Taxman, Faye, Karen Cropsey, Douglas Young, and Harry Wexler. 2007. "Screening, Assessment, and Referral Practices in Adult Correctional Settings: A National Perspective." *Criminal Justice and Behavior* 34: 1216–1234.

Taxman, Faye, Matthew Perdoni, and Lana Harrison. 2007. "Drug Treatment Services for Adult Offenders: The State of the State." *Journal of Substance Abuse Treatment* 32: 239–254.

Taxman, F. S., E. Shepardson, and J. Byrne. 2004. "Tools of the Trade: A Guide to Incorporating Science Into Practice." Washington, D.C.: National Institute of Corrections, and Maryland Department of Public Safety and Correctional Services.

Taxman, Faye S., David Soule, and Adam Gelb. 1999. "Graduated Sanctions: Stepping Into Accountable Systems and Offenders." *Prison Journal* 79: 182–204.

Taxman, F., C. Yancey, and J. Bilanin. 2006. *Maryland's Proactive Community Supervision Initiative: Findings from an Impact and Outcome Evaluation.* College Park: University of Maryland, Bureau of Governmental Research.

Terry, Natalie. 2006. "Returning to Its Roots? A New Role for the Third Sector in Probation." Introduction and Executive Summary. September, Social Market Foundation.

Thompson, Cara, and Brian Lovins. 2012. "Effective Practices in Community Supervision/Correctional Settings (EPICS)." Cincinnati, OH: University of Cincinnati.

Tonry, M. 2011. "Less Imprisonment Is No Doubt a Good Thing: More Policing Is Not. *Criminology and Public Policy* 10: 137–152.

Tonry, M. 2009. "Mostly Unintended Effects of Mandatory Penalties: Two Centuries of Consistent Findings." In *Crime and Justice: A Review of Research,* edited by M. Tonry. Chicago: University of Chicago Press.

Tonry, M. 1987. "Prediction and Classification: Legal and Ethical Issues." In *Prediction and Classification: Criminal Justice Decision-Making,* edited by D. M. Gottfredson and M. Tonry. Chicago: University of Chicago Press.

Tonry, M. 1996. *Sentencing Matters.* New York: Oxford University Press.

Tonry, M. 2004. *Thinking About Crime: Sense and Sensibility in American Penal Culture.* New York: Oxford University Press.

Tonry, M. and Frase, R. 2001. *Sentencing and Sanctions in Western Countries.* New York: Oxford University Press.

Toros, Halil, and Manuel Moreno. 2012. "Project 50: The Cost Effectiveness of the Permanent Supportive Housing Model in the Skid Row Section of Los Angeles County." County of Los Angeles, CA.

Torrey, E. Fuller, Aaron Kennard, Don Eslinger, Richard Lamb, and James Pavle. 2010. "More Mentally Ill Persons Are in Jails and Prisons Than Hospitals: A Survey of the States." Arlington, VA: Treatment Advocacy Center.

Travis, Jeremy, Anna Crayton, and Debbie Makamal. 2010. "A New Era in Inmate Reentry." New York: John Jay College of Criminal Justice.

Travis, Jeremy, Amy Solomon, and Michelle Waul. 2001. "From Prison to Home: The Dimensions and Consequences of Prisoner Reentry." Washington, D.C.: Justice Center, the Urban Institute.

Turner, Susan, P. Greenwood, T. Fain, and J. Chiesa. 2006. "An Evaluation of the Federal Government's Violent Offender Incarceration and Truth-in-Sentencing Incentive Grants." *Prison Journal* 86 no. 3: 364–385.

Turner, S., P. Greenwood, T. Fain, and E. Deschenes. 1999. "Perceptions of Drug Court: How Offenders View Ease of Program Completion, Strengths and Weaknesses, and the Impact on Their Lives." *National Drug Court Institute Review* 2: 61–85.

Ulmer, Jeffrey. 2005. "The Localized Used of the Federal Sentencing Guidelines in Four U.S. District Courts: Evidence of Processual Order." *Symbolic Interaction* 28 no. 2: 255–279.

Ulmer, Jeffrey, Megan Kurlychek, and John Kramer. 2007. "Prosecutorial Discretion and the Imposition of Mandatory Minimum Sentences." *Journal of Research in Crime and Delinquency* 44: 427–458.

UNICEF Innocenti Research Centre. 2012. *Measuring Child Poverty: New League Tables of Child Poverty in the World's Rich Countries,* Innocenti Report Card 10, UNICEF Innocenti Research Centre, Florence, Italy.

United States Government Accountability Office. 2005. "Adult Drug Courts: Evidence Indicates Recidivism Reductions and Mixed Results for Other Outcomes" [No. GAO-05-219]. Washington, D.C.

United States Sentencing Commission. 2010. "Results of Survey of United States District Judges January 2010 through March 2010, June 2010." Washington, D.C.

United States Sentencing Commission. 2013. "Preliminary Quarterly Data Report, Fourth Quarter Release." Washington, D.C.

United States Sentencing Commission. 2013. *Sourcebook of Federal Sentencing Statistics*. Washington D.C.: Author.

Unnever, James, and Francis Cullen. 2010. "The Social Sources of Americans' Punitiveness: A Test of Three Competing Models." *Criminology* 48: 99–129.

Unnever, James, Francis Cullen, and Julian Roberts. 2005. "Not Everyone Supports the Death Penalty: Assessing Weakly Held Attitudes About Capital Punishment." *American Journal of Criminal Justice* 29: 187–216.

Urban Institute. 2013. "The Justice Reinvestment Initiative Experiences from the States." Washington, D.C.: Justice Center, the Urban Institute.

U.S. Sentencing Commission. 1991. *The Federal Sentencing Guidelines: A Report on the Operation of the Guidelines System and Short-Term Impacts on Disparity in Sentencing, Use of Incarceration, and Prosecutorial Discretion and Plea Bargaining*. Washington, D.C.: Author.

Useem Bert, and Anne Piehl. 2008. *Prison State: The Challenge of Mass Incarceration*. New York: Cambridge University Press.

VanBenschoten, Scott. 2008. "Risk/Need Assessment: Is This The Best We Can Do?" *Federal Probation* 72 no. 2.

Van Dijk, Jan, John van Kesteren, and Paul Smit. 2007. "Criminal Victimization in International Perspective: Key Findings from the 2004–2005 ICVS and EU ICS." New York: United Nations Office on Drugs and Crime.

Van Goozen, S. H. M., and G. Fairchild. 2008. "How Can the Study of Biological Processes Help Design New Interventions for Children with Severe Antisocial Behavior?" *Development and Psychopathology* 20: 941–973.

Van Pattan, Isaac, and Randy Matney. 2004. "A Survival Analysis of Probation Supervision: A Closer Look at the Role of Technical Violations." Paper presented at the American Criminal Justice Society Annual Conference 2004.

Vaske, Jamie, Kevan Galyean, and Francis Cullen. 2011. "Toward a Biosocial Theory of Offender Rehabilitation: Why Does Cognitive-Behavioral Therapy Work?" *Journal of Criminal Justice* 39: 90–102.

Vera Institute of Justice. 2013. "The Potential of Community Corrections to Improve Safety and Reduce Incarceration." New York: Center on Sentencing and Corrections, Vera Institute.

Villettaz, P., Killias, M., and I. Zoder. 2006. *The Effects of Custodial vs. Non-Custodial Sentences on Re-Offending: A Systematic Review of the State of Knowledge*. Campbell Systematic Reviews, The Campbell Collaborative, Oslo, Norway.

Vincent, B.S. and P. J. Hofer. 1994. *The Consequences of Mandatory Minimum Prison Terms: A Summary of Recent Findings*. Washington, D.C.: The Federal Judicial Center.

Visher, Christy, and Jeremy Travis. 2011. "Life on the Outside: Returning Home After Incarceration." *The Prison Journal* 9: 102–119.

Vito, G. F. 1989. "The Kentucky Substance Abuse Program: A Private Program to Treat Probationers and Parolees." *Federal Probation*: 65–72.

Volkov, Nora. 2004. "Measuring the Effectiveness of Drug Addiction Treatment." Testimony Before the House Committee on Governmental Reform, Washington D.C.: U.S. House of Representatives. *The Wall Street Journal*. 2002. "Yes, the Death Penalty Deters." June 21, 2002.

Walmsley, R. 2011. *World Population List*, 9th ed. Essex: International Centre for Prison Studies.

Walsh, Anthony. 2012. *Criminology: The Essentials*. Thousand Oaks, CA: Sage Publications.

Walsh, Anthony, and Jonathan Bolen. 2012. *The Neurobiology of Criminal Behavior: Gene-Brain-Culture Interaction*. Burlington, VT: Ashgate.

Warren, R. 2008. *Evidence-Based Practice to Reduce Recidivism: Implications for State Judiciaries*. Washington, D.C.: National Institute of Corrections.

Washington State Institute for Public Policy. 2003. "Washington State's Drug Courts for Adult Defendants: Outcome Evaluation and Cost-Benefit Analysis."

Washington State Institute for Public Policy. 2011. "Return on Investment: Evidence-Based Options to Improve Statewide Outcomes." Olympia, WA: WSIPP.

Warr, Mark. 2000. "Public Perceptions of and Reactions to Crime." In *Criminology: A Contemporary Handbook*, edited by J. Sheley. Belmont, CA: Wadsworth.

Warren, Roger. 2009a. "Arming the Courts with Research: 10 Evidence-Based Sentencing Initiatives to Control Crime and Reduce Costs." Pew Center on the States, Public Safety Policy Brief.

Warren, Roger. 2009b. "A Tale of Two Surveys: Judicial and Public Perspectives on State Sentencing Reform." *Federal Sentencing Reporter* 21: 276–287.

Watkins, K. E., A. Burnam, F-Y Kung, and S. Paddock. 2001. "A National Survey of Care for Persons with Co-Occurring Mental and Substance Use Disorders." *Psychiatric Services* 52: 1062–1068.

Welsh, Brandon. 2004. "Monetary Costs and Benefits of Correctional Treatment Programs: Implications for Offender Reentry." *Federal Probation* 68 no. 2.

Welsh, Brandon, and David Farrington. 2000. "Correctional Intervention Programs and Cost Benefit Analysis." *Criminal Justice and Behavior* 27: 115–121.

Western, Bruce. 2006. *Punishment and Inequality in America*. New York: Russell Sage Foundation.

Widom, C. S. 2000. "Childhood Victimization: Early Adversity, Later Psychopathology." *National Institute of Justice Journal* January: 3–9.

Wiest, K. L., S. M. Carey, S. J. Martin, M. S. Waller, A. Cox, R. Linhares, and D. Crumpton. 2007a. "Indiana Drug Courts: St. Joseph County Drug Court Program Process, Outcome and Cost Evaluation: Final Report." Portland, OR: NPC Research.

Wiest, K. L., S. M. Carey, S. J. Martin, M. S. Waller, A. Cox, R. Linhares, and D. Crumpton. 2007b. "Indiana Drug Courts: Vigo County Drug Court Process, Outcome and Cost Evaluation: Final Report." Portland, OR: NPC Research.

Wilson, David, Ojmarrh Mitchell, and Doris Mackenzie. 2006. "A Systematic Review of Drug Court Effects on Recidivism." *Journal of Experimental Criminology* 2: 459–487.

Wolf, Robert. 2007. "Breaking with Tradition: Introducing Problem-Solving in Conventional Courts." New York: Center for Court Innovation.

Wolf, Robert. 2011. "Reentry Courts: Looking Ahead." New York: Center for Court Innovation.

Wolff, N. 1998. "Interactions Between Mental Health and Law Enforcement Systems: Problems and Prospects for Cooperation." *Journal of Health Politics, Policy, and Law* 23:133–174.

Wooldredge, John, and Timothy Griffin. 2005. "Displaced Discretion Under Ohio Sentencing Guidelines." *Journal of Criminal Justice* 33: 301–316.

Wright, Benjamin, Sheldon Zhang, and David Farabee. 2012. "A Squandered Opportunity? A Review of SAMHSA's National Registry of Evidence-Based Programs and Practices for Offenders." *Crime and Delinquency* 58: 954–972.

Yamatani, Hide. 2012. "The Program for Offenders: Comprehensive Evaluation and Cost/Benefit Analysis of a Community Corrections Facility." Excellence Research, Inc. January 31, 2012.

Yearwood, Douglas, James Klopovic, Richard Hayes, Justin Davis, Charlene Coppersmith, and Yuli Hsu. 2007. "A Discussion of Incarceration and Its Alternatives in North Carolina: A Crime and Justice Perspective from The NC Governor's Crime Commission." The North Carolina Criminal Justice Analysis Center, July 2007.

Yeh, Stuart S. 2010. "Cost-Benefit Analysis of Reducing Crime Through Electronic Monitoring of Parolees And Probationers." *Journal of Criminal Justice* 38: 1090–1096.

Yoshikawa, H. 1995. "Long-Term Effects of Early Childhood Programs on Social Outcomes and Delinquency." *The Future of Children* 5: 51–75.

Zarkin, Gary, Alexander Cowell, Katherine Hicks, Michael Mills, Steven Belenko, Laura Dunlap, and Vincent Keyes, 2012. "Lifetime Benefits and Costs of Diverting Substance-Abusing Offenders from State Prison." *Crime and Delinquency.* http://www.gmuace.org/documents/events/Wednes.10.5/Zarkin_Cowell.pdf.

Zarkin, G. A., L. Dunlap, S. Belenko, and P. Dynia. 2005. "A Benefit-Cost Analysis for the Kings County District Attorney's Office Drug Treatment Alternative to Prison (DTAP) Program." *Justice Research and Policy* 7: 1–26.

Zhang, Sheldon, E. L. Roberts, and Valerie J. Callanan. 2006. "The Cost Benefits Of Providing Community-Based Correctional Services: An Evaluation of a Statewide Parole Program in California." *Journal of Criminal Justice* 34: 341–350.

Zilberstein, Karen. 2013. "Neurocognitive Considerations in the Treatment of Attachment and Complex Trauma in Children." *Clinical Child Psychology and Psychiatry*: 1–19.

Zimring, F. E. 2007. *The Great American Crime Decline.* New York: Oxford University Press.

Zimring, F. E. and G. Hawkins. 1994. *Crime Is Not the Problem: Lethal Violence in America.* New York: Oxford University Press.

Zimring, F. E., G. Hawkins, and S. Kamin. 2001. *Punishment and Democracy: Three Strikes and You're Out in California.* New York: Oxford University Press.